Transformations
of the American
Party System

Political Coalitions from
the New Deal to the 1970s

SECOND EDITION

Transformations of the American Party System

Political Coalitions from the New Deal to the 1970s

SECOND EDITION

Everett Carll Ladd, Jr.

with

Charles D. Hadley

W · W · NORTON & COMPANY · INC ·

NEW YORK

Copyright © 1978, 1975 by W. W. Norton & Company, Inc.

Published simultaneously in Canada
by George J. McLeod Limited, Toronto.
PRINTED IN THE UNITED STATES OF AMERICA.

Library of Congress Cataloging in Publication Data
Ladd, Everett Carll.
  Transformations of the American party system.

  Includes bibliographical references and index.
  1. Political parties—United States. 2. United
States—Politics and government—1933–1945. 3. United
States—Politics and government—1945–
I. Hadley, Charles D., joint author. II. Title.
JK2261.L34 1978   329'.02   77–12307
ISBN 0–393–05660–0
ISBN 0–393–09065–5 pbk.
1 2 3 4 5 6 7 8 9 0

To the Memory of *Clinton Rossiter*

Pro debitis plurimis seras gratias

Contents

List of Figures

List of Tables

Preface

Discussions of contemporary American society and politics are dominated by a sense of the overwhelming newness of it all. As a nation whose beginnings were framed by the breakdown of aristocratic norms, institutions, and social arrangements in the West, by the advent of the egalitarian, industrial, and scientific revolutions, the United States has hardly been a stranger to change. Response to massive societal transformations colors its whole existence. Both the rate and the scope of change, however, have taken on a new extended dimension in the contemporary period.

The signs are scattered everywhere. We see them in the exceptional rapidity with which assessments of directions in American life are advanced and discarded. Just a decade or so ago, serious observers perceived an "end of ideology," and believed, as S. M. Lipset put it critically, that "the growth of affluence in the Western world [was promoting] the emergence of a peaceful social Utopia. . . ." [1] The fundamental problems had been resolved in advanced societies like the United States, the fundamental antagonisms were being washed away. Now in 1977, looking back upon a decade marred by political assassinations, sharp racial conflict, massive domestic protests against the longest and most unpopular war in U.S. history, by a political scandal of such proportions that it destroyed an administration elected less than two years earlier with the largest plurality ever recorded—the notion that this had become a "peaceful social Utopia" seems ludicrous.

There has been some recovery from the emotional depression of Watergate and Vietnam, but the extent of the

[1] Seymour Martin Lipset, "The Changing Class Structure and Contemporary European Politics," *Daedalus* (Winter 1964); as reprinted in his book, *Revolution and Counterrevolution: Change and Persistence in Social Structures* (Garden City, N.Y.: Doubleday Anchor Books, revised edition, 1970), p. 301.

loss of confidence is still striking. The sense of an economic order able to sustain continuing growth and thereby
smother wants in a blanket of expanding abundance has
been replaced with concerns over economic stagnation
and how to "cope with scarcity." Virtually every major
societal institution evokes less confidence today than ten
years ago. "The decline of the West," a theme not heard
since the Depression and war and totalitarian challenge of
the 1930s, is once again being sounded. Change preoc-
cupies Americans, and many of the perceptions of the consequences of change are now colored with pessimism.

The pronounced sense of an ending, and from that, necessarily, of a beginning, colors so much of contemporary
social commentary. Daniel Bell has caught this nicely,
cataloging the frequent, paradoxical appearance of the prefix *post* to denote, as a combined form, the era we are entering.[2] Thus, Dahrendorf writes of *post-capitalist society*,
Etzioni of the *post-modern* era, Lichtheim of a *postbourgeois* order. Boulding sees the U.S. at the *post-
civilized* epoch, while Beer talks of *post-collectivist* politics, and Bell himself heralds *post-industrial society*.
Feuer finds our period *post-ideological;* Leonard foresees
(following McLuhan) the birth of *post–Literature Culture;*
and Ahlstrom captures the religious scene with a trilogy of
posts—post-Puritan, post-Protestant, and *post-Christian*.[3]
Unless we dismiss such fealty to the prefix as the mere following of terminological fashion, we must conclude that

[2] Bell, *The Coming of Post-Industrial Society* (New York: Basic Books,
1973), pp. 51–54.
[3] Ralf Dahrendorf, *Class and Class Conflict in an Industrial Society*
(Stanford: Stanford University Press, 1959); Amitai Etzioni, *The Active
Society* (New York: The Free Press, 1968); George Lichtheim, *The New
Europe: Today and Tomorrow* (New York: Praeger, 1963); Kenneth
Boulding, *The Meaning of the Twentieth Century: The Great Transition*
(New York: Harper & Row, 1964); Samuel Beer, *British Politics in the
Collectivist Age* (New York: Random House, 1969); Lewis Feuer, *Marx
and the Intellectuals* (Garden City, N.Y.: Doubleday Anchor Books,
1969); John Leonard, "Art in the Global Village," *New York Times* (No-
vember 26, 1970); and Sidney Ahlstrom, "The Radical Turn in Theology
and Ethics," *Annals* (January 1970), pp. 1–13.

social change has ushered in a new age thus far understood largely in terms of what is being negated.

An assortment of simple objective indicators testify to the current siege of societal transformations perhaps as eloquently as do sweeping interpretations. If we are now occupied with economic woes, we should not be unmindful of the exceptional gains of the last quarter-century. Personal consumption of goods and services in the United States rose from under 200 billion to about 750 billion dollars between 1947 and 1973. Controlling for the effects of inflation we find that in this quarter-century, the median income for all American families about doubled, jumping from $5,665 to $11,120 (in dollars of 1972 value). More purchasing power was added at the level of individual families in this brief span than in all preceding periods of American history combined. When it is remembered, too, that at the close of World War II the United States was an exceptionally wealthy country by any historical or cross-national comparative standard, the extent of this "abundance revolution" is more sharply hatched.[4]

There have been all manner of consequent developments. Americans have consumed about one and a half times more fossil fuels since World War II than did all inhabitants of the country in all of the preceding years of the nation's existence—a fact which powerfully defines changes in styles of living just as it points up the basis of the current "energy crisis." The *increase* of six million in college and university enrollment between 1947 and 1973 *was about four times greater than the total enrollment in 1940.* Expenditures for toys climbed 500 percent in the last quarter-century, those for cosmetics by 550 percent, while personal spending for recreation increased fivefold, to about $45 billion. In 1947, at the start of the television age, less than .1 percent of U.S. families (or 14,000) pos-

---

[4] The above data are from: U.S. Bureau of the Census, *Current Population Reports: Consumer Income*, Series P–60, No. 87, June 1973, p. 6; U.S. Bureau of the Census, *Statistical Abstract of the United States, 1973* (Washington, D.C.: U.S. Government Printing Office, 1973), p. 322.

sessed TV sets; but in 1973, 96 percent of all families dedi-
cated, as an average, perhaps 25 percent of their waking
hours to the cathode-ray tube.[5]

Such chronicles of the amount of change compressed in
the contemporary period, and of our absorption, our fasci-
nation with its sundry implications, can be endlessly mul-
tiplied. Many of the components of change are not directly
political, and most, surely do not originate in the polity:
They encompass the economy, life styles, culture, values,
virtually the entire sweep of societal interactions. But collectively, these transformations define a new environment
for political life. They delimit a broad new sociopolitical
period in American history—the character of which is confusing, ambiguous because imperfectly comprehended
and because of internal contradictions bred of complexity,
yet still distinct when set against what came before.

Up until a short while ago, as recently, perhaps, as Lyndon Johnson's 1964 electoral triumph, the New Deal
seemed to inaugurate the "political present." The bold
legislative thrust of the Johnson administration, we were
told repeatedly in 1964, built upon, extended, and served
to culminate policy initiatives begun under Franklin Delano Roosevelt. No one questioned, of course, that the
American political agenda reflected change over the first
two decades following FDR's death, but so much continued to seem familiar, explainable, in New Deal terms.
The ascendant position of the Democratic party remained
unshaken—despite Eisenhower's two presidential triumphs—and it was the "old New Deal coalition" which
held sway. Businessmen and unionists were still primary

[5] The above data were compiled from: *Statistical Abstract of the
United States, 1973*, pp. 508, 107–108, 322, 714–715, and 693; U.S.
Bureau of the Census, *Historical Statistics of the United States, Colonial
Times to 1957* (Washington, D.C.: U.S. Government Printing Office,
1960), pp. 354–355, 210, 178, 420, 491. While we have not located any
fully reliable estimates of the average daily television viewing of Americans, *Television Factbook* (Washington, D.C.: National Association of
Broadcasters, 1973) reports that in 1972 average daily use of television
sets in private homes totaled six hours and twelve minutes, about 38 percent of the waking hours.

political antagonists, even if tension separating them diminished after the Depression era. The substance of policy argument, of political conflict generally, appeared as a
natural extension of that nurtured during the 1930s.

Now, in rapid fashion over the past decade, the New
Deal has become "history." What was recently "present"
has become "past," and therein lies much of the confusion
which currently besets American political life.

Conflict rests at the core of all politics. Contending individuals and groups make claims for public action or inaction which are perceived as advancing their interests over
others. It is the prime political feature of our time that the
structure of conflict has been transformed: new collections
of political interests; new packages of concerns and of demands among colliding groups; a basic redrawing of the
political agenda. Inevitably, in such a context, political
leaders find themselves groping. That the lines of conflict
have shifted, that interests, alliances, and party loyalties
are in flux, is obvious, but the sources of such change are
so recent and unprecedented as to becloud the matter of
appropriate response. Old formulas are inadequate, but
what new ones promise adequacy? The perceptible public
pessimism which colors our politics has many causes, from
disillusionments bred of the Indochina war, to political
corruption codified as "Watergate," to uncertainties produced by economic dislocations like the energy crisis.
Contributing to the current mood along with these proximate events, however, is an underlying dimension—one
comprising exceptional social change with its introduction
of altered states of conflict, all the more taxing because so
poorly understood and so contradictory of prior expectations.

The task of this volume is to help clarify the reordering
which has been imposed upon political life by societal
change since the New Deal. Political parties, especially
the partisan coalitions, provide our analytic departure
point. They are so structured and situated that they serve
admirably as the foci of attention in an enterprise con-

cerned primarily with charting the changing directions of
the polity within the larger context of a changing social
order.

A party system took shape during the New Deal, reflective of the character of the prevailing sociopolitical setting,
and specifically of the types of intergroup conflict which
were then generated. The workings of the "New Deal
party system" came to figure prominently in our understanding of the dynamics of American politics. Now in
1975, it is evident to all that this party system has been altered in important regards, and it appears to some that
there has been a fundamental transformation. By systematically examining changes in the party coalitions which
have occurred between the mid-thirties and the mid-
seventies, we hope to add a dimension to the understanding of political change generally in the United
States.[6]

In the course of work on this volume, we have acquired an
especially long list of debts. Seymour Martin Lipset of
Harvard University read much of the manuscript, and was
a continuing source of insight and intellectual guidance.
William Havard of the Virginia Polytechnic Institute and
State University, Austin Ranney of the University of Wisconsin, Walter Dean Burnham of M.I.T., Aaron Wildavsky
of the University of California at Berkeley, Dwaine Marvick of the University of California at Los Angeles, William Schneider of Harvard University, Irving Kristol of
New York University and co-editor of the *Public Interest*,
John Kessel of Ohio State University, James Clarke of the
University of Arizona, and Daniel Bell of Harvard University, gave generously of constructive criticism, encouragement, and observations on the changing dimensions of the
American polity. We wish to express our thanks to Wayne
Shannon, David RePass, George Cole, and Howard Reiter,
colleagues at the University of Connecticut, who offered

[6] The survey materials on which we have drawn are described in the
Appendix: "A Note on Data Sources."

penetrating commentary on the manuscript and whose suggestions for revision and restatement we had, at least on occasion, the good sense to accept.

Whatever merit the reader may find in this volume accrues in large measure from the rich body of data on the American electorate which was made available to us. We have drawn heavily indeed upon Gallup surveys conducted over the entire 1936–1974 span, and are happy to acknowledge the contribution of the Gallup Organization and its vice-president, Irving Crespi, and the Roper Center for Public Opinion Research which serves as a repository for much of the Gallup data. The Michigan biennial election studies made available through the Inter-University Consortium for Political Research; Harris survey data, furnished us through the Louis Harris Political Data Center of the University of North Carolina, and directly by Louis Harris and Associates; studies conducted in the National Data Program for the Social Sciences by the National Opinion Research Center of the University of Chicago; election surveys of Daniel Yankelovich, Inc. (now Yankelovich, Skelly, and White); data from the California Poll, provided by the State Data Program of the University of California, Berkeley; and studies of presidential convention delegates and of the national electorate in 1972, made available through the courtesy of Warren J. Mitofsky, director of Survey and Data Services of CBS News, together constituted an invaluable body of survey materials for our secondary analysis.

We relied upon the facilities of the Social Science Data Center (SSDC) of the University of Connecticut, and Connecticut's Computer Center, for the secondary analysis. Our thanks go to John Löf, Computer Center director, and to his staff; and to Anne-Marie Mercure, William Gammell, Margaret Pyne, Joffre Levesque, Gary Grandon, Jack Davis, and Peter Hooper, all of the SSDC. William D. Slysz, the SSDC's director of Technical Services, advised us on many points of analysis. Diane Reed served as the principal research associate to the project, aided by Susan

Wilcox, Michael Gold, and Michael Dunphy. As in many past endeavors, Eleanor Wilcox typed the several drafts of this manuscript with notable editorial care as well as technical skill.

We deeply appreciate the financial support extended by the John Simon Guggenheim Memorial Foundation, which awarded Ladd a fellowship; by the National Endowment for the Humanities which granted a fellowship to Hadley; by the American Enterprise Institute for Public Policy Research; and by the University of Connecticut Research Foundation. The project simply could not have been completed without this assistance.

Both of us want to add a note of special thanks to Donald S. Lamm and Michelle C. Cliff of W. W. Norton. In timely criticism and equally timely encouragement, as in their sensitivity both to the demands of social science and those of clear exposition, they have been everything one could ask editors to be.

Our families have suffered long and gracefully. Ladd's sins of commission and omission are the greater, if for no reason other than his family—including his wife, Cynthia Northway Ladd, and his children, Carll, Corina, Melissa, and Benjamin—is larger. Mary Turner Hadley deserves equal recognition for forbearance. If these observations have the flavor of flippancy, it is only because we do not regard the pages of this volume an appropriate place to try to express the respect and affection which characterize many families in their joint enterprises variously defined and pursued, and which are surely evident in our own.

As in any collaborative effort, a division of labor was employed in work on this book. Ladd provided the overall direction of the research, secured the necessary financial support, and did the actual writing of each chapter. Hadley, in residence at the University of Connecticut, directed the analysis and presentation of the data and contributed ideas to the direction of the research and writing.

It is something of a ritual to conclude such prefatory remarks by observing that the authors alone should be

held accountable for what they have written. We happily
adhere to this ritual. While our debts are many, we are exclusively responsible for all views and interpretations expressed here.

E.C.L.
C.D.H.

Mansfield Depot, Connecticut
New Orleans, Louisiana
December 1974

A Note on the Second Edition

Two considerations prompted us to prepare this substantially revised edition of *Transformations* now, just two
years after the first edition appeared. One of these is rather
apparent. The 1976 elections are an important chapter in
U.S. electoral history, and we wanted to bring information
on them into our account. The reader will find material updating the various figures and tables so that the Carter-
Ford contest is described as comprehensively as the earlier McGovern-Nixon election. The 1976 voting is located
in the analytic context that we previously introduced.

Updating is a "neutral" act, one involving nothing more
than proper deference to the passage of time. We intend
more than this. Since November 2, 1976, we have been
variously bemused and disturbed by a stream of commentary suggesting that 1976 saw something akin to a New
Deal restoration. The "old coalitions," so fractured in the
late 1960s and early 1970s, allegedly made a forceful reappearance. American electoral politics can once again be
understood in the framework made familiar during the
Roosevelt era.

The latter line of argument is, quite simply, nonsense. The 1976 balloting evidences broad continuities, all right—but to the alignments which began taking shape in the 1960s, not those which developed in the 1930s.

Our list of debts lengthened with preparation of this revised edition. At Stanford University where Ladd was in residence during academic year 1976–77, Anne Diesel and John Devine assisted in the preparation of the new material; while in Storrs, Evelyn Vanden Dolder, Sally Daniels, Diane Reed, and Anne-Marie Mercure, and in New Orleans, Rosemary Sander made important contributions. Yankelovich, Skelly and White, and the Gallup Organization made available their 1976 survey collections, and we could not have undertaken this revision without access to such extensive data of high professional quality. Ladd was on leave during 1976–77 with fellowships from the Rockefeller Foundation and the Hoover Institution of Stanford University, and he wishes to express his thanks for this generous support.

Portola Valley, California
June 1977

Introduction

Views from the Tripod

In ancient Greece, when the priestess of Apollo at Delphi made ready to deliver an oracle, she positioned herself upon a special seat supported by three legs, the tripod. Prophecy was important to the Greeks, and so it has been, in varying forms, to all peoples. We do indeed strain to see the future, knowing that one day it will be our present.

In the United States today, a society far more secular than ancient Delphi, the prophecy most attended to concerns the *political* future, and falls in the province of news commentators and social scientists. Especially because society and polity are now beset by such sweeping change and extreme turbulence, the question of where the system is heading has become notably compelling. And because political parties do not merely reflect the structure of societal conflict but are primary instruments for translating conflict into political responses, they are appropriately a principal focus for political prophecy.

Out of the massive amount of recent commentary on American political parties—changing electoral configurations, partisan realignment, new patterns of conflict between party elites and ranks and file, and the like—a small group of reasonably distinct projections as to the emergent character of the parties-elections system have taken shape.[1] They deserve brief examination here, partly for the insights they offer, and partly because they provide some sense of the extraordinary diversity of the interpretations advanced.

The party system of the United States now in the middle years of the 1970s is undergoing an upheaval. Upon that, most observers agree. This upheaval stems from major changes which have enveloped American society generally, and carries consequences for the substance of public decision making. It will help shape the political future. But a lot of different answers have been given to some basic questions about the future of American party politics. What interests will be decisive? What coalitions will be dominant? What lines of conflict will segment the public? Will majority status remain with the Democrats, shift to the Republicans, move to some third party, or reject any stable partisan home altogether, to reside in shifting coalitions of the moment? The several projections we discuss here speak to such questions.

I. The New Republican Majority

In the immediate post-Watergate period, this argument appears the most clearly implausible—that the thrust of

---

[1] A good many commentators, including one of us, have noted that *political party* is regularly used with varying referents: to include the formal organizational machinery of the party; to encompass those leaders in government and outside it who accept the party label; and to comprise the segment of the electorate at large which variously identifies with the party standard and supports candidates running beneath it. See Ladd, *American Political Parties: Social Change and Political Response* (New York: W. W. Norton, 1970), p. 8; and Frank Sorauf, *Political Parties in America* (Boston: Little, Brown, 2nd edition, 1972), pp. 9–11. While these several components are so obviously interwoven, we will be attending to positions, alignments, and conflict primarily as they involve the mass base of the parties. The phrase *parties-elections system* is cumbersome and so we will use it sparingly. But it is the most precise depiction of what will occupy us: that complex set of interactions whereby the myriad array of contending demands and interests among the citizenry are organized by parties for the purpose of electoral resolution.

various contemporary social and political changes will replace the old New Deal majority with a new majority, conservative in its policy expectations and *Republican* in its
partisan home. Yet if it appears implausible today, we
should remember that it seemed notably more realistic on
the morning of Wednesday, November 8, 1972, and that
the social conditions which nurtured it have hardly all
vanished before the corruption of Watergate.

First, it should be noted that premonitions of a Republican return to majority status, so common in some quarters
between November 1968 and March 1973, are not altogether new. In the first decade after World War II, they
were regularly felt by any number of politicians, journalists, and political scientists. The key ingredient then was
deemed to be affluence: The American middle classes had
long been decisively Republican, postwar prosperity was
expanding dramatically the ranks of the middle class, and
the Republican party would ride growing *embourgeoisement* to national ascendancy.

Visions of a new Republican majority, as these emerged
again in the late 1960s and early 1970s, bear only partial
resemblance to those of the 1950s. The new visions have
been seen by many—with satisfaction by Republican partisans, including Richard Nixon who during the 1972 campaign frequently heralded "the birth of a New American
Majority"; [2] and by some Democratic partisans with more
than a little trepidation. But they were most clearly articulated by conservative columnist and onetime Nixon administration aide, Kevin Phillips.[3]

[2] For a good exposition of the origins of this new majority as Mr. Nixon
perceived them, see the text of his radio address of October 28, 1972,
made available by the Republican National Committee.

[3] Among the many writings on this theme by Phillips, see *The Emerging Republican Majority* (New Rochelle, N.Y.: Arlington House, 1969);
"How Nixon Will Win," *New York Times Magazine* (August 6, 1972), pp.
8–9, 34–38; and "The Future of American Politics," *National Review*, 24
(December 22, 1972), pp. 1396–1398. It should be noted that Phillips has
subsequently repudiated his projection of an emerging Republican majority, while reaffirming most of the analysis of social and political change
which led him to it. For this revised position, see *Mediacracy: American
Parties and Politics in the Communications Age* (Garden City, N.Y.:
Doubleday, 1975).

For Phillips and others of this view, all of the ingredients for basic partisan realignment became present in the United States in the late 1960s. The familiar political agenda drafted in the New Deal era had been rewritten. In part this was due simply to rising affluence in the society: "The Democratic party fell victim to the ideological impetus of a liberalism which had carried it beyond programs taxing the few for the benefit of the many (the New Deal) to programs taxing the many on behalf of the few (the Great Society)." [4] Poverty, decisively majoritarian during the Depression, had become decisively minoritarian by the 1960s. At the same time, all manner of new items, new subjects of contention, had been added to the agenda. The black "socioeconomic revolution," the fraying of nerves and sensibilities before extraordinary changes in life styles and cultural values, crime and violence—these and related matters indicated a world of public concerns scarcely perceptible when the Rooseveltian coalition was put together.

As new problems have arisen, the patterned responses suggested by New Deal liberalism have become increasingly inadequate. Any ideology, any public philosophy, has its day in the sun and then passes into obsolescence as the problems it was designed to deal with are replaced. New problems demand a new public philosophy. The movement from the liberalism of the New Deal to that of the Great Society was one from "innovative policy" to "institutionalized reflex." Just as the insufficiency of laissez faire Republicanism in the face of the Depression crisis defined the end of one sociopolitical era, "so did the breakdown of New Deal liberalism in the face of a social and urban crisis which clearly demands its own ideological innovation." [5]

---

[4] Phillips, *The Emerging Republican Majority*, p. 37.

[5] Phillips, *The Emerging Republican Majority*, p. 38. Theodore Lowi has stressed the inability of New Deal liberalism, as the "old public philosophy," to speak meaningfully to the range of contemporary public concerns. See his *The End of Liberalism* (New York: W. W. Norton, 1969). Phillips comes to very different conclusions than Lowi as to what public

In both the Depression period and the present, large segments of the public have manifested intense concern with the problem of social stability. The scope of social change, in each instance, left the electorate with an abiding fear of chaos. But Americans in the late 1960s and early 1970s saw very different enemies and looked to different policy responses to achieve stability than did their fellow citizens four decades earlier. In place of a conservative establishment (the business community) responsible for governmental inaction in the face of extreme unemployment, corporate malpractice, collapse of the farm economy, and urban workers' needs for adequate working conditions, a liberal establishment's policy failures had come to sustain concern over social health and stability. The populism of the New Deal had a conservative establishment to attack and was directed to the support of liberal programs and policies. The populism of the late 1960s and 1970s, confronting instead a liberal establishment, has led to neoconservative policy responses. Prospects for a new Republican majority have rested heavily upon this populist revolt against an establishment (by definition, elitist) insensitive to the needs of the people (notably white, petit bourgeois, southern, and heartland people).

Brighter prophets of the new Republican majority, like Phillips, did not assume that the ideological transformations of recent years would automatically redound to the Republicans' benefit. The change in structure of conflict presented the *opportunity*, not the *necessity*, of Republican dominance. In December of 1972, before the storm of Watergate broke, Phillips lamented that "confronted by the ideological opportunity of a generation," the Nixon administration had walked into a political scandal "staining the Republican party's image and alienating voters who would have responded to a positive neoconservative blue-

---

responses are called for in light of the antiquation of New Deal liberalism, but he shares the general view that some new public philosophy is required.

print for America." [6] And not only scandal stood in the Republicans' path. Party leaders had to be disabused of the notion that old-style business conservatism would suffice. The new majority is variously repelled and frightened by components of social and cultural change, and in a sense it is conservative; but its conservatism clearly is not of the pro-business sort.

By 1975, Phillips had become convinced not only that prospects for a new Republican majority lay in ruins, but that the GOP, lacking clarity of vision and mission, was no longer a viable claimant of conservative loyalties. A third party challenge from the right in 1976 was almost inevitable. At its core, of course, the argument had always contained the premise that what was really out there was an emerging neopopulist, neoconservative majority—which *might* be brought under the Republican standard. The latter possibility, not the incipient coalition, had been dashed.[7] Some novel political creature, half-Reagan and half-Wallace, would be needed to rally the constituent groups.

II. The New Democratic Majority

One of the most fascinating aspects of the 1972 presidential contest waged between Richard Nixon and George

---

[6] Phillips, "The Future of American Politics," p. 1398.

[7] Phillips is one of a number of political commentators in the conservative camp who now have written off, or almost written off, the GOP. In *Mediacracy: American Parties and Politics in the Communications Age*, Phillips speculates that the Republicans "may succumb to history," but he is far from confident that a new party, in an age of partisan collapse, will be able to organize so as to exploit the ideological opportunity. William Rusher (*The Making of the Majority Party* [New York: Sheed and Ward, 1975]) is much more sanguine about the prospects of a new coalition—even to the point of offering it a name, the Independence party. It is important to recognize that the step, for Phillips and Rusher, from "an emerging Republican majority" to "a disappearing Republican party" is not really a very long one. Both men reflect the old conservative longing for an authentic conservative voice, and the old conservative belief that there really is a conservative majority out there waiting for a party to arise and summon it to its true majoritarian destiny.

McGovern lies in the perception by both candidates and their strategists that America would be ruled in the 1970s and 1980s by a majority vastly different from the one ascendant for the first three decades or so after the Great Depression. Both Nixon and McGovern believed that there was aborning a new American majority. No significant difference separates these two projections on many specifics: For example, that Catholics are far less securely Democratic in the new (heavily racial) ethnocultural conflict of the 1970s than they were in the traditional ethnic (Protestant vs. Catholic) divide; that the white South has broken massively with its ancestral party; that the burgeoning intelligentsia of postindustrial society can be expected to give decisive support to liberal-left policies, and to the Democratic party so long (as seem likely) as it serves as the principal vehicle for such approaches. Overall, however, they differ profoundly about who comprises the new majority, about what this majority wants in the arena of public policy, and in their basic reading of the thrusts of social change.

In the views of Senator McGovern, many of his 1972 campaign associates, others of this wing of the Democratic party, and assorted social commentators, power in the next decade will belong to a "change coalition," a collection of otherwise disparate social groups united by dissatisfaction with the status quo and by a commitment to equalitarian, popular, or liberal changes. The McGovern presidential campaign, together with efforts at party reform spearheaded originally by the Commission on Party Structure and Delegate Selection to the Democratic National Committee (McGovern-Fraser Commission), were predicated on the assumption that this change coalition *could* attain sufficient maturity to capture the presidency in 1972. We know now it did not. Analyses supporting the position that a new Democratic majority would be born in 1972 are nonetheless interesting because they comprise a position considered valid by many for the long run—even though the 1972 birth was aborted.

On July 30, 1972, the distinguished historian, Arthur
Schlesinger, Jr., explained to the readers of the *New York
Times Magazine* the underlying hope of the McGovern
candidacy.[8] According to Schlesinger, a situation prevailed
in the seventies comparable to that of four decades earlier
when Franklin Delano Roosevelt brought together the old
Democratic majority.

What F.D.R. had going for him was a strong conviction of the insufficiency of existing policies, a strong concern for what he
called the "forgotten man," and a strong determination to bring
about genuine change. He represented, in short, the New Politics
of 1932. . . . In the same way, George McGovern stands today
for the rejuvenation of the Democratic party. He is the leader of a
coalition of citizen participation, a coalition for change, as broad
as F.D.R.'s coalition of 1932. This coalition—the young, the
women, the blacks, the blue-collar workers, the suburbanites, the
farmers, the Mexican-Americans, the intellectuals—has already
won him the nomination. . . . He has read more accurately than
anyone else the disquietudes of the nation. . . ." [9]

Campaign rhetoric? Of course. But there can be little
doubt that the basic viewpoint propounded was held
firmly.

Like Phillips and other new Republican majority proponents, Schlesinger perceived widespread popular disen-
chantment with the establishment. Populism was in the air
in 1972. Both new majority arguments found the populace
up in arms against decisions of ascendant elites, alienated,
convinced that government was insufficiently responsive
to their needs, proclaiming their resentments through
third party movements like that headed in 1968 by George
Wallace. But it seems establishments, like beauty, are in
the eyes of the beholder. The people, Schlesinger con-

---

[8] Schlesinger, "How McGovern Will Win," *New York Times Magazine*
(July 30, 1972), pp. 10–11, 28–34. Harvard economist John Kenneth Gal-
braith advanced an almost identical prophecy at this time, "The Case for
George McGovern," *Saturday Review/Society* (July 1, 1972), pp. 23–27.
Gary Hart said much the same thing in *Right from the Start* (New York:
Quadrangle, 1973).

[9] Schlesinger, *op. cit.*, p. 34.

cluded, "are estranged from the political system, hostile to
what they perceive as a selfish and oblivious ruling Establishment and intensely eager for a change." [10] The
target of this popular wrath was a big business elite which
spent money lavishly to prop up a Republican administration with which it had established cozy relations, which
resisted such sensible social and economic reforms as establishing a more equitable tax system, cutting down the
bloated defense budget, assuring improved health care,
and providing a system of income guarantees.

The ingredients for the change majority remain present.
Perhaps the most imaginative exposition on this theme is
that of Louis Harris, extended in a recent book, *The
Anguish of Change*.[11] The American electorate as seen by
Harris—drawing heavily upon his survey research organization's regular inquiries into the state of the national
temper—is oriented to change, and tuned in to a distinctly
new political agenda. There is little support for a candidate of the status quo, and any contender "who thinks he
can win the White House by riding a status quo majority
whose main concern in life is to resist the forces of change
represented by the poor, the blacks, or the youth will find
his demagogic cacophony falling on deaf ears. . . ." [12] A
vastly more knowledgeable and sophisticated electorate is
far from unreceptive to the visions of change the Democrats articulated in 1972, despite McGovern's lopsided defeat. For example, "contrary to the observations of some
political reporters, the 1972 Democratic party reforms
were well received by the public: 'greater representation
of women' was received with favor by 81% to 13% of the
public; 'greater representation of black and Spanish-speak-
ing groups' appealed to a 76% to 17% majority; 'greater
representation of youth as delegates' was approved by 76%
to 19%. . . ." [13]

---

[10] *Ibid.*, p. 11.
[11] Harris, *The Anguish of Change* (New York: W. W. Norton, 1973).
[12] *Ibid.*, p. 265.
[13] *Ibid.*, p. 266.

According to Harris' interpretation of his survey materials, a majority of the public has moved to a progressive
posture concerning the directions of needed change. The
advantaged candidate will be the one who is "at least a
moderate on the race question," since "the zenith of anti-
black feeling may well have been reached in the 1967–72
period"; who emphasizes the shame of national neglect of
"the most wretched and miserable in our midst"; who ad-
dresses himself effectively to such newly muscular problems as those involving the deterioration of the environment, the shortage of energy, the transportation crisis; and
who above all can promise effective action to maintain a
peaceful world.[14] Problems now commanding popular concern inevitably favor candidates and party inclined to a
more activist federal role, because only the federal government can offer the broad central coordination and direction necessitated by their national and even international
scope.

In short, as Harris examined the survey data of a decade,
he saw emerging an electorate whose inclinations were for
change, for increasingly sophisticated public responses,
for an activist federal policy, and generally for progressive
commitments. *The Anguish of Change* did not prophesy
the ascendancy of a new *Democratic* majority, but the
character of the new majority as Harris sketched it is far
closer to the visions of McGovern and Schlesinger than of
Phillips.

In the midst of a period of extraordinary social transformations, serious observers in both parties have seen the
raw material from which can be built a durable new majority. With the construction of this majority, of course, would
come electoral victories, and with such victories consonant
directions in public policy. So much of the language in
both the Republican and the Democratic projections is the
same: alienation, frustration, desire for change, populism,
establishments, and so on. At the core of the disagreement

---

[14] *Ibid.*, pp. 267–272.

is whether a new majority will be built around the white bourgeoisie of suburbia, the South, the Sun Belt, the heartland, around a neoconservative Middle America; or whether it will be assembled from groups demanding equalitarian change rivaling that of the New Deal in scope while different in substance, an alliance comprised notably of nonwhites demanding parity in a white-dominated society, women demanding parity in a male-dominated society, youth moved by visions of a social order far less restrictive than that of the past, and a burgeoning intelligentsia critical of the old order. Not surprisingly, wish has been at least in part mother to perception: Both Democrats and Republicans have seen what they wished to see. But there is more to it than this. So fluid, indeed chaotic, has been the last half-decade that reasonable men and women could plausibly construct diametrically opposed interpretations of where majoritarian electoral weight will rest in the ensuing decade.

III. The Search for the Center

This third argument is less distinct than the two already discussed, but still sufficiently singular to admit attention by itself. It insists that no party commands majority status in national presidential politics today, and that none will unless it comes to command the center, unless it emerges through majoritarian appeals on the issue cluster which dominates the contemporary political agenda.

Probably the most prominent exposition of this thesis is that offered in 1970 by Richard M. Scammon and Ben J. Wattenberg in *The Real Majority*.[15] The United States, they began by noting, has not had a *national* majority party since World War II. Witness the following (as of 1970):

—Three of the last five presidential elections were won by Republicans: Eisenhower twice and Nixon once.

---

[15] Scammon and Wattenberg, *The Real Majority* (New York: Coward-McCann, 1970).

—A Democratic presidential candidate for President had received a majority of the popular vote only once in the last six elections (LBJ in 1964).

—If one added up all the Democratic and all the Republican votes for President since World War II, they would be about dead even: 185,000,000 for Republicans and 186,000,000 for Democrats. Some Democratic era! [16]

Updating these figures to take into account the 1972 balloting, we would note that four of the last six presidential elections have been won by Republicans, that a Democratic presidential candidate has received a majority of the popular vote only once in the last seven contests, and that adding up all post–World War II presidential votes we now find Republicans actually leading the Democrats 231 million to 215 million. Congressional voting has produced consistent Democratic majorities, of course, but so internally diverse are the congressional parties—notably their regional components—that the Democratic majority appears more of name than of substance.

What knocked the Democrats from their majority perch? The answer, for Scammon and Wattenberg, is that the "Voting Issue" which dominated the agenda during the New Deal has lost saliency. Terminology varies, but the concept of a Voting Issue is common to many studies of realignment. For the authors of *The Real Majority*, it encompasses "one big issue . . . motivating millions of voters . . . of surpassing political interest . . . [which] continues to hold sway over the electorate for many consecutive years or even consecutive decades." [17] In the Depression years, a new Voting Issue, shaped around the condition of middle-class poverty, came to be of decisive importance to an electoral majority; and the Democrats controlled the center defined by it. With the growing affluence of the post–World War II era, however, this Voting Issue has been displaced. "As middle-class poverty disappeared, so did some of the Democratic appeal." [18]

---

[16] *Ibid.*, p. 26.
[17] *Ibid.*, p. 30.
[18] *Ibid.*, p. 33.

The late 1950s and early sixties were a time in between voting issues: The old had declined, but without any clear replacement. Then, in the latter half of the sixties, a new cleavage emerged, defined by "a set of public attitudes concerning the more personally frightening aspects of disruptive social change." [19] Ascendant as the new Voting Issue, "at the beginning of the 1970s, the Social Issue appears up for grabs in the decade to come, an issue honestly and legitimately troubling tens of millions of Americans." [20]

According to the Real Majoritarians, important segments of both principal parties have been unaware of how the new Voting Issue cuts, and of what is necessary to achieve a majority around it. Some Republicans, perceiving the political muscle of this issue cluster, have talked of the need to "move to the right," to adopt a "southern strategy," to take advantage of anti-black feelings to capture the Wallace voters, and so on. At the same time, some in the Democratic party have seen success in "a leftward movement."

Under the banner of new politics there is talk of forming a new coalition of the left, composed of the young, the black, the poor, the well educated, the socially alienated, minority groups, and intellectuals—while relegating Middle America and especially white union labor to the ranks of "racists." [21]

Both positions, Scammon and Wattenberg argue, are morally troublesome and analytically wrong. The strategies involve neither a proper way to govern the Republic, nor an effective pursuit of electoral majorities. Good government and winning elections require a search for the center. This center is not a static entity, rather a moveable feast. It comprises the attitudinal middle ground defined by distributions on the Voting Issue at a given point in time. Scammon and Wattenberg recognize the awesome complexity of popular opinion, and the extreme difficulty in talking about an attitudinal center when in fact there ap-

---

[19] *Ibid.*, p. 43.
[20] *Ibid.*, pp. 43–44.
[21] *Ibid.*, p. 280.

pear to be multiple dimensions each with its own center. But they insist that typically one set of issues is disproportionately influential; and that American opinion usually fits the classic bell-shaped curve, with a majority of the people clustered around a position which is substantively centrist—falling between polar views which attract only minoritarian backing. Many conservative Republican and "new left" Democratic strategists, the authors argue, either misread the structure of opinion distributions, or failed to understand what kind of appeals would summon the real majority. National majority status is up for grabs, and can be expected to remain there, because neither Republicans nor Democrats seem to possess the capability to dominate the contemporary center.

The normative posture of the authors of *The Real Majority* is evident enough. Unhappy over the policy directions of the McCarthy-McGovern segment of the national Democratic party, they feel closer to the Humphrey-Jackson wing. The former is chastized as unmindful of majority wishes. Normative assumptions surely intrude upon the interpretation—but this is the condition of social science generally. We are inclined simply to take the argument as one basic interpretation of the future of American electoral politics.

IV. The Era of Partisan Decomposition

This fourth projection shares much in common with the others, assuming an end to the ascendancy of the old New Deal coalitions and the type of conflict structure which nurtured them. The outcome here, however, is not some reconstituted new majority, but rather an extenuation of the rapid thrusts toward partisan decomposition or disaggregation of the last decade. The emergent epoch will be one where no party commands a base of support sufficiently broad and persistent to claim majority status.

In his brilliant study of the unfolding of the New Deal

parties (1951), Samuel Lubell turned to astronomy in search of an appropriate analogy for the historic American major party alignments.

Thumbing back through history, we find relatively few periods when the major parties were closely competitive, with the elections alternating between one and the other. The usual pattern has been that of a dominant majority party, which stayed in office as long as its elements held together, and a minority party which gained power only when the majority coalition split. Our political solar system, in short, has been characterized not by two equally competing suns, but by a sun and a moon. It is within the majority party that the issues of any particular period are fought out; while the minority party shines in reflected radiance of the heat thus generated.[22]

The party decomposition interpretation, rejecting the continued applicability of this model, foresees a period when the principal partisan bodies will lack the political gravitational pull needed to order the system coherently.

Few if any observers question that the American parties have been weakened in the contemporary era, both organizationally and in their command of citizenry loyalties. Party organizations have never been notably strong in the United States, but in recent decades most of the once muscular urban and state machines have withered. The proportion of voters describing themselves as independents, rather than as Republicans or Democrats, has increased notably since the 1950s. Among the young and the college educated today, independents are the largest "party," their numbers exceeding those of self-identified Democrats and Republicans. More importantly, the incidence of independent or split-ticket voting has risen dramatically.

A number of factors associated with the weakening of party organizations and of party regularity in the electorate are widely appreciated. The level of exposure to formal higher education has climbed markedly, and one main ef-

---

[22] Lubell, *The Future of American Politics* (Garden City, N.Y.: Doubleday Anchor Books, revised edition, 1956), p. 212.

fect of this "higher education explosion" has been to extend dramatically the proportion of the population which feels no need for parties as active intermediaries in the voting decision. And with attention focused so much on the style and personal attributes of the contenders, the role of party ties necessarily is weakened. Television projects candidates, not parties.

Some components of this interpretation, then, have passed into consensus. What is distinctive about the argument is its wholistic view of decomposition as the primary, decisive dimension of contemporary change in the parties-elections system. More than any other student of the American political parties, Walter Dean Burnham has developed this diagnosis.

In Burnham's view, fundamental, "critical" electoral realignments have occurred periodically in American political life in response to major disfunctions—disfunctions arising as massive social and economic change produced new political demands which could not be met by the existing parties-elections system.

The socioeconomic system develops but the institutions of electoral politics and policy formation remain essentially unchanged. Moreover, they do not have much capacity to adjust incrementally to demands arising from socioeconomic dislocations. Disfunctions centrally related to this process become more and more visible, until finally entire classes, regions, or other major sectors of the population are directly injured or come to see themselves as threatened by imminent danger. Then the triggering event occurs, critical realignments follow, and the universe of policy and electoral coalitions is broadly redefined.[23]

Now in the 1970s, so many of the major disfunctions required for critical realignment are present. And there is some possibility that such unmet demands will be satisfactorily handled through realignment, "that . . . the excep-

[23] Burnham, *Critical Elections and the Mainsprings of American Politics* (New York: W. W. Norton, 1970), p. 181. See also by Burnham, "The End of American Party Politics," *Transaction*, 7 (December 1969), pp. 12–22.

tionally rapid erosion of the behavioral hold of the old major parties on the American electorate which is now going on may be part of a pre-realignment process during which masses of voters become available for mobilization along other than traditional lines . . . [with] such realignment . . . [involving] the creation of a sixth party system of as yet undefined structure and policy content." [24] But Burnham doubts that any such realignment will occur, in part because "electoral disaggregation carried beyond a certain point . . . make[s] critical realignment in the classic sense impossible. . . ." [25] He charts the inauguration of long-term party decomposition after 1896, a disaggregation arrested in the New Deal era, but which has "very obviously undergone immense, almost geometric, expansion" over the last decade. When the crumbling of the psychological cement binding citizens to parties has progressed far enough, one arrives at an electorate which is "beyond" critical realignment.

Burnham sees, as well, sinister forces behind the weakening of party. Referring to 1972 activities designed to advance the president's position at the expense of the Republican congressional party, he observes that "deliberate elite strategies may reinforce or accelerate trends toward the liquidation of party-in-the-electorate." [26] And the latter development is linked to nothing less than "the disappearance of democracy . . . in the United States." [27] So extreme a foreboding springs naturally enough from the assumptions and arguments which have distinguished Burnham's work: parties are the only available instrument whereby "countervailing collective power on behalf of the many individually powerless [can be marshaled] against the relatively few who are individually or organizationally

[24] Burnham, *Critical Elections and the Mainsprings of American Politics*, p. 92.

[25] *Ibid.*, pp. 91–92.

[26] Burnham, "Rejoinder to 'Comments' by Philip Converse and Jeɪ.old Rusk," *American Political Science Review*, 68 (September 1974), p. 1057.

[27] *Ibid.*

powerful"; [28] the progressive weakening of the citizenry
parties is profoundly conservatizing, for the interests
which can operate effectively as individual units are concentrated largely in the corporate business system; the
possibility of progressive social reform is dependent upon
a strong party structure being able to mobilize constituent
groups in the public and direct their attention in some coherent fashion toward the necessary policy responses.

Samuel Lubell has written on the decline of party from a
different perspective. Success in American national politics, he argues, now is determined primarily by the electorate's evaluation of the "President-manager." [29] On the
one hand, parties have grown weaker. On the other, an extraordinarily augmented presidency has become the fulcrum for electoral choice. Lubell sees the United States
having entered an era of "total elections," in which presidents utilize their exceptional powers over economic life
and foreign policy to orchestrate electoral results. The
elections of 1964 and 1972 were not the first in which
presidents had utilized prerogatives as incumbents to help
promote their reelection, but presidential management of
the society has moved so far that unparalleled resources
are now available to shape the outcome.[30] When things go
wrong, of course, the president is blamed massively and
his party banished from office. Lubell is describing a kind
of plebiscitary presidency, one in which the electorate
comes to vote for or against the incumbent almost exclusively, thereby expressing approval or disapproval of the
current course of the American societal experience.

Party loyalties are lightly held. The Republican coalition
shows little prospect of becoming majoritarian, and "there
does not seem to be much chance of reestablishing the
New Deal coalition in its old form." [31] Party fades into the

---

[28] Burnham, "The End of American Party Politics," p. 20.

[29] Lubell, *The Hidden Crisis in American Politics* (New York: W. W.
Norton, 1971), p. 278.

[30] Lubell, *The Future While it Happened* (New York: W. W. Norton,
1973). See in particular pp. 30–45.

[31] Lubell, *The Hidden Crisis in American Politics*, p. 278.

background before total elections, plebiscitary presidencies, and a massive presidential orchestration (successful or unsuccessful) of social and political life. These developments, along with an apparent inability to establish any long-range pattern in resolution of the conflicts dividing the country, have resulted in "a new alignment of two incomplete, narrow-based coalitions, polarized against each other." [32]

V. Tout Finira Pareil

The final projection is of special interest, because alone among these efforts to foresee the future, it speaks finally of continuity rather than change. *Quoique bouleversé par les changements, tout finira pareil.* It looks, in other words, through the convulsions caused by contemporary change, and detects the ultimate continuation of the New Deal party system. Amid all the prophecies of "an end to the New Deal coalitions," this view foretells their continued vitality, and in particular the continued ascendancy of a coalition very much resembling that which FDR presided over.

The freshest, most cogent and complete statement of this enucleation has been provided recently by James Sundquist.[33] Four issues have emerged in the post–World War II era, Sundquist argues, with at least the potential to precipitate major realignment. That is, there have been four main clusters of public concerns able to mobilize large numbers of voters and which, at the same time, have cut across the axes of conflict of the New Deal period: agitation over communism—foreign and domestic—and how the United States should respond to it; race; Vietnam; and law and order. Sundquist notes the power of each of these,

---

[32] *Ibid.*

[33] James L. Sundquist, *Dynamics of the Party System: Alignment and Realignment of Political Parties in the United States* (Washington, D.C.: The Brookings Institution, 1973).

the turbulence in the body politic each produced, but concludes that for varying reasons—the decline in the intensity of the issue and its capacity to mobilize the citizenry,
or the actions of the threatened party in successfully straddling it—these crosscutting issues of the post–New Deal
years "have not provided the impetus for any major realignment of the party system established in the
1930s. . . ." [34]

Sundquist is not unaware or unimpressed by various of
the elements deemed crucial in the other projections.
For example, the recent growth of independent attitudes
and independent electoral behavior is carefully assessed.
And he recognizes the existence of some long-term trends
bearing on the parties-elections system which are irreversible: media campaigning is not going to be outlawed; old
style political bosses are not going to achieve the ascendancy of a half-century ago; the high affluence and education which makes for independent electoral behavior is
part of a broad, secular progression. But, he concludes, the
measure of change has been overstated. One message
comes across clearly throughout *Dynamics of the Party
System*—that much under the American political sun now
seen as new really isn't. And much which is new represents short-term change. For example, the growth of independent electoral behavior in the 1960s coincides with
deep divisions over race, Vietnam, and the Social Issue.
Because these bisected the existing lines of party cleavage, they blurred inter-party distinctions, created demands
for change which found no adequate expression through
the existing parties. Various groups of independents were
thus spun off: the young, as the group most alienated by
Vietnam; southern white segregationists, most alienated
by the race issue; southern whites and urban northern
Catholics, blocs deeply troubled by the Social Issue. This
is important, surely, in terms of the last decade of American politics, but it appears to Sundquist as essentially of

---

[34] *Ibid.*, p. 32. For a careful discussion of the impact of these crosscutting issues on the party coalitions, see pp. 308–331.

the short term. "The party system is always thrown into turmoil when powerful, crosscutting issues are at work." [35]

The creation of a new party system and the revitalization of an old one, different as they seem, occur in much the same way. In the first case, a new cluster of issues dominates the agenda, cutting across the existing line of party cleavage in a permanent fashion; while in the second instance, the new axis, superimposed on the old, is coincident with it. Looking to the future, Sundquist sees a weakening of the great crosscutting issues of the last decade, and the strengthening of "coincident issues" which will serve to redefine and sharpen the old New Deal cleavage. American politics in the coming decade will increasingly be dominated by "the activist-conservative" and class conflicts dominant throughout the Democrats' Depression and immediate post-Depression ascendancy. The late 1960s and early seventies, in this view, bear striking similarity to the late 1940s and early 1950s.

The message is clear. A national majority in the long run will support activist and equalitarian governmental programs. This position in the agenda of the U.S. as an advanced industrial society is occupied by the Democratic party—which displays no signs of surrendering it. Periodically, crosscutting issues have arisen, and an exhausted electorate has turned to the Republicans to buy time, peace, tranquility. But the mood has passed, and the activist-equalitarian commitments have reasserted themselves.[36] This will happen once again. The New Deal party system will be reinvigorated.

VI. Toward One View from the Tripod

These several attempts at charting direction of the American parties-elections system are not all mutually exclusive, and observers identified with one are frequently

[35] *Ibid.*, p. 353.
[36] *Ibid.*, p. 373.

sensitive to the importance of changes subsumed beneath others. Still, they convey a considerable variety in interpretation, and collectively contain much that is contradictory. In this volume, we will be sorting out and assessing the various propositions, as we try to move to a single integrative statement.

PARTIES AND THE SOCIAL SYSTEM

Like any study of a set of political phenomena, this one proceeds from a conceptual orientation and underlying concerns which should be specified at the outset. In the first instance, parties, elections, and voting are all seen, in a fundamental sense, as *dependent* variables. They exist as parts of the political system which is, precisely, a subunit of the larger social system. As such, they are much more *acted upon* than *acting upon*. The environment in which they move impinges upon them in many more ways than they intrude upon that environment.

Parties are bounded by complex arrays of institutional and statutory constraints. Electorates are buffeted about by ever-changing structures of social conflict. The issues on which voters are asked to take sides; the group antagonisms to which parties must respond in formulating programs, waging campaigns, and in their attempts to build governing coalitions; the contrasting expectations and views as to the course of public life which determine what kind of arena elections will be fought out in, and hence the type of result which the democratic electoral process can obtain; all these are products of forces which lie deep in the fabric of a social order. Similarly, characteristics of voters as participants in party and electoral life are heavily determined by broad dimensions of the society: their educational levels; the channels through which they acquire political information; their degree of satisfaction or dissatisfaction with "the system"; their cultural norms bearing upon electoral participation; and so on.

It is true that parties not only are shaped by, but through their own distinctive properties help to shape the external environment. The flow of influence, however, must be disproportionately toward parties and elections. Sensitive to those areas where attributes of the parties impinge upon polity and society and hence sensitive to the implications of changes in the way parties and elections are organized, we nonetheless emphasize environmental impacts *upon* the parties-elections system.

This line of argument is straightforward enough, but its implications are really quite substantial. We are led to insist that the parties-elections system cannot be understood without careful attention to the complex set of linkages between it and the larger society. A primary research task becomes, then, locating the principal points or areas of encroachment upon parties and elections, and specifying the kinds of impact which result. The job of theory is to suggest the most critical points of linkage, while empirical research then explores the consequences of the flow or interaction across those points deemed the most critical.

The parties-elections system is wonderfully situated to sustain a rich and diverse set of inquiries into the society and polity. When new interest collectivities appear, when groups experience changes of status or otherwise arrive at expectations such that their dominant concerns are transformed, when major new public problems beset the polity, or when issues arise which divide publics differently than did those of the past—then the parties-elections system is transformed. The nature of this transformation both ratifies the cumulative impact of precipitating social and political developments, and helps to determine the manner in which the new conflict is processed or resolved. Parties thus provide a window through which to view and assess the political consequences of many important pieces of social change.

THE QUESTION OF REALIGNMENT

While we will be especially attentive to changes which have occurred in the Republican and Democratic party coalitions since the New Deal, we would not want to categorize the present undertaking as a study of partisan realignment. The assumptions which underlie the literature on "critical elections" and "critical realignment," in particular, are rather foreign to our approach.

V. O. Key, Jr. drew the attention of political science to elections which may be critical, in the sense of involving wider voter movements and more durable shifts than commonly occur, in his well-recognized 1955 article.[37] While the concept of critical elections did not loom large in Key's work, and while in a 1958 article [38] he introduced a major modification, political scientists seized upon the category and have subsequently amended, extended, and applied it in a fairly sweeping fashion. It is truly a case of Key sneezing and political science catching a cold.

It seems to us that attention here has been directed to the wrong class of objects. Elections became the prime units of analysis. So argument developed as to whether one election produced the durable shifts which "critical" implies. Is election X realigning or deviating, converting or maintaining? Do we get out of an intellectual box by shifting the focus to a "critical-election syndrome" [39] or to a "critical period"? [40] And so on. From a social systemic perspective, one can question whether there is any such thing as a critical *election* or set of elections. Instead, it

---

[37] Key, "A Theory of Critical Elections," *Journal of Politics*, 17 (February 1955), pp. 3–18.

[38] Key, "Secular Realignment and the Party System," *Journal of Politics*, 21, (May 1959), pp. 198–210.

[39] Duncan MacRae, Jr. and James A. Meldrum, "Critical Elections in Illinois: 1888–1958," *American Political Science Review*, 54 (September 1960), pp. 669–683.

[40] Walter Dean Burnham, "The Alabama Senatorial Election of 1962: Return of Inter-party Competition," *Journal of Politics*, 26 (November 1964), pp. 823–824. Burnham used this term again in later writings, including *Critical Elections and the Mainsprings of American Politics*.

Concentration on question of new majority may be too superficial

seems, the accumulation of social change periodically reaches critical proportions—in the sense that the structure of conflict shifts so far from that which sustained the old partisan coalitions and cleavages as to render them obsolete. Elections occurring at times when sweeping changes coalesce naturally manifest pronounced shifts of a durable sort in voter behavior. But the election is but one current in the sweeping tide of sociopolitical change.[41]

Critical realignments take place primarily as *effects of* other major changes occurring in the society. Throughout American political history, there have been crucial economic transformations. New social collectivities have arisen, while previously ascendant interests have experienced decline or erosion. Broad redistributions of political power have occurred. New clusters of social issues have arisen in response to a changing societal setting, while issues which once deeply divided the populace have passed into the graveyards of consensus and irrelevancy. The political agenda has been rewritten. And as a result of these forces, the societal environment has at times been so substantially altered as to require some fundamental modifications of the parties-elections system.

Central claim ↓

If this general interpretation is accepted, the prevailing view of the ingredients of a basic realignment—blocs of voters crossing party lines, producing a new majority party—comes to be seen as dangerously incomplete. Almost certainly, if the structure of conflict is drastically altered, large numbers of voters will respond differently in

[41] Key emphasized the social systemic context in his 1958 piece on "secular realignment." He noted that "events and communications of political import play upon the electorate continuously; election returns merely record periodic readings of the relative magnitudes of streams of attitudes that are undergoing steady expansion or contraction. . . . The rise and fall of parties may to some degree be the consequence of trends that perhaps persist over decades and elections may mark only steps in a more or less continuous creation of new loyalties and decay of old. . . . If the general analysis is correct, doubtless secular changes affecting major segments of American society now in process will in due course profoundly affect the party system." Key, "Secular Realignment and the Party System," pp. 198, 209.

the new electoral arena than they did in the old. But the crossing of party lines is of secondary importance. What really matters is that both the policy expectations and social group composition of electoral coalitions is transformed. It may or may not follow that there will be a new majority party—that is, a relatively durable and coherent majoritarian coalition operating under a different party label than the preceding majoritarian coalition.

This seems to us vitally important, because it raises again the matter of what set of phenomena our conceptual scheme leads us to emphasize. If critical realignment brings to mind primarily the emergence of a new majority party, we may attend insufficiently to changes in the parties-elections system which are of much more fundamental importance. The possible appearance of a new majority party does not figure, in our interpretation, as a main ingredient of the contemporary partisan transformation. But the changes taking place are scarcely less dramatic:

1. The Democrats have lost the presidential majority status which they enjoyed during the New Deal era, as new lines of conflict have decimated parts of the old coalition, but the Republicans have not attained presidential majority status. There is no majority party in the presidential arena.

2. There has been an inversion of the old New Deal relationship of social class to the vote. In wide sectors of public policy, groups of high socioeconomic status are now more supportive of equalitarian (liberal) change than are the middle to lower socioeconomic cohorts (within white America); and as a result liberal (often, although not always, Democratic) candidates are finding higher measures of electoral sustenance at the top of the socioeconomic ladder than among the middle and lower rungs. This inversion follows from very basic changes in the structure of conflict in American society, and is likely to be long-term.

3. The Republican coalition has experienced serious erosions, and is weaker now than at any time since the days of the Great Depression, probably weaker, in fact, than at any time since the party's rise during the Civil War era.

4. A "two-tier" party system has emerged, with one set of electoral dynamics operating at the presidential level, and yet another in subpresidential contests.

5. The electorate is far more weakly tied to political parties now than at any time in the past century, and as it has been freed from the "anchor" of party loyalties it has become vastly more volatile.

6. The communications function—whereby party leaders communicate with the rank and file, and the latter in turn send messages up to the party leadership—has historically been a great raison d'être for political parties in egalitarian systems; but this function has increasingly been assumed by other structures, notably those organized around the mass media of communication.

7. A major new cohort of activists has assumed vastly increased importance in the electoral arena, a cohort whose position is closely linked to the growth of the intelligentsia in postindustrial America.

Do these describe a realignment? Well no, not really, although many of the components are obviously related to what *realignment* has suggested. They surely comprise elements of a basic transformation of the parties-elections system—the focus of this book. Attention to realignment as such is just too restrictive. We will be examining a more general set of changes involving parties, elections and voting behavior, as these are occurring in response to a changed social setting.

Part I

Intertwining

1

The Formation of the
New Deal Party System

Fundamental changes comprising a shift from one sociopolitical era to another, with an accompanying alteration of
the political agenda, are the stuff of which major partisan
transformations are made. One such epochal transition was
consummated in the Depression years. Among its many
consequences for American public life was the structuring
of new partisan coalitions. Basic changes were imposed
upon the fabric of inter-party policy conflict. The Democrats attained majority status, and the Republicans assumed an unaccustomed place in the U.S. political order—
becoming, for the first time in their seventy-year history
since formation during the Civil War years, a minority alliance responding to the initiatives of the new majority.

I. Societal Change and the Political
Agenda of the New Deal

The story of the emergence of a distinctively new sociopolitical setting in the 1930s is too long and involved for

retelling here.[1] The plot itself is complex, and all manner
of sweeping events, strategic episodes, actions, and inac-
tions by the principal characters surround the central
theme. We can attend here only to that portion of the story
essential to an understanding of the appearance of a new
structure in party conflict.

LONG-TERM CONSEQUENCES OF INDUSTRIALIZATION

The success of the enterprise of industrial nation building in the six or seven decades after the Civil War produced major alterations of the fabric of American society.
What had been localized and agricultural became urban,
industrial, and interdependent. A massive factory-based
working class took shape, the foot soldiers of industrialization. Inequalities of wealth and power followed this
surge of industrial development. The society came to be
able to produce more and more of goods and services, but
the working classes shared only marginally in the fruits of
this unprecedented economic expansion.[2] And all this
change occurred with minimal public (i.e., governmental)
direction.

---

[1] One of us has attempted to retell it elsewhere, albeit even there in
abbreviated form. See Ladd, *American Political Parties: Social Change
and Political Response*, especially Chapter 5. See, too, Sundquist's *Dynamics of the Party System*, Chapters 9–12.

[2] The rapid industrial growth of the post–Civil War era of American industrial nation building was financed by what most in a later and more affluent generation would call—and what some contemporaries *did call*—
the exploitation of labor. To put it simply, workers put in long hours at
low pay to permit a high rate of profit and capital investment by management. In 1900, the average annual earnings of American industrial workers were around $500 a year, the work week was sixty hours. Not only
were wages low, but they did not rise significantly with the substantial
expansion of productivity between 1870 and 1915. Paul Douglas concluded that there was no improvement whatever in real wages in the face
of the extraordinary expansion of output in this period. Paul H. Douglas,
Real Wages in the United States, 1890–1926 (Boston: Houghton Mifflin,
1930). A more recent investigation by Albert Rees found that the average
hourly earnings of all workers in manufacturing did increase slightly, from

The claims of industrial development required large infusions of labor, and much of this was provided by immigration: Between 1860 and 1929, the United States received the largest in-migration in history, about 32.5 million people, more than half of whom (18.8 million) arrived in the first three decades of the twentieth century; and this great migration transformed the ethnic composition of the country, as 13.5 percent of the total came from Germany, 15.3 percent from Central Europe, 10.2 percent from Russia and the Baltic states, and 13.8 from Italy, as compared to just 10.6 percent from Great Britain.[3] By 1929, many of these new-stock Americans had, or were ready to come of age politically.

In short, the dynamic of the era of industrial nation building carried with it processes leading necessarily to yet another social setting, with a new political agenda, with a new fabric of conflict, with new claimants for power, economic benefits, and recognition. American society was not transformed overnight by the Great Depression. A stream of developments prior to 1929 contributed to the base of what was to be "the New Deal era."

To take just one example, we can find in the first three decades of this century a series of calls for greatly augmented governmental responsibilities in the direction of economic life. The development of the Progressive movement in the early twentieth century was a radical departure in the thinking of the reformist middle classes, a belated recognition of the new world of industrialism. The Progressives were committed to positive government, to the use of governmental powers to restore the balance, to replace an imbalance which had occurred with the extraordinary growth of private business, to manage a far more

16¢ in 1890 (in constant 1914 prices) to 22¢ in 1914. Albert Rees, *Real Wages and Manufacturing, 1890–1914* (Princeton: Princeton University Press, 1961), p. 4. In any event, workers did not benefit proportionately from increased productivity, and crowded tenements, slums, and ghettos emerged as part of the picture of industrial nation building.

[3] These data are from *Historical Statistics of the United States, Colonial Times to 1957*, pp. 56–99.

complicated and interdependent society. In the language
of the time, the Progressives sought to use government
"where necessary as an agent of human welfare"—"Lord,
how we did like that phrase," wrote William Allen White
in his *Autobiography*, " 'using government as an agent of
human welfare.' " [4]

Herbert Croly, through his many writings, was perhaps
the most coherent and insightful proponent of the Progressive vision of the desired new society. *The Promise of
American Life*, which he published in 1909, was a strong
summons to master the social consequences of industrialization, to "unite the Hamiltonian principle of national
political responsibility and efficiency with a frank Democratic purpose which will give a new power to the Hamiltonian system of political ideas and a new power to democracy." [5] Croly urged, then, what the New Deal later
was to substantially provide, a system of governmental nationalism.

The United States of Croly's day found its nationalizing
impulses and direction coming from private business. This
he found inadequate, bankrupt in terms of emergent problems. A new nationalism was needed (what in embryonic
form Woodrow Wilson was to call the New Freedom, and
FDR was to bring into maturity as the New Deal). Croly's
new nationalism would combine democratic or equalitarian impulses historically associated with the Jeffersonian and Jacksonian traditions, and nationalizing impulses historically linked to Hamiltonianism. It would
combine these with government serving as the principal
initiator and director of change. There should be a national
responsibility for humanizing industrialism and managing
it, and government would be the primary vehicle for this
exercise of national responsibility.

Theodore Roosevelt as president and his Progressive

---

[4] White, *Autobiography of William Allen White* (New York: Macmillan
Co., 1946), p. 77.

[5] Croly, *The Promise of American Life*, (New York: Macmillan Co.,
1909), p. 154.

party candidacy of 1912, Woodrow Wilson in his administration's commitment to the New Freedom—all stand as
precursors of the New Deal, reflective of both an emergent
political agenda, and of new interests and perspectives
generated by the unfolding of American industrialism. Industrialization had created a cosmopolitan middle class
committed to national action, to efficiency and expertise,
to the effective administrative regulation of industry for
broad national purposes; and this class, in alliance with
segments of the urban workers and farmers, had begun to
make its impact felt in American national politics well before 1933. Reformist impulses of the nineteenth century
had tended to be agriculture-based, their vision of the
good society locked in a half-mystical, half-real "golden
age" of the past, a localized society of yeomen farmers.
Gradually in the twentieth century, the base of such impulses shifted to urban and industrial America, and fixed
upon "positive government" as the primary instrument.

THE IMPACT OF THE DEPRESSION

The Great Depression which began in 1929 did not so
much *create*, then, as *abruptly signal* the emergence of a
new social setting. It accelerated the process by which the
political agenda was transformed. The enormity of the
problems comprising the Depression permitted a super-
cession in agendas far more rapid and complete than normally occurs in public life. Herein is the unique contribution of the Depression to American politics, what sets
entry into the sociopolitical era we think of in terms of the
New Deal so decisively apart from entry into other basic
settings: never before or since has so clear a transition
been telescoped into the space of five or six years.

The Depression demonstrated that a complex economy
could not be allowed to operate without central direction,
that in place of the "panics" of less integrated economies
there was the potential in the industrial state for system-

shaking collapses. While displacement of the old entrepreneurial elite as the "political class" of the United States appears to have been inevitable in the long run, the 25 percent unemployment rate of 1932 surely speeded up the "deauthorization." Instead of being custodians of prosperity, the business elite suddenly found itself custodians of an extraordinary collapse.

The severity of economic difficulties provided an unusual opportunity for decisive new action. Typically, efforts at major reform encounter powerful collections of interests able to resist successfully anything more than incremental change. The scope of the post-1929 economic debacle, however, swept these normal barriers aside, giving the Roosevelt administration unusual opportunity to restructure political alignments and to move ahead with new programs. Along with all of these structural elements, there was as well the presence of the right person at the right time. Few observers would question that Roosevelt seized effectively opportunities presented by unique circumstances and used them to the fullest in decisively altering the course of American public argument.

A NEW IDEOLOGICAL DIVIDE

The new political agenda of the 1930s involved introduction of a new conflict axis. And this in turn required terminological innovation. We needed a way of describing conflict different from what had transpired before. It was in this context that *liberal vs. conservative* entered common political discourse.

As Louis Hartz has so effectively argued, the United States is hardly a stranger to liberalism in its classical (Lockean) usage: the ideological defense or statement of interests of ascendant middle classes bred of the commercial and industrial revolution.[6] This liberal tradition, a

---

[6] Hartz, *The Liberal Tradition in America* (New York: Harcourt, Brace and World, 1955).

bourgeois ethic, has formed the core of the American political value system, enjoying a uniquely unquestioned status. Liberalism in its New Deal and post–New Deal sense, however, is very different.

The decisive feature of New Deal liberalism was the fusion of what throughout previous American history had been essentially distinct traditions, what Croly insightfully called the "principles" of nationality and democracy, or the "national idea" and the "democratic idea." This the New Deal accomplished by using government for broad national and democratic purposes, notably in the harnessing of industrialism. To understand the fabric of the political agenda upon which the New Deal partisan alignment was constructed, we must recognize what a fundamental departure this linkage entailed.

In the first century and a quarter of American history after regime formation, the principal initiatives on behalf of nation building or national integration rested with one political party, while the more popular, equalitarian, and democratic directions were provided by the contending coalition: reflecting the former were the Federalists, the Whigs, and subsequently the Republicans; the latter, the Jeffersonian Republicans and the Democrats. The effect of this split in partisan-ideological orientations was to associate democratic, reformist impulses with states' rights, limited government, and localism. It is hardly surprising, then, that early proponents of the fusion of the "national" and "democratic" ideas such as Croly entertained severe doubts about the prospects generally, and in particular as to the Democrats' presiding over this new fusion. In Croly's view, the Democrats were the party of the provincial idea, of Protestant fundamentalism in the Bryan wing and of Catholic fundamentalism in its urban North wing, the party of small towns and farms or of urban neighborhoods, a party of localized interests, a party lacking vision of the national idea.

Along with others of like political persuasion in his time, Croly looked to the Republican party, so much the party of industrialization, as the most likely instrument for national reform because such reform could not come from those nostalgic for a rural past. It could come only from those who accepted industrialism while seeking to master its social consequences. The Republicans were the party of the urban middle class, and it was to a portion of that class that Croly was looking, from which Progressivism sprung. "Those who sought political reform," Samuel Hays has written, "were far more involved in a cosmopolitan than a local world. . . . The reform image of an appropriate decision-making system also arose from the cosmopolitan world. The reformers' model was the business corporation. . . ." [7] More than any other political leader of the time, "Teddy" Roosevelt was the person to whom Progressives looked for "vigorous national action" to deal with the social problem.

Perhaps even in 1928 the Republicans, so long the party of the national idea as embodied in the enterprise of industrial nation building, might have seemed a more likely instrument of the new nationalism than the provincial Democrats. But it was not to be. There was surely an element of historical accident. In any event, the opportunity fell to the second Roosevelt. Franklin Roosevelt ran a campaign in 1932 notable for its call for a balanced budget as the principal governmental response needed in the face of the Great Depression. Yet his roots went deep into the Progressive tradition, in office he was flexible and pragmatic, and his administration groped toward a broad series of policy changes. The country was profoundly sympathetic to change because nothing of the old seemed to work, and gradually, over a four- to five-year period, the nucleus of a distinctive governmental response emerged.

Samuel Beer has correctly emphasized the importance of distinguishing between the *democratic overtones* of the

---

[7] Samuel P. Hays, "Political Party and the Community-Society Continuum," in William Nisbet Chambers and Walter Dean Burnham, eds., *The American Party Systems* (New York: Oxford University Press, 1967), p. 177.

New Deal and its bold assumption of *governmental nationalism*. While FDR's policies had clear equalitarian and class components giving them a perceptible affinity with the Jeffersonian "cherishment of the people," a major thrust of New Deal liberalism is lost sight of when focus is confined to the impact on economic interests of various social groupings. For the New Deal carried the national idea ahead to a new stage, promoted nationalizing by integrating into the society segments of the population which previously had been on the margin or excluded. "Through the new doctrine and force of liberalism, the national idea worked to integrate the pluralism of the twentieth century as it had once countered the territorial sectionalism of the nineteenth." [8]

The liberalism of the Roosevelt administration became a nationalizing force as it centralized governmental power, using such authority to meet problems which had been left to the state and local level or to the private sector, to win for such beneficiary groups as labor and new immigrants "a degree of acceptance in the national consciousness and in every-day social and economic intercourse that they had never previously enjoyed." [9]

The New Deal joined the equalitarian and reformist strains which had appeared throughout American political history through governmental nationalism. The thrust of American nation building shifted from the business community to the public sector, as government assumed responsibilities of both a managerial sort and of a social welfare and reformist character so as "to make the nation more solidary, more cohesive, more interdependent of its growing diversity; in short to make the nation more of a nation." [10] In the Roosevelt era, the Democratic party shifted direction decisively, became the liberal coalition; while the Republicans became the partisan instrument of conser-

---

[8] Samuel H. Beer, "Liberalism and the National Idea," *Public Interest* (Fall 1966), p. 75–76.
[9] *Ibid.*, p. 75.
[10] *Ibid.*, p. 71.

vatism—here defined as opposition to the governmental
nationalism embodied in the New Deal.

No study has more effectively chronicled the rise of the
Democrats to majority party status in a transformed social
and political setting than Samuel Lubell's masterful *The
Future of American Politics*. He caught nicely the underlying dynamic between profound social changes and
the transformation of partisan combat. Throughout most of
American history, Lubell notes, one political party has
stood decisively astride the political agenda of the time,
embodying in its programs, imperfectly to be sure, the directions in policy change demanded by majoritarian interests of the society. The minority party has been left, then,
bound to the majority in a fixed way, like a satellite, forced
to follow a course determined by the latter.

As the party of the agenda, the majority alignment has
staked out policy positions to which the minority con-
tinually is forced to respond or react. This has left the latter with two basic courses of action. At times it has said,
"me too, only a bit differently." It has accepted, that is, the
policy orientation of the majority as basically sound, and
has sought to persuade the electorate that it could accomplish the specified objectives somewhat better. Some
in the minority party, of course, do not court the majority
coalition, but instead oppose what it seeks. The minority
party of a two-party system necessarily becomes the principal vehicle for those social groups which resent and resist the prevailing direction of policy movement of the
period. From time to time, therefore, the second party has
served as the vehicle for a frontal challenge to prevailing
policy. In either case, though—when the weaker of the
two big parties acts as a slightly altered copy of the majority, and when it offers a basic challenge to the majority—it
shows its inability to escape the political web of the party
of the agenda. Lubell chose to describe this relationship
with a vivid if somewhat inaccurate astronomical analogy,
referring to long periods when one party moved as the sun

in the American political solar system, with the weaker of the two parties in orbit about it as a moon.

In the 1930s, one majority sun was setting and a new one rising in response to the transformation of American political life. And as Lubell saw, this new partisan ascendancy meant that the Democrats, no longer the Republicans, would provide the structure in which the great issues of the time would be fought out and through which new directions in policy response would be determined. "Civil Rights, how to balance the interests of the newly emergent labor power against those of the rest of the society, the yearning for security against another depression, the hunger for social status of the climbing urban masses—these have been do-or-die problems for the elements in the Democratic coalition." [11]

In a special sense of the word, political parties in the United States have been thought of as progressive when their visions of the desired public order were generally ascendant, when their conceptions of what government should and should not do, how problems should be met, who should rule, correspond to expectations held by decisive segments of the electorate as to the course this nation should follow. It is in this sense that the Republicans were the progressive party for nearly three-quarters of a century after the Civil War, and that the Democratic party of Franklin Roosevelt emerged as the progressive alignment in the transformed political agenda of the New Deal era.

II. The New Democratic Majority: Continuities and Conversions

When a major transformation of the parties-elections system comes under examination, the natural tendency is to focus upon the newcomers—those whose *addition* to a

---

[11] Lubell, *The Future of American Politics*, p. 213.

party coalition proved decisive both in numbers and in policy directions. The New Deal coalitions were formed around a substantial influx of voters into the Democratic ranks, and this we must attend to. At the outset, though, it may be appropriate to look at continuities: elements of the party alliances of the 1930s representing a carrying over of loyalties formed long before the era when the party system was dramatically transformed.

CONTINUITIES: THE CASE OF THE WHITE SOUTH

The most unambiguous instance of a powerful continuity in group attachments from the pre–New Deal years into the 1930s and beyond involves southern whites. They were a prime component in the Roosevelt majority. In the 1932 presidential balloting, the South (with blacks largely excluded from the electorate) went Democratic by a margin of 76 to 24 percent, and all of its 146 electoral votes swelled FDR's total; four years later, the region was again Democratic, by a 76–24 percent margin, and delivered its entire bloc of electoral votes to Roosevelt; while in 1940, Dixie's unswerving allegiance to the Democracy produced a 73 percent vote for Roosevelt as against just 27 percent for Republican Wendell Willkie, and every electoral vote went to the Democratic nominee.[12] The southern congressional delegation reflected this same massive one-party bent as, for example, all 26 of the region's senators and 119 of its 120 representatives were Democrats in 1936.

But white southerners were not, we know, suddenly converted to the cause of the Democracy by events of the New Deal period. From the end of Reconstruction in 1877 up to the Depression, the South without exception, in every presidential election, affirmed its status as the most Democratic section of the country; and with only one ex-

---

[12] In this chapter, as throughout the book, the South includes the eleven states of the Old Confederacy, together with Kentucky and Oklahoma.

ception (1928), Dixie was the most Democratic by a massive proportion. Figure 1.1 points up this impressive continuity in Democratic loyalties among residents of the Old Confederacy. In the McKinley-Bryan contest of 1900, the proportion of Southerners voting Democratic exceeded that among the national electorate-at-large by 15.3 percentage points; and in 1936, at the height of the New Deal, the region's pro-Democratic margin, as compared to the country generally, was exactly 15 points.

Only in 1928, when Al Smith's Catholicism and northern urban style produced a massive defection to Republican Herbert Hoover, did the Democratic portion of the presidential vote in the South drop below 50 percent, and the region's pro-Democratic posture compared to the rest of the country diminish notably. In contrast to the pattern which was to appear later with the Civil Rights revolution, the biggest 1928 Republican gains were achieved throughout the rim South rather than the Deep South. Smith over-

Figure 1.1. Democratic Percentage of the Presidential Vote; Nationally and the South, 1900–1944

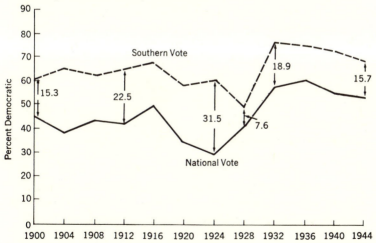

SOURCE: U.S. Bureau of the Census, *Historical Statistics of the United States, Colonial Times to 1957*, pp. 686–687.

whelmed Hoover by 66 to 33 percent in the southern
heartland, while losing the peripheral South decisively, by
44 to 56 percent. The Bible Belt, solidly Protestant heartland of Dixie, stuck with the Catholic Democratic nominee while the outer South was defecting, first because the
former's Democratic attachments were stronger. Less
pluralistic, overwhelmingly rural, with a notably larger
black population historically and hence more obsessed
with race, the Deep South's commitment to the Democracy as the party of white supremacy and regional loyalty
was vastly more complete. The one thing it would not tol-
erate from the national party was any deviation on race,
and in 1928 there wasn't any. Unhappy about Smith, it
nonetheless voted for him. The states of the rim South
were more diverse socially and economically. Their black
populations had never been as large proportionally, and
their politics never so dominated by racial concerns. They
began to industrialize sooner, received a larger population
movement from other sections of the country, and were
less estranged from national life. The Civil War racial support of Democratic allegiance was weaker in the peripheral South, then, and there was more of a socioeconomic
base on which to build an opposition party. Presidential
Republicanism, which refers to voting for GOP national
nominees even though state and local politics remain one-
party Democratic, began in the rim land, and Smith's Catholicism simply gave it a big short-term shove.

This 1928 deviation aside, the South's pro-Democratic
allegiance compared to the rest of the country showed a
strikingly similar pattern during the three decades before
the Great Depression, and in the decade and a half after
FDR first took office. To be sure, the region gave Roosevelt an even higher proportion of its vote in the four presidential elections between 1932 and 1944 than had been its
custom for Democratic presidential candidates in the first
seven elections of the twentieth century. The Democratic
proportion of the total vote jumped approximately 10 percentage points. This gain occurred, seemingly, in response

to forces operating upon the national electorate: gross dissatisfaction with Republican performance during the Depression; the desire for new programmatic initiatives by government; and a general approval of the policies which emerged through Roosevelt's leadership. But overall, the southern voting response proved remarkably constant. Voter turnout in the region remained exceptionally low throughout the Roosevelt years—around 30 percent of the potential electorate, compared to 65–70 percent in non-southern states [13]—reflecting both the disenfranchisement of blacks and the continued depression of incentives to vote resulting from one-partyism.[14] More importantly, the New Deal years in the South simply marked a continuation of more than a half-century of unchallenged Democratic supremacy.

The long-term southern fidelity to the Democratic party which persisted through the Roosevelt era had three great supports. The one best understood comprises the mixture of experiences surrounding race and the Civil War. The Democracy came to function as the expression of white supremacy and regional loyalty. Important as this prop was, it could not have held up one-partyism for so prolonged a period by itself. Parallel support was provided by the region's status as a predominantly rural and farming area, a status which naturally put it in opposition to the business nationalism dominant in the Republican party. Since the Republicans were quickly established after the Civil War as the principal partisan instrument of those interests surrounding industrialization, the Democratic party was the obvious vehicle for the dissenting and minoritarian interests of the agricultural South. The strength of these two

---

[13] These data are from Walter Dean Burnham, "The Changing Shape of the American Political Universe," *American Political Science Review*, 59 (March 1965), pp. 10–11.

[14] Jerrold G. Rusk and John J. Stucker document the constraints resulting in low voter turnout in their interesting "The Effect of the Southern System of Election Law on Voting Participation" (paper delivered at the Mathematical Social Science Board's Conference on the History of Popular Voting Behavior, Cornell University, June 11–13, 1973).

supports naturally permitted construction of a third, tradition. Quite tangible interests underlay the South's commitment to the Democratic party, but once established, that
commitment had a life of its own. For a Southerner growing up in 1910, as in 1935, Democratic allegiance was natural. Wasn't everyone around Democratic? The persistence of party identifications has been often noted
throughout the literature on voting behavior; in the South,
that meant the persistence of Democratic loyalties.

Massive change was to come to the Old Confederacy,
precipitating major shifts in voter loyalties. But these developments awaited events that were to occur after World
War II. There was no New Deal transformation in Dixie.
Its loyalties remained what they had been throughout the
years since the climactic struggle over slavery. White southerners were indeed a major component of the New Deal
Democratic majority, but their loyalties long antedated the
shift in the political agenda which the New Deal represented, standing much more as a continuity than as a conversion.

CONTINUITIES: THE CATHOLIC-PROTESTANT DIVIDE

As a nation built upon great waves of in-migration—
much of it voluntary, some, most notably in the case of
blacks, forced—of peoples of widely varied cultural traditions, the United States has been throughout its history a
setting of major ethnic conflict.

In view of such diversity and the prominence of ethnic
conflict, it is hardly surprising that the attachments and interests of ethnic collectivities historically have been a
prime factor in defining American partisan alliances. And
for more than a century, stretching from well before the
Civil War until the years after World War II, the *Protestant-Catholic* division served as the great organizer of
American ethnic struggles. In the sense intended by this
depiction, *Protestant* and *Catholic* represent not so much
religious as more general ethnocultural traditions. Each of

these loose categories, it is important to note, has subsumed a considerable variety of groups and interests, often
internally at odds. Still, the Protestant-Catholic divide,
more than any other, represented the primary ethnic
frontier for much of American history. And the Democratic
party functioned as the partisan home of large majorities of
Catholic Americans as it did battle with largely Protestant,
and at times anti-Catholic, opponents—the Whigs and subsequently the Republicans.

In their 1840 platform, for example, the Democrats put
themselves on record as flatly opposed to nativist demands
for immigration restrictions, proclaiming that the United
States should be a haven for "the oppressed of every nation," and arguing further that the open door (to immigration) was a "cardinal principle" of their party's creed.
They repeated it in 1844, and again in 1848, in 1852, and
1856, when the Know-Nothings were challenging them on
the national scene. The meaning of this surely was not
lost—on either recent immigrants or the nativists. In the
face of all this the Whigs were silent: not once in their
platforms from 1844 through 1856 (there was no Whig platform in 1840) did they mention immigration. As a major
party, they would not take over the nativist demands for
restriction, but neither would they repudiate such demands.

The electoral response was predictable. Studies of voting behavior by the various ethnocultural groups agree
that old-stock Protestants were not polarized but fairly
evenly divided between the two parties, while Catholics
of whatever ethnic origin were overwhelmingly Democratic.[15] Benson has estimated that in 1844 "about 95 percent of the 'Catholic' voters supported the Democrats in
New York State." [16]

---

[15] See, for example, Edward Pessen, *Jacksonian America: Society, Personality and Politics* (Homewood, Ill.: Dorsey, 1969), especially Chapter
10; and Lee Benson, *The Concept of Jacksonian Democracy* (Princeton,
N.J.: Princeton University Press, 1961), Chapters 8 and 9.

[16] Benson, *op. cit.*, p. 187.

In the post–Civil War period, the South excepted, the
Republicans served as the party of American Protestantism. Such a proposition rests on the same limited and
equivocating association which has normally prevailed between party and social group in view of the diffuse, undis-
ciplined, nonprogrammatic, "many things to many people"
character of the American umbrella parties. From the Civil
War to the Great Depression, the Republicans apparently
retained the allegiance of a clear majority of nonsouthern
Protestants, while the Democrats were the partisan home
of a very large majority of Catholic Americans.

Throughout the late nineteenth and early twentieth centuries, the heterogenous character of the major parties and
their promiscuous search for allies served to blur the relationship between party and position in the ethnocultural
divide. Important here is a fact emphasized by David
Burner, that "the Democracy had attracted the extremes—
the most aggressively Jeffersonian or Populist of the
farmers, particularly in the South, and the most powerful
of the urban immigrant machines." [17] A party thus bifur-
cated inevitably became the battleground when such
issues as prohibition, immigration, and the Ku Klux Klan
assumed high saliency in the national political agenda,
because these two wings were diametrically opposed on
each of these issues. As the struggle was proceeding, the
center of power within the Democracy shifted decisively,
away from the rural, southern and heartland, Protestant
and "dry" (prohibitionist) wing, toward the faction which
can be characterized as urban, eastern, Catholic, and
"wet." This shift was precipitated in large measure by the
great waves of immigration of the late nineteenth and
early twentieth centuries, which swelled the ranks of
urban, new-stock Democrats.

Despite a deep schism within the Democracy between
the rural and Protestant and the urban and Catholic wings,
the party was easily distinguished from the Republicans

---

[17] Burner, *The Politics of Provincialism: The Democratic Party in
Transition, 1918–1932* (New York: Knopf, 1968), p. 6.

on ethnocultural issues in the 1920s. In the South, the (second) Ku Klux Klan worked within the Democratic party, of course—there really wasn't any Republican party—but elsewhere, Burner concludes, "the Klan allied itself primarily with the Republicans and made overtures to the Democracy in most cases only when it desired to widen its already considerable influence. . . . Outside the South the Klan usually assumed a Republican coloration; and at times it encountered organized Democratic opposition." [18] The relatively conservative 1924 Democratic presidential candidate, James W. Davis, denounced the Klan, and Alfred E. Smith, the 1928 nominee, had long been at war with it. There were surely a lot of Democratic prohibitionists, but all three Democratic presidential nominees in the 1920s were wets, and were denounced by the dry forces. The net result of such party differences on the ethnocultural issues of the time was that decisive majorities of Catholic voters fairly consistently backed the Democrats.[19]

---

[18] *Ibid.*, pp. 84–85. The first Ku Klux Klan grew up, of course, in the aftermath of the Civil War. It was exclusively southern. The second Klan, of the 1920s, had different targets and a very different geographic distribution. Strong in a number of northern states, the second Klan considered the Catholic and Jewish immigrants of southern and eastern Europe its prime enemies.

[19] Working with recently discovered interviews which the parties had conducted in a systematic fashion among all voters in certain midwestern towns and counties in the 1870s, for example, Richard Jenson has demonstrated extraordinarily high Catholic support for the Democracy: In Geneseo city and township, Illinois, in 1877, more than 90 percent of old-stock Congregationalists, Methodists, and Baptists were affiliated with the Republican party, while 75 percent of German Catholics, and 100 percent of Irish Catholics were linked to the Democrats; in Hendricks County, Indiana, in 1874, the pattern was much the same, with only 22 percent of Methodists, 31 percent of Presbyterians, 39 percent of missionary Baptists affiliated with the Democracy, as against 83 percent of Catholics. Richard Jensen, "The Historical Roots of Party Identification" (paper presented to the Annual Meeting of the American Political Science Association, New York, September 1969), pp. 2, 13. David Burner has brought together data on the voting of ethnic-religious groups between 1916 and 1932 in several large cities. While these materials are not directly comparable to Jensen's—because an individual may vote for a party other than his own in a given election in response to short-term forces—the Burner investigation nonetheless shows a decided Democratic preference among Catholic Americans.

This brief chronicle of the impact of the Protestant-Catholic ethnocultural tensions upon partisan attachments, and specifically on the long-standing Catholic support for the Democratic party and on white nonsouthern Protestants backing for the Republicans, is not intended to argue that no shifts among these big ethnocultural groups occurred in the New Deal period. Catholics did become more strongly Democratic over the years between 1928 and 1940. But the Protestant-Catholic divide, along with its citizenry party manifestations, had century-old roots in the American experience. The strong backing which Franklin Roosevelt received from Catholics—like that from the white South, a prime support of the New Deal Democratic majority—rested on a well-laid foundation.

This having been said, an element of newness stemming from events of the late 1920s and early 1930s cannot be ignored. With the success of the northern, urban wing in national Democratic politics, symbolized by Smith's capture of the party's presidential nomination in 1928, the Democrats obviously became more attractive to Catholics than they had been during the years of agrarian, southern and heartland, and Protestant ascendancy. And with the coming of the New Deal, Catholic status group attachments to the Democracy were reinforced by economic attachments, since the preponderance of Catholics were in strata benefiting most from the new social policies.

There is some argument among historians as to how much the electoral loyalties of urban Catholics were swayed by the "Al Smith revolution" which antedated the "Roosevelt revolution" of the 1930s. Did some measure of long-term shift involving the electoral loyalties of new immigrants occur as a direct result of the nomination in 1928 of an Irish Catholic from the urban Northeast? [20] Important as this question is, it need not occupy us here. The record makes evident that disproportionate numbers of Catholic

---

[20] For an examination of the literature bearing upon this argument, see Jerome M. Clubb and Howard W. Allen, "The Cities and the Election of 1928: Partisan Realignment?" *American Historical Review*, 74 (April 1969), pp. 1205–1220.

Americans supported the Democracy with notable regularity from the Age of Jackson to the Age of Roosevelt; and that these attachments were strengthened and extended in the 1928–1936 period. Survey materials from the latter half of the 1930s document the heavy commitment of Catholics, compared to white Protestants outside the South, to the Democratic party.

In Table 1.1, we present data drawn from American Institute of Public Opinion (Gallup) surveys on presidential and congressional voting, and partisan self-identification, for 1936–1940. Since our interest here is in the contrasting electoral loyalties of white ethnocultural groups, blacks—at this time a small proportion of the electorate in any case—have been excluded from the computations. And because white southern Protestants behaved politically in such a different manner than their northern co-religionists, materials on this group are presented separately.

Table 1.1. Percentage Democratic of the Presidential and Congressional Vote, and of Party Identification, Whites by Religion and Region, 1936–1940 (Column Percentages)

	White Nonsouthern Catholics	White Nonsouthern Protestants	White Southern Protestants
1936 Presidential Vote	81	52	83
1940 Presidential Vote	70	39	80
1940 Party Identification	62	31	81
1940 Congressional Vote	68	34	87

SOURCE: Southern white Catholics comprise a group too small, in the survey context, to be considered. Survey data on party identification in 1936, and on congressional voting in 1936 and 1938, are not available. Data on 1936 presidential vote are from American Institute of Public Opinion (AIPO or Gallup) studies 150 and 208; on 1940 presidential voting, from AIPO studies 219 and 248; on 1940 party identification, from AIPO studies 208 and 209; and on 1940 congressional vote, from AIPO study 215.

The massive division which prevailed during the New Deal between whites of Catholic and Protestant attachments outside the South manifests itself in all of these data. The proportion of Catholics identifying with the Democratic party in 1936, for example, was exactly twice that for non-southern white Protestants (62 percent as against 31 percent). In the presidential contest of 1940, when Roosevelt's popularity had waned somewhat, Catholics outside Dixie backed him by a margin of slightly better then seven to three, while northern Protestants voted Republican by a proportion of more than three to two. Except in 1936, at the height of popular support for FDR and the New Deal programs—and at the nadir of Republican morale and fortunes—white Americans of those ethnic groups subsumed by *Protestant* outside the South remained overwhelmingly Republican.

When one considers just how internally disparate the categories with which we are working are, the exceptional variety in ethnocultural experience which *Protestant* and *Catholic* subsume, the extent of the differentiation in voter loyalties, by religious group, which are shown in Table 1.1 appear even more impressive. The power of the Protestant-Catholic divide in structuring electoral behavior is sometimes concealed to a degree by a failure to apply the regional differentiation: that is, the Republicans were not precisely the "Protestant party"; they were the party of northern Protestants. Southern white Protestants, by way of contrast, remained securely anchored to the Democracy throughout the Roosevelt years.

The extent of the difference in voting choice between northern Protestants and Catholics is in no way *primarily* a function of the contrasting economic position of the membership of these two religious groups. When we hold socioeconomic status constant (Table 1.7, p. 71), we find the magnitude of Protestant-Catholic electoral differences essentially unaffected. For example, in the 1936 presidential balloting, 35 percent of white Protestants of high socioeconomic status outside the South voted for Roosevelt, just half the percentage (69 percent) for the Democratic nominee among Catholics of the same regional and socioeconomic position.[21] In the 1940 presidential election, the middle status Protestant cohort voted just 32 percent Democratic, as against 58 percent Democratic among their Catholic counterparts; while low SES Protestants outside the South were 49 percent Democratic and, again, their Catholic counterparts a much higher 74 percent for Roosevelt. Religious background had a substantial independent influence upon electoral behavior.

Building upon a strong base in historic attachments, then, the events of the late 1920s and 1930s solidified Catholic support for the Democracy—as the influence of the urban northern wing of the party was enhanced, and the programmatic initiatives of the Roosevelt administration meshed with the interests and perspectives of large numbers of Catholics. At the same time, the ascendancy of the Republicans in the Protestant North, while somewhat shaken, remained impressive. The historic Protestant-Catholic divide figured prominently in the partisan divisions of the New Deal.

---

[21] The early Gallup surveys provide only one continuing measure of socioeconomic status which can be accepted as broadly adequate. Other indicators which we might have liked to employ, such as family income and respondent education, appear only sporadically in the early surveys. Coding of occupational position is inconsistent and incomplete. Furthermore, there is a problem of locating surveys which possess both the requisite measures of socioeconomic status *and* the appropriate voting information. For example, some studies which asked educational background did not solicit information on partisan identification. We were required, then, to work with the one indicator of socioeconomic status which appeared in essentially the same form throughout *all* of the early Gallup surveys. Interviewers were required to specify the status of the respondents (as "wealthy" or "above average," as "average," or as "below average" or "poor") on the basis of such considerations as housing, possession of a telephone, car ownership, and the like. We were able to test selectively the differentiation produced by these semi-subjective interviewer assessments with those yielded by such objective indicators as income and occupation; and find no significant differences in the pattern observed. See Note 11 of Chapter 2, for further description of the Gallup SES indicator.

CONTINUITIES: THE PERSISTENCE
OF NORTHEASTERN REPUBLICANISM

In discussing the prominence of white southerners and Catholics in the New Deal Democratic party, and of white Protestants outside the South in the Republican alliance, an interesting regional link of a more specific sort has been passed over. We attend to it here, in noting the special strength of the GOP among white Protestants in the Northeast.

That the Northeast on the one hand, and the South on the other, have been going in opposite directions in partisan support throughout much of American history is one of the fascinating constancies of this country's electoral experience.[22] A combination of factors—widely variant social and economic developments, the presence of sharply conflicting regionally defined coalitions of interests, and from these the emergence of distinctive sectional subcultures—have propelled the Northeast and South apart. Before the Civil War, the latter region gave consistently high backing to the Jeffersonian Republicans and the Democrats, while the Northeast, especially New England, was the most supportive of the Federalists and subsequently the Whigs. After the Civil War, the South was impelled by a combination of race-related considerations and its status as the most agricultural section during an era when business nationalism was ascendant, to a posture of overwhelming Democratic support. In contrast, as the first section to embark on rapid industrial development, and the home ground of the business establishment, the Northeast manifested the most consistent allegiance to the party of business nationalism—the Republicans—over the years from the Civil War through to the Great Depression. (Today, to move ahead of our story, the Northeast has become the most Democratic region in national politics, while the

---

[22] For an early account, see Richard P. McCormick's "Political Development and the Second Party System," in Chambers and Burnham, *The American Party Systems*, pp. 97–102, 111–113.

states of the Old Confederacy, cut loose from their ancestral home, have proved the most resistant to the initiatives of the national Democratic party, and stand as the most secure Republican base in presidential politics.)

While Catholics, Jews, and blacks in the region marched in a different direction during the New Deal era, northeastern white Protestants continued to be heavily Republican, more so than their co-religionists elsewhere (Table 1.2). Protestant-Catholic tensions, and hence group consciousness, were much more acute in the Northeast, where

Table 1.2. Presidential and Congressional Vote, and Party Identification, White Protestants by Region, 1936–1940 (Row Percentages)

	Demo-cratic	Repub-lican	Other or Inde-pendent
NORTHEAST			
1936 Presidential Vote	48	51	2
1940 Presidential Vote	32	68	—
1940 Party Identification	26	54	20
1940 Congressional Vote	26	73	1
SOUTH			
1936 Presidential Vote	83	15	1
1940 Presidential Vote	80	20	—
1940 Party Identification	81	11	8
1940 Congressional Vote	87	13	—
MIDWEST			
1936 Presidential Vote	52	47	2
1940 Presidential Vote	38	61	—
1940 Party Identification	30	50	20
1940 Congressional Vote	34	62	4
WEST			
1936 Presidential Vote	62	37	1
1940 Presidential Vote	52	47	1
1940 Party Identification	41	38	21
1940 Congressional Vote	45	53	2

SOURCE: See Table 1.1. "Independent" applies to the party identification data, while "other" pertains to presidential and congressional voting.

disproportionate numbers of the new immigrants had settled, and the *religious factor* loomed larger in voting behavior. In the face of the surge to Roosevelt in 1936, a majority of white Protestants in the northeastern states cast
their ballots for Republican Alfred Landon. And four years
later, in the presidential election of 1940, this bloc of the
electorate went for Wendell Willkie over Franklin Roosevelt by better than two to one (68 to 32 percent). Distributions of party identification show the same pattern. In
1940, according to Gallup data, just 11 percent of white
Protestants in the South described themselves as Republicans, a status claimed by 38 percent of this population stratum in the West, 50 percent in the Midwest, and a high of
54 percent in the Northeast. Indeed, self-described Republicans outnumbered Democrats by a full two to one
among white Protestants in the northeastern states, a substantially greater GOP fealty than was evidenced by midwestern Protestants. And a slight majority of white Protestants in the western states were, by 1940, identifying as
Democrats, whereas the white Protestant South proclaimed Democratic attachments by a margin of roughly
seven or eight to one.

The Protestant-Catholic divide, we have noted, historically loomed large in American electoral politics. Like any
such general division it was modified by a variety of in-
truding elements. The interaction of ethnocultural and
regional variables is especially interesting. Throughout
the years of industrial nation building, the Republicans
enjoyed particular strength in the Northeast; and even during the New Deal era, while other groups in the region
moved toward (or continued) strong Democratic preferences, white Protestants in all socioeconomic strata remained firmly committed to their ancestral party. Eight
years after FDR achieved the presidency, northeastern
Protestants were identifying with the Republicans over
the Democrats by a margin of roughly two to one, and voting Republican by the same proportion or greater, in both
presidential and congressional contests. While we have no

comparable data bearing upon the partisan attachments of this stratum of the electorate in, say, 1910, we doubt that it was dramatically (although, almost certainly, it was somewhat) more heavily Republican than after a decade of Depression and New Deal. Long-standing party ties were not readily cast off. Supported by both strong ethnocultural attachments and a regional subculture which was the most supportive of business nationalism, northeastern white Protestant backing for the GOP showed remarkable continuity into the 1930s.

CONVERSIONS: BLACK AMERICANS AND THE PARTY OF LINCOLN

In examining the electoral impact of the New Deal era on the groups considered thus far—white southerners, Catholics, white Protestants outside the South—we have encountered a situation where, while some conversions unquestionably occurred, the dominant note is the continuity of attachments formed in earlier times on through the 1930s. Other strata offer contrasting patterns, however, marked by major conversions. Black Americans are one such group, moving massively in the Roosevelt years from historic Republican ties to a strong commitment to the Democratic party.

A basic set of structural factors bearing on the position of black Americans in the years from the Civil War to the Great Depression are familiar yet so important that they deserve brief mention here. The black population of the United States in 1865 was predominantly southern (more than 90 percent of the total residing therein), rural, and agricultural. While there was some opportunity for electoral participation during and immediately after Reconstruction, the erection of the Jim Crow system, beginning in the 1890s, produced virtual disenfranchisement. After World War I, due partly to the perception of opportunities outside the region and partly because of sheer economic necessity resulting from the mechanization of southern agri-

culture and the consequent elimination of jobs which they
had held historically, blacks began migrating to urban
areas generally but especially to the urban North. The out-
migration of blacks to the North was rapid in the 1920s,
slowed appreciably during the Depression years, and then
expanded steadily over the 1940s, 1950s, and 1960s. Once
the most rural of American ethnic collectivities, blacks
became by the 1970s among the most heavily urban. The
southern black population remained for the most part disenfranchised through the New Deal era: In 1940, only
250,000 or 275,000 blacks were even registered to vote in
the states of the Old Confederacy—just 5 percent of the
voting-age black population. At the same time, as the black
population outside the South doubled in the two decades
after 1920 (reaching approximately 3.6 million in 1940)
possibilities for some measure of significant political participation gradually presented themselves.[23]

The allegiance of blacks—to the extent that any electoral
involvement was permitted—to the party of Lincoln has
been described often enough. Glantz, for example, notes
"a history of strong allegiance to the Republican party in
the 17 elections from Reconstruction through 1932." [24] Although they manifested no particular enthusiasm for Herbert Hoover, and suffered greatly during the early Depression years, black Americans apparently remained
decisively Republican in the 1932 presidential election.
Gosnell found, for example, that Roosevelt received only

---

[23] As noted earlier, the South in the data distributions presented in this
volume includes the eleven states which seceded from the Union during
the Civil War together with Kentucky and Oklahoma. The U.S. Bureau of
the Census, by way of contrast, includes Delaware, Maryland, West
Virginia, and the District of Columbia, along with the above-mentioned
states, in the category southern. This more inclusive definition of the
South accounts for the fact that we report a nonsouthern black population
of 3.6 million in 1940, while the Census was identifying approximately
2.9 million nonsouthern blacks in that year. For the Census tabulations,
see *Historical Statistics of the United States, Colonial Times to 1957*, pp.
11–12.
[24] Oscar Glantz, "The Negro Vote in Northern Industrial Cities," *Western Political Quarterly*, 13 (December 1960), p. 999.

23 percent of the black vote in Chicago in 1932; while Collins reports a 29 percent Democratic presidential vote among blacks that year in Cincinnati.[25]

The New Deal offered little along the lines of a formal legislative or judicial attack on the institutions of white supremacy. But some advances in the position of blacks were achieved as spin-offs from legislation designed to benefit the lower income strata generally; and the group moved into the Democratic camp after 1932. While the numbers of votes thus provided the New Deal Democratic alignment was small—since blacks remained heavily southern and disenfranchised—the conversion thus achieved was to prove of extraordinary long-run import to American partisan competition.

The data presented in Table 1.3 makes evident this process of conversion on the part of black Americans from Republican to Democratic attachments. Roosevelt took about 70 percent of the black vote in both 1936 and in 1940 (at least doubling his 1932 proportion). While his vote dropped off rather sharply (1936 to 1940) among most segments of the population, among blacks it remained essentially constant. In short, the economic programs of the New Deal had made their mark in the minds of black voters, and there was to be no falling off of support. Indication of the major shift which was occuring in the black community is provided by the comparison of partisan identification and presidential vote. In the case of groups like Catholics, strongly wedded to the Democracy long before the New Deal, the correspondence between partisan self-identification and presidential selection in this period is very close. In contrast, it is massively discrepant for blacks. For example, Roosevelt received margins in excess of two to one among black voters in both 1936 and 1940, while blacks were roughly evenly divided in self-

[25] Harold F. Gosnell, "The Negro Voter in Northern Cities," *National Municipal Review*, 30 (May 1941), pp. 264–267; and Ernest M. Collins, "Cincinnati Negroes and Presidential Politics," *Journal of Negro History*, 41 (April 1956), pp. 131–137.

described party loyalties. Here is a classic case, then, of a group pulled strongly to the national Democratic party; yet so recently propelled away from its historic partisan allegiance that it manifested a major lag in party self-identification. Presumably, if the impulses emanating from national party program were subsequently to have changed—that is if the national Republican party had become the principal proponent of policies supported by black Americans—the potential for a permanent or long-term conversion implied by the data in Table 1.3 need not have been realized. Such a shift did not occur, however, and during the ensuing decades, as we shall see below, a drastic change in the partisan self-perception of blacks occurred, bringing I.D. into correspondence with regular vote preferences.

Table 1.3. Presidential Vote and Party Identification of Black Americans, 1936–1940 (Row Percentages)

	Democratic	Republican	Other or Independent
1936 Presidential Vote	71	28	1
1937 Party Identification	44	37	19
1940 Presidential Vote	67	32	—
1940 Party Identification	42	42	16

SOURCE: To achieve a sufficient number of cases for reliability, a number of AIPO surveys, closely proximate in time, were combined: for the 1936 presidential vote, AIPO studies 53, 60, 62, 72, and 104 (with the total *n* [number of respondents] comprising 240 cases); for the 1940 presidential vote, AIPO studies 222, 224, and 225 (*n* = 248); for 1937 party self-identification, AIPO studies 72 and 104 (*n* = 100); and for party self-identification in 1940, AIPO studies 208 and 209 (*n* = 172). "Independent" applies to the party identification data, while "other" pertains to presidential voting.

CONVERSIONS: JEWS ENTER THE DEMOCRACY

Although only about 3 percent of the U.S. population, Jews have obtained a significant measure of political influence. This is due, in part, to a generally high level of political activism; and as well to a high level of attainment in

American social and economic life. Their present position as one of the most heavily and consistently Democratic subgroups in the population is not unimportant, and this pattern of party support flows back directly to a change in allegiance during the New Deal.

More than two million Jewish immigrants came to the United States in the years between 1896 and the outbreak of World War I, most of them refugees from the anti-Semitism and poverty of eastern Europe. These new Jewish immigrants—vastly outnumbering the older Jewish American population—for the most part settled into the tenement houses which composed the slums of New York and, to a lesser extent, other large northern cities. While they contributed disproportionately to the minor parties of the radical left (especially the Socialists), the large majority made their electoral choices between the major parties and, as Lawrence Fuchs has noted, "more voted for Republicans than Democrats in every presidential election from 1900 to 1928, with the possible exceptions of 1900 and 1916." [26] All available aggregate data support this general picture of majoritarian Jewish support for the Republican party until the New Deal. As an example, a full 78 percent of enrolled voters in the fourteenth ward of Boston in 1928, a ward heavily Jewish in makeup, were registered Republicans.

During the Roosevelt years, however, Jews shifted into the Democratic column. Roughly 85 percent of Jewish voters went Democratic in both the 1936 and 1940 presidential contests (Table 1.4).[27] As a group in the process of

---

[26] Lawrence H. Fuchs, "American Jews and the Presidential Vote," in Fuchs (ed.), *American Ethnic Politics* (New York: Harper & Row, 1968), p. 52.

[27] Because Jews are a small proportion of the population, and because the data presented comes from national cross-section surveys, we have found it necessary to combine a number of studies, closely proximate in time, to achieve a number of cases sufficiently large to obtain reliable estimates. Data on Jewish congressional voting in this period is not presented then, because only scattered surveys including information on both religious attachment and congressional vote are available. It can be noted, however, that the survey data which we do have suggests a similarly high Jewish vote for Democratic congressional candidates in these years.

changing party loyalties, Jews (like blacks) manifested a striking discrepancy between the proportion Democratic in presidential balloting on the one hand, and the proportion describing themselves as Democrats on the other. In 1940, Gallup found 84 percent of Jews claiming to have voted for Roosevelt, while only 45 percent thought of themselves as Democrats. An unusually large proportion for the time (32 percent) were self-described independents—representing an ambivalence bred of the opposing pull of old attachments and current policy preferences.

Table 1.4. Presidential Vote and Party Identification of Jewish Americans, 1936–1940 (Row Percentages)

	Democratic	Republican	Other or Independent
1936 Presidential Vote	85	15	—
1940 Presidential Vote	84	16	—
1940 Party Identification	45	24	32

SOURCE: To obtain data on the 1936 presidential vote of Jews, five AIPO studies were combined, 150, 208, 209, 215, and 219. Data on the 1940 presidential vote are from AIPO studies 215, 219, and 248; while the partisan self-identification distributions are based upon AIPO studies 208 and 209.

It might seem unnecessary to go beyond two obvious features of the position in which Jewish Americans found themselves in the 1930s in order to explain their heavy vote for Roosevelt. Along with other Americans of recent immigrant stock, Jews experienced particular deprivation in the Depression and had ample reason to applaud the remedial efforts of the New Deal. At the same time, it is apparent that Roosevelt had the overwhelming support of Jews on behalf of his efforts at intervention against the Fascists and Nazis. To stop with these factors, however, would be to miss another which has proved of much more fundamental importance to the political orientations of Jews over the last four decades. The propensity of Jews to be located on the political left has been so widely dis-

cussed that we need not detail the argument here.[28] Some
observers have linked this liberal-to-left orientation to
aspects of Jewish religious teaching. Most, however, find
its principal source in the historic pattern of discrimination
which forced or disposed Jews to oppose conservative parties—so often aligned against the claim of Jews for equal
rights. Although discrimination was greater in much of
Europe than in the United States at any time, American
Jews did face barriers in employment, in admission to pro-
fessions, and in access to major private universities, along
with sanctions against their participation, even when they
were prosperous and highly educated, in the social activities of the predominantly Protestant affluent strata.

In view of the strong commitment of Jews to liberal values, their partisan switch during the New Deal years probably resulted as much from the Democracy's becoming the
American *liberal party* as from immediate economic and
foreign policy interests. The major shift in the political
agenda achieved during the 1930s, bringing the liberal-
conservative axis to the fore, and the consequent location
of the Democrats on the liberal side of this divide, underlies the change in political loyalties among American
Jews.

The proclivity for a liberal-to-left politics associated
with the Jewish experience was expressed through the absence of class divisions in voting among Jews during the
New Deal, a time when most ethnic groups were sharply

---

[28] For statements bearing on this subject, see Lawrence H. Fuchs, *The
Political Behavior of American Jews* (Glencoe, Ill.: The Free Press,
1956); Werner Cohn, "The Politics of American Jews," in M. Sklare (ed.),
The Jews (Glencoe, Ill.: The Free Press, 1958), pp. 614–626; Nathaniel
Weyl, *The Jew in American Politics* (New Rochelle, N.Y.: Arlington
House, 1968); Nathan Glazer, "The Jewish Role in Student Activism,"
Fortune, 79 (January 1969), pp. 112–113, 126–129; Louis Ruchames,
"Jewish Radicalism in the United States," in Peter I. Rose (ed.), *The
Ghetto and Beyond* (New York: Random House, 1969), pp. 228–252;
Charles S. Liebman, "Toward a Theory of Jewish Liberalism," in Donald
R. Cutler (ed.), *The Religious Situation: 1969* (Boston: Beacon Press,
1969), pp. 1034–1059; and Seymour Martin Lipset, *Revolution and Coun-
terrevolution*, pp. 376–400.

divided along class lines. In both the 1936 and 1940 presidential elections, for example, white Protestants of high socioeconomic status (the South excluded) were solidly Republican, while their ethnic counterparts of low status provided substantial Democratic support. No such class division is found in Jewish voting of the period: about 85 percent of high status Jews in both 1936 and 1940 voted for Roosevelt, with the Democratic proportion at most a few points higher for Jews in the lower social and economic strata.[29] Here, as in numerous other political contexts, we see the effects of a Jewish liberalism or proclivity for liberal candidates and causes cutting across class lines.

CONVERSIONS: A BROAD LOWER CLASS COALITION?

Among the many characterizations of the New Deal coalitions that have been offered over the last four decades, none is more common or salient than that describing the prominence of class lines. The lower socioeconomic strata—numerous in the Depression era of majoritarian poverty—were moved heavily in the short run into the Democratic camp, with some measure of long-term class conversion occurring; while the upper SES groups remained disproportionately Republican. In advancing this view, Samuel Lubell attributes the failure of trade unions in the late nineteenth and early twentieth centuries to achieve a relatively cohesive working-class alliance to the strength of ethnic tensions between old- and new-stock workers: For example, "much of the A.F. of L.'s reluctance to embark on a real organizing drive in the mass production industries reflected the dislike of the 'aristocrats of labor' in the skilled crafts for the immigrant 'rubbish.' " [30] As Lubell sees it, the formation of the Congress of Industrial Organizations between 1935 and 1938 takes on spe-

---

[29] These observations are based upon analysis of the raw data from AIPO studies 150, 208, 219, and 248.

[30] Lubell, *The Future of American Politics*, p. 49.

cial importance, symbolizing or resulting from a sufficient fusing of the interests of immigrant and native workers to make such a political coming together possible. "By 1935, of course, the immigrants had made considerable progress toward Americanization. But the key to the change was the rise of a common class consciousness among all workers. The Depression, in making all workers more aware of their economic interests, suppressed their racial and religious antagonisms. Put crudely, the hatred of bankers among the native American workers has become greater than their hatred of the Pope or even of the Negro." [31] The New Deal, then, witnessed the sharpening of class lines of conflict, and permitted the establishment of a partisan coalition (the Democratic) with a broadly inclusive lower-class or working-class base.

Fred Dutton has pursued this same line of argument, noting that Roosevelt succeeded in politicizing major new forces, notably the working class at large, and thereby transformed the basic lines of partisan division.[32] And as part of his general analysis of the realignment of the 1930s, James Sundquist stresses the high degree of "class bias" which developed in the new alignment:

The party system undoubtedly reflected some degree of class bias before the realignment, but there can be little doubt that it was accentuated by the event. It was in the New Deal era that tight bonds were formed between organized labor and the Democratic party, that ties equally close if less formal and overt were formed between business organizations and the GOP, and that partisan politics for the first time since 1896 sharply accented class issues.[33]

He notes that Walter Dean Burnham and others have called attention to the polls conducted by the *Literary Digest* as interesting confirmation of the heightened class basis of the new alignment: the fact that the *Digest* poll of

[31] *Ibid.*
[32] Frederick G. Dutton, *Changing Sources of Power: American Politics in the 1970's* (New York: McGraw-Hill, 1971), pp. 5–7.
[33] Sundquist, *Dynamics of the Party System,* p. 202.

1932 rather accurately predicted the outcome of the election, even though the *Digest*'s sample was markedly weighted in favor of upper-income groups, indicates that the 1932 Democratic majority must have cut rather uniformly across the various socioeconomic strata; whereas in 1936, still using the same sampling techniques, the *Digest* grossly miscalculated Roosevelt's share of the vote, predicting that he would receive 42 percent when in fact he gained 60 percent.[34] The underrepresentation of low-income groups in the *Digest*'s sample reduced the poll to an absurdity once the lower income categories became much more heavily Democratic than the high status cohorts.

Examples of this general line of analysis can be produced almost endlessly. The point is not, of course, simply that in the midst of extreme economic privation people turned in large numbers to a party promising—and to some measure, achieving—progressive economic change. It is, rather, that the class distinctiveness of the party coalitions was markedly accentuated during the New Deal, that the Democrats established themselves as the working-class party in a broad, national sense, and that this conversion of segments of the lowest strata proved decisive not only to the short-run successes which Roosevelt and his party achieved in the 1930s but to the longer-range structure of American partisan divisions.

So much is unquestionably valid in this line of interpretation that it is important to make clear at the outset that our analysis suggests only the need for a somewhat modified and enlarged view—important enough, surely, but hardly along the order of a major revision. That class divisions were relatively sharp, for the American political context, and that some long-range conversion of lower socioeconomic groups to the cause of the Democracy occurred, appears beyond dispute; but the overall picture of the relationship of class and party in the New Deal agenda is sufficiently complex that some further attention to detail seems in order.

---

[34] *Ibid.*, p. 203.

It may be useful to bear in mind that this general inquiry contains two somewhat distinct facets. On the one hand, there is the question of the extent to which the New Deal Democratic alliance can be described as a broad *working-class* aggregation, in opposition to a distinctly *middle-* or *upper–middle-class* Republican coalition. And there is the somewhat separate question of the relative sharpness of the differentiation in electoral preference of high SES and low SES voters during the New Deal, as compared to what prevailed before and what was to come subsequently.

We need to remind ourselves that class distinctions in patterns of partisan support apply almost exclusively to the electorate beyond the southern states. Within the Old Confederacy, differences by socioeconomic position at the height of the New Deal were extremely modest. In 1936, indeed, they were literally nonexistent (Table 1.5). Eighty-four percent of southerners of high socioeconomic status voted for Roosevelt in the 1936 presidential election, as compared to 82 percent in the middle strata, and 89 percent in the lower categories. Party identification in 1937 showed almost exactly eight southerners in ten, in each of the three basic socioeconomic strata, attaching themselves to the Democracy. Four years later, in 1940, with the waning of enthusiasm for the New Deal among the more prosperous classes generally, some measure of party differentiation by socioeconomic status appeared in the South, but it remained relatively modest.

Looking to the country as a whole, we find in the 1930s some impressive differences in partisan behavior by aspects of social and economic standing—but variations perhaps not quite so stark as casual commentary has suggested. For example, a slight majority of the college-trained voted for FDR in 1936 and nearly half of those employed in business and professional occupations gave him their vote that year. Semiskilled and unskilled workers showed the highest proportion of Democratic identification in 1940, among the various basic occupational cohorts, but a full third (32 percent) of business and professional men aligned with the Democracy (Table 1.6). The other side of these data is the existence of a rather neat declension in Democratic support with movement from the lowest to the highest socioeconomic stratum, whatever the measure used. And the class-related dif-

Table 1.5. Presidential Vote and Party Identification of Southerners, by Socioeconomic Position, 1936–1940 (Row Percentages)

	Democratic	Republican	Other or Independent
1936 PRESIDENTIAL VOTE			
High SES	84	16	—
Middle SES	82	17	—
Low SES	89	11	—
1937 PARTY IDENTIFICATION			
High SES	79	14	7
Middle SES	78	14	8
Low SES	78	14	9
1940 PRESIDENTIAL VOTE			
High SES	65	35	—
Middle SES	79	21	1
Low SES	78	22	—
1940 PARTY IDENTIFICATION			
High SES	74	13	14
Middle SES	79	12	9
Low SES	81	12	8

SOURCE: Data on the 1936 presidential vote are from AIPO studies 72 and 104; for 1937 party identification, AIPO studies 72 and 104; for 1940 presidential vote, from AIPO studies 222 and 224; and for 1940 party identification from AIPO studies 208 and 209. "High," "Middle," and "Low" socioeconomic status are construed here, in Tables 1.6 and 1.7, and in Figure 1.2, on the basis of the Gallup SES indicator. The indicator is described in Note 27 of this chapter, and Note 11 of Chapter 2. "High SES" comprises Gallup's "wealthy" and "above average" or "average plus" categories; "Middle SES" includes the "average" group; while "Low SES" contains persons "below average" or "poor plus," "poor," and "on relief."

ferences in voting *are very substantial* in many instances: witness the fact that the proportion of semiskilled and unskilled voting for Roosevelt in 1940 was more than twice that among the business and professional stratum (68 against 31 percent).

Table 1.6. Percentage Democratic of the Presidential Vote and of Party Identification, by Socioeconomic Standing, 1936–1940 (Row Percentages)

	1936 Presidential Vote	1940 Presidential Vote	1937 Party Identification	1940 Party Identification
EDUCATION				
Some college, college graduate	51	39	NA	NA
High school graduate	60	56	NA	NA
Less than high school	69	67	NA	NA
GALLUP SES INDICATOR				
High SES	44	31	37	27
Middle SES	60	44	46	39
Low SES	73	62	60	51
OCCUPATION				
Business and professional	48	31	38	32
Lower white-collar	NA	50	NA	41
Skilled	NA	57	NA	43
Semiskilled and unskilled	NA	68	NA	54
Farmers (farm owners)	65	50	NA	45

SOURCE: Data on 1936 presidential vote are from AIPO studies 150, 208, and 209; on 1940 presidential vote, from AIPO studies 222, 224, 225, and 248; for party identification in 1937, from AIPO studies 72 and 104; and for party identification in 1940, from AIPO studies 208 and 209. (NA = data not available.)

Region, ethnocultural background, and socioeconomic position were all powerful predictors or determiners of electoral orientations in the New Deal era. We have already noted that white southerners, without regard to economic position, sustained the Democracy. Outside the South, white Protestants were notably more Republican than white Catholics within each socioeconomic stratum; while those of high status were substantially more Republican than persons in the lower strata, within both the white Protestant and the Catholic ethnocultural categories. The mutually supportive character of socioeconomic status and religion is nicely shown, with each contributing decisively to the proclivity of a group for Democratic or Republican support. Thus, in 1936, Catholics of high SES were more Democratic than Protestants of comparable standing by a margin of 34 percentage points; while Protestants of the highest SES cohort were more Republican than those of the lowest stratum by a margin of 25 points. Together, religion and socioeconomic standing account for massive differences in electoral behavior among voters outside the South. In the 1940 presidential contest, to cite an example, just 20 percent of white Protestants of high social standing voted for Franklin Roosevelt, compared to 74 percent of Catholics in the low SES cohort.

Overall, the data presented in Table 1.7 lend themselves to somewhat conflicting interpretations. The differences by class within the two ethnocultural groupings are indeed impressive. Almost certainly, the strong Democratic support among low SES white Protestants outside the South had never been even approached between 1896 and the Great Depression. The fact that the Democrats gained about half the votes of the most disadvantaged white Protestants in the nonsouthern states in the 1940 presidential balloting appears to be ample grounding for the argument that the New Deal Democratic party benefited substantially from conversions in the lower strata. At the same time, it needs to be pointed out that Gallup found Republican Wendell Willkie capturing the majority of the vote among all the various groups of white nonsouthern Protestants, even those most disadvantaged economically; and in 1940 few more than one in three among this population stratum described their party identification as Democratic. To talk about the New Deal Democracy as the party of the poor is just a bit too neat. It was the party of the white South, the party of Catholic Americans, and the party which had made significant inroads among low income white nonsouthern Protestants. But at the end of the Depression decade, in 1940, the Republicans remained the party of white Protestants outside the southern states, even those of the lowest socioeconomic stratum.

Table 1.7. Percentage Democratic of the Presidential Vote and of Party Identification, Voters outside the South by Religion and Socioeconomic Standing, 1936–1940

	1936	
	WHITE PROTESTANTS Presidential Vote	WHITE CATHOLICS Presidential Vote
High SES	35	69
Middle SES	48	81
Low SES	60	83

	1940			
	WHITE PROTESTANTS		WHITE CATHOLICS	
	Presidential Vote	Party Identification	Presidential Vote	Party Identification
High SES	20	16	42	46
Middle SES	32	27	58	60
Low SES	49	36	74	65

SOURCE: Data for the 1936 presidential vote distributions are from AIPO studies 150 and 208; for the 1940 presidential vote, from AIPO studies 219 and 248; and for 1940 party identification, from AIPO studies 208 and 209.

That class lines evidenced an unusually high salience in electoral behavior during the New Deal and the immediate post–New Deal becomes clear from the data presented in Figure 1.2. We have plotted the percentage point difference separating the highest and lowest socioeconomic strata, in terms of their vote for Democratic presidential nominees and the proportion Democratic in partisan self-identification. In all cases, the lower cohort is more Democratic, but the degree to which it is so varies rather strikingly over the last ten presidential elections.[35]

We have chosen to present data on the class differentiation in voting for whites outside the South only. That is, all southerners, and all blacks, have been excluded from these computations. The reason for this choice is evident enough. As we have already pointed out, class distinctions in electoral support have been vastly more modest, even to the point of nonexistence in 1936, among voters in the Old Confederacy, reflecting the greater salience of other concerns. At the same time, black Americans have become so heavily Democratic that their inclusion would produce a peculiar skewing of the lines in Figure 1.2. Blacks were an exceptionally small proportion of the northern electorate in the early years covered by Figure 1.2, but became a rather substantial group in the later years. Class distinctions among black voters are not absent, but racial concerns have moved blacks of all socioeconomic strata into the Democratic camp by major proportions. We see the impact of class on electoral orientations most unambiguously, then, if we confine our attention to whites outside the southern states.

Several interesting aspects of the influence of class lines in partisan differentiation appear in Figure 1.2. First, we see the extent to which the differentiation is election-dependent. The degree of difference in Democratic support from the high to the low strata was very substantial in

---

[35] For purposes of this depiction, we have applied rather demanding standards for inclusion in the "high" and "low" SES categories: The former includes those who have attended college and are working in professional and managerial occupations; while the latter is defined by semi-skilled and unskilled occupational status.

Figure 1.2. Percentage Point Difference between High and Low SES Whites outside the South in Democratic Support; Presidential Vote and Party Identification, 1936–1972

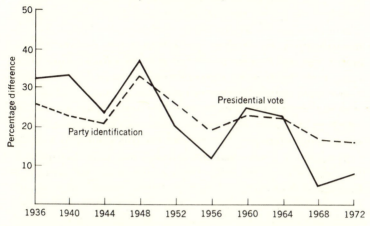

SOURCE: Data from following AIPO surveys: *1936*, 72, 104; *1940*, 208, 209, 222, 224; *1944*, 328, 329, 336; *1948*, 431, 432; *1952*, 507, 508; *1956*, 573, 574; *1960*, 637, 638; *1964*, 699, 701; *1968*, 770, 771; *1972*, 859, 860.

the immediate New Deal period. Then, reflecting a temporary shift in political attention brought about by American involvement in World War II, there was a drop in the 1944 presidential election. The Truman-Dewey contest revived New Deal class concerns, and brought the degree of interclass differentiation to its all-time (to the extent that data are available) high point. There was a marked decline during the Eisenhower years, as the nature of the general's appeal and program reduced the thrust of economic cleavage. The 1950s have often been described as a time of low salience in conflict over economic issues, as Eisenhower led the Republicans to a kind of acceptance of the New Deal, and this is reflected in Figure 1.2. Following the fifties, there was something of a revival of class distinctiveness in voting in 1960 and 1964, and this was followed by an extraordinarily sharp drop-off before the thrust of a distinctly new agenda—emphasizing social and cultural concerns—in 1968 and 1972.[36] (The full impact of class distinctions in the post-1950 period will be dealt with in much greater detail in the chapters which follow.)

It is also interesting to note how closely the line for party self-identification follows that for presidential voting. It is, as would be expected from what we know of the relative stability of self-identification, a flatter line. But the general direction is the same as that for presidential balloting, indicating that the larger element of the political context, the thrusts of the issues of the day, make their weight felt upon the perceptions of party loyalties in the electorate as well as on immediate voting choices.

The most important finding evidenced by Figure 1.2, however, comprises the secular decline in the salience of class differentiations in electoral behavior since the Roosevelt-Truman years. The lines indicating the percentage point difference in Democratic backing between the high and low strata for both presidential support and party self-identification have their peaks and valleys, but the long-term direction over the last thirty-six years is clearly etched. The high and low cohorts were much more sharply distinguished between 1936 and 1948 (with the wartime context a somewhat deviating instance) than they have been at any time since. The oft-observed salience of class distinctions in partisan support of the New Deal period is amply confirmed by Figure 1.2, then. If we had comparable data for the thirty-six years prior to 1936, it is likely that the uniqueness of the Roosevelt-Truman elections would be even more dramatically evident.

---

[36] For further data and interpretation, see Norval D. Glenn, "Class and Party Support in the United States: Recent and Emerging Trends," *Public Opinion Quarterly*, 38 (Spring 1973), pp. 1–20; and Paul R. Abramson's interesting "Generational Change in American Electoral Behavior," *American Political Science Review*, 68 (March 1974), pp. 93–105. See, also by Abramson, *Generational Change in American Politics* (Lexington, Mass.: D. C. Heath, 1975).

CONVERSIONS?: THE ISSUE OF A "GENERATIONAL BULGE"

We have noted that in the 1930s, a major alteration of the American political agenda occurred, and that the Democrats succeeded in transforming themselves into the party of the new agenda, and thereby laid the foundation for their electoral supremacy. This general analysis would sustain the expectation that, with the emergence of a new agenda and a new majority party speaking to it, voters entering the electorate for the first time would show greater long-range allegiance to the new majority than those who were part of the electorate when the old agenda was still largely intact. Party identification, once established, is not readily eroded, and new voters, not having developed stable party attachments, should thereby be drawn in greater numbers to the new majority than persons anchored by partisan attachments and related political perceptions formed under the influence of the old.

Data collected by the Survey Research Center of the University of Michigan in the 1950s strongly suggests that this was indeed the case: "There is reason to believe . . . that a good number of these Republicans who defected into the Democratic ranks during the early years of the Roosevelt era were soon disenchanted. Some erstwhile Republicans never returned to their party, but these party-changers do not appear to have made up a very large part of the long-term Democratic increase. Our inquiries into the political histories of our respondents lead us to believe that a larger component of the gain came from young voters entering the electorate. . . ." [37] The new majority, then, was built upon a kind of generational conversion, a success in attracting a disproportionate share of the emerging electorate.

The authors of *The American Voter* presented materials

---

[37] Angus Campbell, Philip E. Converse, Warren E. Miller, and Donald E. Stokes, *The American Voter* (New York: John Wiley, 1960), p. 153.

from their surveys suggesting that those in the electorate of the 1950s who had begun voting in the 1920s were significantly less Democratic than those who had first entered the electorate in the 1930s and 1940s. Some of these data are summarized by Figure 1.3. What all this means, if valid, is that one of the key group components of the new Democratic majority was defined by age. The entire political generation that came of age politically after 1930, in this interpretation, was more Democratic than the previous generations.

This argument concerning a generational conversion is especially interesting because it links up with an even broader concern in social science, for which the existing literature does not provide a clear and unambiguous guide. As one of us has pointed out in a collaborative study with Seymour Martin Lipset, the basic confusion lies in the contrasting emphases in the literature on the experi-

Figure 1.3. Party Identification of Respondents Born between 1900 and 1930

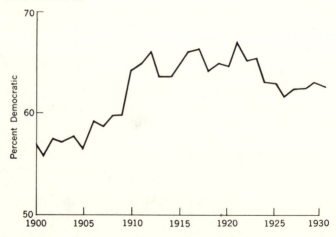

SOURCE: Figure from Campbell, *et al., The American Voter,* p. 154. Based on approximately 10,000 cases, accumulated from seven national samples interviewed between 1952 and 1958.

ences of *political generations* on the one hand, and upon the effects of *aging* on the other.[38]

Scholars such as Karl Mannheim, Sigmund Neumann, and Rudolph Heberle have contended that people form a frame of reference which serves to inform their subsequent values and orientations from major events of the period when they first come to political consciousness, usually in their late teens or early twenties.[39] The prevailing climate in which a cohort comes of age politically, according to this line of interpretation, becomes of decisive importance to its future political orientations.

Those who speak of generations do not suggest, of course, that all or even most people in the same age category react identically to all key political events. Mannheim wrote of "generation units," which are different groups within the same age stratum who adhere to alternative, often conflicting values. More recently, Bennett Berger has noted that "it is essential, when using the concept of generation, in a cultural sense, to specify generations of what, because it is only in a demographic sense that people of the same age-group constitute a homogenous unit. . . ." [40] The rich and poor youth, factory workers and college students, blacks and whites, quite obviously, have not experienced events in the same way. During the Great

---

[38] Lipset and Ladd, "The Political Future of Activist Generations," in Philip G. Altbach and Robert S. Laufer (eds.), *The New Pilgrims: Youth Protest in Transition* (New York: David McKay, 1972), pp. 63–84. The generations-aging confusion has been effectively pointed out, too, by John Crittenden, "Aging and Party Affiliation," *Public Opinion Quarterly*, 26 (Winter 1962), p. 648.

[39] Mannheim, *Ideology and Utopia* (New York: Harcourt Brace, 1936), p. 270; Neumann, "The Conflict of Generations in Contemporary Europe," *Vital Speeches*, 5 (1939), pp. 623–628; also by Neumann, *Permanent Revolution* (New York: Harper and Brothers, 1942), pp. 234–244; Heberle, *Social Movements* (New York: Appleton-Century-Crofts, 1951), pp. 118–127. See, for further arguments along this line, José Ortega y Gasset, *Man and Crisis* (New York: W. W. Norton, 1958), pp. 50–84; and Bruno Bettelheim, "The Problem of Generations," in Erik Erikson (ed.), *Youth: Change and Challenge* (New York: Basic Books, 1963), pp. 64–92.

[40] Bennett M. Berger, "How Long is a Generation?" from his book, *Looking for America* (Englewood Cliffs, N.J.: Prentice-Hall, 1971), p. 29.

Depression, some were reared in families whose real income actually increased, while many had unemployed
parents. Still, the economic privation of the Depression extended to broad segments of the population.

Emphasis upon the effects of aging, on the other hand,
has led to very different conclusions or expectations. For
both social and psychological reasons, many have argued,
people tend to move from the political extremes as they
grow older, toward a more moderate or centrist position.
Actions defined by society as deviant—e.g., delinquent,
bohemian, and radical—have tended to be largely phenomena of youth.[41] As they grow older, the overwhelming
majority of deviants become respectable and settle down.
In politics, this has generally meant that young people, as
they age, tend to move toward the political center, as then
defined. Parties of the extreme left and right almost invariably draw disproportionate influence from the young
voters.

Aristotle wrote incisively on the contrasting political orientations associated with different age strata.[42] And Max
Weber reiterated an aspect of Aristotle's analysis when he
suggested that the young are more disposed to an "ethic of
ultimate ends," the older to the "ethic of responsibility."
That is, the latter seek to accomplish what limited good is
practically possible even though to do so may mean to
compromise with evil, whereas new generations try to protect their sense of virtue by refusing to compromise.[43]

The argument is indeed a complex one. From our standpoint here, however, it may be reduced to a fairly simple
question: Did significant segments of those who came of
age during the New Deal as a result of the decisive experiences of that time undergo a kind of generational con-

[41] On this theme, see David Matza, "Subterranean Traditions of
Youth," Annals, 338 (November 1961), pp. 102–118.

[42] The Rhetorica of Aristotle, in Richard McKeon (ed.), The Basic
Works of Aristotle (New York: Random House, 1941), especially pp.
1403–1406.

[43] From Max Weber: Essays in Sociology, edited and translated by
H. H. Gerth and C. Wright Mills (New York: Oxford University Press,
1946), especially pp. 120–128.

The Formation of the New Deal Party System 79

version, manifesting itself in an inclination of the entire group to give a markedly higher level of support to the Democratic party than those who came of age prior to the Great Depression? Or, in contrast, do we find simply the young more inclined to support the Democrats during the New Deal and subsequently as the more *change-oriented* of the two parties, but with no noticeable persistence of any generational distinction?

To try to deal with this question we have extensively analyzed a broad collection of Gallup survey materials from the 1930s on through into the 1970s. Taken together, these data raise serious questions as to whether any significant generational conversion occurred during the New Deal. Perhaps most conclusive on this point are the distributions of partisan identification and presidential vote presented in Tables 1.8 and 1.9. What we have done is to replicate broadly, using a range of Gallup materials, the thrust of the analysis conducted by the Michigan investigators. Table 1.8 shows, for example, the proportions of the electorate reporting Democratic party identification in

Table 1.8. The Percentage of the Electorate Describing Themselves as Democrats, 1940–1972, by Year of Birth

Percentage Democratic Identification

BIRTH YEAR	1940	1944	1948	1952	1956	1960	1964	1968	1972
1901–1905	45	42	45	47	40	54	55	44	—
1906–1910	45	44	47	50	45	45	55	46	44
1911–1915	48	47	47	51	50	55	53	45	39
1916–1920	42	47	52	52	49	55	58	45	46
1921–1925		51	48	51	48	55	52	45	38
1926–1930			45	48	44	49	52	45	38
1931–1935					44	45	49	41	39
1936–1940						49	44	37	36
1941–1945							50	37	37
1946–1950								39	36
1951–1955									36

SOURCE: Data from AIPO studies: *1940*, 208, 209, 224, 225; *1944*, 316, 328, 329; *1948*, 430, 431, 432, 433; *1952*, 505, 506, 507, 508; *1956*, 572, 573, 574, 576; *1960*, 636, 637, 638, 640; *1964*, 699, 701, 702, 704; *1968*, 770, 771, 773, 774; and *1972*, 857, 858, 859, 860.

each presidential election year from 1940 through 1972, by the years in which they were born—and from this, by the years in which they came of age politically. It is clear from this extraordinarily large volume of survey materials—four separate studies, and between 6,000 and 13,000 cases, in each year—that there is no "bulge" of any magnitude in Democratic allegiance among those who entered the electorate during the Great Depression and the presidency of Franklin Roosevelt. For example, in 1952 we find that the percentage Democratic among those who first came to political maturity during the Harding and Coolidge presidencies—in the roaring Republican 1920s—is almost exactly the same as that for those reaching voting age during the Depression and the New Deal. The proportion describing themselves as independents is higher among the youngest voters than among the older age groups, throughout the period.

Reporting on presidential vote by age cohorts for the 1940–1972 span, Table 1.9 also demonstrates a total absence of any New Deal bulge. And there does not appear

Table 1.9. Percentage of the Electorate Backing the Democratic Presidential Candidate, 1940–1972, by Year of Birth

Percentage Democratic Presidential Vote

BIRTH YEAR	1940	1944	1948	1952	1956	1960	1964	1968	1972
1901–1905	55	51	47	44	39	54	69	36	—
1906–1910	54	51	46	43	42	49	69	35	32
1911–1915	55	58	51	46	49	54	65	39	29
1916–1920	54	57	54	46	46	60	74	41	33
1921–1925		61	52	45	47	62	69	37	30
1926–1930			49	50	43	58	72	41	29
1931–1935					45	54	69	41	28
1936–1940						51	70	37	32
1941–1945							72	43	33
1946–1950								45	46
1951–1955									43

SOURCE: Same AIPO studies as enumerated in Table 1.8 with the exception of 1944 where study 316 is excluded and studies 336 and 337 are included.

The Formation of the New Deal Party System   81

to be appreciably greater Democratic support among
young voters generally, with the notable exception of the
1972 presidential election. Neither the aging nor the generation thesis finds much support here.[44]

Other forms of analysis add further confirmation. In
Table 1.10 we present data on the proportion of the sev-

Table 1.10. Percentage Democratic in Presidential Vote and Party
Identification, Age Cohorts by Region and Religion, 1936–1940
(Row Percentages)

1936

PRESIDENTIAL VOTE

| | SOUTH | NON-SOUTH | |
Age	White Protestants	White Protestants	White Catholics
18–29	86	51	81
30–39	85	55	84
40–49	85	54	80
50–59	81	49	78
60 +	79	51	81

1940

| | SOUTH | | NON-SOUTH | | | |
| | White Protestants | | White Protestants | | White Catholics | |
Age	Presidential Vote	Party Identification	Presidential Vote	Party Identification	Presidential Vote	Party Identification
18–29	78	88	39	31	71	57
30–39	79	85	42	32	66	66
40–49	82	78	38	29	62	61
50–59	80	75	36	29	63	55
60 +	76	75	39	33	72	68

SOURCE: Data on 1936 presidential vote from AIPO studies 150 and 208; on
the 1940 presidential vote from AIPO studies 219 and 248; and on party
identification in 1940 from AIPO studies 208 and 209.

[44] It is perfectly possible, of course, that within certain special subpop-
ulations a mix of social factors linked to aging may produce a situation
whereby members are in fact conservatized as they grow older. Lipset
and Ladd ("The Political Future of Activist Generations") appear to have
located this in the case of the college educated.

eral age cohorts voting Democratic, and identifying with
the Democratic party, in 1936 and 1940—controlling further for region and ethnocultural background. Three distinctive subgroups are contained in Table 1.10: southern
white Protestants; their co-religionists outside the South;
and white Catholics outside the South. In each case, the
youngest voters—who first entered the electorate in the
Roosevelt era—do not show any different pattern of partisan support than their older counterparts. In each of the
ethnocultural and regional groupings, there is simply no
consistent or substantial variation by age. These surveys
conducted during the 1930s and in 1940 *neither reveal a
New Deal political generation, nor sustain a picture of the
young being consistently more supportive than the old of
the party of change.*

It is still striking, in view of all that has been written
about the stability of partisan identification, that the
various age cohorts showed so little difference in party
allegiance during the New Deal epoch. White Protestants
outside the South, for instance, who first became voters
during Roosevelt's tenure in office, were no more inclined
in 1940 to describe themselves as Democrats than those
who came of voting age during periods of maximum Republican ascendancy.

Table 1.10 presents data on the partisan orientations of
age cohorts by region and religion. If we apply yet other
controls, such as socioeconomic status, we find the same
pattern. In the 1936 presidential contest, to take one example, people of low socioeconomic status under 30 years
of age voted for Roosevelt by a margin of 71 to 28 percent,
compared to 71 to 27 percent for the 30–39 cohort, 70–29
percent for the 40–49 age grouping, 66–30 percent for the
50–59 cohort, and 67–31 percent among voters 60 years of
age and older.

Conversions indeed occurred during the 1930s. But
there is little indication of any generational conversion, of
any bulge in Democratic support among new members of
the electorate. The overall picture suggests a remarkable

uniformity in political response—whether voting or party identification—across the various age cohorts in the New Deal era.

III. The Democratic and Republican Party Coalitions of the 1930s: Conclusions in Overview

Our focus has been upon the social group composition of the respective New Deal coalitions, and upon changes in social group alignments following from the substitution of a new agenda of politics. Before attending to this subject in summary fashion, one additional facet of the partisan alignment of the New Deal period should be considered—that involving the relative success each party had in mobilizing its own supporters in the elections of the period, and in appealing to the unaligned.

Roosevelt was notably successful in maintaining the support of people who thought of themselves as Democrats and in attracting independents to his cause. Examining all of the presidential elections since 1936, one finds only three (out of ten) in which a majority of self-described independents voted Democratic: One of these was 1964, in the extraordinary Johnson landslide; the other two were elections of the New Deal period, those of 1936 and 1940. In the 1936 presidential balloting, Roosevelt attracted the support of three independents out of every four who went to the polls, strikingly greater success than any Democratic candidate has attained subsequently, including Johnson in 1964. FDR also kept Democratic identifiers in the fold, while making significant inroads among Republican adherents. Again looking at the ten presidential contests since 1936, we find only three in which the proportion of self-ascribed Democrats defecting to the Republican nominee failed to exceed that of Republican identifiers voting Democratic. And once again, the Johnson landslide of 1964, and the 1936 and 1940 Roosevelt victories, offer the three exceptions. According to Gallup survey materials 98 percent of Democratic identifiers voted for Roosevelt in 1936, while 14 percent of Republican adherents crossed over and voted Democratic. Apart from the matter of continuities and conversions among social groups, then, the New Deal era stands out as a time of particular Democratic success in mobilizing their own identifiers and in attracting independents and Republicans.

An interesting blend of continuities and conversions served to define the New Deal party coalitions, specifically to support the Democrat's new found majority status. Two groups so very far apart in their ethnocultural backgrounds, styles of life, and type of residential setting, provided primary sustenance for FDR's majority: old-stock white southerners, overwhelmingly Protestant and heavily rural; and new-stock Catholics, concentrated in the urban North. Neither group was a newcomer to the Democracy. Both had partisan roots long antedating the Great Depression and the New Deal. They had often rested together uneasily in the same party, and from roughly 1914 until the Depression their struggles for contrasting policy objectives, and for control of nominations, consumed the party. Both white Protestants of the South and Catholics of the North shifted even more decisively to the Democratic camp during Roosevelt's tenure, and as importantly in terms of the success of the party, achieved a kind of *quid pro quo* whereby the northern wing dominated presidential nominating politics while the southern camp retained exceptional influence in Congress. The bitter internecine struggles evident in, for example, 1924 when the Smith and McAdoo forces struggled for ascendancy, were largely submerged. This development followed in large part from the near-disappearance of significant policy differences between these two wings of the party during the New Deal—although they had been so sharply at odds in the preceding period. When the lines of conflict shifted so that the principal axis separated those favoring governmental nationalism on behalf of a more equalitarian distribution of the fruits of industrial growth (the liberals) from proponents of the old business nationalism, southern Protestants and northern Catholics could rest comfortably on the same side. Here is a good illustration of the inseparability of political agenda, group interests within the agenda, and social group composition of the parties. The strong support for New Deal programs provided by the Catholic North and the Protestant South invites further attention below.

The decisive shift in party loyalties of blacks and of Jews toward the Democrats was clearly precipitated by the new alignment of party program and policy conflict inaugurated by the New Deal. Jews rallied to the Roosevelt Democratic party because it was the *liberal* party; while blacks shifted less, it appears, for general ideological reasons than because the immediate economic programs which FDR initiated meshed closely with group needs. In the case of both groups, the partisan conversion proved to be of less import in the short run than it was to be for the future of party competition. Neither blacks nor Jews were numerically decisive in the contests of the 1930s and early 1940s. For the longer run, the location of an overwhelming majority of black Americans in the Democratic camp was to have a profound impact, in the support provided, and in the inter-party and intra-party battles which necessarily followed. Jews came to contribute heavily to the intellectual and the financial leadership of the Democracy. So the shifts occurred in response to the change of agenda in the 1930s and the broad alterations of party programs which that entailed, but had relatively little to do with the outcome of electoral contests during the New Deal itself.

Much has been made of the salience of class lines in the party divisions of the 1930s and, as we have seen, this is broadly justified. Voters of high and low socioeconomic standing were more sharply distinguished in electoral commitments in 1936, 1940, and 1948 than in any of the subsequent presidential elections, and probably more than in any of the preceding contests. The New Deal and immediate post–New Deal era provided the high-water mark of class saliency in American electoral politics. At the same time, it confuses things inordinately to describe the New Deal Democrats as the working-class party. Never during Roosevelt's tenure in the presidency did the Democrats establish themselves as the majority party among nonsouthern white Protestants of working-class or generally low socioeconomic standing. The old ethnocultural underpinnings, with Republicans the Protestant party, were not removed by the relatively high salience of class concerns in the New Deal agenda.

Contrary to some earlier analyses, it does not appear that generational conversion contributed significantly to the transformed status of the Democrats. Neither the current (New Deal) electoral orientations of the various age cohorts, nor later voting commitments by time of entry into the electorate, sustain the argument that those who first came of political age in the midst of the decisive events of the Depression and New Deal era were more heavily attracted to the Democracy than those who had previously formed political perceptions and party loyalties.

Viewed strictly in terms of numbers, three population groupings contributed decisively to the New Deal Democratic party. Southern white Protestants, Catholics, and nonsouthern white Protestants of the lowest socioeconomic stratum together accounted for roughly three-fourths of all Americans of voting age in 1940 who thought of themselves as Democrats.[45] By way of contrast, these three groups provided only about 40 percent of the smaller cadre of Republican identifiers. Or to put these findings somewhat differently, white Protestants of moderate to high socioeconomic status outside the South accounted in 1940 for more than half of all Republican identifiers, as contrasted to less than one-fifth of Democratic adherents.

Striking as these differences are, attention to them can detract from appreciation of the breadth of conversions

---

[45] These data are based upon analysis of a large collection of studies conducted by the Gallup Organization, especially AIPO studies 208 and 209. See Note 21 of this chapter for further details on Gallup measures of socioeconomic status.

that established the Democratic ascendancy. We have argued that party coalitions have attained majority status in the American experience when they served as the party of the agenda, when they represented a public philosophy which attained widespread acceptance as positive, forward-looking, progressive. The effect of the Depression, and the espousal of governmental nationalism by the Roosevelt administration, was to transform the Democrats into the party of the new political agenda. In that status, they broadened the base of their appeal across a variety of population groupings. It is possible, of course, to locate those collectivities which contributed most heavily. But we miss the larger dynamic of the conversion process if we fail to note the remarkable uniformity in increased support across the population spectrum. As an example, the Democrats enjoyed a higher proportion of support within the working class than among business and professional people in the 1930s; but in 1937, 38 percent of all those in business and professional positions considered themselves Democrats, while 40 percent identified as Republicans, and 22 percent as independents. Our analysis of all available survey data for the 1936–1941 period suggests strongly that the Democrats advanced (from their position before the 1930s) by a relatively consistent measure in most population groups. There was a process of conversion, then, relating to a perception rather widely held that the Democracy under FDR, more than its Republican opposition, spoke effectively to the salient concerns and problems defining a social and political era.

2

The Extension of the
New Deal Party System

The New Deal as such lasted less than a decade, from Roosevelt's inauguration on March 4, 1933, up to the outbreak of war in Europe which shifted attention away from domestic social reform toward questions of involvement in the greater international struggle. But the New Deal era surely extended beyond the 1930s—if the era is seen encompassing those years when the political agenda formulated during the thirties continued to dominate or structure public debate. Roughly the three decades from the Depression on through the 1950s assume coherence as a sociopolitical setting around continuing efforts to establish a new order of public-private relationships in response to the condition of mature industrialism. The managerial state was erected and fleshed out. A massive urban working class, product of the successful enterprise of industrial nation building, was accommodated within the structure of industrial decision making and national political life. Overall productive capacities were extended enormously, and the pressures to use these for a much larger measure of popular enrichment and economic security were strong and persistent.

We get a direct sense of the continued persistence of the

New Deal era throughout the 1940s and 1950s from the continued vitality and coherence of the liberal-conservative divide. *Liberalism vs. conservatism* had been erected in the 1930s as the primary axis of ideological or policy conflict in the United States. Involved here was a profound shift in the argument over the directions of nation building as the newer governmental nationalism challenged its older business counterpart, the former promoting equalitarian and reformist social policies, the latter tending to oppose them. Substantial change occurred between 1935 and 1960 in the specific substance of public policy argument, but the broad outlines of the division which took coherence under FDR continued to shape political conflict.

Attention to the boundaries of the New Deal period is consequential because of the powerful relationship between society and party. It has been the American experience that a basic structure of partisan alignments, once established, has persisted—as long as the sociopolitical setting upon which it rested remained essentially intact. If a sociopolitcal order erected during the New Deal persisted throughout the 1940s and 1950s, then, this should be manifested in important continuities within the party system.

I. Change Within Continuity

In his *Dynamics of the Party System,* James Sundquist expresses some uneasiness with the "society and party system" relationship which we have developed.[1] Among other things, Sundquist maintains that it is possible for major new issues reshaping partisan division to arise without anything so sweeping as a shift to a new sociopolitical setting. To the extent that he is arguing that new conflict structures have been formed without the precipitant of

---

[1] Sundquist, *Dynamics of the Party System,* pp. 275–276.

fundamental social change in the United States—a democratic polity which has a high level of institutional stability—we would disagree.[2] On the other hand, to the extent that Sundquist is pointing to the party-society relationship as complex and dynamic, we would very strongly agree. It would border on the nonsensical to suggest that once a sociopolitical setting is established and a party system reflecting the social group composition and interest configurations of that society takes root, this party system must persist in an essentially static manner up to the point where convulsive changes usher in a new social era.

The American political experience reveals a much more interesting and complicated pattern with several key components which are worth singling out. (1) Almost immediately after a new party system has been established, it begins to experience *inherent extensions*. Once a majority party, for example, has established its position of particular sensitivity and responsiveness to what Samuel Lubell called "the problems with which the newer generation has

---

[2] It is essential to reiterate that the generalizations which we are offering about the relationship of party and society are meant to apply only to democratic polities with very well-established structures of stability in political institutions—and specifically, to the United States. Consider, by way of contrast, a society where several contending interests each offer drastically different versions of the desired constitutional order. In such a context, a major redefinition of conflict can occur if one group succeeds in supplanting another, as through a coup d'état. In such an instance, the underlying social structure has not been substantially altered. There was nothing approaching constitutional consensus. One group simply won out, temporarily at least, in a struggle for power. When a society has achieved a high measure of consensus around its constitutional arrangements, however, the source of lasting change in the structure of conflict must be transformations of the social system: For example, the appearance of broad new sets of political interests, drastically altered expectations within the citizenry, marked increases in the numerical strength of established interest groups, and the like.

The matter is complex, and an almost infinite array of further qualifications and exceptions can be developed. The basic point, nonetheless, seems sufficiently well established and precisely stated for the purposes of this volume. The dynamic whereby major new political issues have been generated in the United States comprises the instrument of fundamental social change.

grown up . . . ," [3] once it has become, in other words, the party of the agenda, it reaps the return in electoral support among population groups which subsequently have come to consider themselves beneficiaries of the new thrusts in social policy. And it loses support among other groups which have found serious fault with these new policies, as their implications have become clear. (2) Then, there is the element of *natural maturation*. The socioeconomic composition of a party coalition can change enormously as its membership grows up or ages. Once a set of partisan attachments have been formed, they tend to persist; and if the social status of certain constituent groups is significantly modified, through natural maturation the coalitions may be importantly transformed even though no realignment of the classic sort (people crossing from one party to another) has occurred. (3) Further changes may occur through *habitual reinforcement*. Under the impetus of a set of powerful political issues and circumstances, a group's historic fealty to one party may be interrupted. But before the first onslaught of these forces, established loyalties may keep important segments of the group in their old electoral pattern. The social change has occurred, the new political agenda precipitating the group's shift in partisan loyalties has emerged, but there is a lag. After several elections in which the same forces remain present, however, the voting choice they suggest no longer appears strange or heretical. The forces of habitual loyalty which once anchored the group to one party gradually serve to bind it to another. (4) A very different sort of transformation which occurs within a single societal setting/party system configuration comprises *localized transformations*. When we consider the boundaries of a sociopolitical era, our frame of reference is the national experience. Frequently, however, developments have occurred within one sector of the society with important implications for electoral behavior in that unit—while the overall national pattern has con-

[3] Lubell, *The Future of American Politics*, p. 35.

tinued to manifest compelling continuities. The transformations to which we refer here may be localized in a geographic sense—confined to one section of the country—or their localism may connote confinement to specialized groups and interests which lack any particular territorial coloration. The key point is that the transformation may be powerful in one sector, while leaving the broad national pattern essentially intact.

To note the persistence of a party system, then, is not to describe some static phenomenon. Once formed at the onset of a sociopolitical period, party coalitions are variously extended, reinforced, changed through a natural maturation of their members, and otherwise modified as the sociopolitical period unfolds. New issues arise, old ones lose salience, in a dynamic, ever changing political landscape. In the course of its evolution, a given party system may experience a bundle of transitions which collectively are far from inconsequential. The sense of a party system lasting over a period of time, then, should avoid any suggestion of stasis and call attention instead to the continuing evidence of lines of electoral cleavage *ordained by the inauguration of the sociopolitical setting.*

II. Evolution of the New Deal Coalitions

The two decades or so after the New Deal provide a nice illustration of the phenomenon we have been describing—the persistence of a party system involving a plethora of natural extensions and enlargements. The old New Deal coalitions were much in evidence in 1960, but not as static carryovers of the partisan bodies of 1935. Patterns of social group attachments to the respective coalitions, policy disagreements between Democratic and Republican adherents, the relative strength of the major parties—all of these reveal impressive continuities. But the natural evolution of the New Deal parties carried with it as well certain transformations.

The 1940s and 1950s constituted a time when changes initiated during the Depression and New Deal epoch were incorporated into a new political landscape. But as we suggested above, "assimilation" does not quite capture the complexity of the process. Neither does James Sundquist's "aftershocks of the New Deal earthquake," by which he meant state or local realignments bringing the various regions "into conformity with the realignment established in the country as a whole in the 1930s. . . ." [4] It is appropriate to turn to the substantial body of survey materials available on party attachments, policy orientations and electoral loyalties for the 1940s and 1950s, to make clearer the long-term impacts upon the party coalitions of changes wrought in the Depression decade.

GROWTH OF THE DEMOCRATIC MIDDLE CLASS

The advance in the prosperity of Americans from the Depression to the end of the 1950s is substantial by any measure. Per capita personal income (expressed in constant 1958 dollars) reached a depression low of $898 in 1932; by 1939, it had returned to $1,195, about the 1929 figure; then it jumped to $1,805 in 1950, and to $2,133 in 1959. Median family income, in the same constant dollars, doubled in the twenty years after 1939—from $2,725 to $5,337. Such an increase in affluence drew a growing segment of the population into a socioeconomic position commonly referred to as middle-class. The proportion of families earning $6,000 or more a year (in dollars of 1960 purchasing power) jumped from 18 percent in 1939 to 44 percent in 1959; while the proportion over $8,000 per year tripled, from 9 to 27 percent.[5]

---

[4] Sundquist, *Dynamics of the Party System*, p. 218.

[5] These data are adapted from U.S. Department of Commerce, *Survey of Current Business*, vol. 29, no. 8 (April 1949), p. 15; vol. 41, no. 5 (May 1961), p. 16; and vol. 49, no. 4 (April 1969), pp. 26–27.

The impact on the citizenry parties of this dramatic surge in national wealth and the accompanying changes in political interests—from getting "Pa" off relief to putting "Pamela" through college—is not made in all ways evident by an examination of survey data, but a number of things are brought out rather well. For one thing, the Democracy *did not suffer* from growing affluence. A coalition forged in a climate of privation of acute economic needs was not weakened by the dramatic upturn in the overall prosperity of its members.

Many knowledgeable observers in the late 1940s and early 1950s believed that growing national prosperity, and particularly the expansion of the middling classes, would usher in a new era of Republican supremacy. Politicians such as Senator Robert A. Taft, scholars like Professor Edward Banfield, pollsters including Louis Harris, journalist-commentators like Frederick Lewis Allen, all entertained in one way or another the idea of a class-precipitated conversion to Republicanism.[6] The idea of conversion sometimes surfaced in discussions about the effects of that vast population movement from cities to that quintessential home of the new middle class, the suburb. That there was an inherent contradiction between Democratic support and middle-class status, comes perhaps as a legacy of an over-romanticization of the working-class character of the New Deal Democratic party. If being a Democrat and having relatively high socioeconomic status were in some way contradictory, then the extraordinary increase in prosperity and status associated with the middling classes should have precipitated some substantial conversion to Republicanism.

The "conversion thesis" had a number of flaws. For one,

---

[6] For representative statements see Banfield, "The Changing Political Environment of City Planning" (paper delivered at the American Political Science Association Annual Meeting, Washington, D.C., 1956); Harris, *Is There a Republican Majority?* (New York: Harper and Brothers, 1954); Allen, "Crisis in the Suburbs: The Big Change in Suburbia," Part II, *Harper's* (July 1954), pp. 47–53.

it overestimated the extent of the middle-class–working-class electoral split even in the Depression context, when it was greatest. The lower classes were never so uniformly Democratic or the middle classes so solidly Republican as some conventional wisdom proclaimed them to be. A massive contradiction between middle-class standing and Democratic support never existed.

There is more than this, however, to the fallacy underlying the conversion expectation. Implicit in it were the assumptions (1) that the character of the amorphous middle class would remain essentially unchanged while its numbers increased; and (2) that the Democratic appeal of the 1930s—clearly to those experiencing economic distress—could not be readily adapted to a condition of relative abundance.

Actually, the composition of the middle classes was transformed as large numbers of Americans climbed the socioeconomic ladder during and after World War II. In a climate of expanded prosperity, the natural maturation of the Democratic coalition of the thirties brought many of its members to middle-class standing. And frequently, they carried old Democratic ties with them as they moved up the status ladder. People who were economic have-nots in the 1930s—and their children—retained Democratic loyalties as their social and economic position improved, a process which Samuel Lubell described so nicely just as it was occurring.[7]

The middle class, historically, has been largely entrepreneurial, a class which grew up with industrialization;

---

[7] Lubell wrote (1952) that "the Democrats generally have been thought of as the 'poor man's party' and, at the outset of the New Deal, they certainly were mainly an aggregation of economic 'have nots.' The rising prosperity of the last twenty years, however, has subtly transformed the internal makeup of the Democratic coalition, lifting many of its members to a 'have' status. . . . [I]n large part, as the poor and underprivileged prospered and climbed they remained loyal to the Democratic party. The new middle class, which has developed over the last two decades, seems as Democratic by custom as the older middle class elements are instinctively Republican." *The Future of American Politics*, pp. 61–62.

and in turn it possessed political orientations and interests associated with entrepreneurial activity. With World War II, however, a vast new middle class began to take shape, bearing little in common with the old. Advanced industrial society requires much less manual labor, whether of factory or farm, and in turn can sustain an expanded professional and managerial stratum. Reflecting this occupational change, a literature discussing the character, life styles, problems, and behavior of white-collar man sprang up in the 1950s.[8] While the base for the ascendancy of the professional and managerial stratum formed gradually, it was in the first decade after World War II that the social and political importance of this group was brought home to observers of the American scene.

In *White Collar*, C. Wright Mills observed that coming to grips with the behavior of the new middle class had proved difficult because its boundary lines were vague: "We can easily understand why such an occupational salad invites so many conflicting theories and why general images of it are likely to differ. There is no one accepted word for them; white collar, salaried employee, new middle class are used interchangeably." [9] The category is indeed loose and generally inclusive, but if we construe the new middle class as comprising those employed in professional and managerial occupations, we see it to be set off decisively from the self-employed, entrepreneurial old middle class. And the growth of the middle classes between 1940 and 1960 clearly occurred primarily in the former camp. In this twenty-year span, the number of persons in professional and managerial occupations increased by 7 million (7.3 to 14.5 million); while the number of self-

[8] Among the most interesting contributions to this literature are Mills, *White Collar* (New York: Oxford University Press, 1951); David Riesman, Nathan Glazer, and Reuel Denney, *The Lonely Crowd* (New Haven: Yale University Press, 1950); and William H. Whyte, Jr., *The Organization Man* (New York: Simon and Schuster, 1956).

[9] Mills, *op. cit.*, p. 291.

employed persons actually declined, from 10 to just over 9 million.[10]

The Republican attachments of the old middle class are evident. The Republican party served the cause of industrial nation building, and received the support of an apparently large majority of the middle classes associated with this enterprise. Because it had generally sought and benefited from Republican policies, its opposition to the departures of the New Deal offers no surprise. By way of contrast, the new middle class lacked the stakes of the old in earlier Republican programs. Because its members occupied positions created by the economy of advanced industrialism, they found nothing incompatible between their interests and governmental programs and policies introduced as public responses to advanced industrialism. Indeed, a significant segment depended as much upon governmental nationalism as the old middle class had benefited from business nationalism. Since the Democrats served as the principal architects of the new governmental nationalism and the new liberal state which was its product, the fact that broad segments of the new middle class perceived no conflict—indeed, saw a congruence— between Democratic support and their socioeconomic status followed naturally.

As the economic privation of the 1930s passed, then, and as important segments of the growing middle classes came to endorse the general policy directions of the new liberal state, the Democratic party was necessarily transformed in tone and style. The Democracy abandoned much of the rhetoric of the class struggle on which it had capitalized in the 1930s; and the *new middle class qua Democratic identifiers*, finding many like themselves in the party, saw nothing contradictory in being people of rising social position and being Democrats.

---

[10] These data are from: U.S. Bureau of the Census, *Statistical Abstract of the United States, 1952*, pp. 186–187; and *1973*, p. 233.

The conversion hypothesis, though not totally invalid, ill-fitted the dynamic of the 1940s and 1950s. The socio-economic structure of the Democratic coalition changed substantially as important segments of its membership rode the wave of growing prosperity, and as the party's programs and policies became securely fixed as compatible with the needs and aspirations of much of the new middle class.

Survey data demonstrate a rather dramatic relative strengthening of the Democratic position within the middle classes. Looking at presidential and congressional voting of members of the professional and managerial stratum, for example, we see that these middle-class occupational cohorts gave decisively lower support to the Democrats than did the population at large in the elections through 1948. Fifty-five percent of the general public voted for Roosevelt in 1940, compared to just 31 percent of professionals and businessmen—a difference of 24 percentage points. Fifty-one percent of all voters, but just 32 percent of these middle-class occupational groups supported Democratic congressional candidates in the 1944 elections.

Beginning with the 1950s, however, the variation between the vote of the entire electorate and that of the professional and managerial stratum shrinks notably, with a reduction evident in both congressional and presidential balloting. The margin between the professional-business cohort and the public at large, along the order of 15 to 20 percentage points in the 1940s, dropped to between 5 and 10 points in the 1950s. Most striking are the gains in Democratic congressional support within the managerial stratum. Forty-seven percent of businessmen and professionals backed Democratic congressional candidates in 1956, only 4 percent below the national Democratic congressional support. And in 1960, Democratic congressional candidates received the support of half (49 percent) the voters from the professional and managerial stratum. This middle-class occupational cohort, then, which gave Democratic candidates for the national House of Representatives roughly one-third of its votes in the early 1940s, was delivering roughly half of its vote to congressional Democrats by the end of the 1950s.

These data in one sense understate Democratic gains among the middle classes over the 1940s and 1950s. For at the same time the Democrats were drawing a higher proportion of electoral backing from professionals and businessmen, these occupational groups were constituting a larger proportion of the total electorate.

Other representations of the middle class reveal the same shift over the last two decades of the New Deal era. In his surveys over this entire span, Gallup employed a composite measure of socioeconomic status.[11] The principal categories of this indicator defined persons of above average, average, and below average status. The first of these best approximates what the term *middle class* nor-

---

[11] "Economic status" for the 1935–1948 Gallup Polls was ascertained by the interviewers who made an assessment of the neighborhood in which respondents lived for the categories "wealthy," "average plus," "average," "poor plus," and "poor"; while those "on relief" or receiving "old age assistance" were identified from an occupation question. The classification scheme was supplemented with information on telephone subscription, automobile ownership, and specific occupation. In 1940, moreover, George Gallup checked the validity of the classification using family income and self-ascribed class position data.

Gallup's basic sample for this earlier period, always corrected against Bureau of the Census information, was based on a quota of persons in each of the economic categories. By 1952, TV ownership replaced that of telephones and the classification scheme was reduced to three—"average plus," "average," and "poor." Further, by 1956, and through 1960, the threefold economic status classification was more objectively based on rent paid or the amount of rent a *home owner* estimated he could afford, would he have had to rent his home. The rent figures were then arrayed under four population headings from the city size question—"rural farm" and "non-farm," 2,500–49,999, 50,000–499,999, and 500,000 + —divided into thirds, and aggregated into "upper," "middle," and "lower."

See George Gallup and Saul Forbes Rae, *The Pulse of Democracy* (New York: Simon and Schuster, 1940), pp. 110–116; George Gallup, *The Sophisticated Poll Watcher's Guide* (Princeton, N.J.: Princeton Opinion Press, 1972), pp. 45–61; and the explanatory note in the codebook for AIPO No. 638. For a more technical discussion of "economic status" and its validity: Hadley Cantril, *Gauging Public Opinion* (Princeton, N.J.: Princeton University Press, 1944), pp. 288–296.

mally connotes, even though it contains as well persons of
the very highest social standing, while average encompasses the more prosperous manual workers.[12] The above
average cohort in 1940, 1944, and 1948 was overwhelmingly Republican, consistently conferring over two-thirds
of its electoral support in presidential and congressional
contests to the Grand Old Party. Again in the 1950s, however, Democratic allegiance in this cohort jumped notably—reaching nearly half of the total in congressional
contests. The gap in Democratic support separating the
above average stratum from the electorate at large dwin-
dled appreciably, to approximately 5–10 percent. By the
end of the period, this middle, or perhaps more precisely
upper–middle-class cohort had moved far from the decisively Republican standing of its counterpart of the Depression and immediate post-Depression years. Still more
Republican than the population at large, it divided its vote
roughly along the lines of the national electorate.

We find the same pattern exactly when we examine the
partisan identification of the above average cohort. In the
1940s, this group's Republican allegiance exceeded its
Democratic attachments by a margin of roughly two to one
(53 percent Republican, and 24 percent Democratic, for instance, in 1948). By the 1950s, however, it divided evenly
in its party loyalties. The big Republican edge had disappeared. While it is jumping somewhat ahead of our story,
it should be noted that the pattern revealed by Table 2.1
and Figure 2.1 was not proved evanescent, some peculiar
product of the Eisenhower "era of good feeling." The massive Republican dominance in the middling classes, evident in the 1930s and 1940s, vanished in the 1950s never
(or at least not yet) to return.

Some attention should be directed to the exceptional
shift shown by our data for the 1948–1952 period. Quite

[12] The "above average" category is a rather demanding one, closer
overall to what we commonly understand to be upper-middle class. In
1940, for example, 20 percent of the public was located in the above
average category; in 1960, 33 percent.

Table 2.1. Presidential and Congressional Voting of Persons of
Above Average Socioeconomic Status, 1940–1960; with Comparisons to the Electorate at Large

	Percentage Democratic	
	PRESIDENTIAL VOTE	CONGRESSIONAL VOTE
1940		
(a) Above average	31	33
(b) All voters	55	51
Percentage difference;		
(a) minus (b)	−24	−18
1944		
(a) Above average	33	31
(b) All voters	53	51
Percentage difference;		
(a) minus (b)	−20	−20
1948		
(a) Above average	23	29
(b) All voters	50	52
Percentage difference;		
(a) minus (b)	−27	−23
1952		
(a) Above average	32	46
(b) All voters	44	50
Percentage difference;		
(a) minus (b)	−12	− 4
1956		
(a) Above average	33	NA
(b) All voters	42	NA
Percentage difference;		
(a) minus (b)	− 9	
1960		
(a) Above average	41	48
(b) All voters	50	55
Percentage difference;		
(a) minus (b)	− 9	− 7

SOURCE: Data from following AIPO studies: *1940*, 215, 219, 224; *1944*, 329,
336; *1948*, 430, 431, 432; *1952*, 506, 507, 508; *1956*, 574, 576; and *1960*, 638,
640. Above average includes respondents classified "average plus" and
"wealthy" or "upper."

Figure 2.1. Partisan Self-Identification of Persons of Above
Average Socioeconomic Status, 1940–1960

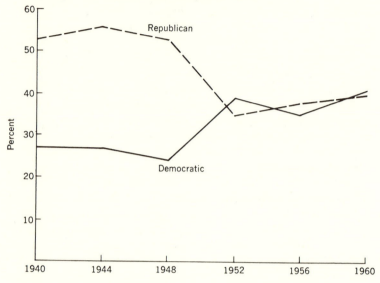

SOURCE: Data from following AIPO surveys: *1940*, 208, 209; *1944*, 329;
1948, 431, 432; *1952*, 507, 508; *1956*, 574, 576; *1960*, 638, 640.

clearly, our argument bearing on the underlying precipitants of Democratic gains in the middling classes cannot
account for so massive and abrupt a transition. Nothing in
the data contradicts the basic dynamic we identified, but
the shift is just too rapid and too precisely fixed. Since
analysis utilizing a variety of different measures of middle-
class status and a wide array of separate surveys all revealed the same thing, we must conclude that the survey
data are probably not in error. The most likely interpretation is that the 1948 election was a curious hangover, a
contest out of keeping with the larger sociopolitical reali-
ties of the time in which it was waged. The nature of Truman's "bloody shirt" campaign—labeling the Republicans
the party of Depression as the post–Civil War Republicans
had typed their Democratic antagonists the party of rebel-
lion—together with the exceptional uncertainties of the

immediate postwar years, produced a "Depression-like" configuration in class voting. In fact, the programs of the Democratic new liberal state were not antithetical to the interests of much of the new middle class and that larger political reality quickly took hold in the electoral politics of the 1950s.

Studies conducted by Michigan's Survey Research Center in the 1952–1960 period indicate the extent of Democratic gains among the middle to upper strata through another indicator in many ways the most direct and revealing—family income.[13] Respondents to these SRC surveys were located in one of three income categories: substantially above the national median family income at the time; around the median; and substantially below the median family income. In all cases, we constructed the "above the median" or high income category so that it would contain the top 25 to 30 percent of the population. Throughout the 1952–1960 span, this high income cohort showed a greater proportion of Democratic than of Republican identifiers. Forty percent of this group described themselves as Democrats in 1952, for example, compared to 35 percent identifying as Republicans; in 1960, the percentages were 40 and 32 respectively. Republican electoral support within the high income cohort in congressional contests—much less subject than presidential voting, of course, to the short-term impact of candidate personal attributes—declined steadily throughout the period, from 59 percent in 1952, to 52 percent in 1956, 50 percent in 1958, and just 47 percent in 1960.

Republican allegiance among Americans of middle to high social and economic status remained substantial throughout the period, and was consistently higher than within the lower socioeconomic cohorts. The pronounced GOP advantage within the middle classes which characterized electoral competition in the Roosevelt and Truman years disappeared, however, late in the New Deal era.

---

[13] With but a few exceptions for the period before 1960, Gallup questionnaires did not contain an income question.

This growth of the Democratic middle class in one sense
reflects "secular realignment"—a process which V. O. Key
described in terms of long-range social and economic
changes affecting the composition of various population
groups, thereby altering their party loyalties and in turn
the partisan balance.[14] But the emergence of a partisan situation in which the Democrats as much as the Republicans could lay claim to being a middle-class party is better
understood as a natural extension of the New Deal partisan transformation. The substance of party competition
was dramatically altered during the 1930s. The Democrats
emerged as the party of governmental nationalism, and
proceeded to initiate a range of programs which defined
the new liberal state. Nothing in the broad outlines of this
development contributed to a fundamental cleavage between the Democratic party and the socioeconomic status
we describe as middle-class. Governmental nationalism
clashed with the old liberal state, and with the interests
and perceptions of the entrepreneurial middle classes associated with that state, but was hardly incompatible with
middle-class standing in any generic sense. As various deprived groups rose in socioeconomic positions, as the
boundaries of the middle classes were altered as a consequence of broad economic transformations, more middle-
class components appeared who considered Democratic
allegiance both fully consistent with their interests and
natural. Indeed, one must assert that the success of the
Democracy in establishing itself as the party of the
agenda, that is, of governmental nationalism, *ordained the
growth of its support among the middle classes.*

STATUS POLARIZATION AND THE ISSUE DIMENSION

There has been some disagreement as to whether the
distance separating the higher and lower socioeconomic

---

[14] Key, "Secular Realignment and the Party System," pp. 208–210.

status groups in electoral behavior and various political attitudes has remained roughly constant since the New Deal
or has declined—and if the latter, why. This argument obviously relates to the point we have been exploring, of
growing Democratic strength in the expanded middle
classes after 1948.

Philip Converse introduced the concept *status polarization* to indicate "the degree to which groups at opposing
ends of the status continuum have taken up mutually an-
tagonistic value positions in the politico-economic
sphere." [15] Drawing upon the election studies of Michigan's Survey Research Center in the 1950s and a 1945 survey by Richard Centers which together permit comparable
class or status definitions,[16] Converse concluded that "it is
beyond dispute" that a "sizeable decline" in status polarization, in the distance between the middle and working
classes, occurred over the 1945-1956 span.[17] A decade and
a half after the Converse study was published, Paul
Abramson's investigation confirmed its basic findings, that
the distance in voting choice separating the middle from
the working classes had declined, and added the likely
projection that "unless unforeseen events occur . . [it]
will continue to decline." [18]

Robert Alford took issue, however, with the conclusion
of Converse and his Michigan colleagues concerning the

---

[15] Philip E. Converse, "The Shifting Role of Class in Political Attitudes
and Behavior," in E. E. Maccoby, T. M. Newcomb, and E. E. Hartley (editorial committee), *Readings in Social Psychology* (New York: Holt Rine-
hart & Winston, 3rd edition, 1958), p. 394. The concept is also dealt with
in Campbell, *et al., The American Voter,* Chapter 13.
[16] The study by Richard Centers is fully reported in his book, *The Psychology of Social Classes* (Princeton, N.J.: Princeton University Press,
1949).
[17] Converse, "The Shifting Role of Class in Political Attitudes and Behavior," pp. 391-393.
[18] Paul R. Abramson, "Generational Change in American Electoral Behavior," p. 105. Abramson goes beyond Converse's treatment to discuss at
length the relationship between age and class on the one hand, and voting choice on the other. We will pick up these arguments in Chapters 4
and 5.

depression of status polarization or class voting. Comparing the proportion of manual workers and of the non-
manual occupational strata voting Democratic in presidential contests from 1936 through 1960, Alford argued that
"there has been no substantial shift in the class bases of
American politics since the 1930s, despite the prosperity
since World War II and despite the shifts to the Right in
the Eisenhower era. . . . No evidence of either a decline
of class voting or any substantial change in the pattern of
class voting among major United States regions or religious groups has been found." [19]

Our own studies make clear, however, that there has in
fact been a substantial secular decline in the degree to
which the higher and lower strata are distinguished by
their electoral choices since the Depression and the immediate post-Depression years. Figure 1.2 comparing the
presidential vote of high status (college-educated, and
business and professional occupations) and low status
(semiskilled and unskilled laborers) groups from 1936
through 1972 testifies to this. So do the data presented in
Tables 2.1 and 2.2, and in Figure 2.1. The materials which
Alford presents are not incorrect in and of themselves, but
they provide an incomplete picture. He has examined only
presidential voting—not other measures of electoral attachments and support—and he has compared only two
grossly inclusive occupational cohorts—manual and non-
manual workers. A composite picture is necessary. If one
applies a variety of measures of socioeconomic status, and
looks at the full array of electoral choices for the entire
1936–1972 period—and particularly, in view of our focus
in this chapter, at the 1940–1960 span—the secular diminution of status polarization is amply documented.

At the same time, we cannot accept Converse's explanation of the source of this decline. His argument contained
the following points. First, given a fairly constant structure

---

[19] Robert R. Alford, *Party and Society: The Anglo-American Democra-
cies* (Chicago: Rand McNally, 1963), pp. 226–227, 248.

to the distribution of wealth in an industrial society such as the United States, class voting will be higher in times of depression and lower in periods of prosperity. There are, however, other intervening considerations. Wars, by depressing concern with domestic economic questions, and entailing effects not clearly distributed along class lines, temporarily reduce status polarization. Still other "prominent elements in the election situation" can serve to reduce temporarily the cleavage between socioeconomic groups in electoral choice—notably, "a magnetic presidential candidate" able to generate "a broad public appeal which defies status lines." [20] Our own analysis suggests, instead, that the higher and lower socioeconomic strata became less differentiated in voting after the Roosevelt and Truman years more because of changes in the composition of the middle classes—from entrepreneurial toward professional and managerial—and because the broad new middle class has proven generally receptive to the policy thrusts of governmental nationalism and hence to the Democrats as the party of governmental nationalism.

A number of elements, some already presented, support this interpretation. Class voting was high in 1944, much higher than in the 1950s (or in the 1960s and 1970s), even though a major war was going on. The composite picture of status polarization in 1944 compared to 1948 shows it only marginally less pronounced in the former year. Much more revealing, although it could be nothing more than speculation in 1958, is the persistence of a secular decline in status polarization. The middle and working classes were less differentiated in 1956 with a magnetic Republican presidential nominee than they were in 1948, when issues rather than candidates held center stage; but the middle and working classes were even less distinct electorally in 1968 and 1972 than they had been in the Eisenhower years. A larger dynamic has been at work, in-

[20] Converse, "The Shifting Role of Class in Political Attitudes and Behavior," pp. 395–397.

volving the composition of the social classes and their relationship to an unfolding political agenda, and it is to this that we must look for the source of the altered relationship of class and party.[21]

The decline of working-class–middle-class distinctiveness in voting from the 1940s through the 1950s was paralleled, as we would expect, by a decline of class differences over salient policy questions—a conclusion sustained by our examination of data from more than fifty Gallup and SRC surveys conducted between 1940 and 1960. The respective status groups can be compared as to their opinions on an extraordinary array of social and economic policy questions throughout the time span, and a general picture does emerge: The higher and lower status cohorts consistently displayed much more "opinion distance" on the basic New Deal and post–New Deal programs in the 1940s than in the 1950s. There is a basic problem in such comparisons, of course, because with but a few exceptions we lack precisely comparable questions throughout this twenty-year period. The same general areas are covered: governmental regulation of business, and of the labor movement; more governmental management of the economy; the use of government to develop various social welfare programs for the society. But the wording of questions used to probe these policy areas varies significantly, and this naturally muddles the comparison.

Still, meaningful comparisons emerge from composite pictures. For example, a wide range of questions were asked between 1936 and 1948 soliciting orientations toward trade unions, whether or not they should be subject to greater or lesser regulation, whether legislation governing unions—principally the Wagner and Taft-Hartley Acts—was too restrictive or insufficiently so, and in general whether the development of an active trade union movement was to be applauded or disapproved. The dif-

---

[21] Aspects of this theme are more appropriately developed in Chapters 4 and 5.

ferences separating business and professional personnel from manual workers, or distinguishing those of above average socioeconomic status (as measured by the Gallup indicator) from others of below average status, were massive, often in the range of 30 to 40 percentage points. On the other hand, by the late 1950s and early 1960s roughly similar pro-con questions on unionism showed relatively narrow inter-class variations. A January 1961 Gallup survey, for example, asked respondents whether they gave general approval or disapproval to the thrusts of the trade union movement. Sixty-eight percent of those of above average status, compared to 72 percent of those below average, indicated approbation.[22]

Table 2.2 illustrates this same pattern of inter-class decline in policy differentiation in attitudes toward governmental regulation of business. The 1940 and 1961 ques-

Table 2.2. Opinions on Government Regulation of Business, Selected Occupation Groups, 1940 and 1961

1940 Question: "During the next four years, do you think there should be more regulation or less regulation of business by the Federal Government, than at present?"

	MORE	ABOUT SAME	LESS
Professional/managerial	14	16	70
Manual	40	26	35

1961 Question: "Do you think the laws regulating business corporations are too strict, or not strict enough?"

	NOT STRICT ENOUGH	ABOUT RIGHT	TOO STRICT
Professional/managerial	37	47	16
Manual	38	49	13

SOURCE: For 1940, AIPO No. 219KT; and for 1961, AIPO No. 650.

—————

[22] AIPO Survey No. 640, January 10, 1961. "In general, do you approve or disapprove of labor unions?"

tions are only roughly comparable in phrasing; but both test sentiment as to whether regulation of business should be expanded or curtailed, is too strict or not strict enough. The opinion differences separating the professional and managerial and the manual strata in 1940 are extraordinarily large: 70 percent of the former, as against 35 percent of the latter, wanted less regulation of business by government. In 1961, by way of contrast, opinion distance between these two strata on the general question of business regulation had disappeared completely.

The point being made requires especially careful qualification. The array of opinion measures with which we are required to work is exceptionally disparate, with basic policy areas explored through all manner of contrasting questions. General approximations can be made as to the shifting magnitude of inter-class variations, nothing more precise. This composite picture shows that on regulation of business and unions, social welfare programs, and the like, higher status groups were notably further apart from lower status groups in the New Deal and immediate post–New Deal years than in the 1950s and early 1960s. This is not to suggest that inter-class differences disappeared in the policy realm, any more than in voting. The magnitude of variation in both attitudes and behavior did decline.[23]

---

[23] Philip Converse has provided further confirming data on this point. He compared findings of the 1956 Michigan election study with those of Richard Centers's 1945 survey. Working both with subjective class assignment and with occupational status, Converse demonstrated that the higher and lower status cohorts had become much less differentiated on such basic economic policy matters as the responsibility of the national government to assure full employment, government-sponsored health insurance, and governmental control of private business, in 1956 than they had been eleven years earlier. Converse, "The Shifting Role of Class in Political Attitudes and Behavior," pp. 391–393. Erickson and Luttbeg have subsequently made the same argument, noting that "the relative difference in economic liberalism between people of high and low status occupations appears to have declined during the post–World War II era." They also observe that one element in this reduced policy differentiation involves the fact that "the more prosperous [occupational cohorts] have become less resistant [to governmentally directed social welfare]." Robert S. Erikson and Norman R. Luttbeg, *American Public Opinion: Its Origins, Content and Impact* (New York: John Wiley, 1973), p. 170.

The middle class of 1940 differed from that of 1960 in a number of salient ways. Composition was different, both because of changes over this span in the occupational mix of the society—involving the growth of the new middle class—and because lower status cohorts rode the wave of postwar prosperity to higher socioeconomic standing. By any of the varying measures that can be constructed for the category, the middle class of 1940 was much more resistant to the thrusts of governmental nationalism—compared to the working class—than was its counterpart two decades later. What we have called "inherent extensions" and "natural maturation," then, transformed a broad social category, altering its opinion orientations on basic social and economic questions, and changing significantly its electoral orientations. The natural rhythm of the alignment established during the Depression contributed in the postwar years to an appreciable growth of the Democratic middle class.

ETHNIC CONFIGURATIONS

In discussing the political orientations of higher SES cohorts in the American population, we have stressed the relative strengthening of the Democratic position, as part of a natural unfolding of the New Deal alignment. This development takes on major importance: Had the Democrats failed to become a party with broad support among the middle and upper status groups, they would have found their claim to majority status in serious jeopardy amid the economic transformations and generally rising prosperity of the postwar years. Such an emphasis upon change in electoral distributions should not take us too far, however, from a recognition of impressive electoral continuities. For as we have noted, the changes which occurred did so on the whole within the boundaries of a basic pattern of electoral alignments constructed during the New Deal. This sense of underlying continuities together with an evolutionary process within the New Deal party system be-

comes manifest in partisan divisions separating the principal ethnocultural groups. Throughout the New Deal era,
the pronounced Republican base among white Protestants
outside the South is evident, as is Democratic ascendancy
among newer ethnic collectivities—notably blacks, Jews,
and Catholics.

Blacks were brought into the Democratic coalition
through new economic initiatives of the Roosevelt administration. They remained there securely throughout the
1940s and 1950s. Table 2.3 shows, for example, that
roughly two-thirds of the black electorate supported Democratic candidates for president and Congress in all of the
elections in the two decades after 1940.

Table 2.3. Presidential and Congressional Vote, and Party
Identification of Black Americans, 1940–1960 (as Percentages)

	1940	1944	1948	1952	1956	1960
PARTY I.D.						
Democratic	42	40	56	66	56	58
Republican	42	40	25	18	24	22
Independent	16	21	19	16	20	20
PRESIDENTIAL VOTE						
Democratic	67	68	77	76	68	76
CONGRESSIONAL VOTE						
Democratic	65	55	64	78	67	69

SOURCE: Data from following AIPO studies: *1940,* 208, 209, 215, 222, 224,
225; *1944,* 328, 329, 336, 337; *1948,* 430, 431, 432, 433; *1952,* 506, 507, 508,
509; *1956,* 572, 573, 574, 576; and *1960,* 637, 638, 640. In 1948, the
Democratic and Progressive (Henry Wallace) presidential vote totals have
been combined.

Not too much should be made of minor variations in the
proportion of blacks shown voting Democratic from one
election to another. Survey data reveal general voting configurations. But they lack sufficient accuracy, especially in
the case of a group like blacks who are a small proportion
of the electorate—about 4.5 percent in 1952—to justify
reading substantive conclusions into shifts of a few percentage points. Even combining surveys, the number of

black respondents in the data base with which we are
working remains small and hence susceptible to a substantial margin of error. It is highly questionable, to take one
example, whether the black vote for Democratic congressional candidates jumped by 14 percentage points between 1948 and 1952.[24] The overall pattern, nonetheless,
seems clearly etched. Black Americans voted solidly Democratic throughout the period, at around the two-thirds
level of support.

One notable change in electoral affinities among blacks
did occur, in the area of party identification, as habitual reinforcement made Democratic attachments as natural as
Republican loyalties had been over the seven decades or
so after the Civil War. During the Roosevelt years, we
noted, there was a massive discrepancy between the partisan self-identification of blacks and their electoral behavior. In 1944, the proportion of blacks describing themselves as Republicans equaled that identifying as
Democrats, even though two-thirds of black voters supported the Democratic presidential candidate. The attrac-
tion of national Democratic programs shaped the vote, but
old loyalties, manifested in party self-identification, persisted for a time. By the Truman years, however, the conversion was complete. Data on the partisan self-perception
of blacks after 1948 reveal as decisive a commitment to the
Democracy as does actual electoral performance. Democratic programs and policies continued to be more supportive than the Republican of the interests of blacks as a
deprived group, and the lingering appeal of the party of
Lincoln dimmed notably.

The conversion of blacks to the Democratic party,
rounded out and reinforced after the 1930s, occurred in
the context of the New Deal party system. It was rooted

---

[24] The Survey Research Center of the University of Michigan, found
the black vote for Democratic congressional candidates in 1960 considerably higher than that reported by Gallup, 83 as against 69 percent. Such
variations inevitably occur when the number of cases (in national surveys) is small.

primarily in economic policy. Black Americans were clustered at the bottom of the socioeconomic ladder. The
Democrats were the more liberal of the two major parties,
offering more than their Republican opponents in social
welfare legislation. Throughout the 1930s, 1940s, and
1950s, however, the Democrats did not become associated
with bold new civil rights initiatives. While the national
Democratic party under Truman initiated some significant
civil rights actions, the most dramatic breakthrough, sig-
naling the end of the Jim Crow system in the South, was
mandated by the Supreme Court in the 1954 *Brown* decision—written by a chief justice who had been the Republican governor of California and was appointed to the Court
by a Republican president. Throughout the 1940s and
1950s, the Civil Rights movement for the most part looked
South. The Civil Rights revolution had not yet attained
broad national political import. The Republican and Democratic parties did not display the clear-cut differentiation
in civil rights that was to follow as the politics of race
became nationalized during the 1960s. Blacks were drawn
to the Democracy in the period we are considering, then,
by the thrusts of New Deal and post–New Deal economic
policies. The result was a strong measure of Democratic
support in the black electorate, but not the total liquidation of Republican backing which followed in the new
party system of the 1960s and 1970s.

The black population of the United States remained
massively rural and southern in 1940—with nearly 70 percent residing in the states of the Old Confederacy. By
1960, however, about half of all black Americans resided
outside the South. And the black electorate grew substantially over these two decades, from less than one million
registered voters in 1940 to over five million at the time of
the Kennedy-Nixon presidential contest. Much of the
ground was thus laid for the increased political strength of
blacks, and for their participation in a politics of race that
was national rather than essentially southern—developments which were to loom large in the transformations
ending the New Deal party system.

Although attributable to a somewhat different dynamic, the movement of Jews from the Republican party during the New Deal era followed a pattern similar to what we have seen for blacks. Jews were brought from the Republican to the Democratic camp in the 1930s in response to the internationalism, the economic policies, and more generally the broadly liberal commitments of the Roosevelt administration. Since nothing intervened to interrupt the converting stimuli—for the Democrats remained the liberal party and the strong Jewish commitments to liberal programs continued—the latter years of the New Deal era witnessed a reinforcement of Democratic attachments. By the 1950s, Jews were the most heavily and consistently Democratic of all ethnocultural groups in the United States.

Table 2.4. Presidential and Congressional Vote, and Party Identification of Jews, 1940–1960 (as Percentages)

	1940	1944	1948	1952	1956	1960
PARTY I.D.						
Democratic	45	NA	53	56	58	65
Republican	24	NA	13	9	8	8
Independent	32	NA	35	36	34	27
PRESIDENTIAL VOTE						
Democratic	84	91	72	72	71	85
CONGRESSIONAL VOTE						
Democratic	NA	NA	65	76	70	85

SOURCE: Data from following AIPO studies: *1940*, 208, 209, 215, 219, 248; *1944*, 336, 337; *1948*, 430, 431, 432; *1952*, 506, 507, 508, 509; *1956*, 573, 574, 576, 579; and *1960*, 637, 638, 640. In 1948, the Democratic and Progressive (Henry Wallace) presidential vote totals have been combined.

While both blacks and Jews heavily supported the Democracy in the New Deal period and experienced a common conversion from earlier Republican attachments, the social experience of these two groups stands in striking contrast. Jews gained dramatically in socioeconomic status after World War II, while blacks remained disproportionately among the most deprived. This brings us back to a

point made earlier, that Jewish support for the Democrats
did not come primarily as an expression of class politics.
Lawrence Fuchs noted, in examining the vote of Jews in
Boston for the 1952 Eisenhower-Stevenson contest, that
"differences in Stevenson's strength . . . cannot be accounted for by differences in socioeconomic status." [25] Our
analysis of Gallup survey materials confirms the general
validity of this observation. Jews of the highest socioeconomic status were usually somewhat more Republican
than the lowest status cohorts; but class differences in voting in all cases prove markedly less pronounced among
Jews than among Protestants and Catholics. The sources of
the strong proclivity of Jews for liberal policies, described
briefly in the preceding chapter, are to be found in the historic pattern of discrimination experienced by the group
and transmitted through its political culture.

The ethnocultural division in white America between
old stock and new stock—summarized rather effectively as
Protestant vs. Catholic—long antedated the New Deal but
assumed a prominent place in the New Deal party alignment. White Protestants in the South and black Protestants
throughout the country, for reasons bearing no connection
to their religious group status, provided generally strong
Democratic backing; but in only one election of the New
Deal era (1936) and indeed in only one election from the
Civil War through 1960, did *white, nonsouthern Protestants* cast a majority of their votes for a Democratic presidential nominee. Between 1940 and 1960, white Protestants outside the southern states never gave as high as 40
percent of their presidential votes to a Democratic nominee, while their Catholic counterparts never failed to return a Democratic majority. Congressional voting and partisan self-identification form a similar pattern. Some
variations are necessarily introduced by contrasting mixes
of candidates and issues, but it is not unfair to suggest as a
composite picture that only one-third of white northern [26]

[25] Fuchs, "American Jews and the Presidential Vote," p. 56.
[26] Northern refers to the states outside the Old Confederacy, excluding
as well Kentucky and Oklahoma.

Protestants backed the national Democratic party over the 1940–1960 span, while nearly two-thirds of the Catholics were in the Democratic camp.

Figures 2.2–2.4 fill in the complexity missing from the composite picture. Presidential and congressional voting, and partisan self-identification, are shown for northern white Protestants and Catholics over the two decades after 1940. The gap separating these groups in all forms of electoral attachments and behavior over the period is wide, but not uniform. Catholics and Protestants are most dissimilar at the beginning and end of this period, closest during the Eisenhower years. Northern Catholics, for example, produced a Democratic presidential vote 30 percentage points higher in 1944, then 24 points higher in 1948, 22 points in 1952, only 17 points in 1956, and then a massive 40 points in the 1960 Kennedy-Nixon election (Figure 2.3). The intergroup variation in partisan identification followed a similar, although as expected, somewhat flatter progression, from a 31 point differential in 1940, to 23 points in 1948, 24 in 1952, a low of 20 in 1956, and once again a high of 32 points in 1960 (Figure 2.2).

Two candidacies appear to account for most of the change in electoral distance between Protestants and

Figure 2.2. Percentage of White Non-South Protestants and Catholics Identifying as Democrats, 1940–1960

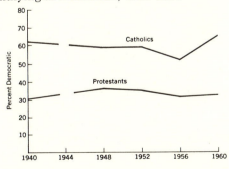

SOURCE: Data from following AIPO surveys: *1940*, 208, 209; *1948*, 431, 432; *1952*, 507, 508; *1956*, 573, 574; *1960*, 637, 638; data for 1944 not available.

Figure 2.3. Percentage of White Non-South Protestants and Catholics Voting Democratic in Presidential Contests, 1940–1960

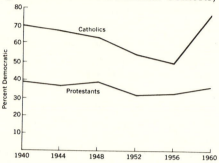

SOURCE: Data from following AIPO surveys: *1940*, 219, 248; *1944*, 336, 337; *1948*, 431, 432; *1952*, 507, 508; *1956*, 573, 574; *1960*, 637, 638.

Figure 2.4. Percentage of White Non-South Protestants and Catholics Voting Democratic in Congressional Contests, 1940–1960

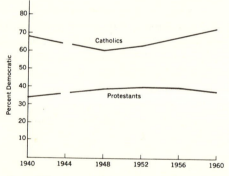

SOURCE: Data from following AIPO surveys: *1940*, 215; *1948*, 430, 431; *1952*, 506, 507; *1956*, 572, 573; *1960*, 637, 638; data for 1944 not available.

Catholics over the New Deal period—those of Eisenhower and Kennedy. Eisenhower advanced beyond previous Republican efforts in virtually all population subgroups, including northern white Protestants. But he improved much less in 1956 over Dewey's 1948 performance within the Protestant cohort (7 points) than among Catholics (14 points). This does not indicate that the defections of the Eisenhower interlude derived from religious background.

Our analysis of Gallup data supports Converse's findings based on Survey Research Center materials that in the 1950's "rates of defection were essentially the same for Protestant and Catholic *Democrats* alike." [27] Roughly comparable rates of defection among Democrats nonetheless produced a much larger shift in the Catholic cohort— because it was so much more heavily composed of Democrats than its Protestant counterpart.[28]

The 1960 presidential contest, pitting a Catholic against a Protestant for only the second time in American history, produced a major convulsion in religious voting. As Figure 2.3 demonstrates, Kennedy improved to an extraordinary extent over the Truman-Stevenson performance among Catholics, and his 77 percent of the vote in this cohort was surpassed only by the 81 percent FDR received in the 1936 Democratic landslide. The electoral distance between northern white Protestants and Catholics—42 points—was by a decisive margin the greatest of the New Deal era. To a lesser but still substantial extent, the religious polarization precipitated by the 1960 presidential contest showed up in partisan self-identification and in the congressional voting of that year.

Taken alone, the presidential vote shown in Figure 2.3 suggests that the Protestant vote was unaffected by the Kennedy candidacy, while the Catholic vote surged toward the Democrats. This is a bit misleading. For one thing, southern Protestants are not included, and Kennedy lost heavily in this still Democratic group.[29] In addition,

[27] Philip Converse, "Religion and Politics: The 1960 Election" (unpublished paper, Survey Research Center, University of Michigan, 1962), pp. 4–5. A shortened version of this paper was published in Campbell, *et al., Elections and the Political Order* (New York: John Wiley, 1966), pp. 96–124.

[28] According to Gallup data, 16 percent of northern *Catholics* who considered themselves Democrats defected to Eisenhower in 1956, and the same percentage exactly of northern white *Protestant* Democrats crossed over into the general's camp.

[29] For a more detailed discussion of this defection of white Protestant Democrats in the South, see Philip Converse, Angus Campbell, Warren Miller, and Donald Stokes, "Stability and Change in 1960: A Reinstating Election," in Campbell, *et al., Elections and the Political Order,* pp. 88–92.

the actual vote of Catholics in the Eisenhower elections was notably depressed below the "normal" vote of this strongly Democratic cohort. The 1956 Eisenhower base among Catholics, in other words, shows an unusually high level of Republican support; and some substantial measure of return to the Democratic camp, approximating the "normal" vote, would have been expected had the 1960 Democratic nominee not been Catholic. Kennedy's Catholicism in fact brought the Democratic percentage among Catholics from *below* to *above* the norm.[30] At the same time, it is significant that Kennedy actually improved marginally over Stevenson's showing among northern white Protestants, while gaining dramatically among Catholics. The pronounced religious polarization of 1960 resulted more from the positive impact of the Catholic candidacy among Catholic voters than from negative ramifications of that candidacy among Protestants.

Looking at data for the entire 1940–1960 span, we find further confirmation for our observation (in Chapter 1) that electoral differences between northern Protestants and Catholics do not follow primarily from their contrasting economic positions. When socioeconomic status is held constant (Table 2.5, p. 123) the magnitude of religious differences in voting is largely unaffected. There are curious variations from year to year. For example, Protestants and Catholics of low socioeconomic status in 1948 are shown to be notably more dissimilar in congressional voting than their high SES counterparts; while in 1956 and 1960 exactly the opposite applies. Such discrepancies probably result from sample error—extraordinarily magnified by the small number of cases in detailed subgroup analysis. Only composite picture analysis offers a remedy. And on the whole, the magnitude of Protestant-Catholic divisions stays the same when class is held constant.

Demonstration that electoral differences between white

---

[30] This subject has received careful consideration by Converse, "Religion and Politics: The 1960 Election."

Protestants and Catholics outside the South were both large and—taking into account variations necessarily introduced by specific candidacies and election situations—strikingly consistent, only touches the surface of a very complex set of relationships between the religious factor and electoral choice. Various studies have demonstrated, for example, the presence of quite disparate orientations in political attitudes and behavior among the different strains of Protestantism, and among the varying ethnic groups making up the Catholic electorate in the United States.[31] Religion affects electoral choice in different ways, as a supplier of beliefs, for instance, and as a determiner or indicator of status. What is most striking, though, and what occupies us here, are broad matters of the composition of the two party coalitions. The Protestant-Catholic ethnocultural frontier, politically potent since the Age of Jackson, its partisan significance heightened in the late 1920s and 1930s, remained influential throughout the New Deal era. The Republicans were as decisively the Protestant party—of white Protestants outside the South, that is—at the end of the 1950s as they had been during the Depression years. And despite the pronounced gains in socioeconomic status and in the general measure of acceptance in American life experienced by Catholics in the quarter-century after 1935, their support of the Democracy stood undiminished. It was only after 1960, with the emergence of a new ethnocultural frontier, that the historic Protestant-Catholic divide began to lose its grip on American electoral life.

THE DECISIVE ROLE OF CLASS AND RELIGION

We have pointed to the general secular decline of class voting since World War II, and in particular to the growth

---

[31] For an especially rich treatment of such differences and their sources, see Lipset, "Religion and Politics in the American Past and Present," in his *Revolution and Counterrevolution*, pp. 305–373.

of Democratic support within the expanded middle class. Important as these developments are, they do not suggest the disappearance of class distinctions as the New Deal era progressed. In its varying constructions, *class* remained a factor of considerable importance in differentiating electoral behavior. So too, as we have seen, did religion. Together, class and religion differentiated American electoral behavior throughout the New Deal period to an extent dwarfing all other general causal elements. Indeed, outside the South, the interaction of religion and class is very much the story of the New Deal partisan configurations.

Table 2.5 shows this nicely. Presidential and congressional voting, and partisan self-identification, are presented for white northern Protestants and Catholics by their socioeconomic standing.[32] Several aspects of the distributions in Table 2.5 are striking. There is the neatness and the consistency of the pattern produced by religion and class. Protestants of high socioeconomic status provided more Republican backing than their middle SES counterparts, who voted more heavily Republican than low SES Protestants—in all instances. The same set of distributions applies to Catholics. In every case, northern white Protestants of high socioeconomic status appeared as the most Republican cohort; while low status northern Catholics were the most solidly Democratic group.

The degree of differentiation imposed by these two variables is extraordinary. In 1940 congressional voting, for example, just 22 percent of high status northern Protestants voted Democratic, as against 72 percent of low status northern Catholics. Sixteen years later, in 1956, 30 percent of the former group backed Democratic congressional can-

---

[32] The population has been divided into high, middle, and low socioeconomic status categories. The "high SES" category contains those in business and professional occupations who are as well college educated; the "middle SES" group includes skilled, and clerical and sales workers; while "low SES" comprises semiskilled and unskilled workers. This construction of the status cohorts is the same applied in Figure 1.2.

Table 2.5. Democratic Support in Presidential and Congressional Voting, and in Partisan Identification, by Class and Religion, 1940–1960 (as Percentages)

	1940			1944			1948			1952			1956			1960		
	PRES.	CONG.	I.D.	PRES.	CONG.	I.D.	PRES.	CONG.	I.D.	PRES.	CONG.	I.D.	PRES.	CONG.	I.D.	PRES.	CONG.	I.D.
High SES																		
White Non-South Protestant	20	22	16	27	NA	NA	21	22	22	19	21	20	22	30	15	18	16	13
White Non-South Catholic	42	44	46	43	NA	NA	36	35	32	30	36	34	35	56	37	62	58	45
Middle SES																		
White Non-South Protestant	32	27	27	37	NA	NA	33	35	29	32	39	35	31	39	33	36	41	36
White Non-South Catholic	58	60	60	66	NA	NA	58	56	52	53	61	56	49	66	47	76	75	65
Low SES																		
White Non-South Protestant	49	42	36	47	NA	NA	57	53	51	39	51	40	42	54	39	52	52	46
White Non-South Catholic	74	72	65	73	NA	NA	74	74	63	61	70	64	51	74	57	85	80	72

SOURCE: Data from following AIPO studies: *1940*, 208, 209, 215, 219, 248; *1944*, 336, 337; *1948*, 430, 431, 432; *1952*, 506, 507, 508; *1956*, 572, 573, 574; *1960*, 637, 638.

didates, compared to 74 percent of the latter. In no instance, involving either presidential voting, congressional
voting or partisan identification, did the Democratic proportion among high status white northern Protestants exceed 30 percent. And the Democrats never failed to attain
majoritarian support among low status northern Catholics—typically receiving a commanding margin.

As S. M. Lipset rightly pointed out in a review of this
same subject, "the gross character of the indicators of class
and religious voting make it impossible to reach any defi-
nite conclusion concerning the relative weight of 'class' as
contrasted to 'religion' as a determinant of party choice." [33]
It can be added that quite different conclusions appear as
alternate definitions of socioeconomic status are applied.
The trichotomized version employed in Table 2.5 emphasizes class variations in voting by isolating sharply dissimilar groups in the polar categories: college-educated business and professional people on the one hand, and
semiskilled and unskilled workers on the other. The
cruder "manual-nonmanual" distinction employed by Alford and Lipset somewhat blurs the impact of class by
putting a number of dissimilar occupational groups
together.

The class dimension obviously loomed larger than the
religious factor in the *class-salient* 1948 election, while
religion dominated in the *religion-salient* 1960 contest.
But over the period, the most that can be ventured is that
religion and class each exerted a powerful independent
impact upon electoral behavior, shaping the New Deal coalitions in a remarkably predictable and consistent manner.

THE SCOPE OF THE DEMOCRATIC MAJORITY

The national Democratic party held majority status
throughout the New Deal era. Like most complex political

---

[33] Lipset, "Religion and Politics in the American Past and Present," p.
340.

phenomena, however, the precise scope of this majority status from the 1930s through 1960 invites ambiguities, as Figures 2.5, 2.6, and 2.7 attest.

The distribution of partisan self-identification in the electorate shows an uninterrupted Democratic ascendancy over the Republicans from 1936 through 1960. And on the whole, the Democratic margin widened as the New Deal era progressed (Figure 2.5). The aggregate national vote in

Figure 2.5. Distribution of Party Identifiers, Gallup Data, 1937–1960

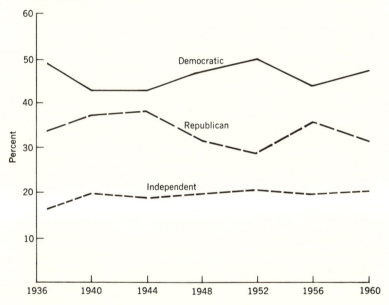

SOURCE: Data from following AIPO surveys: *1937*, 72, 104; *1940*, 208, 209; *1944*, 328, 329; *1948*, 429, 431, 432, 433; *1952*, 504, 505, 507, 508; *1960*, 635, 636, 637, 638.

the biennial House of Representatives contest follows a somewhat similar pattern: After the Democrats' surge in the Depression year elections, their proportion of the total House vote dipped perceptibly, but then began a modest secular rise throughout the 1950s (Figure 2.7). The presidential vote line, however, flows in the opposite direction.

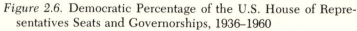

Figure 2.6. Democratic Percentage of the U.S. House of Representatives Seats and Governorships, 1936–1960

SOURCE: *World Almanac and Book of Facts* (New York: New York World-
Telegram); *1937*, p. 927; *1941*, p. 822; *1945*, p. 720; *1949*, p. 58; *1951*, p.
92; *1956*, p. 72; *1960*, pp. 66–68, 70; and *Historical Statistics of the U.S.,
Colonial Times to 1957*, p. 691.

After the solid Roosevelt majorities, the Democrats were
never again in the period to achieve an absolute majority
of the presidential vote, although their candidates obtained pluralities and hence victories in 1948 and 1960.

One part of this discrepant pattern results from the natural unfolding of a party system. For seven decades after
the Civil War, the Republicans held majority status—and
by a decisive margin from 1896 through to the Depression.
Then, economic collapse served to introduce a new axis of
conflict in national politics, and to provide the vehicle for
the transformation of the Democrats into the party of the
new agenda. Roosevelt at once attained sweeping victories, but the underlying configurations in party loyalties—better expressed in the partisan self-identification of

the electorate and in congressional voting—more gradually reflected the thrust of the new alignment. Party loyalties became more solidly and securely Democratic partly through a natural change in the composition of the electorate which was occurring as old voters died and the young came of voting age. The shift also resulted in part because the new policy directions offered by the Democrats achieved an increased acceptance that made its claim to majority standing as familiar as the Republicans' had once been.

Presidential voting responded to a different dynamic—much more affected by particular mixes of candidate attributes and the issues of the day. The enormous tensions and "time for a change" thirsting of the Truman years, Eisenhower's magnetism, Kennedy's personal appeal and his Catholicism, are all cases in point.

Figure 2.7. Democratic Percentage of the Aggregate Popular Vote for President and for U.S. House of Representatives, 1936–1960

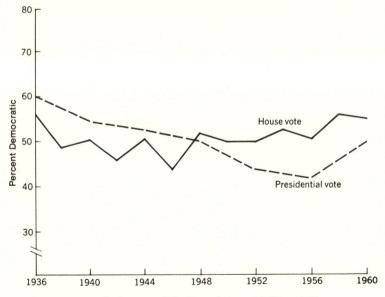

SOURCE: *Statistical Abstract of the United States, 1973,* p. 364.

Still granting that a greater volatility operated in presidential voting, the overall scope of the Democratic majority, its programmatic base, and its social group underpinnings remained notably stable throughout the New Deal era. At the time of Kennedy's victory in the 1960 presidential contest, few signs of deterioration of the New Deal party system could be detected. The political agenda, necessarily modified, still reflected the basic commitments of the Roosevelt administration and the conflict these precipitated; and the Democrats' position as the party of governmental nationalism maintained the allegiance of most components of the original coalition. But social change is a continuing process, and by 1960 it had brought some erosion of the New Deal alignment. The most dramatic instance was offered by the historic bastion of Democratic fealty, the Old Confederacy. For if no substantial national transformation had emerged, a significant local metamorphosis was already well underway. To that we turn in the ensuing chapter.

3

First Rendings

The Case of the South

From Reconstruction on through the New Deal, no region rivaled the South in strength of attachment to the Democracy. By the 1970s, however, no section was so unsupportive of the national Democratic party. This massive shift in electoral loyalties has necessarily altered the structure of inter- and intra-party relations, contributing powerfully to the end of the New Deal party system. And at the same time, it reflects basic changes in the fabric of American politics. Because of this, and because southern electoral transformations became evident before those of comparable scope appeared elsewhere in the country, the case of the South serves as a good intellectual bridge between the New Deal system and that now groping for definition.

I. The South and the New Deal: Issue Congruence

Various sources of the South's long-standing attachment to the Democracy have been described endlessly, and were reviewed earlier in this volume. Too often overlooked, however, is the extent to which the policy thrusts of the New Deal struck a responsive chord in Dixie. The

1970s' picture of the South as the most conservative region
of the country leads frequently to the notion that it has
always been "to the right." This tendency to impose the
present upon the past is furthered by the recognition that
majorities of southern whites historically have proved reactionary on civil rights. Typical of the failure to appreciate the degree of southern support for the New Deal is
James Sundquist's observation that "the South . . . had
managed, without leaving the national Democratic party,
to accept the Wagner Act, minimum wages, public housing, public power, federal welfare programs, the Farm Security Administration, deficits and debt and devaluation of
the dollar, Roosevelt's 'purge,' and his attack on the Supreme Court." [1] Supposedly, old loyalties kept the region
supportive of the Democrats *in spite of dissatisfaction
with the central Roosevelt programs*. But in fact, as we
shall see, the South *gave higher approval to New Deal
policies* than any other section in the country.

William Havard effectively refutes the notion that southern Democrats in Congress have served as a reactionary
force since the days of John C. Calhoun.[2] He notes that the
progressivism of Woodrow Wilson's administration owed
an enormous debt to radical agrarian forces of the South
represented in Congress. On issues such as the regulation
of financial and industrial enterprise, increased income
taxation, and the tariff, southern Democrats not only provided a substantial portion of the votes for the Wilsonian
position but much of the leadership as well. And as Havard points out, this trend of southern support for efforts to
harness business nationalism "continued and was in some
ways accelerated in the early days of the New Deal." [3]

Havard recognizes that much southern support for the
New Deal flowed from agrarian-based resentment of the

---

[1] Sundquist, *Dynamics of the Party System*, p. 258.
[2] William C. Havard, Jr., "From Past to Future: An Overview of Southern Politics," in his edited volume, *The Changing Politics of The South*
(Baton Rouge: Louisiana State University Press, 1972), pp. 703–710.
[3] *Ibid.*, p. 705.

business nationalism embodied in the Republican party; that the region, both its leadership and its electorate, "remained in the nineteenth century agrarian mold of the Democratic party," [4] rather than going over to an urban-based governmental nationalism. But, as he correctly points out, "it was the radical rather than the reactionary agrarian tendencies of the South that manifested themselves most clearly in elections and in congressional behavior during the period under consideration; and in the eras of government finance, taxation, social security, easy credit, provision for employment, and public regulation—as well as in agricultural innovation—the radical agrarianism of the South (a heritage of the nineteenth century) coincided with and even promoted general programs that inaugurated the changed relation among the public, party and government that characterized postcapitalist developments from the 1930s onward." [5]

As striking and unambiguous as the congressional support is the endorsement which the New Deal received from the southern electorate at large. We have become so accustomed to a view of white southerners as more conservative than their counterparts elsewhere in the country that it is hard not to be at least a bit surprised by the extent to which they were the regional group most supportive of New Deal initiatives.[6] An exhaustive analysis of Gallup survey data from the 1930s and early 1940s, however, documents this position conclusively. In 1936, southern whites supported a compulsory old age insurance program at a higher level than did the denizens of the Northeast,

---

[4] *Ibid.*

[5] *Ibid.*, pp. 705–706.

[6] Blacks in the South strongly supported New Deal measures. But it would be a mistake to conclude that the high measure of southern backing for the New Deal was a function of the fact that this region had the largest proportion of blacks of any region of the country. Blacks were largely excluded from electoral participation. Such was the disenfranchisement imposed upon them that in 1940 only 250,000 southern blacks were registered voters. The opinion data we present here are for southern whites only.

the Midwest, or the West.[7] Roosevelt's plan to pack the Supreme Court in order to prevent it from blocking New Deal legislation received notably greater backing in the South than elsewhere.[8] Fifty-nine percent of respondents in the South in March 1939 felt that the Roosevelt administration's policies toward private business had been about right or even too friendly, compared to just 44 percent of northeasterners.[9] Sixty-two percent of southerners answering an October 1940 Gallup survey indicated that they favored even more or about the same amount of federal regulation of business in the ensuing years, as against just 44 percent of westerners, 48 percent of residents of the Northeast, and 51 percent of midwesterners.[10]

Residents of other regions, more than southerners, reflected fears that the convulsive changes of the Depression period posed a serious threat to "the American way of life." In 1941, Gallup asked whether "you think our country is in any real danger from any of these groups [those "which are trying to change our form of government"]?" The proportion in Dixie responding in the affirmative (45 percent) was lower than in the West (53 percent), the Midwest (51 percent), or the Northeast (51 percent).[11] Southerners were less inclined to perceive "subversive" thrusts in the turbulence of the late thirties and early forties.

In only one area did southern whites furnish less support for policy directions associated with the New Deal than the residents of other regions. Trade unions and legislation benefiting the trade union movement drew somewhat more opposition in the South than in the industrial and rapidly unionizing Northeast.

The greater approval which Roosevelt and his programs

[7] AIPO Survey No. 53, September 26, 1936.
[8] AIPO Survey No. 72, March 1, 1937.
[9] AIPO Survey No. 150, March 3, 1939.
[10] AIPO Survey No. 219, October 24, 1940.
[11] AIPO Survey No. 247, September 9, 1941.

received in Dixie extended beyond the domestic scene to foreign affairs. As the United States moved closer to involvement in the war with Nazi Germany, the rank and file of southerners proved more internationalist and interventionist than their fellow citizens elsewhere.[12] Fifty-three percent of white southerners in October 1940 favored changing neutrality legislation so that American ships could carry war supplies to England, compared to 36 percent of residents of the Midwest, 40 percent in the Northeast, and 42 percent in the West.[13] That same month, 70 percent among southern whites wanted to grant England U.S. loans to buy materials needed for its war effort, a position taken by only 50 percent of northeasterners and 42 percent of residents of the Midwest.[14] Eighty-two percent of southerners, as of December 1940, indicated willingness to "pay more taxes to meet costs of the defense program," the stance of just 65 percent of the residents of the Northeast.[15] In September 1941, only 11 percent of southern respondents believed that Roosevelt had gone "too far" in aiding Britain. Thirty-one percent of midwesterners held to this position.[16] Southern support for Roosevelt, then, was reinforced by agreement with the thrusts of his interventionist foreign policy, just as it was sustained by relatively high approval of his domestic programs.

To argue, as we have, that southern support for the Democracy during the New Deal stemmed not only from historic antipathy toward the Republicans but as well from a high measure of congruence between what the New Deal

[12] Southern support of active American intervention in foreign affairs in the World War II period has been frequently described. Especially valuable are Charles O. Lerche, Jr., *The Uncertain South: Its Changing Patterns in Foreign Policy* (Chicago: Quadrangle Books, 1964); and Alfred O. Hero, *The Southerner and World Affairs* (Baton Rouge: Louisiana State University Press, 1965).

[13] AIPO Survey No. 215, October 9, 1940.

[14] *Ibid.*

[15] AIPO Survey No. 226, December 16, 1940.

[16] AIPO Survey No. 248, September 17, 1941.

accomplished and what southerners wanted done, should not dull appreciation of several qualifications. Some powerful opposition to the New Deal developed early in the South. Since responses to Roosevelt programs were conditioned not only by ideological preferences but as well by partisan considerations, the fact that the southern electorate comprised Democratic identifiers disproportionately surely contributed to the high measure of support which we have found in the region. Democrats are more likely to support a highly charismatic Democratic president than are Republicans, and the South was heavily Democratic. At a somewhat more technical level, we should note that while the southern electorate showed up consistently higher in its support for both the foreign and domestic initiatives of the Roosevelt administration, the regional differences are not typically massive.

Still, the overall picture is striking. The South did not just *manage* to accept social welfare legislation along with greater governmental controls in economic life without leaving the national Democratic party. More than the Northeast, the Midwest, or the West, it *desired* such actions. Far from shaking southern loyalty to the Democracy, the New Deal reinforced it. To be sure, power within the national Democratic party was gravitating toward the urban North, but in the 1930s and early 1940s this hardly posed any perceptible threat to the rank and file of southern Democratic adherents. And while, aided mightily by hindsight, we can see that the attachment of black Americans to the national Democratic alliance made disaffection of southern whites from the party unavoidable once the Civil Rights movement could lay serious claim on national policy, this development was hardly foreseen in the 1930s. More than any other region, the South backed Roosevelt and the New Deal—both the domestic and the foreign manifestations. Through World War II, the South and the Democracy rested in a context of issue congruence, not dissonance.

II. Exit the South

In the presidential election of 1944, southern voters gave FDR 69 percent of their ballots, compared to a 55 percent Democratic proportion in the western states, 52 percent in the Northeast, and just 49 percent in the Midwest. It was the last time—certainly up to the present, but as well, it seems, for the foreseeable future—that the South would be decisively Democratic presidentially, the last time that its Democratic loyalties would dwarf those of other regions. A major local transformation was about to unfold.

No other shift in a region's voting pattern approaches in magnitude and secular persistence that occurring throughout the South over the last quarter-century (Figure 3.1). From 1900 through 1944, Democratic presidential candidates secured two-thirds of the total vote in Dixie.[17] (Extending the frame further, back to 1876, does not alter this proportion significantly.) In 1948, however, a pronounced falling off of southern backing for the national Democratic party occurred, one from which there has been no recovery.

The prime precipitant of this electoral change was race. At the Democrats' 1948 convention, there was a bitter floor fight over an amendment to substitute a strong civil rights plank for the weaker one which the platform committee had recommended. The battle for the strong plank—which was finally carried by a vote of 651.5 to 582.5—was led by Hubert H. Humphrey, then a young Minneapolis mayor. After losing, some southern delegates walked out; and anti-Truman southerners later met in Birmingham to nominate South Carolina Governor J. Strom Thurmond for president on a states' rights and white supremacy platform. The 1948 Democratic intra-party struggle is important not

---

[17] Of the 47.5 million presidential ballots cast in the South over these eleven elections, 31.5 million, or 66 percent of the total, went to Democratic nominees.

so much in itself as in its reflection of long-term developments which would unavoidably split the party: (1) a national civil rights movement gathered force after World
War II; (2) in the partisan context, this movement found
expression and support largely within the ranks of northern Democrats; (3) a large proportion of southern Democrats remained strongly opposed to the advances in civil
rights which the national party was coming, haltingly to be
sure, to sustain.

Confronted with the States' Rights party challenge in
1948, Truman won just over half (52 percent) of the southern popular vote. The Democrat's proportion was slightly
lower still over the next three elections—reflecting such
disparate factors as Eisenhower's broadly nonpartisan appeal, Kennedy's Catholicism, changing socioeconomic
composition of the region, and emergent racial protest.
Then in 1964, for the first time, the Republicans actually
surpassed their national performance in the southern popular vote, admittedly for naught as they went down to
gargantuan defeat. They duplicated this superior southern
showing in their 1968 and 1972 victories. Nixon received
71 percent of all votes cast in Dixie in 1972, as against 60
percent in the Midwest, 59 percent in the West, and 58
percent in the Northeast. The South has proved less hospitable to national Democrats than any other region since
1960, while it has given Republican presidential nominees
a higher measure of support than any other section during
two of the last three contests.

Figure 3.1 compares the Democrats' southern performance to the party's national vote since 1932; and includes
as well comparable data on the Northeast. Throughout this
chapter we will be attending to the South-Northeast contrast, because of the uniquely compelling tension between
the politics of these two regions. Throughout much of
American history, they have been polar opposites, and
have marched to different drummers. New England was
the Federalist bastion early in the nineteenth century
while the South Atlantic states were solidly Jeffersonian.

Figure 3.1. Percentage Deviation from the National Democratic Presidential Vote, the South and the Northeast, 1932–1972

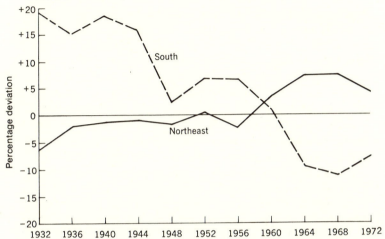

SOURCE: *Historical Statistics of the United States, Colonial Times to 1957,* pp. 686–687; *Statistical Abstract of the United States, 1969,* pp. 356–357; *1973,* p. 367.

Between 1832 and 1852, the Whigs were strongest in New England, weakest in the southern states. Abolitionist sentiment during the 1850s and into the Civil War years manifested its greatest strength in the Northeast, and notably in New England—while, needless to say, it was weakest in the South.

The half-century or so after the Civil War witnessed a highly sectional politics in which a series of political movements based in the South and West challenged the Northeast: the Readjusters, Independents, Greenbackers, Populists, and the Bryanites. Again, the Northeast and the South were the most directly polar regions, with the former the primary locus of that collection of interests directing the processes of industrial nation building, represented politically through the Republican party. The South, the conquered provinces, remained overwhelmingly rural and agricultural. Industrialization contributed to a profoundly sectional politics because its varying rates produced such divergent economic needs and status from one region to another. For example, personal per capita income, between 1880 and 1930 was dramatically higher in the Northeast than elsewhere in the country, and much lower in the South than elsewhere.[18]

During the New Deal, the old "Republican Northeast, Democratic South" distinction still retained its basic validity. But over the last quarter-century, as the South has shifted from the most to the least Democratic region presidentially, the Northeast has moved from being the most Republican to the most heavily Democratic section.[19]

Various factors contributing to the present partisan manifestations of what is a long-standing divergence of the two regions will be brought out more fully as we proceed. Still, it might be useful to attend to some of the more salient elements in summary fashion here.

The antipathy of many white southerners to a national Democratic party which has been in the forefront of endeavors to advance the civil rights of blacks is well understood, and surely has contributed powerfully to the precipitous falling off of southern backing for Democratic presidential nominees. But broader social and economic forces can be seen at work. The last region to industrialize, the South after 1950 began industrializing with a passion. Much of this new business enterprise has behaved like its counterpart in the Northeast three or four decades earlier: It has been, for example, militantly anti–trade union, opposed to large-scale governmental intervention in social and economic life, and generally conservative. The region, then, has acquired powerful interest collectivities around

---

[18] See Richard A. Easterlin, "Regional Income Trends, 1840–1950," in Seymour E. Harris (ed.), *American Economic History* (New York: McGraw-Hill, 1961), p. 528.

[19] Detailed explanation of the processes associated with the polar political positions of the Northeast and South through much of American history lies beyond the present study. One of us has explored the subject at some length elsewhere. See Ladd, *American Political Parties: Social Change and Political Response, passim.*

industrialization that are quite conservative and which consider the Republicans a natural home.

Philip Converse has noted the partisan importance of migration patterns associated with southern industrialization. He observes that since 1950 the South has been losing Democrats while receiving a lot of in-migrants who are Republican. "Furthermore, unlike the South-to-North migration, the North-to-South stream is selective along partisan lines: It turns out that the non-southerners moving into the South are actually *more* Republican than the non-southerners they leave behind." [20] There has been, in other words, a high measure of selectivity in the post-1950 migration, with the in-movement disproportionately of high status people, while the out-migration has been comprised heavily of those of low status. According to Converse, in 1956 only one-quarter of North-to-South white migrants were blue-collar workers, while about two-thirds of white southerners moving North and more than four-fifths of blacks leaving the region were located in the blue-collar sector.

In social science, the whole is sometimes more than the sum of its parts. This appears to be the case with the pronounced transformation of southern political orientations. We have noted that during the New Deal the South was the most liberal section of the country—providing the highest measure of support for national Democratic programs. And below we will document in some detail the South's currently unassailable claim to being the most conservative section, the one most opposed to the broad sweep of contemporary extensions of the liberal vision. In part, it seems likely, this profound shift has occurred as a result of developments associated with socioeconomic change, and the attendant replacement of old agrarian radicalism with new industrial conservatism. In part, too, it has followed as a massive offshoot of regional resentments

[20] Philip E. Converse, "A Major Political Realignment in the South?" Allan P. Sindler (ed.), *Change in the Contemporary South* (Durham, N.C.: Duke University Press, 1963), p. 210.

that were in the first instance race based, but which now
dwarf the parent plant. Believing that they had been un-
justly made pariahs by political elites strongly represented
in the national Democratic party, and associated in some
sense with a northeastern establishment, white southerners have entered upon a broad resistance to all manner
of new initiatives associated with the leadership structure
of the Northeast. William Havard was referring to this
when he noted that, "today, in addition to the race question, southern opposition seems based as much on objections to the postindustrial, centralized, welfare-oriented,
intellectualist, bureaucratically organized political culture
of the Northeast as anything else. Both Goldwater and
Wallace—the former something of a throw back to the classical liberalism of the American industrial revolution and
the latter something of a 'spoiled' Populist—attacked the
news media, 'soft-headed' intellectuals, and the life-styles
of the urban east at least as much as they did their political
opponents." [21] Resistance was an important part of the
southern political subculture in the years of industrial nation building—when it often meant support for liberal, reformist types of programs. The South remains resistant,
but now directs its ire at the extensions of liberalism prominently associated with such elite strata as intellectuals,
leaders of the communications media, the high governmental bureaucracy, mature business enterprise, and the
like, groups hardly the exclusive province of the Northeast
(just as, for that matter, industrial development and the
leadership thereof was not exclusively a northeastern preserve in an earlier era) but which are nonetheless prominently associated with a northeastern establishment. The
South is a dissenting region in 1977, as it was in 1900. But
it now dissents from the programs of a liberal establishment, rather than the business nationalism of an earlier ascendant elite. So times have changed and the South has
changed, but the social bases of oppositionism remain.

---

[21] Havard, "From Past to Future: An Overview of Southern Politics," p.
714.

Still other factors enter into the broad southern transformation. The support for interventionism which seemed progressive in the World War II context becomes hawkish or militaristic when carried over with much the same motivation into the Vietnam era. The South's disproportionate reflection of Protestant fundamentalism is not new, but appears more decisively conservative in the face of various cultural changes associated with the contemporary agenda. But as we have said, the whole appears more than the sum of these individual parts. In response to them as a collective melange, a regional political subculture has emerged in the 1960s and 1970s which is more resistant to contemporary demands for change than that of any other section in the country—whereas the South of 1937 was relatively supportive of change-related demands then manifesting themselves and dominating political argument.

The disproportionate Republicanism of the Northeast over the long sweep of American industrial nation building, we have noted, rested heavily upon the region's status as the principal locus of elites and efforts and interests surrounding industrialization. The Republicans gave partisan guidance to industrial development under business aegis, and were properly rewarded in the region which was at once the custodian and prime beneficiary of the emergent industrial state. Interestingly enough, contemporary variations on the theme which made the Northeast the Republican center have now carried the region heavily Democratic. The New Deal brought about a basic shift in the national political agenda, in which initiatives associated with governmental nationalism supplanted the older business nationalism. The controlling impulses here, clearly, involved no repudiation of industrialism, rather an effort to harness it and manage it and humanize it. The key point seems to be the essential harmony between the thrusts of the New Deal and the condition of advanced industrialism. To be sure, business elites in the Northeast bitterly resisted elements of Roosevelt's programs in the 1930s and immediately thereafter. But this tension quickly vanished as business, together with other sectors in the in-

dustrial order, became important claimants and beneficiaries of "the new industrial state." [22] Just as the configuration of interests in the Northeast in 1920 reflected, more
than that of any other region, the condition of the closing
stages of industrial nation building; so the configuration
today most fully approximates or represents postindustrial
society.

Other related changes contribute to the northeastern
transmogrification into the most liberal and Democratic
section of the country. There has been, for example, an important shift in population composition. As blacks have
moved from the decaying manual agriculture of the South,
reducing that section's population from 25 percent black in
1940 to 20 percent black in 1970, the nonwhite population
has increased somewhat more in the Northeast than in any
other part of the country. The 1970 Census showed the
Northeast 11 percent nonwhite, up from 5 percent three
decades earlier. Black Americans provide important sustenance for extensions of liberal programs, and specifically
of support for the national Democratic party.

The emphasis we have placed on the South-Northeast
tension in a sense oversimplifies. Like any analytic ab-
straction, it suggests more coherence than reality offers. As
an analytic category, the Northeast ends with the western
boundaries of New York and Pennsylvania. Patterns related to postindustrial development obviously do not.
Still, there are reasons for keeping with the traditional
regional distinctions. The Northeast and the South are
sharply differentiated socially and politically at present, as
they have been throughout American history. They do reflect alternate lines of development. And in their respective experiences we find an important component of the altered partisan alignments appearing in contemporary
America. The Northeast is a generally satisfactory analytic
counterpoint—as long as we remember it is only that—to

---

[22] From very different perspectives, this point has been made effectively by Theodore J. Lowi, *The End of Liberalism;* and John Kenneth
Galbraith, *The New Industrial State* (Boston: Houghton Mifflin, 1967).

the South in a series of developments which have transformed national political life.

The sharply divergent electoral patterns, South and Northeast, which we have noted in presidential voting are evident in the full range of partisan behavior. Figures 3.2 and 3.3 display shifts in partisan identification in the Northeast and in the South, from 1937 through 1974. Through the 1940s and 1950s, the Democratic bulge in Dixie was enormous. In 1940, 80 percent of southerners described themselves as Democrats, compared to 13 percent as Republicans and 8 percent as independents. Eight years later, when race-related defections appeared at the presidential level, the distribution was virtually identical: 73 percent self-described Democrats, 16 percent Republican, and 11 percent independents. The margin between the proportions Democratic and Republican then began a pronounced secular declination, with big drops occurring in the mid-1950s and late 1960s, followed by some recovery in the 1970s. As Figure 3.2 shows, this shrinkage has occurred through a dramatic growth in the proportion of southerners rejecting any major party identification and describing themselves as independents, rather than from a jump in Republican identifiers. While only 11 percent of the southern electorate proclaimed independent status in 1948, 35 percent assumed this posture two decades later.

The failure of the Republicans to improve substantially upon their "self-identification" base is striking in view of the party's marked improvement in electoral performance. Indeed, according to Gallup data, the proportion of Republican identifiers has actually declined in the last twenty years, from 22 percent in 1956, for example, to just 18 percent in 1974. A good indicator of declining Democratic fortunes in the South, Figure 3.2 serves as a poor measure of Republican development. Although GOP presidential fortunes have improved enormously in the South over recent elections, while there have been significant increases in the party's share of the vote for lesser offices, and a substantial strengthening of Republican organizations, especially in metropolitan areas, this has not been accompanied by some overall conversion to Republicanism. Large numbers of white southerners appear to have arrived at an electoral status in which they think of themselves as either Democrats or as independents, but at the same time are perfectly willing to vote frequently for Republican contenders.

The apparent permanency of the pattern deserves attention. In the past, it has been common to view the growth of independents in the southern electorate as entry into a kind of halfway house between old to new party loyalties. It was presumed that the increased legitimization of the southern Republican party, and Republican voting becoming common for growing segments of the electorate, would manifest themselves in a growing body of Republican identifiers.[23] Since by 1974 this has not occurred, we must conclude that it may not at all, and that a strengthening of the Republican party in Dixie without an increase in Republican identifiers may be the permanent order of things. Indicative here is the fact that in 1972, young southerners, who came of age politically in an era of Republican "respectability" in their region, were no more likely than their oldest co-regionists to identify as Republicans.[24]

Apparently, a combination of two factors—the persisting acceptability of many state and local Democratic leaders, and the general weakening of party loyalties evident throughout the nation—has yielded an electorate able to produce Republican victories with a fair degree of regularity, in the absence of a Republican "identification" party any larger than one-fifth of the electorate. We should has-

---

[23] See, for example, E. M. Screiber, " 'Where the Ducks Are': Southern Strategy versus Fourth Party," *Public Opinion Quarterly*, 35 (Summer 1971), pp. 157–167.

[24] The partisan self-identification of white southerners in 1972 (Gallup data) are as follows, in the order Republican, Democrat, and independent: for those ages 18–29, 17, 36, and 47; for the 30–39 cohort, 17, 48, and 36; for the 40–49 cohort, 19, 46, and 36; and for those 50 years and older, 19, 56, and 25.

ten to add that this aspect of the southern experience is essentially duplicated elsewhere in the country. According
to Gallup, just 18 percent of southerners described themselves as Republicans in 1974 but only 23 percent of the
national electorate adopted a Republican association.

Figure 3.2. Partisan Identification in the South, 1937–1974

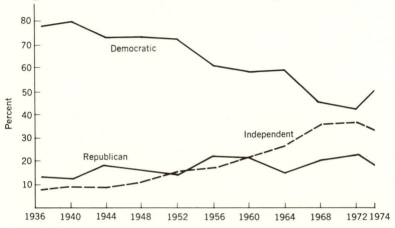

SOURCE: Data from following AIPO surveys: *1937*, 72, 104; *1940*, 208,
209; *1944*, 328, 329; *1948*, 431, 432; *1952*, 507, 508; *1956*, 573, 574; *1960*,
637, 638; 1964, 699, 701; *1968*, 770, 771; *1972*, 859, 860, *1974*, Gallup
Poll, *Hartford Courant* (July 18, 1974), p. 23.

As the Democratic margin in the area of self-identification has declined in the South, it has increased notably in
the East. Figure 3.3 indicates that throughout the 1930s,
1940s, and 1950s, northeastern Republicans competed
rather evenly with Democrats in the contest for voter
loyalties. In 1940, 1944, and then again in 1956, Republican identifiers actually outnumbered Democrats. The tide
shifted in the 1960s. And the Democrats now enjoy a large
margin in this area where for so long after Roosevelt the
Republicans had maintained a competitive position.

The internal heterogeneity of the relatively amorphous
American party coalitions has worked to the advantage of
southern Democrats. They have been able to stake out

Figure 3.3. Partisan Identification in the Northeast, 1937–1974

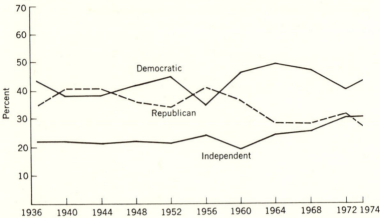

SOURCE: Data from the following AIPO surveys: *1937*, 72, 104; *1940*, 208, 209; *1944*, 328, 329; *1948*, 431, 432; *1952*, 507, 508; *1956*, 573, 574; *1960*, 637, 638; *1964*, 699, 701; *1968*, 770, 771; *1972*, 859, 860, *1974*, Gallup Poll, *Hartford Courant* (July 18, 1974), p. 23.

positions, in many cases fully acceptable to majorities of their local electorates, continuing to prosper even as the national party has been reduced to a kind of regional ruin. In 1972, for instance, when McGovern secured only 29.5 percent of the popular vote in the South, 69 percent of congressmen elected from the region were under the Democratic banner. Still, as Table 3.1 shows, Republicans have made notable congressional gains in Dixie. Ninety-seven percent of congressmen from southern states in 1948 were Democrats; in 1964, the proportion was down to 85 percent; and in 1972 it dropped to 69 percent. Over this same period, northeastern Democratic representation in Congress has increased, although modestly, and since 1966 Democrats have constituted a higher percentage of the northeastern delegation to the national House than they have of the midwestern or western delegations. While in 1950 just five percent of southern congressmen but 55 percent of northeastern representatives were Republicans, by 1972 and proportions had become, respectively, 31 and 44 percent.

Table 3.1 Democratic Party Strength in the
United States House of Representatives, by
Region, 1948–1974 (in Percentages)

Year	Percentage Democratic			
	Northeast	Midwest	South	West
1948	50	42	97	49
1950	45	28	95	45
1952	38	26	92	33
1954	45	34	92	35
1956	41	36	92	45
1958	56	53	93	55
1960	53	40	93	56
1962	53	38	88	59
1964	66	53	85	68
1966	60	36	77	55
1968	60	37	74	52
1970	60	44	74	57
1972	56	42	69	55
1974	68	57	76	67

SOURCE: Bureau of the Census, *Statistical Abstract of
the United States: 1954; 1959; 1964; 1966;* and *1973;*
respectively, pp. 354; 353; 377; 375; and 374; and
Congressional Directory: 1975, pp. 200–210.

These data on the Democratic share of regional delegations to the House of Representatives leave unstated one
important component of the argument we have been developing. Not only has Republican representation increased in the South while Democrats have picked up
strength in the Northeast, but northeastern representatives
of both parties are decidedly more liberal than their partisan counterparts in other sections, while southern congressmen are by far the most conservative. This point has
received impressive documentation in a study by Stephen
D. Shaffer.

Shaffer developed "conservatism" scores for every
member of the U.S. House of Representatives over the
years 1959 through 1973—the Eighty-sixth through
Ninety-fourth Congresses—by combining the rating of the
Americans for Constitutional Action (ACA) with the in-

verse of the Americans for Democratic Action (ADA) scores.[25] He then averaged his individual rating for state and regional delegations. In 1972, Shaffer found, the composite conservatism score for northeastern representatives was 40—on a zero to 100 scale with zero the *least conservative*—compared to scores of 56 for midwestern congressmen, 54 for western congressmen, and 82 for southern representatives. In Figure 3.4, the conservatism ratings for all congressmen, and for those from northeastern and from southern states are presented for the entire 1959–1973 span, as deviations from the House of Representatives composite score. As late as 1963, southern congressmen proved only modestly more conservative than the average; northeastern representatives only modestly more liberal. But over the ensuing decade, the margin widened substan-

Figure 3.4. Percentage Point Deviation from the National Congressional Conservative Score (Averaged ADA/ACA Scores) for the Northeastern and Southern House of Representatives Delegations

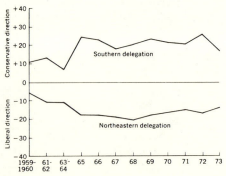

SOURCE: Stephen D. Shaffer (unpublished study, University of New Orleans, 1974).

---

[25] Shaffer (unpublished study, University of New Orleans, 1974). Data cited with the permission of the author. ACA and ADA scores were combined in an effort to partially reduce biases inherent in any single scheme—utilizing one rating system developed by an avowedly conservative organization, and another by a decidedly liberal group.

Figure 3.5. Percentage Point Deviation from the National Democratic Congressional Conservative Score (Averaged ADA/ACA
Scores) for the Northeastern and Southern Democratic House
of Representatives Delegations

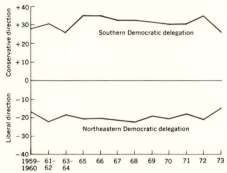

SOURCE: See Figure 3.4.

Figure 3.6. Percentage Point Deviation from the National Republican Congressional Conservative Score (Averaged ADA/ACA
Scores) for the Northeastern and Southern Republican House
of Representatives Delegations

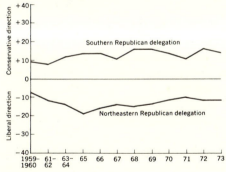

SOURCE: See Figure 3.4.

tially, with the delegations of these two regions moving to
the poles. The contrast in conservatism scores for northeastern and southern *Democrats* is even more striking. In
1972, for example, the composite score for all southern

Democratic representatives was 79, as against just 23 for
Democratic congressmen from the Northeast. Southern
Republicans stood well to the right of all Republicans,
while northeastern GOP representatives assumed a place
to the left of their party.

As would be expected, the Republicans have made their
most modest gains in local electoral contests in the
South—where ideology looms less large and personal attributes along with historic party ties are the most impressive. But even at the local level, significant Republican advances have occurred over the past two decades. In 1954,
just 86 of 1,559 representatives to lower houses of southern state legislatures (5.5 percent) were Republicans. A
decade later, there had been a modest increase, to a total
of 130 Republicans in 1,542 seats (8.4 percent). By 1972,
however, Republican representation had climbed to 280
out of 1,516 representatives, or 18.5 percent. Republican
delegations of substantial size (here defined as 20 percent
or more of the entire membership) operated in the
Virginia, North Carolina, South Carolina, Florida, Kentucky, Tennessee, and Oklahoma State Houses of Representatives.[26]

A number of strands of the argument presented thus far
need to be woven together before we try to break new analytic ground. A falling away of southern support for the national Democratic party began occurring in the midst of
the New Deal era. This disaffection was enormously
heightened after 1964 and the South, so long the section
most supportive of the Democracy, became most resistant
to national Democratic candidates and programmatic initiatives. Two main components of the withering of Democratic loyalties in the region are evident: massive regional
resentment of new policy directions, most immediately in
the area of race but extending to a more diffuse ideological
protest, sometimes expressed through third party movements such as the States' Rights Democratic party of 1948
and the American Independent party of 1968; and a less

---

[26] These data are from Bureau of the Census, *Statistical Abstract of the
United States: 1960; 1966;* and *1973;* respectively, pp. 358, 378, and 377.

dramatic but notable secular expansion of regular Republican electoral support. As a counterpoint to this major southern disaffection, the Northeast has moved steadily, although gradually, toward the Democratic camp. Long the principal regional locus of business nationalism articulated through the Republican party, the section has become most supportive of post–New Deal liberalism and the Democratic party.

III. The Southern Partisan Transformation: Stages and Sources

The Democratic decline in Dixie has occurred through a pattern of Republican gains and third-party protests which have not been uniform throughout the South. At its low ebb in the early years of this century, the Republican party was a feeble collection of blacks (the relatively few not disenfranchised), patronage hangers-on, and "mountain Republicans." [27] The first substantial Republican presidential surge occurred in the 1928 presidential election, when the Democrats nominated a Roman Catholic, Alfred E. Smith of New York. This short-term gain was achieved, then, when the national Democratic party came into the hands of its northern and urban wing.

In 1928, the Republicans managed to get 52 percent of the region's vote, but their fortunes differed markedly between the outer and the Deep South.[28] Hoover won five

---

[27] The principal concentrations of mountain Republicans were in southwestern Virginia, western North Carolina, and eastern Tennessee. Slavery never extended into these upland areas, and in 1860–1861 their inhabitants showed little enthusiasm for secession and the planters' war. Key has summarized it nicely: "The upland yeomanry did not want to fight a rich man's war; the Democratic party was or at least became the planters' party and the war party. The Democratic party forced the hills into the War, and for this it has never been forgiven." *Southern Politics* (New York: Knopf, 1949), p. 283.

[28] Throughout most of our analysis and commentary, the South employs the definition which Gallup has used consistently in his survey research: the eleven states of the Old Confederacy plus Kentucky and Oklahoma. In the discussion which follows, as we distinguish between the rim South

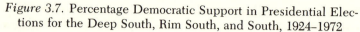

Figure 3.7. Percentage Democratic Support in Presidential Elections for the Deep South, Rim South, and South, 1924–1972

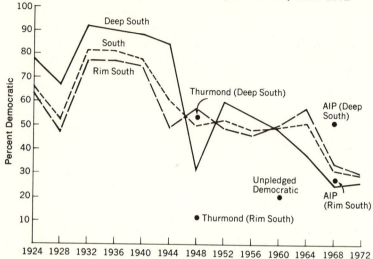

SOURCE: *Historical Statistics of the United States, Colonial Times to 1957,* pp. 686–687; *Statistical Abstract of the United States, 1969,* pp. 356–357; *1973,* p. 367. "AIP" is the American Independent Party, the vehicle for the candidacy of George C. Wallace in 1972.

southern states with 62 electoral votes, and all were in the rimland. As Figure 3.8 shows, his share of the popular vote was 20 percent lower in the Deep South. While the Republican presidential vote was inflated everywhere in Dixie in 1928, the pattern between the rim and the heartland was the familiar one. As a collection of states more overwhelmingly rural, less diverse, far more obsessed with race because of their much larger black populations, the Deep South manifested a degree of one-partyism vastly more extreme than in the peripheral Confederacy. The position of the Democrats as an instrument of white su-

and the Deep South, however, we will confine analysis strictly to the Old Confederacy. The Deep South states are South Carolina, Georgia, Alabama, Mississippi, and Louisiana; while Virginia, North Carolina, Tennessee, Florida, Arkansas, and Texas comprise the outer or rim South.

Figure 3.8. Percentage Republican Support in Presidential Elections for the Deep South, Rim South, and South, 1924–1972

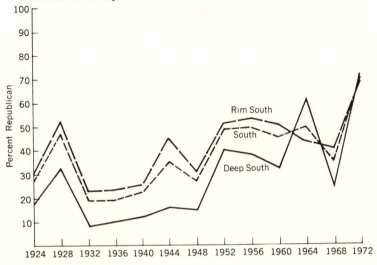

SOURCE: See Figure 3.7.

premacy and regional loyalty was unchallenged. Turnout in presidential contests in Deep South states was extraordinarily depressed. With race-related concerns far less dominant and with a much broader socioeconomic base on which to build an opposition party, the rimland sustained a higher measure of presidential Republicanism in every contest up until 1964.

A significant secular gain in support for Republican presidential candidates took place in the rim South throughout the New Deal era, with the proportion Republican of the total subsectional vote increasing from 23 percent in 1932 to 25 percent in 1940, 45 percent in 1944, and then across the 50 percent line into majority status in the Eisenhower elections of 1952 and 1956. The Republicans carried Florida, Tennessee, Texas, and Virginia in 1952; these same four rim-South states, plus Louisiana, in 1956; and Florida, Tennessee, and Virginia in 1960.

The major electoral inroads into national Democratic allegiance evident in 1948 did not result, however, from the
gradual construction of a Republican party of the same
general policy and constituency base as elsewhere in the
country—that is, a relatively more conservative aggregation—but rather from a regional third-party protest.
Angered by the civil rights commitments of the national
party, the States' Rights Democratic party was launched.
The Republicans failed to carry a single southern state, but
the States' Rights party took four. And where in 1928 the
defections from the national ticket occurred in the rimland, in 1948 they occurred in deepest Dixie.

In the 1960s and 1970s, currents working against the national Democrats in the South came together, forming an
overall configuration resembling that of earlier decades in
some regards but differing notably in others. There was a
firm sociopolitical base for the Republicans as the more
conservative party, and large numbers of southerners had
become quite accustomed to voting Republican in presidential elections. At the same time, as civil rights matters
reached high saliency, and as the national Democrats took
a stance clearly committed to advancing the position of
black Americans, racial protests by angry whites against
the national party became intense, notably in the southern
heartland. But for the first time, the convergence of various
sundry resentments into a more generalized conservative
protest became evident. And for the first time, as well, the
Republicans functioned as the primary partisan outlet for
such widespread regional resentment.

In 1960, burdened by his Catholicism, along with the
more general secular transformations we have discussed,
John Kennedy lost the rim South to Nixon in the popular
vote; each won the electoral vote of three states. The
Democratic nominee ran well ahead of his Republican opponent in the Deep South, however, but lost the electoral
vote of two states—Alabama and Mississippi—to slates of
unpledged electors entered as a protest. Then in 1964, historic voting patterns were completely scrambled as the

Republican nominee became the expression of southern protest—protest which had a strong racial coloration but which extended beyond race. The GOP did better in the Deep South than in the rimland for the first time, sweeping all five states of the former. It should also be noted that the 1964 election appears to have had a long-term importance which, of course, election statistics by themselves cannot reveal, in legitimating Republicanism. A white southerner could henceforth acknowledge Republican adherence without feeling the slightest tinge of regional disloyalty. The old Civil War repute of the GOP as "unsouthern" was pretty much erased.

The Republicans again contested strongly for southern support in 1968, but were positioned as a more moderately conservative center party between Wallace on the right and the national Democrats on the left. In the Deep South, the American Independents as the party of racial protest won decisively, and the national Democrats were reduced to one quarter of the vote, their lowest in history. By way of contrast, it was a close three-way race in the rim states, with the Republicans ending up on top.

Then, in 1972, with Wallace struggling for his life following an assassination attempt and hence out of the race, the Republicans swamped their Democratic opponents in a two-way contest as decisively as had been their fate to lose throughout much of the post–Civil War experience. The GOP share of the vote in the South exceeded that in nonsouthern states by some 12 percentage points, even though the party benefited from a truly national landslide. That the Nixon candidacy in 1972 served as a vehicle for articulating southern resentments concerning the flow of national policy is evident, but more than at any time in the preceding two decades the regional reaction was more diffuse ideologically, much less clearly tied to race. The Republican base was stronger in the rim South, but the ideological protest assumed more force in the Deep South. When these two crosscutting currents came together, the electoral result was an interesting one: the temporary dis-

appearance of overall differences between the vote distribution in the rim South and in the heartland.

Few aspects of the American political future now seem
clear, certainly not the future of southern electoral politics.
Still, there is a secure Republican base in the rim South,
one unlikely to be eroded. At the same time, the very
diversity of the rimland which nourished presidential Republicanism in the years of Democratic dominance now
seems capable of sustaining an at least modest revival of
national Democratic fortunes. As for the Deep South, it
seems destined to manifest a continuing alienation from
national politics, and to intervene nationally through some
form of single-party protest—at times turning to the Republicans, in other instances providing core support for
conservative third-party resistance. Under the Democratic
banner at the state and local levels, this Confederate heartland is unlikely to provide a secure base for national Democratic candidates beyond that offered by the black minority.

Impressive as the change in southern electoral patterns
appears working with the total regional vote, we see an
even more pronounced shift when blacks and whites are
separated—for the obvious reason that these two groups
have been going in opposite directions over the past forty
years. In 1940, as for the preceding half-century, the southern black population was largely disenfranchised. No more
than 250,000 blacks were registered voters in the states of
the Old Confederacy on the eve of World War II, just 5
percent of those of voting age. In only a few localities—
principally in cities of Tennessee, North Carolina, and
Virginia—was voting by significant numbers of blacks accepted.[29] In the 1940s, there was some expansion of the
black vote, primarily as a result of court decisions striking
down discriminatory practices. After two decades of litiga-
tion, for example, the Supreme Court finally condemned

---

[29] For further discussion of black electoral participation in the South,
see Ladd, *Negro Political Leadership in the South* (New York: Atheneum, 1969), especially pp. 1–47.

the white primary in the landmark *Smith* v. *Allwright* decision.[30] Between 1952 and 1960, black registration in the South increased by about 400,000, to 1.4 million. By the fall of 1964, however, 1,900,000 blacks were registered in the eleven states of the Old Confederacy. The largest part of this increase was recorded in the eight months preceding the November 1964 election. Efforts of civil rights organizations and the crumbling of southern white resistance to the Voting Rights Act of 1965 contributed to this rather dramatic expansion. Over the last decade, even in the face of a new out-migration of blacks from the region, the number of black voters has expanded further, cresting at 3.6 million in 1973.[31]

So the black electorate has grown appreciably, from a cipher to approximately 17 percent of the total number of registrants in the southern states. And black voters in the South, as throughout the country, have become even more supportive—now overwhelmingly so—of the national Democratic party. The drop in white support for Democratic presidential nominees, then, has been more precipitous than the data presented thus far suggest. Figure 3.9 shows the virtual decimation of national Democratic allegiance presidentially within the ranks of southern white Protestants between 1940 and 1972. In 1940, 80 percent of this group, the historic center of regional Democratic loyalty, voted for FDR. The Democratic presidential proportion then dropped off steadily. A major withering away occurred around 1948, followed by a kind of plateau, and

---

[30] *Smith* v. *Allwright*, 321 U.S. 649 (1944). The Court ruled that the conduct of a primary election under no circumstance could be considered a purely private activity. Because of the central position of primaries in the electoral process, the state has entrusted each party with the power to determine qualifications for primaries. This delegation of a state function thus makes the party's action state action. And the Fifteenth Amendment, of course, forbids the states to deny any citizen the right to vote "on account of race, color, or previous condition of servitude."

[31] David Campbell and Joe R. Feagin, "Black Politics in the South: A Descriptive Analysis," *Journal of Politics*, 37 (February 1975), p. 133. Cf. the registration figures reported in Bureau of the Census, *Statistical Abstract of the United States, 1973*, pp. 378, 381.

then total collapse in the late sixties. Only 14 percent of southern white Protestants voted for George McGovern in 1972.

During the New Deal, southern white Protestants were the most heavily Democratic ethnogeographic collectivity in the United States. They were followed, fairly closely in Democratic fealty, by northeastern white Catholics. The lines of these two groups—in terms of the proportion voting Democratic—crossed intermittently in the forties and fifties, diverged markedly in the face of Kennedy's candidacy in 1960 and have since remained far, far apart.

Figure 3.9. Democratic Presidential Support, Southern White Protestants, Northeastern White Protestants, Northeastern White Catholics, and Blacks, 1936–1972

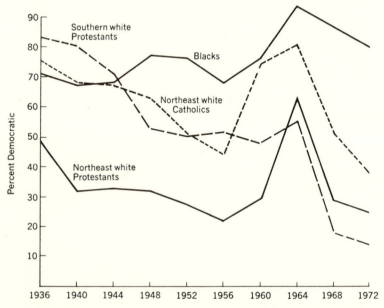

SOURCE: Data from following AIPO surveys: *1936,* 53, 60, 62, 72, 104, 150, 208; *1940,* 219, 222, 224, 225, 248; *1944,* 329, 336, 337; *1948,* 431, 432, 433; *1952,* 507, 508, 509; *1956,* 573, 574, 576; *1960,* 637, 638, 640; *1964,* 699, 701; *1968,* 770, 771; *1972,* 859, 860.

White Protestants in the Northeast, less Democratic than their southern co-religionists by some 35 to 50 percentage points during the New Deal, became in the 1960s and 1970s notably more Democratic. Black support for the Democracy, as Figure 3.9 indicates, has increased over this period of three and one half decades, from an already substantial base in 1936, to a massive eight to one plurality in the two Nixon presidential victories.

We have noted that the big change in partisan self-identification in the South has involved a shrinking of Democratic attachments and a very large increase in the proportion describing themselves as independents. Table 3.2 shows that while this pattern is indeed the predominant one, it applies more decisively to southern white Protestants. In 1940, this group identified with the Democrats over the Republicans by a margin of seven to one. The proportion of self-proclaimed Democrats fell by an extraordinary 46 percentage points between 1940 and 1972, however, while Republican identifiers increased notably, from 11 to 26 percent. Independents surged from 8 to 39 percent. Since blacks entering the electorate are almost exclusively among Democratic identifiers, both the Republican and independent categories show more substantial gains when analysis is confined to southern white Protestants.

Quite appropriately, there has been considerable interest surrounding the electoral orientations of the growing professional and managerial stratum of the "new South." Following rapid industrial development, this group has expanded substantially, and it possesses resources and skills which give it an importance in electoral politics beyond what numbers alone would confer.

In Table 3.3, presidential and congressional voting, along with the party identification of this cohort are examined for the entire 1936–1972 period. During the New Deal years, what there was of a professional and managerial stratum in the South behaved electorally much as the population at large. It was heavily Democratic. The first substantial divergence became evident after World War II.

Table 3.2. Partisan Identification of All Southerners and Southern White Protestants, 1940–1972 (as Percentages)

	1940	1944	1948	1952	1956	1960	1964	1968	1972
DEMOCRATIC									
All Southerners	80	73	73	72	61	58	59	45	42
Southern white protestants	81	NA	74	73	63	60	53	38	35
REPUBLICAN									
All Southerners	12	18	16	14	22	21	15	20	22
Southern white protestants	11	NA	15	14	22	22	17	22	26
INDEPENDENT									
All Southerners	9	9	11	15	17	21	26	35	36
Southern white protestants	8	NA	11	13	15	18	30	39	39

SOURCE: Data from following AIPO surveys: *1940*, 208, 209; *1944*, 328, 329; *1948*, 431, 432; *1952*, 507, 508; *1956*, 573, 574; *1960*, 637, 638; *1964*, 699, 701; *1968*, 770, 771; *1972*, 859, 860.

Table 3.3. Presidential and Congressional Vote, and Partisan Identification of the Southern Professional and Managerial Stratum, 1936–1972 (Column Percentages)

	1936	1940	1944	1948	1952	1956	1960	1964	1968	1972
PRESIDENTIAL VOTE										
Democratic	76	67	67	44	32	40	38	53	22	23
Republican	22	32	31	42	68	59	61	45	55	75
Other	2	—	2	14	—	1	1	2	24	2
CONGRESSIONAL VOTE										
Democratic	NA	81	72	68	77	69	67	58	47	52
Republican	NA	19	28	30	23	31	31	40	50	45
Other	NA	—	—	1	—	—	2	1	3	3
PARTY IDENTIFICATION										
Democratic	76	80	71	66	67	57	50	49	30	31
Republican	12	7	23	14	16	20	23	20	29	30
Independent	13	12	6	20	17	22	26	31	41	39

SOURCE: Data from following AIPO surveys: 1936, 53, 60, 72, 104; 1940, 208, 209, 215, 219, 224; 1944, 328, 329, 336, 337; 1948, 430, 431, 432; 1952, 506, 507, 508; 1956, 572, 573, 574; 1960, 637, 638; 1964, 699, 701; 1968, 770, 771; 1972, 858, 859, 860.

In the 1948 presidential election, for example, this group
was notably more Republican than the southern electorate
generally, and less inclined to support the racial protest
candidacy of J. Strom Thurmond. During the Eisenhower
years, professional and managerial workers in the South
voted heavily Republican, by a margin (of roughly two to
one) comparable, for the first time, to that of their peers in
the northeastern states. And this Republican tendency has
persisted through the sixties and into the seventies, with
the one exception of the 1964 Johnson-Goldwater contest
when a modest majority of the group backed the Democratic nominee.

Beginning with 1964, another interesting divergence occurred between the voting of professional and managerial
workers in the South, and in the Northeast. The southern
professional stratum was 20 percentage points *less Democratic* than its northeastern counterpart in the Johnson-
Goldwater contest; and in 1972, just 23 percent supported
McGovern's candidacy, as against 39 percent of the cohort
in the northeastern region.

Congressional voting shows much the same pattern, although the magnitude of the shift is less pronounced since
some southern congressional seats have remained uncon-
tested by the Republicans, or weakly contested, and since
many southern Democratic representatives are ideologically well to the right of their national party. By the late
1960s, professionals in the South were dividing their congressional vote evenly between Democratic and Republican nominees. And, reflecting the pronounced South-
Northeast tension which we have been describing, very
much evident among groups of high socioeconomic status,
and specifically at the elite level, southern professional
and managerial workers were providing *less support* for
the relatively conservative array of southern Democratic
congressional candidates than their northeastern counterparts furnished for the much more liberal Democratic congressional contenders of their region.

Much of the commentary on the growth of southern Republicanism has focused upon developments in metropolitan areas. The rapidly growing cities of the new South have, of course, been the prime centers of industrial development—which is seen providing socioeconomic underpinnings for Republicanism. The North-to-South migration, furthermore, has flowed largely to urban rather than rural areas. And as more rapidly changing and socially diverse sectors, the metropolises are thought to be less tradition-bound in partisan behavior. Working with aggregate data, Donald Strong and Bernard Cosman have demonstrated that there was a substantially higher measure of Republican support in the urban than in the nonurban South during the Eisenhower elections; and Professor Cosman, carrying his analysis back to 1920, found this same pattern for earlier elections.[32]

Surveys add a dimension hard to come by through analysis of aggregate voting materials, especially as they permit us to pare off groups whose presence only confuses analysis. Here, we are primarily concerned with the relative degree of Republican support of metropolitan *whites* in the South, as contrasted to their rural counterparts. With survey data, we can easily make this comparison for the entire period since the New Deal.

Republican presidential strength among metropolitan-area southerners increased sharply over the three presidential elections after 1936. While Alfred Landon was the choice of just 15 percent of this cohort, Thomas Dewey received the votes of 46 percent of urban southerners in 1948. The pattern among rural southern whites was quite different, revealing only a modest increase over the twelve-year span. In the face of both traditional national Democratic loyalties and the Thurmond protest candidacy,

---

[32] Donald S. Strong, "Durable Republicanism in the South," in Sindler (ed.), *Change in the Contemporary South*, pp. 179–180; and Bernard Cosman, "Republicanism in the Metropolitan South," (unpublished Ph.D. dissertation, University of Alabama, 1960).

Dewey made notable inroads in the urban areas, gains he could not match in the rural South (Table 3.4).[33]

Eisenhower brought Republican backing among metropolitan whites above the 50 percent line for the first time in 1952. It has remained above 50 percent in every subsequent presidential election, except 1964 when Johnson secured a majority. By way of contrast, presidential Republicanism never attracted a majority of rural southern whites until 1972. The cities have been much more hospitable to Republican efforts throughout *most* of the span we are considering.

The exceptions to this are themselves revealing. The 1964 Goldwater candidacy, associated with white racial protest, proved as strong in rural areas as in the urban centers. And the more diffuse ideological protest manifested by the repudiation of McGovern in 1972 produced a decidedly larger Republican vote within the rural white population than among urban and suburban whites of the region. In the two cases, then, when Republican presidential nominees served directly as vehicles for southern resentments and protests—which is not to argue, of course, that the Goldwater and Nixon candidacies were only or primarily instruments of regional reaction—the GOP did better in rural areas than it did in the metropolitan centers.

There is an obvious parallel between Republican performance in the rim as against the Deep South, and in metropolitan compared to rural Dixie. Figure 3.8 shows that the Republicans were stronger in the rim South than in the heartland in all but two presidential elections since the New Deal, again those of 1964 and 1972. A broader socioeconomic base for Republicanism exists in the outer and metropolitan parts of the region; but at the same time, these areas are more heterogeneous, more diverse socially and economically, less enveloped in a politics of resent-

---

[33] "Metropolitan" here includes cities of 100,000 population and over, plus the suburbs, or surrounding urbanized area of these core cities. "Rural" comprises the farm population, along with towns of 2,500 or fewer people.

Table 3.4. Republican Voting Strength among Metropolitan and Rural Whites in the South, 1936–1972 (as Percentages)

Vote	1936	1940	1944	1948	1952	1956	1960	1964	1968	1972
PRESIDENTIAL										
Metropolitan whites	15	33	34	46	55	55	51	43	57	76
Rural whites	18	21	29	28	49	43	44	44	36	85
CONGRESSIONAL										
Metropolitan whites	NA	25	27	29	25	30	34	32	54	49
Rural whites	NA	14	17	19	22	29	32	37	40	50

SOURCE: Data from following AIPO studies: *1936*, 53, 60, 72, 104; *1940*, 208, 209, 215, 219JV, 219KT, 224; *1944*, 328, 329, 336, 337; *1948*, 430, 431, 432; *1952*, 506, 507, 508; *1956*, 572, 573, 574; *1960*, 637, 638; *1964*, 699, 701; *1968*, 770, 771; and *1972*, 858, 859, 860.

ment. So the normal pattern breaks down when Republicanism becomes the primary vehicle for articulating resistance. And in these cases—1964 and 1972, to date—whites of the rural and Deep South surpass their rimland and urban brethren in Republican support.

IV. The South in Contemporary America: Issue Divergence

We are hindered in contemporary descriptions of ideological divides by the inappropriateness of our analytic categories. *Liberal* and *conservative* are New Deal terms, speaking effectively to the structure of conflict erected in the days of Roosevelt, but imperfectly catching many of the axes of conflict which distinguish the contemporary agenda. Still, if they are impaired depictions and often confuse rather than clarify by evoking images from another political world, *liberal* and *conservative* are all we have. They remain the only widely used categories for locating ideological or policy divisions in the United States.

Having duly acknowledged our dissatisfactions with the categories, let us proceed to use them. The outstanding feature of present-day sectional cleavages is the inversion of the positions of the South and the Northeast. Stripping *liberal* and *conservative* to their bare bones—depicting support for or opposition to the extensions of equalitarian change under governmental aegis—we can say that the South was the most liberal section of the country during the New Deal and is now the most conservative, while the Northeast has moved to the liberal pole.

Herein lies the underlying source of the en masse exodus of the white South from the national Democratic party, and the less impressive but still substantial entry of the Northeast into the Democracy in the new alignment. The Republicans are the more conservative of the two major parties, and are the natural home today for the South as the most conservative section. And similarly, the national Democrats are carrying forth the torch of liberalism, articulating the contemporary liberal vision, and the Northeast as the most liberal region appropriately serves as a focus of national Democratic allegiance.

In Tables 3.5–3.7, and in the text discussion, the responses of Americans to a wide array of different policy matters and disputes are set forth illustratively, attending to the regional variations. Although we present only thirty questions posed by national survey organizations between 1964 and 1972, the picture provided by this modest selection represents faithfully the response structure across the entire realm of policy disputes.[34]

We present regional differentiations in five issue areas: domestic social and economic issues; defense and foreign policy; civil rights matters; questions involving crime, protests, and cultural change; and finally what we have called "symbolic issues." Considering the range in policy choice covered, the consistency of the sectional pattern is compelling. The Northeast occupies one pole, followed by the

---

[34] A main problem confronting any comparative analysis policy preferences within the mass public involves the exceptional variety of opinion measures encountered in the vast collection of available surveys—a point we have discussed at length in *Political Parties and Political Issues: Patterns in Differention Since the New Deal* (Beverly Hills, Calif.: Sage Publications, 1973). Specifically here, we must acknowledge that items could be selected from the array of available data to prove several different theses bearing upon regional differentation. The variety of measures used, imperfections inherent in the survey enterprise, the casualness with which some segments of the public hold their positions on various issues—all these factors contribute to certain inconsistencies which cannot be ignored.

The only defense, given this situation, lies in numbers. From extensive analyses of opinion distributions, we have found that truth emerges in general patterns detectable through a large body of survey information. Any one question, any one survey can be misleading. But patterns are often deeply etched when the whole array of responses is laid out. Comparing regional responses, we located opinions on more than 300 separate policy questions asked of mass publics between 1964 and 1972. These data were categorized by policy area, and items were selected for inclusion in Tables 3.5–3.7 and in the accompanying text on the basis that they faithfully revealed the larger mosaic.

Table 3.5. Positions on Domestic Social and Economic Policy, by Region, 1964–1972

Question Text	South	North-east	Mid-west	West
1. "Congress has considered a compulsory medical insurance program covering hospital and nursing home care for the elderly. This medical care program would be financed out of increased social security taxes. In general, do you approve or disapprove of this program?" *% Disapprove*	39	26	38	39
2. "The minimum wage is now $1.25 per hour. Do you think that this should be increased, decreased, or left as it is for the next year or two?" *% Left as is*	45	32	42	50
3. "It has been suggested that to keep poor people from being attracted to big cities where welfare payments are higher, welfare payments be equalized—that is, based on the cost of living in each area. Does this sound like a good idea or a poor idea?" *% Poor idea*	25	16	17	10
4. "Would you agree or disagree with the following statement? All except the old and the handicapped should have to take care of themselves without social welfare benefits?" *% Agree*	57	40	42	36
5. "There is much concern about the rapid rise in medical and hospital costs. Some feel there should be a government insurance plan which would cover all medical and hospital expenses. Others feel that medical expenses should be paid by individuals, and through private insurance plans like Blue Cross. Where would you place yourself on this [7 point] scale . . . ?" *% [6 & 7]* *Favoring private insurance plans*	42	26	34	31
6. "Some people feel that the government in Washington should see to it that every person has a job and a good standard of living. Others think the government should just let each person get ahead on his own. Where would you place yourself on this [7 point] scale . . . ?" *% [6 & 7] For getting ahead on own*	36	25	31	27

SOURCE: Data from following AIPO and Michigan surveys: 1964, 699 (Q.1); 1965, 716 (Q.2); 1968, 773 (Q.3); 1972, CPS Election Study (Q.4–6).

West, and then the Midwest, with the South at the opposite end of the spectrum.

Northeastern residents are more supportive than their
counterparts in the other regions of efforts involving the
use of governmental power to promote social welfare. In
1964, they provided the greatest backing for government-
directed medical insurance. They were the most in favor,
in 1965, of increasing the minimum wage. They most
strongly favored as of 1972 government action to guarantee
everyone a job and a fair standard of living. Southerners,
by way of contrast, tended to be the most resistant in these
and related areas. They were the least attracted by proposals to provide a uniform base in welfare payments
around the country. Much more than residents of other
regions, they argued that all but the old and infirm should
have to care for themselves without public welfare benefits. They were the most resistant to federal health insurance plans, the most resistant to federal economic management as through wage and price controls.

In the social and economic realm, the South has clearly
shifted ground since the New Deal. Then, it gave the
highest measure of backing to the emergent governmental
welfare initiatives. On foreign policy and defense questions, a somewhat different regional transformation has occurred. In the years before World War II, southerners appeared the most interventionist—a position which came to
be seen as "progressive internationalism." By the 1960s
and 1970s, much of this old response pattern was still evident, but it has come to be seen differently. More than
their brethren of other regions, Table 3.6 shows, southerners are suspicious of the intentions of the Soviet Union,
doubtful about the possibility of a peaceful resolution of
differences. They are more willing to increase American
troops in western Europe as a barrier against Russian
armies in the eastern European states. They most opposed
recognition of mainland China and its admission to the
United Nations. They have been far more supportive of
maintaining or increasing defense spending. And while

Table 3.6. Positions on Defense and Foreign Policy, by Region, 1964–1972

Question Text	South	North-east	Mid-west	West
1. "Do you believe it is possible or impossible to reach a peaceful settlement of differences with Russia?" % Impossible	39	28	28	30
2. "People are called 'hawks' if they want to step up our military effort in Vietnam. They are called 'doves' if they want to reduce our military effort in Vietnam. How would you describe yourself—as a 'hawk' or a 'dove'?" % Hawk	76	66	77	75
3. "Do you think North Vietnam is sincerely interested in finding a peaceful solution to the war, or not?" % Not interested	80	67	71	67
4. "It has been suggested that the U.S. send 100,000 troops to West Germany to remain there until the Russians remove their troops from Czechoslovakia. Do you favor or oppose this proposal?" % Favor	40	30	31	32
5. "Do you think Communist China should or should not be admitted as a member of the United Nations?" % Should not	71	56	57	56
6. "Some people believe that our armed forces are already powerful enough and that we should spend less money for defense. Others feel that military spending should at least continue at the present level. How do you feel—Should military spending be cut, or should it continue at least at the present level?" % Continue at present level	75	55	57	60
7. "With regard to Vietnam, some people think we should do everything necessary to win a complete military victory, no matter what results. Some people think we should withdraw completely from Vietnam right now, no matter what results. Where would you place yourself on this [7 point] scale . . .?" % [6 & 7] For complete military victory	28	16	16	16

SOURCE: Data from following AIPO and Michigan surveys: 1964, 701 (Q.1); 1968, 757 (Q.2), 761 (Q.3), 769 (Q.4); 1969, 774 (Q.5); 1972, CPS Election Study (Q.6, Q.7).

the long Vietnam struggle elicited contradictory responses from many Americans, southerners proved to be among the most supportive of the Vietnam endeavor; and in 1972 gave the most sustenance to the position that the United States should do whatever is necessary to obtain military victory. On all these questions, northeasterners clung securely to the opposite end of the policy continuum.

Civil rights questions not surprisingly reveal some of the largest sectional differences. In 1964, 54 percent of southerners held to the point of view that whites have a right to keep blacks out of their neighborhoods if they choose, the public posture of 30 percent of midwesterners, 28 percent of westerners, and only 13 percent of inhabitants of the Northeast (Table 3.7). They have, in general, most vigorously defended the old racial order. Some change in the regional civil rights pattern becomes evident in the 1970s, with the nationalization of the politics and policies of race. While southerners are still the most resistant to civil rights initiatives, a pronounced declination of sectional differences, compared to the mid-1960s, is apparent. For example, northeasterners and southerners in 1972 were not far apart on the question of school busing to achieve integration. The regional political subcultures are divergent, along quite consistent lines, but hardly impervious to concrete interests. Busing is a national issue, manifesting strong white resistance throughout the country.

The contemporary political agenda is suffused with concerns which Richard Scammon and Ben Wattenberg have placed under the rubric "the Social Issue." [35] Crime, protests and demonstrations, new life styles, the broad sweep of cultural change are all part of the package. Regional differences in this realm are particularly large. Whether legislation should be enacted forbidding possession of handguns by all persons except law enforcement officials, for example, found 63 percent of southerners as of January 1965 against gun control, compared to only 28 percent of

---

[35] Scammon and Wattenberg, *The Real Majority.*

Table 3.7. Positions on Civil Rights Issues, 1964–1972

Question Text	South	North-east	Mid-west	West
1. "Which of these statements would you agree with: White people (colored people) have a right to keep Negroes (colored people) out of their neighborhoods if they want to. Negroes (colored people) have a right to live wherever they can afford to, just like white people." *% Keep Negroes out*	52	13	30	28
2. "Do you think the Johnson Administration is pushing integration too fast, or not fast enough?" *% Too fast*	64	31	40	39
3. "Do you think that private organizations such as country clubs and college fraternities and the like should or should not have the right to exclude otherwise qualified Negroes from membership?" *% Should*	73	38	48	42
4. The same question text as Question 1. *% Keep Negroes out*	41	14	23	16
5. "Some people feel that the government in Washington should make every possible effort to improve the social and economic position of blacks and other minority groups. Others feel that the government should not make any special effort to help minorities because they should help themselves. Where would you place yourself on this [7 point] scale . . . ?" *% [6 & 7] Should help themselves*	39	28	28	29
6. "There is much discussion about the best way to deal with racial problems. Some people think achieving racial integration of schools is so important that it justifies busing children to schools out of their neighborhoods. Others think letting children go to their neighborhood schools is so important that they oppose busing. Where would you place yourself on this [7 point] scale . . . ?" *% [6 & 7] Against busing*	85	78	84	80

SOURCE: Data from following AIPO and Michigan surveys: *1964*, SRC Election Study (Q.1); *1965*, 713 (Q.2, Q.3); *1968*, SRC Election Study (Q.4); *1972*, CPS Election Study (Q.5, Q.6).

northeasterners.[36] Sixty-five percent of the former, as
against 46 percent of the latter, indicated in the fall of 1968
that they disapproved of protest meetings and marches
even when such activities had obtained permits from local
authorities.[37] Forty-two percent of southerners felt that the
Chicago police did not use enough force in dealing with
demonstrators at the 1968 Democratic Convention in Chicago, the viewpoint of 34 percent of westerners, 31 percent of midwesterners, and only 24 percent of northeastern
denizens.[38] The stand that abortion should never be permitted, or allowed only under imminent threat to the
health of the mother, was expressed by about 50 percent of
northeastern and western respondents, but by 70 percent
of southerners.[39] The 1930s were a turbulent time, one of
sweeping social change on which the South was relatively
supportive. But the turmoil and profound cultural transitions of the 1960s and 1970s find the South decidedly
more resistant than any other section.

Symbolic issues include matters of political self-perception, affect toward various political groups, questions
which locate the respondent's sense of his political iden-
tity but which involve only intangible consequences. Inclination to associate oneself with positions described as
conservative or with those labeled liberal furnishes a
prime illustration of this symbolic posture. Southerners
react most positively to things conservative, northeasterners most warmly to those which are liberal. In 1964, 41
percent of southern respondents to a Gallup survey said
that the conservative wing of the Republican party best
represented their political views, the stance of just 15 percent of northeasterners.[40] Fifty-one percent in the South,
as against 37 percent in the Northeast, described themselves as "very conservative" or "fairly conservative" in
the fall of 1970.[41] During the New Deal, southerners, more

---

[36] AIPO Survey No. 704, January 5, 1965.
[37] SRC Election Study, 1968.
[38] *Ibid.*
[39] CPS Election Study, 1972.
[40] AIPO Survey No. 701, November 4, 1964.
[41] AIPO Survey No. 815, October 7, 1970.

than residents of any other region, favored a "liberal" Supreme Court. But in 1969, 74 percent in the region wanted new appointments to the Court to reflect "conservative" positions. Seventy-two percent of midwesterners, 65 percent of westerners, and a comparatively low 58 percent of northeasterners endorsed such conservative appointments.[42]

The present regional configuration departs sharply, then, from that of the New Deal era. Supportive of Roosevelt's domestic and foreign policy initiatives, the South has moved to a position of resistance and reaction vis-à-vis the extensions of liberalism and the current thrusts of societal change. It should be noted that the shift in the position of the South has been even more pronounced than the data we have presented at first suggests. To underscore the point that Roosevelt's programs had widespread southern backing, we excluded blacks from the early regional tabulations. Black southerners have been included, however, in the data just presented. The extent of the white southern reversal and reaction thus is even more dramatic.

The sectional differentiation of mass publics is duplicated at the elite level. The southern congressional delegation, we have noted, provided strong backing for New Deal programs, but it is now decidedly the most conservative regional bloc in Congress. Northeastern representatives, presumably both leading and following larger configurations of opinion in their area, stood to the left of the other regional delegations throughout the 1960s and into the seventies.

The modest body of *survey* data on elite opinion displays comparable distributions. In the fall of 1973, Louis Harris and his associates conducted a national survey of state and local leaders, as part of a larger inquiry into how Americans viewed the way they were governed, and specifically how confident they were in the workings of the political process. The Harris inquiry had the sponsorship of

---

[42] AIPO Survey No. 781, May 20, 1969.

the Senate Subcommittee on Intergovernmental Relations.[43] Harris found southern leaders consistently the
most conservative, with the northeastern leadership generally the most liberal—although matched closely by state
and local leaders from the West.

The Knight Newspapers surveyed all 2,696 delegates
and alternates to the 1972 Republican Convention and received completed questionnaires from a very high 73 percent (1,961 individuals) of this group. Southern delegates
show up decidedly the most conservative, and those from
the Northeast decisively the most liberal. Sixty-six percent
of those from the southern states, compared to 54 percent
from the West, 45 percent from the Midwest, and only 36
percent from the Northeast identified themselves as political conservatives. The idea of a guaranteed income for all
Americans similarly found northeastern and southern delegates at the opposite poles, claiming support from 38 percent of the former as against 17 percent of the latter.
Requirement of a police gun permit for purchase of any
firearm was backed by 73 percent of northeasterners, 57
percent of midwesterners; but 59 percent of Republicans
from the South and 59 percent from the western states opposed the prerequisite. Seventy-three percent of the
southern Republican delegates owned guns, compared to
44 percent of their northeastern brethren. And so it goes
through the whole array of questions covering attitudes
and behavior.

In recent years, there have been a number of indications
that the intense southern swing toward conservatism and
protests reached its maximum extension in the 1964–1972
period, and that some reverse movement has begun.
Within the huge Democratic freshman class that matricu-

---

[43] The survey data were made available to us through the courtesy of
the Louis Harris Center of the University of North Carolina. For a published report of the findings, see *Confidence and Concern: Citizens View
American Government,* a survey of public attitudes by the Subcommittee
on Intergovernmental Relations of the Committee on Government Operations, United States Senate (Washington, D.C.: U.S. Government Printing
Office, 1973).

lated to Congress in January 1975 were a number of new-South types who made a point of describing themselves as "national Democrats." [44] The nationalizing of the politics of race, symbolized by such events as the South Boston busing protest of the mid 1970s, removed one source of regional estrangement. A number of moderate liberals such as Sanford of North Carolina, Askew of Florida, and Carter of Georgia moved out of the South in the 1970s looking for a national constituency. One of them found what he was seeking. Jimmy Carter became the first politician from a Deep South state to win a major-party presidential nomination (and the presidency) since Zachary Taylor of Louisiana in 1848. Taylor was a Whig. The Great Virginians (Jefferson, Monroe, Madison) aside, no political figure from the southern heartland other than Carter has ever won the presidential nomination of the Democratic party.

Although such developments are important, one must avoid the temptation of drawing too much from them. The Carter nomination and election do symbolize a decline in southern political distinctiveness—both in the way others view the region and in the perceptions of southerners of their own political interests. But southerners remain significantly more conservative than their counterparts in other sections of the country.

Viewed broadly, the South's rejection of the Democracy appears as a harbinger of the end of the New Deal party system. When the southern exodus began in earnest in the Truman years, the New Deal party system stood largely intact nationally. By the late 1960s, when alienation of the white South from the national Democratic alliance had gone about as far as it could go, the New Deal party conformation was everywhere in disarray.

Many elements in the collapse of the Roosevelt alignment remain to be considered. But the experience of the

---

[44] For an interesting discussion of changes in the policy makeup of the southern Democratic delegation, see Roy Reed, "House Voting a Reflection of Liberal Trend in South," *New York Times*, February 25, 1975.

South and her antipodal sister, the Northeast, instruct us as to the larger pattern of realignment. A rural, agrarian, radical Dixie could rest comfortably in the Democracy in the economics-dominated agenda of the 1930s. A newly industrializing, petit bourgeois South could not remain Democratic as the agenda came to include civil rights and a host of extensions of the liberal and equalitarian vision.[45] In large part because of the economic configurations located within the region, the Northeast has had an establishmentarian flavor throughout most of American history. So long securely behind the Republicans as the party of business nationalism, northeastern elites in postindustrial America have swung most decisively behind the extensions of governmental nationalism articulated through the Democratic party.

Could one imagine, in the New Deal context, a conservative and rabidly anti-Democratic South rallying behind Republican protest candidacies in opposition to a liberal and increasingly Democratic Northeast? Of course not. The regional alignments now in evidence are incompatible with the New Deal party figuration. That they have come into being offers powerful testimony to how much that structure has already crumbled.

---

[45] For a valuable complementary analysis of political transformations in the South, see Numan V. Bartley and Hugh D. Graham, *Southern Politics and the Second Reconstruction* (Baltimore: Johns Hopkins University Press, 1975).

Part II

Unraveling
and Reweaving

4

Postindustrialism
and the Party System
The Setting

Depending upon analytic aspirations, either continuities or changes can be seen to offer an impressive point of focus in studies of the American party system. Both yield important insights. From the vantage point of cross-national comparison one sees, whether in 1900, 1935, or 1975, a distinctively consistent *American* type of party system: comprising organizationally amorphous *bourgeois* parties, each fully at peace with the persisting consititutional order, equally heir to reigning assumptions of classical liberal and democratic theory. But if one views the party system from within rather than from without, taking as a given the existence of a *genus factiones Americanae* and inquiring as to its phylogeny, the degree of departure from the New Deal order of things becomes striking. From this latter perspective, a new party system has taken shape, responding to a new sociopolitical period.

Many of the basic transformations the parties-elections system is now experiencing follow from shifting patterns of conflict. They are occurring because a bundle of new items have been added to the political agenda while old issues have been scratched, because various groups respond differently to the new than to the old—come, for example, to oppose change prescribed in the one where they had endorsed reforms associated with the other. And the whole structure of alliances and antagonisms is altered, too, as groups themselves develop, change composition in important regards, assume contrasting needs, interests, and perspectives. The composition of the American party coalitions has been transformed, from what it was in the New Deal era, because of the transformation of conflict which has occurred with entry into a sociopolitical setting most aptly described as *postindustrial.*

I. Societal Change and the Emergent Political Agenda

One must be wary about proclamations of entry into some new social epoch. For one thing, there is an understandable tendency for social commentators, searching for what is new, to overstate the case, to make societal mountains out of social molehills, to "extrapolate tiny momentary changes into Necessary Historical Tidal Forces." [1] Then, too, there is the perennial question of when in the flow of continuous change a distinctively different social circumstance is deemed to have been reached. To a significant degree, such determinations are dictated by the level of analysis. The broader the perspective, the further back one stands, the less frequently "decisive change" occurs. Thus, trying to provide a conceptual organization for all human history, Arnold Toynbee locates just twenty-one civilizations, of which Western society stands as one.[2] From a less lofty stance, however, Western society can be seen to fragment into all manner of contrasting stages and eras. Our analytic vantage point stands far below Toyn-

[1] We owe the latter depiction to Paul Weaver, personal correspondence, 1971.

[2] Arnold J. Toynbee, *A Study of History* (London: Oxford University Press, abridgement of Volumes VII–X, 1957), pp. 355–356.

bee's summit, a mere foothill, really, but the view still takes in an abundance of detail; and it suggests that a new, still imperfect stage in the American sociopolitical experience has been taking shape over the last decade and a half.

THE MEANING OF POSTINDUSTRIALISM

Stages in the social development of the United States have been variously conceived and named.[3] *Postindustrial society* is the terminological and conceptual child of sociologist Daniel Bell.[4] In the decade and a half or so since Bell fathered it, the idea of postindustrialism has been variously expanded upon, refined, reformulated, and renamed.[5] If the term has become common intellectual prop-

[3] Ladd has argued for the conceptual utility of perceiving the 185 years of U.S. history since regime formation, with their myriad streams of societal unfolding, as forming four distinct sociopolitical periods: *American Political Parties: Social Change and Political Response*. The third (in chronological sequence), the mature industrial state which gave birth to the New Deal and the Roosevelt party system, has already been discussed. The fourth, taking shape over the last decade and a half and still imperfectly defined, now occupies us. Other conceptual schema, of course, have identified different attributes of this complex reality, and ordered the span of time differently. The nature of such an intellectual enterprise, finding underlying patterns or unity in the labyrinthian structure of social change, has been nicely described by Daniel Bell. He notes that "social frameworks are not 'reflections' of social reality but conceptual schemata. . . . *Nomen est numen*, to name is to know, is an ancient maxim. In the contemporary philosophy of science, *nomen* are not merely names but concepts, or prisms. A conceptual schema selects particular attributes from a complex reality and groups these under a common rubric in order to discern similarities and differences. As a logical ordering device, a conceptual schema is not true or false but either useful or not. . . . Conceptual prisms are logical orders imposed by the analyst on the factual order." Bell, *The Coming of Post-Industrial Society*, pp. 9–11.

[4] Bell first introduced the term and an explanation of the social condition it was meant to convey in a series of lectures given in 1959. He has noted that the term actually appeared earlier, with a quite different meaning, in an essay which David Riesman wrote on "Leisure and Work in Postindustrial Society," printed in the compendium *Mass Leisure* (Glencoe, Ill.: The Free Press, 1958).

[5] Surely the most elaborate effort appears in the works of Bell himself. His major statement is contained in *The Coming of Post-Industrial Society*. Zbigniew Brzezinski probes related concerns in *Between Two Ages: America's Role in the Technotronic Era* (New York: Viking Press, 1970).

erty, the precise sense in which we employ it must be our own.[6] As we understand it, the postindustrial order centers decisively around the precipitants and consequences of several interrelated developments: affluence; advanced technological development; the central importance of knowledge, national communication processes, the growing prominence and independence of the culture; new occupational structures, and with them new life styles and expectations, which is to say new social classes and new centers of power.

As a result of technological changes, the wealth of the society has been enlarged to a point where the majority of the population is beyond subsistence concerns. Because of affluence thus construed, a mass public can partake of values previously limited to only a few—for example, higher education. The massive extension of formal higher education means that the intelligentsia—those trained in the use of ideas, those involved in the culture—has attained unprecedented numbers. Since the intelligentsia is so large, the communications media which serve as its instrument—debating and transmitting views on the culture, and delimiting the public agenda—achieve a centrality, a measure of independence, a degree of political influence quite without precedent. They become a primary power center.

A technologically advanced society requires a mammoth intellectual stratum to direct its sundry operations, but at the same time only a technologically advanced system can generate enough wealth to afford such a stratum. The relationship between a *civilisation technicienne* of mass prosperity and the intelligentsia, then, is symbiotic. Science, technology, knowledge generally, are obviously creations of intellectuals and their client groups. But the intelligentsia depends upon the largess of advanced industrialism.

---

[6] *Postindustrial* does carry an admission of intellectual fuzziness. After all, we speak of industrial, not "postagrarian" society. When there is a clear sense of the new, its essential features are embodied in its name. Only when uncertain do we describe the new as "after the old." But the conceptualization is what matters; final naming can wait.

II. Social Structure: The Place of the Intelligentsia

In our effort to delimit precisely the distinctive features of postindustrial America, let us look first to class composition. Entrepreneurial business has largely passed from the scene. It is no longer a major interest collectivity. Managerial business remains an important stratum. But it experiences peculiar fracturings which could not have been contemplated in earlier periods. Increasingly large segments of the broad new middle class, of the professional and managerial community—primarily those at once the most affluent and secure and most closely associated with advanced technology—cease to function as defenders of business values. More to the point, they cease to think of themselves as "business" in the historic sense. They become incorporated into a rising new class, the intelligentsia, responding to intellectual values and orientations rather than those traditionally associated with business.[7] At the same time, part of the business community, especially those linked to newer enterprises and the top managers, continue to promote business values and reflect relative conservatism.

The intelligentsia, dramatically enlarged, operates as a distinctive social and political class of postindustrial America. It expresses powerful commonalities. Its members are generally secure in their affluence. More importantly, they share contact with intellectual activity—which does not mean, of course, that they participate in high culture or advanced intellectual pursuits—with that extraordinary nexus of 2,500 colleges, 8.8 million college

---

[7] Public opinion analyst Louis Harris has drawn up his survey data in developing one aspect of this argument. Noting that in postindustrial America, "at the key executive level, more people [are] employed in professional than in line executive capacities," he stresses the finding that "the one quality that divided most professionals from line executives in business organizations was that professionals felt much more beholden to their outside discipline—whether it be systems engineering, teaching, scientific research, or other professional ties—than to the particular company or institution they worked for." The Anguish of Change, p. 45.

students, 600,000 professors, 900,000 artists, authors, and editors. They are linked by a communications network of unparalleled scope and pervasiveness, an instrument of technology (e.g., television) and wealth and intellectual sophistication.[8]

The high media or national communications instruments cease in their coverage of public affairs to be vehicles of business, instead respond to and reflect interests and values of intellectuals and their client groups.[9] The size of the intelligentsia gives the communications instruments, and the culture generally, a degree of independence never before attained.

This incorporation of the national communications media—whether the principal television networks, or the major magazines communicating culture and politics, or the great newspapers including the *New York Times* and the *Washington Post*—into the intellectual stratum is a matter of fundamental importance to the class structure and behavior of postindustrial society. In one way or another it has been commented upon by a variety of contem-

---

[8] College training, an experience shared by more than 35 million Americans, defines the outer boundaries of the intelligentsia. We use *intelligentsia* to include those persons whose background and vocation associates them directly in the application of trained intelligence. It includes, that is, not only intellectuals—people involved in the creation of new ideas, new knowledge, new cultural forms—but as well that larger community whose training gives them some facility in handling abstract ideas, or whose work requires them to manipulate ideas rather than things. Thus, school teachers, scientific and technical workers, the burgeoning managerial class which directs the bureaucracies both private and public, people involved in other aspects of the "knowledge industry" than teaching such as editorial staff of newspapers, magazines, and television networks, college-trained housewives who maintain a keen interest in cultural and political ideas although at least temporarily out of the labor force—all these and others in comparable positions comprise the stratum.

[9] It is well known, of course, that commercial television networks are almost wholly dependent upon business for support of their programming, through advertising. We are referring here to the relatively high degree of autonomy which news departments and public affairs presentations have obtained. The content of network news is hardly dictated by business sponsors.

porary observers. A. James Reichley of *Fortune,* for example, has argued that a major shift in orientation took
place over the past half-century among American journalists. Prior to World War II, the communications media
were dominated by business orientations, and displayed
anti-intellectual attitudes. Over the last two or three decades, however, Reichley argues, journalists especially at
the national level have tended to see themselves as part of
the intellectual community and have taken their cues from
it. In large part, this shift has taken place because incom-
ing cadres of journalists have been exposed to higher education.

> The new journalists have tended to be better educated and more
> professional—and strongly influenced by prevailing currents of
> opinion in the academic community. . . . Even the top journal-
> ists who are not college graduates . . . operate in a milieu in
> which liberal intellectual attitudes are pervasive. The suggestion
> of one critic that many national journalists now function as a kind
> of "lesser clergy" for the academic elite is not far from correct.[10]

The national journalists are behaving like intellectuals.
And "like intellectuals" means, more than anything else,
adopting an adversary role.

That the intellectual community is inherently questioning, critical, in contention with the established governmental order, comprises a very old and well-developed
theme. The great nineteenth-century French social com-
mentator, Alexis de Tocqueville, attributed to intellectuals, to the *philosophes,* a major role in the French Revolution, asserting that they "built up in men's minds an
imaginary ideal society in which all was simple, uniform,
coherent, equitable, and rational in the full sense of the
term. It was this vision of the perfect state that fired the
imagination of the masses and little by little estranged
them from the here-and-now." [11] Studying the 1848 revo-

---

[10] Reichley, "Our Critical Shortage of Leadership," *Fortune,* 84 (September 1971), p. 93.
[11] De Tocqueville, *The Old Regime and the French Revolution* (Garden
City, N.Y.: Doubleday Anchor Books, 1955), pp. 146–147.

lutionary eruption, the English historian Lewis Namier described it as "primarily the revolution of the intellectuals—la révolution des clercs." He saw the 1848 events as the "outcome of 33 creative years," in which intellectuals across Europe fostered, in Lamartine's words, "a moral idea, of reason, logic, sentiment . . . a desire . . . for a better order of government and society." [12] Raymond Aron has written generally of "the tendency to criticize the established order [as], so to speak, the occupational disease of the intellectuals." [13] Within the contemporary United States, the socially critical and questioning bent of intellectuals has been documented by a large number of observers, such as Ladd and Lipset for the academic community, and Charles Kadushin for literary intellectuals.[14]

The main source of this oppositionist posture so commonly associated with intellectual activity goes to the very core of the intellectual role. That role involves the creation of *new* knowledge, *new* ideas, *new* forms of cultural expression. Reality is held up to the test of the ideal, the theoretic. Various observers of intellectual life have pointed to the ways in which emphasis on critical work and creativity within specific sectors or fields often has led the more original to formulate general critiques of society. The role predisposes those participating in it toward a critical and questioning stance, to what Lionel Trilling so insightfully described as the "adversary culture." [15]

The adversary role of intellectuals is not new. What is new is the incorporation of mass communications media

---

[12] Namier, *1848: The Revolution of the Intellectuals* (Garden City, N.Y.: Doubleday Anchor Books, 1964), p. 2.

[13] Aron, *The Opium of the Intellectuals* (New York: W. W. Norton, 1962), p. 210.

[14] Ladd and Lipset, *The Divided Academy: Professors and Politics* (New York: McGraw-Hill, 1975); and Kadushin, *The American Intellectual Elite* (Boston: Little, Brown, 1974). For further discussion of the oppositionist stance of American intellectuals, see Lipset and Richard B. Dobson, "The Intellectual as Critic and Rebel: With Special Reference to the United States and the Soviet Union," *Daedalus*, 10 (Summer 1972), pp. 137–198.

[15] Trilling, *Beyond Culture* (New York; Viking Press, 1965), pp. xii–xiii.

into the intellectual stratum—and hence into an adversary role. This incorporation is now receiving recognition. Samuel Huntington has observed that "the national media . . . increasingly came to conceive of themselves in an adversary role vis-à-vis the executive government. At stake were not merely conflicting personalities and differing political viewpoints, but also fairly fundamental institutional interests. The media have an interest in exposure, criticism, highlighting, and encouraging disagreement and disaffection within the executive branch. The leaders of the executive branch have an interest in secrecy, hierarchy, discipline, and the suppression of criticism. The function of the press is to expand political debate and involvement; the natural instinct of the bureaucracy is to limit it." [16]

Theodore White has written extensively on the emergence of the adversary press. Like Reichley, he has commented on the higher levels of formal education of the contemporary journalistic community, a cadre "far more at home in the university seminar than at the police lineup or the football locker room . . . [whose] learning and . . . moralities made them a formidable group." [17] As an upshot, White argues, "the national media have put themselves into the role of permanent critical opposition to any government which does not instantly clean up the unfinished business of our time." [18]

Unfortunately, this profound transition in the role of the communications media, linked to massive growth of the intelligentsia, has too often been depicted in partisan and polemical terms. Journalists understandably resented and reacted against the attacks of disgruntled Republicans, as for example, the thunderbolts hurled by then Vice-President Spiro Agnew in his November 1969 Des Moines

---

[16] Samuel P. Huntington, "Postindustrial Politics: How Benign Will It Be?" *Comparative Politics*, 6 (January 1974), pp. 184–185.

[17] Theodore H. White, *The Making of the President, 1972* (New York: Atheneum, 1973), p. 247.

[18] Theodore H. White, "America's Two Cultures," *Columbia Journalism Review* (Winter 1969–70), p. 8.

address. The debate has settled on such sterile questions as: Are the communications media biased against the Republicans? Is there a liberal bias generally in the reporting of the national news? Did the press try to "get" Nixon? Did the press "prove" itself through a superb performance in covering the Watergate scandal? Such issues may matter to certain partisans, and may even matter in other analytic contexts, but they are quite removed from the point being made here.

We have posited the centrality of a massive new middle class, notably of its upper reaches comprising a broad professional and managerial stratum, as a distinctive feature of postindustrialism. In turn, important elements of this stratum can be identified by another facet involving role and place in the social structure—contained in the term *intelligentsia*. The potential for political influence of the intelligentsia in contemporary America lacks historical precedent. Sheer numbers contribute to this influence. More important, still, is the occupation by the cohort of an especially strategic place in setting the contemporary political agenda.

Whenever they have been present, of course, intellectuals and their client groups in the intelligentsia have been engaged in symbolic formulations for society. They have had a hand in agenda setting. But the entire character of this enterprise has been transformed and enlarged through the sociopolitical structure now prevailing. The wealth of the society permits large segments of a mass public to participate in the world of ideas. The contemporary university complex provides the source and common meeting ground for an expanding intelligentsia. The national communications media serve as vehicles for transmitting ideas on the culture and the polity throughout the intelligentsia; and the latter's size and market power (as purchasers of communication) have freed the media from their earlier dependence upon business. Here are the building blocks for a significant new power center. Its decisive resource is control of the political agenda, influence over how problems are conceptualized, which are deemed to have the highest priority, what responses are worthy of credence and which merit only rejection.

At earlier points in the American industrial experience, control over the means of production stood as a more substantial resource. The coercive power of business over workers proved dominant—until it was tempered by governmental regulations; by the replacement of an entrepreneurial elite with coherence of purpose by a managerial elite with little sense of social direction beyond what was needed to keep the firms over which they exercised temporary custody prospering; by vastly extended affluence which gave large segments of the mass public independence from the most immediate economic worries and hence independence from economic sanctions. As raw economic power as a resource was diminished, as positive government assumed greater scope and responsibilities, determination of the public agenda became an ever more impressive instrument of national power.

? 1980s

Both the limits and the scope of the argument need emphasis. There is no suggestion that the members of the intellectuals-intelligentsia cohort always agree, anymore than business or any broad social collectivity act with essential coherence. No sinister conspiracy is afoot, no unnatural or inherently unhealthy transformation of power relationships. At every point in American history, there have been decisive power centers: collectivities whose resources proved very influential in charting national direction. It is a key characteristic of postindustrial society that a network centering around a massive intelligentsia has come to possess such requisite resources.

III. Social Structure: The White Working Class

The New Deal era stands as the political high-water mark of the urban, white working class. It was in this period that this class received primary governmental recognition and support: legislation guaranteeing the right to organize and bargain collectively; minimum wage legislation; social security benefits; various extended guarantees of safety, healthfulness, and the general humaneness of working conditions. Legislation securing these benefits was not directed exclusively toward urban, white workers, but this group was the principal claimant and beneficiary.

During the New Deal years, the trade union movement took form and attained its highest measure of influence in the governing processes. The new political climate which followed the Depression, together with the general encouragement of the Roosevelt administration, formal legislative support provided by the Wagner Act, and the vigorous initiatives of a new generation of labor leaders, produced a surge in membership—reaching 10 million on the eve of World War II and more than 14 million when the war ended. This was the heroic age of American labor.

In the late 1940s and 1950s, however, union membership as a proportion of the nonagricultural labor force leveled out, and in the 1960s and 1970s embarked upon an actual decline. In 1955, 33.2 percent of all workers in nonagricultural pursuits were unionized; but by 1965 the proportion was down to 28.4 percent, in 1970 to 27.4 percent, and in 1974 to just 26.1 percent. Not only had the American labor movement come to represent a declining portion of the work force; but the sectors where it held the greatest promise of expansion lay outside the traditional industrial, blue-collar sector. Government employees constitute a big growth area. For example, between 1964 and 1970, the membership of the American Federation of Government Employees jumped from 139,000 to 325,000; in the same period, the State, County, and Municipal Workers Union grew from 235,000 to 444,000 members.[19] Perhaps the most dramatic illustration of the "whitening" of organized labor involves the increase in numbers and influence of the American Federation of Teachers. In 1964,

---

[19] *Statistical Abstract of the United States, 1972*, p. 242.

AFT national membership was just 100,000, but a decade later it had reached 440,000.[20] In October 1973 Albert Shanker, then head of the New York AFT and subsequently the union's national president, received appointment to the national council of the AFL-CIO, recognition never before extended to a white-collar union. As the AFT has grown, other teacher's associations which previously rejected the unionization and collective bargaining model have become de facto trade unions— with the National Education Association the most prominent example of this shift. So white-collar unionism shows clear signs of growth; while in their historic posture as representatives of an urban working class, trade unions experience a decline reflective of the shrinking base in the American sociopolitical structure of urban blue-collar workers.

If the white, urban, blue-collar, trade union stratum has lost ground, it has also become an "established" collectivity, in contrast to its "new claimant" status during the New Deal era. Most members of the urban working class were economic have-nots in the 1930s, either experiencing immediate economic privation or operating with precious little margin over subsistence needs. As such, they supported government-directed changes in the economic order. And the trade union movement which gathered momentum in the 1930s organized this have-not working class, and served as one of the principal new claimants for economic betterment and security and influence. These objectives were in large measure attained, through governmental intervention and economic growth. The unionized labor force has moved up the socioeconomic ladder. For this group, the victory over economic privation has been won. Producing a wonderfully American semantic contradiction, this segment of the *working class* had become *middle-class*.

---

[20] Data provided by the national office of the American Federation of Teachers, September 1974.

The economic gains of a large portion of the blue-collar work force are quite dramatic. In 1973, the median earnings of families whose head was a skilled manual worker was $13,576, $3,000 higher than the national median family income ($10,512); and the median family income of these skilled workers was more than double that of their counterparts twenty-five years earlier. Forty percent of these families in 1973 had incomes over $15,000, while just 25 percent earned less than $10,000.[21] The new income structure does not spell wealth, does not preclude economic worries. It does point, for the most part, to an economic status beyond subsistence concerns, to a level of consumption well within the boundaries of what "middle class" has come to connote: a private home, at least one automobile, the opportunity for vacation and travel, and at least modest luxury-goods purchases.

The political consequences of having a large portion of the working class—especially that represented by labor unions—within the middle class have hardly been obscure. A decade ago, Stewart Alsop suggested that "the fire has gone out in labor's belly." And so it has, because we no longer have a large coherent class of have-not wage workers. Alsop recalled Franklin Roosevelt's packing Cadillac Square in Detroit with a half-million cheering workers at Labor Day rallies. He contrasted this to the mere 30,000 who turned out for Lyndon Johnson in 1964, when Johnson was at his most popular and his opponent, Barry Goldwater, provided the clearest target given labor in many moons. Why then the poor turnout? "The workers who crowded shoulder to shoulder into Cadillac Square to hear Franklin Roosevelt regarded themselves as 'little guys' or 'working stiffs.' . . . The poor, and those who regarded themselves as poor, were in those days a clear majority of the population." [22] Alsop went on to point out

[21] U.S. Bureau of the Census, *Current Population Reports*, Series P–60, No. 96, "Household Money Income in 1973 and Selected Social and Economic Characteristics of Households," (Washington, D.C.: Government Printing Office, 1974), p. 10.

[22] Alsop, "Can Anyone Beat LBJ?" *Saturday Evening Post* (May 1967), p. 28.

that the Detroit trade unionist in 1964 occupied a far different position, having been drawn to the warm and inviting bosom of the middle class. Not at all an exploited and forgotten man, he was more inclined to go power boating than participate in solidarity rallies; and more importantly, no longer sustained the drive for social change.

The head of the American labor movement, AFL-CIO President George Meany, has spoken insightfully of the transfiguration of labor's place in the postindustrial era. In a 1969 interview with the *New York Times*, Meany was willing to accept both "middle-class" and "conservative" as descriptions of the membership of the labor movement.

Labor, to some extent, has become middle-class. When you have no property, you don't have anything, you have nothing to lose by these radical actions. But when you become a person who has a home and has property, to some extent you become conservative. And I would say to that extent, labor has become conservative.[23]

A working class which is middle-class and conservative. Yes, that is a distinctive feature of postindustrialism. And it follows, primarily, from the condition of affluence.

IV. Social Structure: The Age of Affluence

The United States has been a relatively wealthy country throughout its history. Its citizenry was dramatically better off than those of other nations in the middle of the nineteenth century, as in 1975. But the now common depiction of America as an "affluent society" expresses something quite distinct from mere relative prosperity. For it to have any real analytic bite and utility, *affluence* must refer to a condition occurring when a critical mass, a decisive majority of the population of a country, no longer confronts problems related to subsistence. It is one in which literal economic privation is the concern of the few rather than of

---

[23] "Excerpts from Interview with Meany on Status of Labor Movement," *New York Times*, August 31, 1969.

the many. Over the sweep of history this condition has been attained only since 1950 and then only by a handful of countries.

Americans did not awake one morning to discover the pleasures and pains of affluence, but entry has come recently and rapidly. The American majority during the years just after World War II surely was not poor, but like its counterparts in all previous periods of American history, the margin over basic subsistence in its income was small. In 1947, for example, the median family income in the United States was $3,000 ($5,665 in dollars of 1972 purchasing power), and 81 percent of all families earned less than $5,000. These Americans clearly had little left over when food, clothing, and shelter were taken care of.

In the last quarter-century, the extraordinary advances of the U.S. economy have propelled American society into affluence. The median family income about doubled between 1947 and 1973, increasing from $5,665 to $11,120, controlling for the effects of inflation by expressing income in terms of the purchasing power of the dollar in 1972. The percentage of families earning $10,000 and over, again in these same constant dollars, quadrupled—from 15 to 60 percent—over this quarter-century span.

We must be quite precise as to what these data mean. They surely do not mean that a majority of Americans became rich over the 1950s and 1960s. Obviously that did not happen. They do not suggest that some economic nirvana was attained, in which most people found all or a large portion of their economic desires satiated. Nor do they suggest that majorities of the population reached a status in which they no longer had economic worries or concerns. Since our sense of how well we are doing grows out of a perception of how others are doing; since what constitutes an acceptable living standard is revised upward as the economic wherewithal of the society increases; because expectations can rise at least as fast as the gross national product; economic satisfaction can never be attained. And economic dislocations such as inflation and recession in the mid-1970s prove unsettling and restricting for millions of people, including many who are in no sense poor. Finally, the concept of societal affluence is not blind to the persistence of literal economic deprivation among an all too substantial minority of the population. But what affluence does mean—an escape of the majority from subsistence concerns and preoccupations—is truly momentous.

If a substantial majority of families in the United States in 1947 received incomes sufficient to meet their subsistence needs with some modest margin, then the doubling of the median family income over the subsequent quarter-century must be considered largely "above-subsistence." Thus, an entire array of consumption values previously limited to a small elite have come within the grasp of a large segment of the population. Some elements of the new consumption patterns occupy us largely by their curiosity value, as gaudy, ostentatious displays of unprecedented national wealth. When pet food manufacturers compete in the mass communications media with contrasting claims as to which product best titillates the palates and provokes approbation of discerning canines; when 7.4 million outboard motors with an average horsepower of thirty-eight are in use, and 7.2 million people take up motorized snowmobiling; when expenditures for liquor and tobacco, jewelry and cosmetics, private autos and pleasure boats, and various forms of recreation in 1974 almost equalled the total amount Americans expended for all personal consumption, including food, clothing, and shelter, thirty-five years before; we gain a clear picture of a new world of consumption.[24] But affluence carries with it a

---

[24] This comparison, of spending for luxury goods in 1974 to total personal expenditures in 1940, has been formulated on the basis of dollars of constant purchasing power. If actual, unadjusted figures were employed, of course, contemporary luxury goods buying would appear to dwarf all personal consumption before World War II. Some might question including private automobiles, radios, and television sets as luxury items. While they have apparent leisure uses, it can properly be said that they serve necessary transportation and communication functions *in this type of society*. Our objective was simply to locate an area of consumption decidedly divorced from subsistence matters.

range of social and political implications far more profound than what is suggested by increased consumption.

The shape of operative political interests changes, as do
the political relations and roles of the various economically defined interest groups. Individuals and groups can
be expected to pursue their economic interests. But what
do they deem these interests to be? In the affluent society,
important interest collectivities emerge around education,
science, research and development. While there has been
a leveling off of college enrollment after the frantic surge
of the 1960s, there can be no doubt that with 8.8 million
students in academe, higher education, historically an
elite value, has become a popular concern. There were
fewer than 250,000 college students at all levels and in all
sorts of institutions of higher learning in the United States
at the turn of this century. At the outset of World War II,
the college student population numbered less than 1.5
million. But between 1960 and 1974, the college population *increased* by 5 million. This big jump in enrollment
testifies not only to the possibilities of affluence, of course,
but also to the drastic change in job and skill needs of a
more technologically advanced system. Still, only a society
of mass-extended affluence can afford to support 9 million
people of peak physical capacities in "unproductive" college work. Higher education, in the past an interest of only
the few, has become the pursuit of a very large portion of
the American public. There may well be ups and downs in
terms of societal interest in the educational enterprise, but
the basic pattern we have sketched will be a persistent
feature of postindustrialism.

Because education looms larger as a value which an affluent society wishes to purchase, it is able to make impressive claims for public support. Thus, expenditures for
education by all levels of government, which stood at just
$2.7 billion in 1940, climbed to $19.4 billion in 1960, and
jumped to over $80 billion in 1974.[25] In the same manner,

---

[25] U.S. Bureau of the Census, *Statistical Abstract of United States,
1974*, p. 109.

the affluent society expends sums of unprecedented magnitude on scientific research and development. In 1940, all branches of the national government spent $74 million for R and D. Two decades later, federal R and D expenditures had climbed to $7.3 billion, and in 1974 they exceeded $17 billion.[26]

Groups organized around the education and research sector have become major interest collectivities in American society. In the 1930s, studies of interest groups, quite appropriately, focused on business, labor, and agriculture. In the 1970s, such studies cannot omit the education and scientific establishment. Government has become the principal supplier of funds expended on education and science. As John Kenneth Galbraith pointed out, the costs of technological development have become too high for even large corporations to assume. And they have fallen to the public sector, as "the underwriting of sophisticated technology by the state has become an approved social function." [27]

Other sorts of changes occur with entry into affluence. In his influential The Other America, Michael Harrington observed that "the majority poor of a generation ago were an immediate (if cynical) concern of political leaders. The old slums of the immigrants had the votes; they provided the basis for labor organizations; their very numbers could be a powerful force in political conflict." [28] That day is gone—forever. The minority poor of an affluent society, lacking as well the requisite skills and resources for effective political action, can obtain influence only if and when alliances with groups which are not poor can be attained.

---

[26] These data are from the U.S. Bureau of the Census, Historical Statistics of the United States, Colonial Times to 1957 p. 613 and Statistical Abstract of the United States, 1974, p. 533. There was a leveling off of federal R and D expenditures in the early 1970s which, given a high rate of inflation, meant an actual decline in support. The long-term growth masks the immediate decline and the frustrations the latter has evoked.

[27] Galbraith, The New Industrial State, p. 164.

[28] Harrington, The Other America (Baltimore: Penguin Books, 1963), p. 14.

Perhaps the most dramatic changes attendant on affluence have occurred in expectations and values. With the emergence of the industrializing state after the Civil War, the U.S. embarked upon a century-long quest for the condition we describe as affluence; and while the physical and economic consequences of the quest were at least partially foreseen, the social-psychological and political products were misperceived—to the extent they were thought of at all.

V. Patterns of Conflict: Consequences of Abundance

Affluence transforms societal conflict, but it does not produce an end of conflict or even necessarily a reduction in its intensity. The *conflict-creating capacities of affluence* were spectacularly unanticipated as recently as a decade and a half ago.

As the New Deal era drew to a close in the 1950s, the fires of conflict had been dampened. During the Depression, government assumed vast new responsibilities in economic life, and this precipitated sharp divisions between advocates of the old and new public-private relationships. By the late 1950s, however, New Deal controversies had lost much of their heat. In its basic outlines, the Rooseveltian state was no longer at issue. The political agenda drawn up under Roosevelt's aegis ceased provoking serious divisions within the public.

The undeniable success of the economy led both supporters and critics of the American system to foresee an abundance-induced era of good feeling—understood by the former as the ability of the economic order to meet the needs of the lower strata, thus freeing them from privation and inaugurating a state of bliss; and by the latter, as sustaining powerful new instruments of social control, suffocating conscious discontent in a blanket of material needs artificially induced and promptly surfeited.

Something important was indeed taking place. Throughout the West generally, a long chapter in political transition was ending, one distinguished by the painful transit from ascriptive class to egalitarian societies and, almost simultaneously, by system-shaking divisions over what would be the dominant sociopolitical relationships in the emergent egalitarian order. The conditions of this transition had produced the deep schisms between capitalism and socialism, communism and fascism, a struggle of "total ideologies" because core social, economic, and political arrangements were at issue. And while America, having achieved in de Tocqueville's words "a state of democracy without having to endure a democratic revolution," followed a notably different course of political development than the European mother countries, it still had to complete a stormy passage from entrepreneurial capitalism to "managed" capitalism of the New Deal variety. The dramatic growth of mass prosperity, occurring in this context, contributed to a pervasive sense that deep political divisions were being eroded throughout the United States and the rest of the developed world. The *fundamental* problems had been resolved, the *fundamental* antagonisms had been removed.

Marx has cast a long shadow over Western political thinking generally, but nowhere is it longer than in the notion that "real" conflict has economic roots. Since the economy was meeting mass needs or wants to an unprecedented degree, real conflict must necessarily have been withering away. The first brush with affluence in the 1950s and early 1960s produced across a broad segment of the intellectual community the conviction that severe conflict had embarked upon a secular decline—a conviction which found articulation notably in the "end of ideology" literature. The amount of attention and controversy elicited by the end of ideology theme, and the extent to which the phrase developed a life of its own and was constantly invoked, appear due to its being seen an apt expression of a

larger intellectual milieu, of the feeling that growing affluence was producing a republic without significant stress.[29]
Now in the mid-1970s, the "decline of conflict" thesis
seems curiously implausible.

In the last decade and a half, Americans have begun to
learn the larger societal truth of the old polite cliche that
"money doesn't buy happiness." An age of affluence gen-
erates new and historically unprecedented types of conflict and dissent.

One area where the reduction of classical economic tensions for a large majority of the population has had the
result of opening the door to new tensions involves the
problem of distinction. In scarcity-bound societies, the
possession of wealth was (is) an important badge of distinction. If you have wealth, you know you are an important person and will continue to be such as long as you re-
tain your wealth. If you are poor, but see a chance of
becoming something other than poor, the accumulation of
wealth is an avenue to prestige. But in a society of mass-
extended affluence, the power of wealth is circumscribed;
obeisance cannot be commanded so readily when the
many are relatively well off. Only the super-rich now
enjoy distinction along with their wealth. Thus the affluent of an affluent society more often assume a relatively
critical posture vis-à-vis the society and the polity in part
because their economic standing neither confers the satisfaction which would submerge other dissatisfactions nor
creates the mentality of a privileged class ready to defend
its position against all challengers.

[29] Lipset, "The Changing Class Structure and Contemporary European
Politics," as reprinted in his book, *Revolution and Counterrevolution,*
p. 301. More perceptive observers such as Lipset and Aron were careful to
make clear that what they saw fading away was not conflict generally, but
a particular form of *ideological class conflict* which had emerged in
Europe with the Industrial Revolution. See also by Lipset, "The End of
Ideology?" in his book, *Political Man* (Garden City, N.Y.: Doubleday
Anchor Books, 1963), pp. 439–456. By Aron, "Fin de l'age ideologique?"
In Theodore W. Adorno and Walter Dirks (eds.), *Sociologica* (Frankfurt:
Europaische Verlaganstalt, 1955), pp. 219–233; and *The Industrial Soci-
ety* (New York: Simon and Schuster, 1968), pp. 92–166.

Affluence does, however, increase dissatisfactions, and hence conflict, by contributing to a mentality of demand, a vastly expanded set of expectations concerning what is one's due, a diminished tolerance of conditions less than the ideal. There is a kind of "entitlement" revolution which, whether one views it positively or negatively or as some mixture of the two, contributes powerfully to a new structure of political conflict. Andrew Hacker has written insightfully on this theme.[30] He argues that the United States is now "a freer and more democratic society" than ever before in its history, if *democracy* is seen to encompass "a temper of mind and spirit" rather than a strictly formal political condition. "Ordinary people in this country now have a higher estimate of their endowments and broader conceptions of their entitlements than ever before." [31] The sources of this changed condition are largely economic, to be found in the vast unfolding of technology which makes possible widespread material prosperity. Prior to mass-extended affluence, "habits of deference" were broadly suffused throughout the population. In a sense, Hacker is arguing, people imposed upon themselves all sorts of limitations as to what was appropriately their station or role in the society. Now, especially within the burgeoning new middle classes, a heightened sense of entitlement frequently brings people into collision one with another, and with the architects of public policy.[32] All of this leads Hacker to see America becoming "an ungovernable nation," in which people are at once so indulgent of their own private interests and so insistent that government remedy all manner of social inequities as to create a kind of "demand overload." [33]

---

[30] Hacker, *The End of the American Era* (New York: Atheneum, 1970).
[31] *Ibid.*, p. 4.
[32] Hacker did not argue that even in an age of affluence all Americans had arrived in the middle class. He insisted, however, that "at this point . . . a majority of the economy's productive citizens hold its [middle class] attitudes, either in objective fact or subjective outlook." *The End of the American Era*, p. 29.
[33] *Ibid.*, pp. 137–138.

Conflict arises in societies when there is a clash between what is offered and what is expected. Injustice is
not some objective condition, apparent as such to most
people in most settings. We see something as unjust when
we compare things as they are in a given sector to what we
believe we have a right to expect them to be—and find a
substantial gap. This insight is not a new one. Nearly a
century and a half ago, de Tocqueville reminded his
readers that millions of human beings over many centuries
in aristocratic societies accepted the permanent subordinate status to which the peasantry was assigned as part of
the natural order of things. Revolutionary assaults on aristocratic societies appeared not because the objective reality became worse, but because large numbers of people
came to question the legitimacy of the long-established
social inequalities of aristocratic orders. "Men are not cor-
rupted by the exercise of power, or debased by the habit of
obedience; but by the exercise of a power which they believe to be illegitimate, and by obedience to a rule which
they consider to be usurped and oppressive." [34] We might
paraphrase de Tocqueville in this manner, without doing
any injustice to the thrust of his argument: "People are not
led to protest as intolerable a given condition so much
because of objective reality; as by their perception that
what is is not as it should be." Precisely because an affluent society can deliver so much, because its expanded resources create the impression that all good things are possible if only people honestly pursue them, because so
many of the things which have vexed humanity historically and made life "solitary, poor, nasty, brutish, and
short" have been removed, the standards by which acts,
conditions, and problems are judged to be intolerable have
been dramatically enlarged or softened.

One of the most important consequences of the entitlement revolution manifests itself notably among the

---

[34] Alexis de Tocqueville, *Democracy in America* (New York: New
American Library, 1956), p. 31.

upper-middle classes, and involves a sense of "participa-
tory entitlement." Involved here is the conviction of one's
importance, and from this the sense that one's interests
and values generally, and one's political views specifically, should be recognized and attended to seriously by
the society. Daniel Yankelovich and Ruth Clark, in their
survey research among college students, note a heightened emphasis on the importance of self-realization, self-
fulfillment, and self-expression.[35] As part of this, they report a marked lessening of "automatic obedience to, and
respect for, established authority . . ."; and a far greater
insistence that in all areas of one's life—job and career
pursuits as well as private interpersonal relationships—
one should be able to find a high measure of fulfillment individually defined. "The emphasis is now self-directed—
self-expression, creativity, self-development, physical well
being, self-fulfillment both on and off the job." [36] Around
this basic insistence on self-fulfillment a new value system
has taken shape and has continued to develop. Values
which were espoused by a distinct minority just a few
years ago are now held, in many instances, by majorities of
college youth.[37]

The orientations which Yankelovich and Clark describe
are not directly political, of course; and indeed the authors
suggest that part in parcel with the growing emphasis on
self-realization is the shift away from concern with social
reform. It is likely, however, that there is as well a profound political consequence. To demand the opportunity
for a higher measure of self-fulfillment is to demand new
recognition as a participant in the society. Rather than simply following norms and standards prescribed by various
central institutions, one insists on the opportunity to personally participate in, even direct, the setting of such

---

[35] Yankelovich and Clark, "College and Non-College Youth Values,"
Change (September 1974), p. 46. See, too, Yankelovich, *The New Morality* (New York: McGraw-Hill, 1974).
[36] Yankelovich and Clark, *op. cit.*, p. 46.
[37] *Ibid.*

norms. One does not self-fulfill in a vacuum. The society
must respond in various ways to permit the enterprise to
go forward. If business corporations, for example, make
work demands which conflict with requirements set by the
individual participant for his or her self-fulfillment, dissatisfactions necessarily arise. The quest for an enlarged
scope of individual participation in and direction of the
setting of societal goals and practices becomes a necessary
part of the demand for greater self-realization.

Individualism has historically been a prominent component of the ideological configuration known as "the American creed." But as Samuel Huntington points out, "the
major periods of fundamental change in American history
have occurred when social forces have emerged to rein-
vigorate the creed and hence stimulate new attacks on established authority." [38] In the affluence of postindustrial
America, the long-standing commitment to individualism
is enlarged and extended. The underlying value is not a
new one, but its meaning and application gets transformed.

As the transformation occurs, however, other developments in the society move to create an inhospitable climate. The advancement of technology makes for a society
of increasing scale: big government; big business; the
dominance of large bureaucratic structures in all sectors;
big metropolitan complexes as the distinctive residential
setting; a massive national communications system; a definition of public problems and their resolution which
requires large commitments of resources and puts them
quite beyond the reach of individual action. Just as people
come to expect enlarged opportunities for meaningful individual participation, structural features arise in the society reducing these opportunities. This is so even if the
larger value system of the society, and the orientations of
those who direct its principal institutions, become more
receptive to self-fulfillment expectations. Consider the

[38] Huntington, "Postindustrial Politics," p. 188.

young, middle-level executive who works for Sears in Chicago, or for First National City in New York. Can he attain a high measure of individual direction of the major social institutions which affect his life? Can the perception of meaningful individual participation in these institutions be obtained? Contrast his situation to that of such equally representative citizens of an earlier America as a general store proprietor in Elmira, New York in 1900, or a farmer near Wooster, Ohio in 1845. Certainly the latter did not have greater control over matters national and global, but they did have greater control over the institutions and processes which directly and immediately affected them.

Not only are the institutions with which one deals typically much larger in contemporary technological society than in earlier periods, but the environment with which one has to deal, which affects one's life, becomes vastly extended. A decision made in Moscow *could* result, in a matter of minutes, in death and destruction in Washington. Oil pricing policies effected in Saudi Arabia quickly disrupt the budgets of millions of North Americans. In a small town an individual could see a fairly direct connection between his voice and vote on the one hand and governmental response on the other; he still has his voice and vote in the metropolitan region today, but the connection between these and any kind of governmental response has been stretched almost to the point of interruption.

Over the last decade, the charge that "the system isn't working," that major institutions are unresponsive, has been made with increasing frequency. Some might be inclined to see the myriad expressions of dissatisfaction with the system as the exclusive product of immediate events and failures: It is hard to live through a decade of political assassinations, riots, a long and enormously costly and highly unpopular war in Southeast Asia, and the Watergate scandals, without being affected by them. The system obviously has not been working as most people wanted it to work in some fundamental areas. But even if in the next decade catastrophes such as Vietnam and Watergate are avoided, the clash resulting from heightened claims for individual participation and the inherent unresponsiveness of an advanced technological society will nonetheless create profound dissatisfactions with societal performance. And the sense of dissatisfaction will be particularly pronounced among those who make the most expansive demands for individual self-fulfillment—that is, among the affluent and highly educated strata, especially their younger cohorts.

One manifestation of these new sensitivities is the rise of utopian political thinking, understood as measuring the adequacy of things as they are by the standard of the ideal. Interesting as an expression of the new utopianism, and at the same time as an analysis of the type of conflict it precipitates, is Charles Reich's *The Greening of America*. Reich proclaimed that in contemporary America "a life of surfing is possible, not as an escape from work . . . but as a life—if one chooses"; and insisted that for those "who have tasted liberation and love, who have seen the promised land, *the prospect of a dreary corporate job, a ranch house life*, or a miserable death in war is *utterly intolerable*." [39]

The Greening and the very substantial reception it received are strong testimony to the growth of utopianism in political thought. Has there been any other society in history where an author would not be subject to unrestrained ridicule for proposing that "a life of surfing is possible" for *anyone who chooses?* In a world in which millions of human beings still face starvation, is it not extraordinary to argue that "the prospect of a dreary corporate job," and "a ranch house life" are totally intolerable? For most human beings in most of history, a corporate job and a pleasantly situated ranch house would be material achievement beyond the wildest dreams. But perspectives change markedly in an affluent society, especially in the relatively

---

[39] Reich, *The Greening of America* (New York: Random House, 1970), pp. 219–220. Emphasis added.

insulated, prosperous suburbs where it is quite literally true that "everyone is well off."

For all its overstatement, *The Greening* contains some important insights. Reich sees clearly that mass-extended abundance, far from necessarily calming the waters of conflict in a society, may in fact be very disruptive. He heralds the birth on a significant scale in the United States of *privileged radicalism*—rejection of the system by segments of the population which have benefited most from its material achievements. The policy thrusts of privileged radicalisms will vary, but there are commonalties, products of the class base, which define the genre. Privileged radicalisms are distinguished by their idealism, by a strongly utopian strain of thought. They find their greatest support among young affluent people who have the time, leisure, freedom from pressing responsibilities of job and family, intellectual training, and disposition to adhere to what Max Weber called the "ethic of ultimate ends"—all of which are conducive to utopianism and idealism.

The argument that an affluent society inclines its members to heightened sensitivities or higher standards in evaluating the adequacy of various societal norms and practices extends well beyond the matter of utopian thinking. People simply expect much more in the performance of leaders and of the various social institutions, and this appears to result in their becoming dissatisfied much more easily.

Consider, for example, the inquiries made by Harris and by the National Opinion Research Center (NORC) into citizenry assessments of leadership performance in all major social agencies—medicine, higher education, organized religion, business, labor, the communications media, each branch of the national government, etc.[40] Both organizations show a depressing decline in popular endorsement

---

[40] The question is worded: "As far as people in charge of running [read list of institutions] are concerned, would you say you have a great deal of confidence, only some confidence, or hardly any confidence at all in them?"

of the nation's leadership over the last decade. Indeed, Harris concluded in March 1976 from his continuing investigations that "public confidence in major U.S. institutions is at its lowest point since the Harris Survey began making such measurements ten years ago." [41] The NORC work sustains a similar if somewhat more ambiguous assessment.[42]

According to the Harris data, 72 percent of Americans in 1966 said they had "a great deal of confidence" in the leadership of American medicine; in 1977, however, the proportion was just 43 percent. The comparable figures for higher education are 61 and 37 percent; for the military, 62 and 27 percent; for major business firms, 55 and 20 percent; for Congress, 42 and 17 percent.

This erosion of trust and confidence undoubtedly has many sources. The most commonly encountered explanation emphasizes the palpable failures of the time: a long and unpopular war; inflation; the Watergate scandals; increasing levels of crime and violence. Such factors are surely important.

Our sense that these are only one of the main contributors is reinforced, however, by the breadth of the decline in satisfaction, touching every area of national life, and by the continuing slippage in many sectors. The performance of medicine, organized religion, and business, for example, was more lowly rated in the generally more positive atmosphere of 1977 than it had been in the more obviously troubled climate of 1974.[43]

----

[41] *The Harris Survey*, March 22, 1976. Data for 1966–1975 are reported in *The Harris Survey*, October 6, 1973, and in *The Harris Survey Yearbook of Public Opinion*, 1971, p. 60. In March 1977, Harris reported increasing confidence in the country's leadership, but with the single exception of the presidency, the rise was either modest or nonexistent. And in virtually all cases the 1977 confidence levels were well below those which prevailed a decade earlier, *The Harris Survey*, March 14, 1977.

[42] The National Opinion Research Center data are from the 1973, 1974, 1975, and 1976 General Social Surveys.

[43] Ladd has evaluated a broad assortment of survey data on national confidence and satisfaction in "The Polls: The Question of Confidence," *The Public Opinion Quarterly*, 40 (Winter 1976), pp. 544–552. There is

Such findings lead us to the tentative judgment that, even if large and apparent failures are removed for a time from the social and political scene, discontent will continue at a very substantial level. The American citizenry expects much more than it did in the past in all areas of social performance. A substantial segment of the population is better informed, more cognizant of the gap between the calling and the coming, entertains heightened sensitivities about inequities and sundry shortcomings. There is, in short, a transformation of consciousness in affluent, postindustrial systems which is part of the permanent order of things. Unable to envision this or any other society not riddled with significant failures—although surely progress can be made in many specific areas—we anticipate that heightened expectations and sensibilities will produce a more demanding and restive public.[44]

VI. *Patterns of Conflict: Liberalism Upside Down*

One further development involving affluence but other phenomena as well needs to be brought into sharper focus. A new class-ideology alignment has taken form over the past decade as part of the general transformation of political conflict. Broadly interpreted, the New Deal experience sustained the proposition that liberal policies would find their greatest measure of support among lower-class voters and that conservatives would be strongest within the high socioeconomic strata. Now, in many although not all in-

---

not agreement in these data on whether an overall recovery of confidence has occurred since the Watergate low, and if it has, how much. It is evident that dissatisfaction has continued to build up in a number of important areas.

[44] We know of no available information which can settle conclusively the relative contributions of an accumulation of specific failures on the one hand, and of the altered consciousness of affluence on the other, to the increasing discontent and distrust evident in the last decade. We believe that the underlying premises of our argument emphasizing the latter are sound, but recognize that only American societal experience over time, serving as a kind of laboratory, will produce definitive evidence.

stances, groups at the top are more supportive of positions deemed liberal than those at the bottom.

THE SCOPE OF THE INVERSION

An examination of survey data reveals the extent to which high socioeconomic groups in the United States now stand "to the left" of the middle- to low-status cohorts, and the broad policy range over which this applies. However "high socioeconomic status" is defined, members of the category appear more socially critical, more supportive of cultural change, more inclined to extensions of the idea of equality than the lower strata. This relationship is clear and unambiguous among whites. Black Americans are an exception—disproportionately in the lower socioeconomic strata and at the same time very highly supportive of change. The long history of discriminatory treatment to which blacks have been subjected readily explains their generalized aversion to the status quo and their generalized commitment to extending equality. All of the following survey distributions are for the white population only, in order to bring into sharper focus the inversion which has occurred there but which is not yet widely evident in the black community.

In the 1930s, 1940s, and 1950s, high SES cohorts in the United States were more conservative in a rather consistent fashion than the middle- and low-status groups. The former were more inclined to describe themselves as conservatives, to reject parties and causes labeled *liberal,* and were generally more opposed to programs associated with New Deal liberalism. The high strata were more internationalist than the middle and low cohorts, and they displayed a somewhat greater sensitivity to civil liberties causes, but on the whole their relative conservatism was clear.[45] This normal New Deal configuration involving

---

[45] For further data on the policy orientations of Americans by their socioeconomic position, see, by Everett Ladd and Charles Hadley, *Political Parties and Political Issues: Patterns in Differentiation Since the New Deal* (Beverly Hills, California: Sage Publications, 1973).

policy stance carried over into the early 1960s. For example, in 1964 Gallup asked his national sample which way they would like to see public policy move: "go more to the Left . . . or go more to the Right." [46] Of professionals, 42 percent picked "Left," the position of 59 percent of blue-collar workers. Of those employed in professional and managerial jobs and college educated, 33 percent said "go more to the Left," as against 55 percent of unskilled workers. In the civil rights area, high-status whites had begun by 1964 to show somewhat greater sympathy with black demands than low SES whites, but even here the differences were not large. The question of whether blacks should stop demonstrations "now that they have made their point," for example, found professionals and trade unionists taking almost identical positions. [47] As recently as 1966, questions like the legitimacy of employing the death penalty for persons convicted of murder yielded minimal differences among whites by social and economic status: 40 percent of professionals and 46 percent of the college educated, compared to 41 percent of blue-collar workers and 41 percent of unskilled workers indicated they favored the death penalty. [48]

Over the last ten years, however, a shift of considerable magnitude has occurred. It has been as rapid a break from the past as it has been extensive. In most policy areas, whites in the higher socioeconomic status categories have become decisively more liberal than the middle and lower cohorts. There are exceptions in economic policy, but even these are being reduced or removed.

The symbol *liberal* is much more in favor at the top than at the bottom. In 1970, 35 percent of whites in professional and managerial jobs described themselves as liberals, the position of just 18 percent of unskilled workers. [49] In the spring of 1975, the National Opinion Research Center found 41 percent of college graduates calling themselves

[46] AIPO Survey No. 702, November 18, 1964.
[47] AIPO Survey No. 699, October 6, 1964.
[48] AIPO Survey No. 729, May 17, 1966.
[49] AIPO Survey No. 815, October 7, 1970.

liberals, compared to 35 percent of those with some college, 21 percent of high school graduates, and 22 percent of persons with less than a high school education.[50] Yankelovich has reported that 25 percent of Americans with incomes over $25,000 a year (1974) accept the designation liberal, as against 18 percent of those earning $5,000 or less.[51] A September 1976 NBC poll showed 40 percent of people with graduate training describing themselves as liberals, compared to 30 percent of those with bachelor's degrees, just 22 percent of high school graduates, and only 16 percent of the grade school educated.[52]

On questions involving race relations it is much the same. In 1968, Gallup found 64 percent of professionals in favor of "open housing" legislation, compared to 37 percent of skilled workers and 32 percent of whites in semi-skilled or unskilled manual labor positions.[53] Busing to achieve school integration was endorsed in 1975 by only a distinct minority of Americans, but the proportion was nearly twice as high for college graduates as for the grade school educated.[54] At the time, 28 percent of those with less than high school education, but only 19 percent of college graduates, argued that the country was spending too much to improve the condition of black Americans.

Other, "newer" extensions of equality find much more sustenance among upper-status groups. In 1972, 62 percent of professionals, in contrast to 41 percent of manual workers, expressed support for the position that men and women should have an equal role "in running business, industry and government." [55] The idea that there is "too much concern with equality" was rejected strongly in 1974 by 25 percent of those earning $25,000 or more a year but by only 16 percent of persons with incomes under $5,000;

---

[50] NORC General Social Survey, 1975.
[51] Yankelovich, Skelly and White, Survey No. 8400, March 1974.
[52] NBC News National Poll No. 55, September 16–18, 1976.
[53] AIPO Survey No. 769, September 24, 1968.
[54] NORC General Social Survey, 1975.
[55] University of Michigan, Center for Political Studies (CPS), 1972 Election Survey.

by 28 percent of the college educated but just 15 percent of the grade school educated.[56]

Matters involving cultural change and new life styles, which have crowded into the agenda over the past decade, show some of the largest differences between the top and the bottom. The argument that abortion "is morally wrong and should not be legally permitted" was rejected without reservation by 69 percent of college-educated Americans in 1974, compared to 41 percent of high school graduates and 27 percent of persons with less than a high school education.[57] Of respondents from families with annual incomes of $5,000 or less, 66 percent strongly agreed that the government should "crack down more on pornography," a position taken by only 18 percent in the $25,000 and higher cohort.[58] About half of the poorest Americans, in contrast to just one-third of the richest, strongly believed that too much permissiveness is hurting the U.S. badly.[59]

Even in domestic economic policy, there has been movement toward an inversion of the old class relationships, although it has not moved as far as in the social and cultural arenas—for the rather obvious reason that people of middle to low socioeconomic status in many instances remain beneficiaries of ameliorative economic legislation. In 1972, 46 percent of professionals indicated they favored increasing the tax rates for people with high incomes, while a slightly higher 48 percent of blue-collar workers took this position.[60] In the spring of 1973, 67 percent of professionals and a slightly smaller 64 percent of blue-collar workers asserted that the country was spending too little "on improving and protecting the nation's health."[61] Also, 51 percent of manual workers and a higher 59 percent of professionals argued that we were spending too little on programs to solve the problems of

[56] Yankelovich, Skelly and White, Survey No. 8400, March 1974.
[57] *Ibid.*
[58] *Ibid.*
[59] *Ibid.*
[60] CPS 1972 Election Survey.
[61] NORC General Social Survey, 1973.

the big cities.[62] Even when asked which they preferred, "the government creating jobs by putting money into things like railroads, housing, and schools, or by cutting back on existing programs and trying to achieve a balanced budget"—the proportion of executives and professionals wanting to go the balanced budget route (49 percent) was only slightly higher than the percentage of blue-collar workers (46 percent) endorsing this approach.[63] The argument has been made that too many dollars that should go for social welfare programs have been channeled into the defense budget. But the 1972 CPS study and the 1974 and 1975 NORC surveys show the high SES cohorts more in favor of cutting the military budget than their low SES counterparts, though the former remain generally more internationalist.[64] In the summer of 1976, 56 percent of college graduates, 43 percent of those with some college training, 42 percent of high school graduates, but only 32 percent of the grade school educated opposed increases in the budget for national defense.[65]

Seventy-four percent of grade school trained Americans, as against 66 percent of college graduates, professed strongly that "the right to private property is sacred." [66] And 29 percent of our poorest citizens, but only 18 percent of our richest, thought that "in the past 25 years, the country has moved dangerously close to socialism." [67] The proportion among the grade school educated who favor more governmental regulation of business is exactly the same as it is among the college educated.[68] It is hard to find much of the working-class awareness and markedly greater antipathy for business which characterized distributions in New Deal years.

---

[62] Ibid.

[63] Yankelovich, Skelly and White, Survey No. 8530, August 1976.

[64] CPS 1972 Election Survey; and NORC General Social Surveys, 1974, 1975.

[65] Yankelovich, Skelly and White, Survey No. 8530, August 1976.

[66] Yankelovich, Skelly and White, Survey No. 8400, March 1974.

[67] Ibid.

[68] Ibid.

Political opinions are complex things. Rather modest changes in question wording can shift responses significantly. Exceptions can surely be found to the pattern outlined above. But the growing conservatism of lower-class whites vis-à-vis the upper social strata is shown clearly in scores of recent surveys.

SOURCES OF THE INVERSION

Three interrelated arguments form the explanation of the inversion sketched above: (1) The composition of the several broad social classes or strata has changed, and so has their social and political character. (2) The thrusts and meanings of liberalism (and, of course, conservatism) have been altered. (3) Because of this, the high SES cohorts (as now composed) are much more liberal (as now defined) than were their counterparts of times past.

The first element has already been discussed. We argued earlier in this chapter that much of the white working class has become bourgeois, and behaves as the bourgeoisie has historically—anxious to protect a status achieved often at considerable effort and sometimes tenuously held. It is no longer comprised primarily, as it was in the Depression era, of economic "have nots." And it is not now nearly so inclined to the idea of social change. A substantial component of the higher SES groups in the United States has become incorporated into the intelligentsia, and shares in at least some of the critical, change-demanding orientations long associated with intellectual life. The upper strata today are not, predominantly, a business class, and surely are not an embattled business class of the 1930s model—feeling that it must man the barricades against a change-crazed "mob."

The shift in the meanings and objectives of liberalism is another, and somewhat complicated, story. The complication is compounded because Americans have imposed one more obstacle in the path of intelligent public discourse of political matters through an insistence upon using *liberal* and *conservative* with several different meanings. First, the entire U.S. political tradition is described, quite appropriately, as liberal. This usage brings to mind Louis Hartz's great book, *The Liberal Tradition in America*. Liberalism here is a body of ideas associated historically with the emergent middle classes of the seventeenth and eighteenth centuries. It stands in opposition to classical conservatism—the defense, again historically, of aristocratic norms, values, and institutions. In the New Deal era, as Samuel Beer pointed out, liberalism came into common usage with a quite different meaning.[69] Liberals were those who favored a major expansion of intervention by the state, the shift of responsibility for guiding the society from the private (chiefly business) sphere to the public sector. State intervention was on behalf of new beneficiary groups, notably the industrial working class. In this context, conservatives were those who continued to hold to the desirability of the old "business nationalism," those who opposed the New Deal state.

Now, *liberal* and *conservative* are receiving other applications. We are told, for instance, that Senator Henry Jackson is of the "conservative wing" of the Democratic party—although Jackson's liberal credentials are impeccable in both the classical and the New Deal senses of the term. Lewis Coser, Irving Howe, and their associates write of "the new conservatives," in whose intellectual ranks they place such as Nathan Glazer, Norman Podhoretz, and Daniel Patrick Moynihan.[70] They recognize explicitly that the perspective in question does not resemble business conservatism. The new conservatives are not New Deal conservatives. Rather, they are New Deal liberals who have come to emphasize a "limits of politics" approach as a result of being seared by public failures of the past decade. Although there is a good bit of disagreement at the

[69] Samuel H. Beer, "Liberalism and the National Idea," *The Public Interest* (Fall 1966), pp. 70–82.

[70] Lewis A. Coser and Irving Howe (eds.), *The New Conservatives: A Critique from the Left* (New York: Quadrangle, 1974).

level of specifics, there is fairly widespread agreement on
a general usage of *conservatism* which encompasses people who, while remaining faithful to New Deal liberal ten-
ets, draw back from certain contemporary facets of social
change and extensions of the idea of equality.

All the basic understandings of *liberal* and *conservative*,
of course, revolve around equality. The latter concept historically has received varying interpretations, has been
taken to require different public policies. The "beneficiary
groups" have thus changed, and so have the "contributory
groups." Liberals are in some sense partisans of the idea of
equality, but the idea has been taken to mean different
things and so the liberal ranks have shifted.

The thirst for change which characterized the working
class in the New Deal era has been quenched by the affluence of the last three decades. Many of the current pressures for equalitarian change, moreover, ask for sacrifices
from the lower or "lower-middle" social strata. In contrast
to the 1930s, when policy innovation often involved efforts
by the working class to strengthen its position vis-à-vis the
business strata, some of the most tension-laden areas
where equalitarian change has been sought over the past
decade have found the white working class (or lower-
middle class) and the black underclass confronting each
other. More secure in their position, less threatened by
such quests for societal transformation, typically residing
some distance from the "front," the upper social strata
have come easily to a more change-supportive posture.

The equalitarianism of the New Deal tended to be majoritarian in terms of its targeted beneficiaries. The contemporary variety is minoritarian and often asks more of
the middle-to-lower strata than of the top.

The dominant concerns or objectives of equalitarianism
have shifted. Representative of the current emphasis are
the busing of school children to achieve higher measures
of racial integration, a rejection of the "equality of opportunity" definition of the egalitarian society with stress instead on "equality of result," and heightened concern over
extensions of civil liberties, notably the rights of the ac-

cused. The beneficiaries of such commitments on the whole are quite different from those of New Deal equalitarianism.

Even in the area of domestic social spending, lower-middle income cohorts have moved in striking fashion toward contributor status; at the same time, the relative contributor burden of upper-income groups has expanded more modestly. Public expenditures for health, education, and welfare have grown at an extraordinary rate over the past two decades—from $49.9 billion in 1953 to $410.5 billion in 1975, an increase of over 800 percent in current dollars and just under 400 percent in dollars of constant (1975) purchasing power. (Over the same span, military expenditures jumped 240 percent in current dollars and just about held even in constant dollars.) This major growth in domestic spending has been sustained in part by increases in the effective tax rate. And for those families earning incomes around the national median, the rise has been much steeper than for upper-middle and upper-income families. Those at the median experienced a *doubling* of the proportion of their income going to taxes between 1953 and 1975, compared to a *50 percent* increase among families with incomes two to four times the median.[71] Families earning four times the median in 1953—about $20,000—paid 20.2 percent of their income in taxes, while those at the median paid 11.8 percent; twenty-two years later median income families were taxed 22.7 percent of their income, while the rate for those earning four times as much had climbed more slowly, to 29.5 percent.

Trying to sum up the meaning of these data, David Broder commented that it is "no wonder there is a tax revolt in this country." [72] We think it might be more appropriate to draw the following conclusions: No wonder there is an inversion of the New Deal class order. The top

---

[71] Advisory Commission on Intergovernmental Relations, *Significant Features of Fiscal Federalism—1976 Edition*, Part I (Washington: ACIR, 1976).

[72] David S. Broder, "The Shift in Spending and Taxes," *Washington Post*, August 4, 1976.

doesn't pay a much higher share of its income in taxes than does the lower middle, even though it has much more of a cushion, and the burden of an expanding role for the states has in one sense been borne disproportionately by the lower-middle cohorts.

Social policies may be described as liberal on grounds that they employ the state for objectives widely perceived as equalitarian. But the equalitarian thrust may in fact be modest, and what there is of it may not be majoritarian in terms of beneficiaries. Furthermore, such policies need not make any special demands on privileged minorities. If they are modestly equalitarian and at the same time define contributors as the many rather than the few, they may come to be perceived by a large segment of the upper strata as "good buys"—that is, supportive of values, such as basic system stability, which the upper-status cohorts can appreciate, at a reasonable price.

Liberalism in the mid-1970s has a different mix of beneficiaries and contributors than it did in the 1930s. Its programmatic thrusts have changed. This is another part of the explanation for the inversion of the New Deal class order, but again it is incomplete. A strict self-interest calculus is useful. It is important to recognize that high-status Americans, as a group, have a greater "interest" in liberalism than did their counterparts four decades earlier. There are other dimensions, however, which the self-interest calculus does not capture. The most important element involves the role, and the measure of autonomy, of ideology. The political beliefs and orientations people hold are not simply products of their most proximate interests.

In the contemporary setting, the more prosperous strata are in fact frequently the most demanding and sustaining of social and cultural change, rather than the most resistant to such changes. The crude Marxist model suggests just the opposite, of course—that real conflict is economic, between the rich and the poor, with the rich generally satisfied and the poor at least intermittently dissatisfied and producing demands for change. But in an affluent society, with classical economic tensions muted, a new set of rela-

tionships and precipitants is introduced. Just as much of
the working class has come to think "bourgeois," so substantial numbers of higher SES Americans have been
brought into the intelligentsia and manifest a decidedly
"postbourgeois" ethos.

One of the first to write with some precision about this
phenomenon, of Marx being stood on his head by the new
cleavages, the blanketing of old tensions, the rise of the
white working class to middle-class standing, the detach-
ment of much of the upper-middle class from traditional
business concerns and their incorporation into the intelligentsia, was the sociologist C. Wright Mills. A decade
and a half ago, Mills made light of "some New Left
writers" who clung fiercely to the notion of the working
class "as *the* historic agency" of social change, labeling
their fixation upon workers "a legacy from Victorian Marx-
ism." [73] Under some historical conditions, to be sure, industrial workers have operated as "a-class-for-them-
selves," and have served as the decisive instrument for
change. But such a condition was not present in the
United States. Instead the intelligentsia was emerging as
the primary lever.

Entry into the contemporary era involves the placing of
a wide range of new issues on the political agenda. In particular, there are important shifts occurring with the introduction of new value configurations. An affluent, much
more highly educated, more leisured public casts off many
of the older norms and standards of behavior. The survey
work conducted by Daniel Yankelovich and his associates
offers a more precise indication of the rapid circulation of
new moral norms including more liberal sexual attitudes, a
weakening of automatic respect for established authority
structures, a decline of "old fashioned" patriotism; chang-

---

[73] C. Wright Mills, "The New Left," in a collection of Mills's essays,
Power, Politics and People, edited by Irving Louis Horowitz (New York:
Ballantine Books, 1963), p. 256. The piece was first published in the *New
Left Review* (September–October 1960).

ing orientations toward work, marriage and family, and the relative importance of material achievement in defining success; and a heightened concern with individual self-fulfillment and expression.[74] Not surprisingly, since the transition to the new social setting and the new value configurations is very recent, conflict arises as some sectors sustain while others oppose the emergent value structure. In this conflict pattern, age and socioeconomic position are the most important differentiating variables. The young, less socialized into the value structures of the old order, become for better or worse more receptive to the new; and within each age cohort, higher SES groups, more exposed to bodies of ideas encouraging change and experimentation and inclining to the prospective that the old is often unnecessarily narrow and restrictive, give a larger measure of backing for the new life styles and mores than their counterparts of lower socioeconomic status.

Table 4.1 shows some representative distributions. The variation by age on questions involving extramarital sex, abortion, and the use of marijuana are very sharp. Thus, 59 percent of college-trained Americans under 30 years of age favor marijuana's legalization, but support for legalization drops to 36 percent of the college stratum in the 30–49 age category and to just 22 percent of those 50 years and older. The differences by education are equally impressive. Homosexual relations are considered "always wrong" by 82 percent of noncollege people over 50, compared to 63 percent of this age group who have attended college; by 60 percent of the young (under 30) noncollege population but by only 42 percent of the young college educated. By a two to one majority, college-trained persons under age 30 maintain that a pregnant woman, married but simply not wanting to have any more children, should be able to obtain a legal abortion. Among Americans not exposed to academe and 50 years of age and older, however, two out of every three oppose legalizing abortion.

---

[74] Daniel Yankelovich, *The New Morality* (New York: McGraw-Hill, 1974).

Table 4.1. Orientations toward Changing Social and Cultural Norms, Cohorts Defined by Education and Age

	Everyone
Please tell me whether or not *you* think it should be possible for a pregnant woman to secure a *legal* abortion if she is married and does not want any more children? (Percentage answering *Yes, should be possible*) [1]	45
Do you think the use of marijuana should be made legal, or not? (Percentage *favoring legalization*) [1]	28
. . . What is your opinion about a married person having sexual relations with someone other than the marriage partner—is it always wrong, almost always wrong, wrong only sometimes, not wrong at all? (Percentage answering *always wrong*) [1]	68
What about sexual relations between two adults of the same sex—do you think it is always wrong, almost always wrong, wrong only sometimes, not wrong at all? (Percentage answering *always wrong*) [1]	67
There are many possible ways for people to show their disapproval or disagreement with governmental policies and actions. . . . How about taking part in protest meetings or marches that are permitted by the local authorities? Would you approve of taking part, disapprove, or would it depend on the circumstances? (Percentage *disapproving*) [2]	41

SOURCE: [1] National Opinion Research Center, General Social Survey 1976.
[2] Center for Political Studies, American National Election Study 1972.

College-educated, under 30 years of age	Non-college, under 30 years of age	College-educated, 30–49 years of age	Non-college, 30–49 years of age	College-educated, 50 years and older	Non-college, 50 years and older
64	46	60	38	54	35
59	44	36	20	22	14
47	60	48	72	67	82
42	60	47	74	63	82
14	25	26	44	51	59

In general, support for elements loosely grouped under "new life styles and values" has become incorporated in the new liberalism. And it has come much more from the higher than from the lower social classes. Has there been any period in which the culturally avant-garde has been a lower-class or petit bourgeois phenomenon? Cultural experimentation by the upper classes is not new. The size of the upper classes is new, as is the boldness of their assault on older values and life styles. A broad array of issues, around which the upper social groups are "naturally" more change supporting than the lower-middle and working classes, now dominates the political agenda.

There is another, quite different, ideological component of the inversion. It has become progressively easier for groups of high socioeconomic status to support policies of the kind described above because the old ideological objections to intervention by the state have been so greatly weakened. We must remember that upper classes of the New Deal years opposed the interventionist programs of the Roosevelt Administration not only because they saw threats to their ascendancy and economic costs in the programs but also because they *believed* that private solutions were intrinsically preferable to public ones. Philosophical disagreements over the proper scope of government were deep and widespread.

The American establishments have long since abandoned this view. While some people still oppose the prevailing levels of governmental intervention as a matter of principle, Lowi was broadly correct when he argued that "statesmen simply no longer disagree about whether government should be involved. . . . Once the principle of positive government in an indeterminable but expanding political sphere was established, criteria arising out of the very issue of principle itself became irrelevant." [75]

During the New Deal era, it was possible to distinguish

[75] Theodore Lowi, *The End of Liberalism* (New York: W. W. Norton, 1969), pp. 67, 57.

people who thought of themselves as liberals from those who described themselves as conservatives rather sharply by their attitudes on the size and scope of government. In 1964, "the size of government issue split the population along classical liberal/conservative lines." [76] That year, 25 percent of the liberals said government was too big, the position also held by a massive 71 percent of the conservatives. In 1968, continuing to follow views on this issue through University of Michigan Election Study data, Nie and Andersen found that the direction of the relationship remained the same but its strength had begun to decline. By 1972, there was no longer any difference between liberals and conservatives as to the size of government, with 57 percent of the former and 60 percent of the latter taking the position that government was "too big." This is not to suggest that self-described liberals and conservatives took the same view on the range of public issues. In fact, policy differences proved exceptionally sharp. But mass publics along with the "statesmen" to whom Lowi referred are no longer divided in any coherent ideological fashion on the question of the size and scope of government.

RECAPITULATION

Over the last decade, a decisive inversion has taken place in the relationship established during the New Deal of class to sociopolitical commitments. The high social strata now consistently provide a greater measure of support for liberal programs and candidacies than do the lower strata. This is no temporary phenomenon. No return to the New Deal pattern should be expected. The sources of the inversion lie buried deeply within broad transformations of the society and its political conflict. An under-

---

[76] Norman H. Nie with Kristi Andersen, "Mass Belief Systems Revisited: Political Change and Attitude Structure," *The Journal of Politics*, 36 (August 1974), p. 556.

standing of the inversion yields more general insights into the character of contemporary politics.

What we now call liberalism frequently makes the old New Deal majority contributors rather than beneficiaries. Lower-status whites more often feel threatened than encouraged by current extensions of equalitarianism. There has been a significant *embourgeoisement* of the working class. The high socioeconomic cohorts, which had such a distinctive business coloration in the 1930s (and earlier), have changed their social and political character—notably through the growth of the professional stratum. Such developments are central to the inversion described herein. They comprise one primary feature of the postindustrial era in the United States.

VII. Patterns of Conflict: Ascending and Declining Interests

Samuel Huntington has observed that periods of movement from one type of social setting to another witness ascensions and declines—in terms of numbers, economic position, and social standing—among various social groups. Some collectivities are products of the emergent social relationships and thereby on the rise; whereas others are part of a social order being displaced.[77] Huntington then sees three distinctive types of cleavage commonly appearing with the transition from one societal setting to another: between the ascendant and the declining groups; within the ranks of groups on the rise; and among the declining social forces. While he applies this to the current movement to postindustrialism, his prototype is the great historic shift from agrarian to industrializing societies. In the latter context, there typically was a pronounced division between the old and the new, between an urban bourgeoi-

---

[77] Huntington, "Postindustrial Politics," pp. 177–182.

sie and working class on the one hand, and the agricultural classes on the other. But fissures also developed within the industrializing sector, notably between the capitalists and their labor force. And while their society itself was being eclipsed, the haves and have-nots of the agrarian order fought things out, as in the struggle between land-owners and peasants.

Useful though the "ascending-declining" distinction is, as a starting point for capturing the decisive features of conflict which appears with passage to a new social set-ting, it requires some modification, specifically when ap-plied to the contemporary industrial era. The intelligentsia can properly be described as an ascendant collectivity, its numbers, economic position, social status, opportunities for influence, and the like, vastly expanded over what they were in the New Deal/industrial period. And in a similar fashion, the urban working class and the trade unions ap-pear to be an interest collectivity in relative decline. The influence of the former on the contemporary polity vastly surpasses what it exercised in the Roosevelt era, while the impact of the latter has been diminished notably. This is a basic secular shift which speaks to the changing structure of American society. Such a division between ascending and declining strata need not always be raw and overt, of course. But it appears prominently, as in the struggle be-tween components of the intelligentsia and the labor movement for control of the destinies of the Democratic party. The intelligentsia, in alliance with other groups in-cluding elements of the black underclass, wrested control of the national Democratic party from its urban, blue-collar, and union wing in 1972. That is why the divisions were so sharp, so tension-laden. George McGovern was opposed not simply because his views were rejected, al-though that obviously played a part, but because he was the symbol of a larger struggle between ascending and declining forces, a struggle manifesting itself in the Demo-cratic party but reaching beyond that into the society. This struggle will not soon go away, although the balance for the long run has shifted to the "new politics" professional and managerial, intelligentsia community.[78]

Still, ascending-declining needs to be supplemented by yet another distinction, "established vs. newly claimant," to be fully persuasive. Black Americans, for example, must be seen as an ascending group in postindustrial America, but at the same time their position obviously differs profoundly from that of the new middle class. Blacks are ascending because postindustrial society, with its greater affluence and concomitant emphasis upon opportunities for individual realization and expression, and hence its equalitarianism, ordains the demise of the old biracial system which locked the vast majority of the black population in a subordinate position. However slow the process of change, however frustrating it appears for many experiencing it, the position of blacks in postindustrial America approaches equity much more decisively than in earlier stages of American social experience. But if blacks are ascending, they clearly are not established; rather, they are ascending and newly claimant. On the other hand, the white unionized labor force is declining—vis-à-vis the new middle classes—and yet remains an older, already established interest, in comparison to blacks.

Just as the shift from one social setting to another involves conflict between ascending and declining forces, so it typically contains a struggle between groups declining/established, and those which are ascending/newly

---

[78] Decline should not, of course, be equated with disappearance. Organized labor remains a vigorous and prominent force in Democratic presidential politics and the efforts by DNC Chairman Robert Strauss in 1973 and 1974 to reconcile the contending groups may indeed achieve a kind of success. Beyond that, politics has always made for strange bedpersons, and the desire for victory will undoubtedly lead many in both of these amorphous camps to reconcile differences on occasion in the interest of electoral success. Still, the transition in the influence of ascending and declining strata will not be reversed, any more than the successful wresting of dominance by the rising urban and industrial forces from the declining rural and southern wing of the Democracy between 1915 and 1935 was reversed.

claimant. The struggle between the white working class and the black population conforms easily to the archetype. The efforts of blacks to advance, and the stresses and strains accompanying governmental and extragovernmental efforts to promote this change, impacted most heavily on previously established collectivities now in relative decline. The urban white working class comprises a substantial segment of the latter.

Other variations on this conflict pattern can be seen. On the one hand, the growing new middle class frequently finds itself at odds with the urban and industrial working class whose base is shrinking. This conflict takes a variety of related forms: suburbs vs. cities; professional and managerial groups vs. unions; intelligentsia vs. the petite bourgeoisie. At the same time, important ruptures appear within the ascending strata. The intelligentsia itself often divides—on ideological rather than economic interest grounds. Components of the professional and managerial stratum linked to business enterprise find themselves at odds with groups focusing more directly around intellectual activity, such as scientific and technical personnel, teachers, governmental planners, and the personnel of the communications industry. Finally, there is a primary division between older established interests now in relative decline, encompassed by the trade union movement, and ascending but newly claimant collectivities, of which black Americans are the most prominent example. Such a conflict structure is not found in any earlier stage of American societal experience, and may appropriately be considered a distinctive configuration of postindustrialism.

5

Postindustrialism
and the Party System
The Coalitions

In every democratic polity, the makeup of party coalitions is derivative, owing in large part to social structure and social conflict. To know the composition of the major collectivities, and the manner in which they are divided by the ascendant disputes of the day is to know how, inevitably, the populace will come to distribute itself in electoral decisions. It is altogether natural, then, that changes in social structure and social conflict which define the emergence of the postindustrial era in the United States have dramatically altered the party coalitions.

I. Collapse of the Democratic Presidential Majority

Throughout the New Deal era, the Democrats were possessed of a natural presidential majority. That they have now lost this majority status is due in part to the inability of any political party in the contemporary setting to command sufficiently firm and long-standing loyalties to give it that relative security of ascendancy which "the majority

party" connotes. The weakening of voter loyalties to political parties generally requires extended treatment, and re-
ceives it in the following chapter. Here, however, we examine what might be considered classic symptoms of a
partisan transformation—social groups coming to find reason to withdraw support from a party to which they previously had granted it. So while both factors contributing
to the collapse of the Democratic majority—the phenomenon of partisan disaggregation and more specific rejections
by certain social groups of the national Democratic party's
policy course—are in fact closely intertwined, for convenience we will attend only to the latter in this chapter.

When over the period of eight presidential elections, a
party which had been thought of as the majority wins only
half the time, secures an absolute majority of the popular
vote only twice, and gains only 48.7 percent of the two-
party presidential vote (compared to 51.3 percent for its
"minority" opponent)—there is a good prima facie case
that its days of ascendancy are over. This has been the fate
of the Democracy in the presidential elections of
1948–1976. The GOP won twice during this span with
Eisenhower, a candidate whose personal attributes were
so obviously disruptive of traditional party voting and
issue divisions. But it also won twice with Nixon, and
came very, very close on three other occasions with
Dewey, Nixon, and Ford.

The long secular decline of support for the national
Democratic party among southern whites was charted in
Chapter 3. Figure 5.1 shows the more recent falling off of
Democratic presidential support among other groups prominently associated with the New Deal majority. During
the Roosevelt era, manual workers, big city dwellers, and
Catholics, together with southern whites, consistently
gave much higher majorities to the Democratic presidential nominee than did the public at large. The country was
Democratic, and these groups were notably more Democratic than the country. By the elections of 1968 and 1972,
however, this Democratic margin had vanished. Blue-

collar whites, for instance, 12 percent more Democratic than the populace generally in the 1940 election, 12 percent more Democratic in 1948, by 1968 gave the Democrats a proportion of their ballots only 3 points higher than the entire electorate, and in 1972 were actually *4 points less Democratic than all voters.* We see a comparable decline in the relative margin of Democratic support among such overlapping groups as big city, working-class whites outside the South, and urban Catholic voters (Figure 5.1). Southern white Protestants, of course, showed the most dramatic reversal, moving from 26 percent more Democratic than the country generally in 1940 to 19 percentage points less Democratic in the election of 1972. Not only was the Democratic presidential vote nationally exceptionally low in the elections of 1968 and 1972, 43 and 38 percent respectively; but none of the groups of whites prominently associated with the New Deal majority—urban, blue-collar, Catholic, and southern—were significantly more Democratic than the national electorate, and some actually fell below the meager national standard.

One might be more inclined to dismiss the 1968 and 1972 vote distributions as products of an aberrational time were it not for the fact that they are revealed by Figure 5.1 as extensions of a secular trend. The Eisenhower years marked the transition point from the New Deal coalitions to those now emergent, just as it stands as a time of passage between the agenda of the industrial state and that of postindustrialism. The white South crossed the line, that is, became less Democratic than the country, after 1956. The Democratic drop-off there has been steady since the Eisenhower years. Among components of the old New Deal Democratic majority outside Dixie, however, 1960 saw a brief revival, when John F. Kennedy, a young charismatic contender of Catholic and urban North background, rallied the New Deal faithful one last time. For the northern white constituents of the Roosevelt majority, then, it is 1960 that is the aberrant election, running against what is otherwise a clear secular Democratic decline.

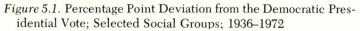

Figure 5.1. Percentage Point Deviation from the Democratic Presidential Vote; Selected Social Groups; 1936–1972

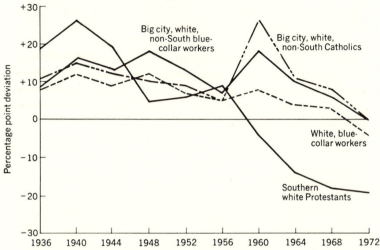

SOURCE: Data from following AIPO surveys: *1936*, 72, 104, 150, 177; *1940*, 208, 209, 215, 219, 248; *1944*, 328, 329, 336, 337; *1948*, 430, 431, 432, 433; *1952*, 506, 507, 508, 509; *1956*, 572, 573, 574, 576; *1960*, 635, 636, 637, 638; *1964*, 697, 699, 701, 702; *1968*, 769, 770, 771, 773; *1972*, 857, 858, 859, 860.

Data on the absolute vote distributions for the membership of these groups adds to what is provided by the relational data of Figure 5.1 in presenting a picture of the withering of the Democratic presidential majority. None of these pillars of the New Deal Democracy have given the Democrats a majority of their presidential ballots since 1964. Big city Catholics outside the South, for example, were just 49 percent Democratic in 1968, 38 percent in 1972. Blue-collar whites allotted just 44 percent of their ballots to Humphrey in 1968, only 34 percent to McGovern four years later. Trade union members voted decisively Republican in the 1972 presidential election, the first time in the history of the modern trade union movement (since passage of the Wagner Act, that is) that they gave majority support to the GOP.

Data on partisan self-identification of these old New Deal Democratic constituents provides still further indication of the Democratic presidential decline. Self-identification patterns are much more stable than those for presidential voting, of course, but they do shift; and our data indicate that not only are many of the strata which were primary supports of the New Deal Democratic majority now vastly less Democratic in their presidential voting, but also that they are much less inclined to think of themselves as Democratic. Fifty-one percent of white manual workers described themselves as Democrats in 1940 and the proportion held roughly the same over the next two decades—55 percent in 1948, 53 percent in 1952, and 57 percent in 1960. By 1968, however, the proportion Democratic for the first time dropped below the 50 percent line, to 46 percent, and in 1972 it stood at just 39 percent. In 1940, 65 percent of urban Catholics identified with the Democracy, and twenty years later the proportion was essentially constant at 71 percent; but it dropped to 50 percent in 1968, and again for the first time dipped below the 50 percent line in 1972, to just 45 percent. Three-fifths of southern white Protestants were describing themselves as Democrats as late as 1960, but in 1972 only 35 percent of this group continued to see themselves attached to their ancestral party.

The party identification data in Table 5.1 reveal short-term fluctuations as well as a long-term trend. The notable Democratic dip in 1972 occurred in part because of strong dissatisfaction with the McGovern candidacy throughout large segments of the old Democratic electorate. A more acceptable nominee would not only have received more votes, but would have helped maintain Democratic identification among these cohorts which once had been so strongly loyalist. Two years later, in contrast, McGovern's candidacy was fading from memory, and the national political climate was proving decidedly inhospitable to Republican growth. Watergate, inflation, and recession all redounded to the disadvantage of the incumbent

Table 5.1. Party Identification of Select Social Groups, 1940–1974
(as Percentages)

	1940	1952	1960	1968	1972	1974
BIG CITY, WHITE, BLUE-COLLAR WORKERS, OUTSIDE THE SOUTH						
Democratic	53	57	62	52	42	47
Republican	21	20	19	21	23	19
Independent	26	23	19	27	36	33
BLUE-COLLAR WHITES						
Democratic	51	53	57	46	39	46
Republican	29	25	26	22	24	21
Independent	20	22	17	32	37	33
BIG CITY CATHOLICS, OUTSIDE THE SOUTH						
Democratic	65	60	71	50	45	51
Republican	13	17	12	22	24	17
Independent	22	23	17	28	32	31
SOUTHERN WHITE PROTESTANTS						
Democratic	81	73	60	38	35	43
Republican	11	14	22	22	26	24
Independent	8	13	18	39	39	32

SOURCE: Data from following AIPO surveys: 1940, 177, 208, 209; 1952, 506, 507, 508, 509; 1960, 635, 636, 637, 638; 1968, 769, 770, 771, 773; 1972, 857, 858, 859, 860; 1974, 889, 897, 899, 903, 906.

administration and necessarily, then, to the Grand Old Party. The proportion of Democratic identifiers rose between 5 and 8 percentage points in each of the groups represented in Table 5.1. But such responses to proximate events should not obscure the basic underlying development: Big city whites, Catholics, blue-collar workers, and southern whites have been leaving the Democratic presidential party in elections of the postindustrial era, and they are much less inclined than they were during the New Deal years to think of themselves as Democrats.

There is no indication that this secular shift will be reversed. The mid-1970s Democratic revival shown in Table 5.1 brought the party back to roughly its 1968 standing among its old loyalists; it was still far behind its position of the 1940s and 1950s.

The collapse of the Democratic presidential majority does not require, of course, the ascension of a secure Republican majority. As subsequent analysis in this and the following chapter should make clearer, a new Republican majority neither exists nor appears in the offing.

How do we know that the sixties and early seventies are not an aberrational time in American national politics, in the sense of temporarily disrupting the regular flow of partisan competition? How do we know that James Sundquist is not right in his expectation that "the New Deal party system will be reinvigorated"? [1] Well, of course, we don't know for sure. But the overall partisan pattern we have begun to locate, one facet of which is the disappearance of Democratic supremacy in the presidential arena, appears very likely to persist. The falling off of Democratic support in many of its old bastions seems to have followed naturally from the transformations of conflict characteristic of postindustrialism. As working-class whites have moved up to middle-class status they have ceased to be a principal focal point of demands for equalitarian social change; and as such give less backing to the Democrats as the primary partisan instrument of liberal extensions than they did during the New Deal epoch when liberalism encompassed policies consonant with their interests. When the white South stands in resistance or reaction to a broad array of social and cultural changes which are promoted more by the national Democratic party than by its Republican counterpart, it is·inconceivable that this group would provide Democratic sustenance comparable to what they offered during the New Deal, when the resistance of the region to business nationalism coincided with the New

---

[1] Sundquist, *Dynamics of the Party System,* p. 373.

Deal Democratic attack on business ascendancy. When an urban white working class as an established but declining interest collectivity confronts blacks as a newly claimant and ascending force on the urban battleground, and when the national Democrats give decisively more support to the latter collectivity than do Republicans, it is inevitable that urban white backing for the national Democratic party will weaken. It seems virtually certain that the passing of regular and substantial Democratic support will be a long-time thing.

Urban whites, manual workers, Catholics, and southern whites were change-demanding groups in the agenda of the New Deal. And they supported the more change-initiating or liberal of the two major parties, the Democrats. In the postindustrial setting, these groups are relatively conservative—not in the New Deal sense of the term, of seeking to bring back the ascendancy of business nationalism and to dismantle the managerial state, but relatively resistant to components of social and cultural change, to extensions of equalitarianism. And it is because the Democrats are the prime partisan custodian of the new liberalism in national politics that they can no longer count upon the new white bourgeoisie for a high measure of electoral sustenance.

II. Inversion of the New Deal Class Order

We noted in Chapters 1 and 2 that class lines evidenced an unusually high salience in the electoral behavior of the New Deal and immediate post–New Deal years, and that cohorts of lower socioeconomic status were markedly more Democratic than the high status cohorts at that time than they have been since 1950.[2] While fully accurate, this pre-

[2] We pointed out (Chapter 1, pages 67–68) that the South stood out as an exception to this general relationship, with class differences in presidential voting in the region virtually nonexistent during the New Deal.

liminary commentary has severely understated the scope and significance of the transformation now occurring in the relationship of class to electoral choice.

Over the past decade there has been something of an inversion. We observed in the preceding chapter that the familiar New Deal relationship of social class and ideology has been dramatically altered. And now in many instances, groups at the top are as Democratic as those at the bottom—in some cases, more Democratic. We see some evidence of an emergent curvilinear pattern, with the top more Democratic than the middle but the middle less Democratic than the bottom.

Table 5.2 reviews the classic pattern of class voting as it persisted throughout the New Deal era and into the early 1960s. What had been well established as the traditional

Table 5.2. Democratic Percentage of the Presidential Ballots, White Voters by Socioeconomic Position, 1948–1972

	1948	1960	1968	1972
ALL				
High SES	30	38	36	32
Middle SES	43	53	39	26
Low SES	57	61	38	32
WOMEN				
High SES	29	35	42	34
Middle SES	42	52	40	25
Low SES	61	60	39	33
UNDER 30 YEARS OF AGE				
High SES	31	42	50	46
Middle SES	47	49	39	32
Low SES	64	52	32	36
College-educated	36	45	47	45
Noncollege	56	49	33	30

SOURCE: Data from following AIPO surveys: for *1948*, 430, 431, 432, 433; *1960*, 635, 636, 637, 638; *1968*, 769, 770, 771, 773; *1972*, 857, 858, 859, 860. High SES includes persons having upper white-collar and managerial occupations who have had college training. Middle SES includes persons having lower white-collar or skilled manual occupations. Low SES includes persons having semiskilled and unskilled occupations, service workers and farm laborers.

configuration held neatly for the several sets of groups represented in this table and indeed for all of the various socioeconomic status groupings which we can locate with survey data. Thirty-eight percent of whites of high socioeconomic status, for example, voted for Democratic nominee John Kennedy in 1960, compared to 53 percent for Kennedy among middle SES whites, and 61 percent of low status white voters. By 1968, the relationship had changed markedly. For the most part, the top gave a higher measure of backing to the relatively more liberal Democratic nominee than did the bottom. Humphrey was supported by 50 percent of high status whites under thirty years of age, but by only 39 percent of their middle SES age mates and by just 32 percent of young, low status electors. The newly emergent conformation was even clearer in 1972, when the somewhat distorting factor of the Wallace candidacy was removed. Among whites—for again blacks constitute a deviating case of voters disproportionately in the lower socioeconomic strata but overwhelmingly Democratic—those with college training were more Democratic than those who had not attended college; persons in the professional and managerial stratum were more Democratic than the semiskilled and unskilled work force; and so on. McGovern was backed by 45 percent of the college-educated young, but by only 30 percent of their age mates who had not entered the groves of academe. Comparing 1948 and 1972, we see a reversal of quite extraordinary proportions.

Table 5.2 also suggests the emergence of a curvilinear relationship between class and support for relatively more liberal as opposed to more conservative candidates. McGovern was weakest among the middling strata: among whites holding positions as skilled workers; among women of middle socioeconomic status; among young people holding positions as skilled manual workers. On the whole, McGovern's strength was greatest among those of high status, lowest within the ranks of the middling strata, and somewhat higher again in the lower reaches of the socioeconomic distribution.

Some qualification is in order. While a massive transformation of the relationship of class in voting has obviously occurred, the old pattern has not been everywhere obliterated. If blacks are included, the lower socioeconomic strata still appear more Democratic than the higher cohorts. Even within the white population, some distributions from the 1968 and 1972 presidential contests show the top more Republican than the bottom—although in all cases by a margin markedly reduced from that of the New Deal era. The proportion of professional and managerial whites backing McGovern was 3 points lower than that of blue-collar whites. On the other hand, comparing professionals alone (excluding businessmen) to manual workers, we find the former 4 percentage points more Democratic than the latter, the first time since the availability of survey data that this inversion has occurred. And for the first time in the span for which we have survey materials, the college educated in 1972 gave the Democratic nominee a higher percentage of their vote than did the noncollege population. So while there are some exceptions, depending upon how the high and low status publics are defined, an inversion of the New Deal relationship has indeed occurred.

Even though this inversion is most notable in presidential voting, the general *direction* of the shift is evident at other levels as well. In Table 5.3, we compare the congressional vote of the several socioeconomic strata for the elections of 1948, 1960, 1968, and 1972. There has been no overall falling off of Democratic congressional support, indicating the emergence of a two-tiered party system about which we will have more to say shortly. And the old class voting structure shows more persistence here than at the presidential level. The weakening of traditional class voting is still evident, however, especially among young voters. In 1947, just 36 percent of high status voters under thirty cast their ballots for Democratic congressional candidates, as against 66 percent of their low status age mates—a margin of 30 points between these two groups.

By 1968, the direction was the same—with those of low status more Democratic than their high status counterparts—but the margin had shrunk to just 8 points. In 1972, even the direction had shifted, as 60 percent of the high status young, 53 percent of their age mates of middle status, and only 51 percent of those of low status, cast ballots for Democratic congressional contenders.

Table 5.3. Democratic Percentage of the Congressional Ballots, White Voters by Socioeconomic Position, 1948–1972

	1948	1960	1968	1972
ALL				
High SES	33	46	42	48
Middle SES	49	60	51	49
Low SES	63	66	55	54
WOMEN				
High SES	35	41	42	48
Middle SES	49	57	49	45
Low SES	64	64	55	56
UNDER 30 YEARS OF AGE				
High SES	36	49	46	60
Middle SES	54	54	51	53
Low SES	66	59	54	51
College-educated	42	51	46	55
Noncollege	60	55	52	53

SOURCE: Data from following AIPO surveys: for *1948*, 430, 431, 432, 433; *1960*, 635, 636, 637, 638; *1968*, 769, 770, 771, 772; *1972*, 857, 858, 859, 860.

For some observers, the 1974 balloting showed the evanescent character of the forces which had contributed to inversion.[3] Yes, issues arose in the 1960s which divided

---

[3] See, for example, James L. Sundquist, "Hardly a Two-Party System," *Nation* (December 7, 1974), pp. 582–586. Sundquist believes the 1974 electoral results support an argument he had developed previously (*Dynamics of the Party System*), that the New Deal alignment remains essentially intact.

the populace along new lines, different from those of the
New Deal years, and thereby scrambled the old class-party
relationships. But the conflict of the 1960s lacked staying
power, according to this view, and it has faded as quickly
as it once arrived. By 1974, issues running coincident with
the basic line of cleavage of the New Deal party system
had reasserted themselves.

As soon as Vietnam, race questions, and the social issue gave way
to class questions and issues of governmental intervention in the
economy, the existing party system [that of the New Deal] took
on meaning once again. In 1974, the questions were whether
people were going to have jobs, whether their wages would keep
pace with the prices in the grocery store, whether oil company
projects were too high, who was going to bear the brunt of inflation and of taxes. These aroused class feelings. . . . Sensing that
they were threatened, people of traditional Democratic leanings
turned instinctively to *their* party.[4]

This argument contains a large element of truth—and a
fundamental flaw. It fails, in the first instance, to account
for what actually happened in the 1974 voting. Examining
the data in Table 5.4, we see that the Democrats *did* do exceptionally well among low status voters. Working-class
whites, who had deserted McGovern (although not the
congressional Democrats) in 1972, overwhelmingly endorsed Democratic candidates for House and Senate, and
those running for lower offices, in 1974. Economic worries, together with a Watergate reaction, did in fact submerge the social and cultural issues which were so prominent between 1964 and 1972.[5] Even in this time of
economic woe, however, when the economic dimension of
conflict loomed larger than it had in the preceding years,
there was no return to the class-party relationship of the
1930s and 1940s, even to that which persisted into the
early 1960s. The Democrats did not do as well among
whites of high socioeconomic status in 1974 as among low

---

[4] Sundquist, "Hardly a Two-Party System," p. 385.
[5] Gallup has provided survey confirmation of this. See *The Gallup
Opinion Index* (November 1974), especially pp. 1–2, 29–31.

status whites, but considering the circumstances they came remarkably close.

The contrast between the 1974 vote distributions and those of 1964—the great congressional landslide a decade earlier—is sharp. The Democrats did no better among middle to lower status voters in 1974 than in 1964, apparently not quite as well, but they bettered their performance markedly within the high status cohorts. While conditions in both elections evoked memories of the New Deal—some said Goldwater wanted to repeal it, and some felt we were entering anew in 1974 the situation which precipitated it—there was no reappearance of class voting in the more recent of the two contests. The distance between high and low status voters, immense in 1964, was modest a decade later. Indeed, where noncollege whites under thirty years of age were 18 percentage points more

Table 5.4. Democratic Percentage of the Congressional Ballots, White Voters by Socioeconomic Position, 1964 and 1974

	1964	*1974*
ALL		
High SES	48	57
Middle SES	65	62
Low SES	74	67
WOMEN		
High SES	44	60
Middle SES	64	61
Low SES	74	68
UNDER 30 YEARS OF AGE		
High SES	50	66
Middle SES	70	68
Low SES	74	73
College-educated	53	69
Noncollege	71	69

SOURCE: Data from following AIPO surveys: for *1964,* 697, 699, 701, 702; *1974,* 915, 916.

Democratic than their college-educated age mates in the
former election, there was no difference at all between the
vote of these two cohorts in 1974.

Nothing in the above commentary offers any comfort to
the Republicans. They were badly—almost identically, in
the overall percentages—beaten in the 1964 and 1974 congressional contests. The 1974 results actually seem a bit
more gloomy for the GOP, since the party lost even its old
base among high status voters, a base which had remained
relatively secure in the general Goldwater rout. It is essential to note that the Republicans lost *differently* in 1974
than during the New Deal era. The old New Deal coalitions were not put back together in the 1974 balloting. Indeed, the only thing which 1934 and 1974 appear to have
in common is that Democratic congressional candidates
trounced their Republican opponents on each occasion.
Can anyone seriously describe a contest in which Democrats secured the support of two-thirds of young, college-
trained, professional and managerial white voters as a
New Deal–type election?

We have another basic element in the disruption of the
New Deal alignment. In the party system which FDR
built, the top had been decisively more Republican than
the bottom. A structure of class voting was erected, remained intact and became natural. It was natural in the
context of the social group composition and political
agenda of the industrial state. It is in no sense natural in
postindustrial America. Among its other dimensions, the
contemporary realignment comprises an inversion of the
old class relationship in voting, an inversion first evident
at the presidential level but likely to penetrate the entire
range of electoral contests where broad policy issues can
intrude. Increasingly, Democratic performance at the top
of the socioeconomic ladder will approach, even surpass,
that at the bottom.

Nothing about this transition, momentous as it is, should
surprise any thoughtful observer. The position of the
lower socioeconomic strata as decidedly the most suppor-

tive of Democratic nominees derived from a particular social and political setting. The composition of contending interests, the ideological climate, the fabric of conflict, the very structure of the society, have now changed, requiring new electoral alignments.

If Marx has been stood on his head; if the top of the socioeconomic pyramid on the whole gives a higher measure of sustenance than does the bottom to the changes involving values, life styles, social relationships, and a range of extensions of equalitarianism, then it should give more backing to the national Democratic party than to its Republican opposition. For much more than the Republicans, the Democrats nationally, especially the wing which McGovern represented in his successful quest for the 1972 presidential nomination—a wing which may well be the most influential in the national Democratic party, in spite of Carter's 1976 success—serve as the partisan instrument for that varied array of social and political changes which we lump together under "extensions of liberalism."

Things are usually more complicated than they appear on the surface. Before leaving the inversion of the New Deal class-electoral relationship, we should offer an illustration of the turbulence that so commonly lies beneath the surface calm. We have noted that the college educated, so much more Republican than the electorate at large during the New Deal years, had by the late sixties and early seventies become at least as Democratic, and in fact it seems slightly more so, than the country. As Figure 5.2 suggests, however, this relatively straightforward if important transformation conceals a number of involved and in some cases contradictory lines of development.

In the years up through 1956, the college educated were indeed more Republican than the country—everywhere outside the South. College-educated southerners behaved politically like their other co-regionists: they were disproportionately Democratic. At this point, college-educated Americans below the Mason-Dixon line and those above it began moving in opposite directions. College-educated southerners became less Democratic than the national electorate in 1960 for the first time, and they continued their precipitous plunge through 1964. By that year, the southern line had crossed those for all three nonsouthern regions (Figure 5.2). And in 1964, college-educated voters in the Northeast became the first of their educational stratum, probably in American history, to be more supportive of a Democratic presidential nominee than the general public. By the late 1960s, college-educated northeasterners were providing Democratic presidential nominees with a notably higher level of backing than these nominees were receiving from the public generally. College-educated westerners manifest a progression line very much like those in the Northeast, only somewhat less so:

Figure 5.2. Percentage Point Deviation from the Democratic Presidential Vote, College Educated by Region of Residence, 1956–1972

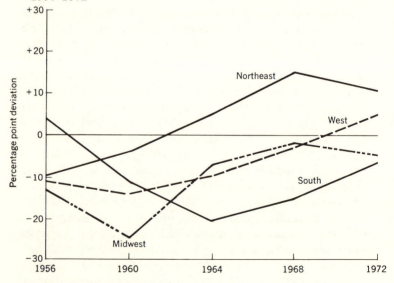

SOURCE: Data from following AIPO surveys: *1956*, 572, 573, 574, 576; *1960*, 635, 636, 637, 638; *1964*, 697, 699, 701, 702; *1968*, 769, 770, 771, 773; *1972*, 857, 858, 859, 860.

that is, they have become markedly more Democratic vis-
à-vis the public at large, but have not moved so far in this
direction as the northeastern contingent. By the late 1960s
and early 1970s, all four regional groups were moving up
in Democratic support compared to the country, but the
distributions were a crude inverse of what they had been
in the New Deal era. The northeastern college contingent
was now the most heavily Democratic, that from the South
the most Republican.

III. Erosions of the Republican Citizenry Party

If the Democrats have cause for concern, having lost
ground in the presidential arena, surrendering the majority
standing which was theirs during and immediately after
the New Deal; the Republican party's overall position is
much bleaker. Despite four presidential victories in the
last six elections, they have not only failed to achieve majority party status, but have less prospect of becoming the
majority than they entertained in the closing years of the
New Deal era.

In view of the general relationship between social
change and the opening of opportunities for a minority
party, a relationship widely perceived if often imperfectly
articulated, it is hardly surprising that many observers
began to sense a Republican opportunity in the 1950s.
American society obviously had changed in some very important regards since the New Deal. The ascension of the
industrial working classes, represented in the growth of
the trade union movement, had reached its apogee and
was about to decline. New middle classes were gaining
strength in numbers and influence. Could not the Republican party harness this change, ride to majority status on
the new middle class as it had on the growth of the business classes in the era of industrial nation building? Later
on, at the end of the 1960s, it was even more apparent that
the social conditions which sustained the New Deal alignment had receded into history. So some politicians and po-

litical commentators began thinking of "an emerging Republican majority." Kevin Phillips gave that phrase to his book, but the idea was already in the air. As we examine the data, there never was any indication that the Republicans were in fact attaining majority status. What was evident—and this is momentous enough—was that America was passing into a new social setting, with a new structure to political conflict, that basic realignment was inevitable, and that herein was an *opportunity* for the minority party.

The opportunity has not been seized. Responsibility for this failure does not rest exclusively with the Republican party. As we will discuss at length in the following chapter, the new party system, unlike the old, will not allow any coalition to entertain the type of majority status which the Republicans achieved around the turn of the century or which the Democrats subsequently attained. Part of the contemporary transformation involves partisan disaggregation, a broad secular weakening of party loyalties.

But the failure does rest partially with the Republican party, and with a leadership which was insensitive to the full dimensions of the changing societal arena. Our interest here is in describing the scope and content of changes involving the party coalitions, not in offering a primer for party leaders, so we will not attempt to deal in detail with the range of strategic miscalculations. It is relevant and appropriate to note that while Republican leaders "looked down"—observing, for example, the disaffection of white southerners and subsequently components of the working classes from the national Democratic party, they did not "look up" at the emergent political class or classes of the new society, at the latter's needs, interests, orientations, and expectations as to public life. Before the New Deal, the Republicans were the party of the American establishment, although that term was not applied then to the dominant business interests. Even during the New Deal era, the GOP remained an establishment party, in the sense that it held the loyalties of disproportionate numbers of those groups who controlled major social institutions, notably the economy. But as we have pointed out, entry into

postindustrialism has involved the ascendancy of new political classes, principally of a broad professional and managerial stratum, or with substantial overlap and a somewhat different perspective, a massive new intelligentsia.
The one opportunity for the Republicans to dramatically
strengthen their position required that they become the
primary partisan vehicle of these new political classes.
This they have not done. For the Republicans to have attained this position, it would have been necessary for
them to develop an ideological perspective, a public philosophy, which offers compelling answers to dominant
questions raised by the transformed society and polity. We
sometimes forget that the Republicans were the progressive party during the years of industrial nation building.
More than the Democrats, they offered a series of answers
that were consonant with the directions of social change.
The country was embarked upon industrial nation building. The Republicans offered a set of positions which were
supportive of that enterprise. They earned the allegiance,
thereby, of the political classes of the day.

Now, it is apparent to many that New Deal liberalism is
insufficient. The answers it yields are inadequate to the
demands of the new society. But the Republican leadership has not moved as far as its Democratic counterpart
toward articulating a new public philosophy reflective of
new concerns. Its position has been essentially reflective,
even reactionary in a literal sense, reacting against components of change which are disliked, but not producing an
alternative vision. The political classes of a new social setting look to a party whose basic appeal is progressive—in
the quite precise and limited sense of being consonant
with the flow of the societal change. This is natural
enough. Since the very ascendancy of the new classes is
the result of new directions the social system has taken,
they could hardly be expected to reward a party opposed
to these directions. If "progressive" means following the
line of development in which the society is progressing,
the political classes will always require a progressive
party. The Republicans have not become that.

As the composition of the American establishment has changed, the Republicans have seen their grip on the establishment weakened. Their hold on that loose array of groups and interests which might be said to exercise disproportionate influence in the society has slipped.

The evidence is all around. The intellectual community has grown in numbers and importance. But the Republican position has grown weaker, not stronger, within the intellectual community. There has been, we know, a long-standing tendency of intellectuals generally to be critics, and of American intellectuals to be socially critical from a generally liberal perspective.[6] So Republicans as the more conservative party have long had good reason not to expect the intellectual community to be one of their strongholds. But if generally liberal compared to the public at large, intellectuals and their apprentices are a variegated group, and they are for the most part among the advantaged rather than disadvantaged segments of the populace. During the New Deal era, there was substantial Republican support within the intellectual stratum. Over the last two decades, it has declined, rather than holding even or increasing.

In 1948, for example, college faculty were only 6 percentage points less Republican than the electorate generally. In 1972, however, presented with a potential opportunity as the positions of the Democratic nominee brought him into a cross-fire of intra-faculty arguments and alienated a substantial segment of traditionally liberal national Democrats, the Republicans wound up relatively much weaker among professors than they had been in the 1940s; the 1972 professorial vote was 18 percentage points below the Republican vote within the electorate at large.[7]

---

[6] For extensive analysis of this subject, see Ladd and Lipset, *The Divided Academy: Professors and Politics.*

[7] For further data and explanation of faculty voting, see Ladd and Lipset, *Academics, Politics and the 1972 Election* (Washington, D.C.: American Enterprise Institute for Public Policy Research, 1973), Chapters 3 and 4. See, too, by the same authors, *The Divided Academy,* Chapter 9.

Data on the politics of college students show a similar progression. S. M. Lipset has noted, for example, that Harvard University students, generally more liberal and Democratic than their counterparts at other campuses around the country, were solidly Republican in presidential preference up until the 1960s. The respectable straw-polls conducted by the *Harvard Crimson* indicated that Thomas Dewey was the choice of 56 percent of the Harvard student body in 1948, while just 25 percent favored Truman. In 1952 and 1956, Adlai Stevenson demonstrated considerable appeal in Harvard Yard, but he still ran behind Eisenhower in the university-wide student balloting. It was not until 1960 that a Democratic presidential nominee was recorded as the choice of a majority of Harvard students, when the *Crimson*'s straw-poll found Kennedy securing about three-fifths of the student vote. In the elections of 1964, 1968, and 1972 the Harvard student body, so solidly Republican during the New Deal when Harvard alumnus Franklin D. Roosevelt was the popular Democratic standard-bearer, supported the Democratic presidential nominees by overwhelming margins.[8] Harvard is certainly part of the American intellectual establishment, and probably most would concede it to be part of the American establishment generally, a training ground for so many of the top leaders of government, business, science, the arts, and culture. Through the New Deal, its student body was Republican. By the 1970s, Harvard students have become strongly Democratic.

While the absolute distributions are different from

---

[8] For a discussion of the Harvard student straw vote historically, see Lipset, "Political Controversies at Harvard," in Lipset and Riesman, *Education and Politics at Harvard* (New York: McGraw-Hill, 1975), Chapter 8. There have been changes in the social group composition of the Harvard student body since World War II, of course, but these are not sufficient to account for the partisan shift. The representation of blacks has increased, but blacks remain less than 10 percent of Harvard students. The proportion Jewish is about the same now as in 1948. Harvard students are still an enormously privileged group, in terms of social background, compared to the public at large.

campus to campus, the student populations of the 1930s and 1940s had been generally Republican, following the normal class distributions of the time: groups of higher socioeconomic status tended to be Republican, and college students were drawn largely from the middle and upper-middle classes. During the Eisenhower years, as well, students were solidly Republican in presidential politics, supporting Eisenhower by margins well in excess of the general public.[9] By the late 1960s, however, the national college student population was decisively Democratic—or, more precisely, heavily anti-Republican, since large numbers of students were self-described independents consistently voting against Republican presidential nominees. Gallup found a marked drop-off in Republican allegiance among students continuing during the late sixties and early seventies. In 1966, 26 percent of college students described themselves as Republicans, 35 percent as Democrats, and 39 percent as independents; by 1970, Republican identifiers in the student population had declined to 18 percent, compared to 30 percent self-described Democrats and a massive 52 percent independents; and in 1974, the Republican proportion stood at its all-time low of 14 percent, as against 37 percent Democratic, and 49 percent in the independent category.[10] Among graduate students, an almost unbelievably low proportion of 9 percent identified with the GOP, while 43 percent thought of themselves as Democrats, and 48 percent as independents.[11] A 1972 CBS election day survey found 54 percent of students in the 18–24 category voting for McGovern, 16 points higher than the proportion among the public at large.[12] Gallup reported in October 1972 that 68 percent of graduate students planned to vote for

---

[9] For supporting data, see Lipset and Ladd, "College Generations: From the 1930's to the 1960's," *Public Interest*, 25 (Fall 1971), pp. 105–109.

[10] *The Gallup Opinion Index*, No. 109 (July 1974), p. 15.

[11] *Ibid.*

[12] CBS News Election Day Survey, data made available to the Social Science Data Center, University of Connecticut, courtesy of CBS News.

McGovern, compared to just 31 percent for the Republican incumbent Richard Nixon.[13]

These current distributions are really quite extraordinary. Not only are college students an important component of the intelligentsia, but from their ranks will come the bulk of the leadership of all of the principal institutions in the United States. When only 14 percent of all students and just 9 percent of graduate students profess an affinity for the Republican party, the extent of the latter's decline, and even more the scope of its potential decline, among the political classes becomes evident.

And the position of the GOP is even bleaker than these data suggest. Among students at major colleges and universities, Republican electoral support falls below that within the general student population. For both faculty and students, the most prestigious and influential sectors are the most solidly Democratic.[14]

What we have noted for students and faculty and other segments of the intellectual community applies in all essential regards to the higher and ascendant socioeconomic strata in the United States. Earlier in this chapter, we noted the inversion of the old New Deal class relationship, one element of which is the contemporary position of high socioeconomic status white voters as more supportive of Democratic presidential nominees than their middle and lower SES counterparts. Data on partisan identification and congressional vote from the New Deal through to the present demonstrate even more sharply the dramatic decline of Republican backing among the higher status cohorts.

In Figures 5.3 and 5.4, we compare the Democratic and Republican proportions of party self-identification and congressional vote throughout the New Deal era and into the contemporary period, for three groups of high socioeconomic status, all of which have expanded greatly as the

---

[13] *The Gallup Opinion Index,* No. 88 (October 1972), p. 3.
[14] For supporting data and analysis, see Ladd and Lipset, *The Divided Academy,* Chapters 5 and 9.

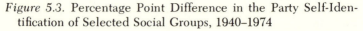

Figure 5.3. Percentage Point Difference in the Party Self-Identification of Selected Social Groups, 1940–1974

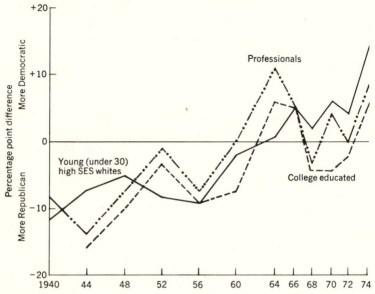

SOURCE: Data from following AIPO surveys: *1940*, 208, 209; *1944*, 328, 329; *1948*, 430, 431, 432, 433; *1952*, 506, 507, 508, 509; *1956*, 572, 573, 574, 576; *1960*, 635, 636, 637, 638; *1964*, 697, 699, 701, 702; *1966*, 724, 729, 737; *1968*, 769, 770, 771, 773; *1970*, 814, 815, 816, 817; *1972*, 857, 858, 859, 860; *1974*, 889, 897, 899, 903, 906.

society has moved into postindustrialism. The college educated, people employed in professional occupations, and young whites of high socioeconomic status—defined as the college educated employed in professional and managerial positions—are not the only representations of the high socioeconomic strata and the intelligentsia which we could make, but they faithfully illustrate developments occurring in the larger stratum.[15]

---

[15] A word concerning how these figures should be interpreted is very much in order. We are presenting survey materials, and it must be borne in mind that even the most carefully executed survey investigations contain a significant margin of error, especially when one looks at subgroups within the sample population. The finding contained in Figure 5.4 that young high status whites voted for Republican over Democratic congressional candidates in 1952 by a margin of 33 percentage points—66 per-

Figure 5.4. Percentage Point Difference in the Congressional Voting of Selected Social Groups, 1940–1974

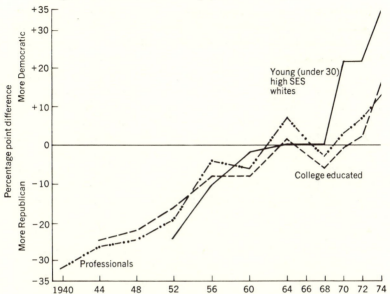

SOURCE: Data from following AIPO surveys: *1940*, 208, 209; *1944*, 328, 329; *1948*, 430, 431, 432, 433; *1952*, 506, 507, 508, 509; *1956*, 572, 573, 574, 576; *1960*, 635, 636, 637, 638; *1964*, 697, 699, 701, 702; *1966*, 724, 729, 737; *1968*, 769, 770, 771, 773; *1970*, 814, 815, 816, 817; *1972*, 857, 858, 859, 860; *1974*, 915, 916.

cent Republican, 33 percent Democratic, 1 percent for minor party candidates—should be taken only as an indication of the strongly Republican direction to the group's vote. The margin in the "real world" may have been 35 percent, may have been 25 percent. So these graphs covering a period of three and one half decades should be read as faithful indicators of general directions, but not of precise magnitudes. We have attempted to reduce the margin of error by combining a number of surveys for each year, thus in effect increasing the size of the sample upon which the distributions are based.

It should also be noted that the figures reveal the effects of short-term as well as long-term changes. In 1964, for example, with the Democrats basking in the high popularity which the Johnson administration temporarily entertained and with the Republicans burdened by the Goldwater candidacy, Democratic congressional candidates reaped gains among virtually all social groups in the population including those represented in our graphs. Here, we are not especially interested in these short-term movements, but with the larger progression over time, a progression reflective of transformations of the American sociopolitical setting.

One basic fact comes through with absolute clarity from the data presented in these two figures: groups of high socioeconomic status were solidly Republican throughout the New Deal era; sometime around the end of the 1950s and early 1960s, there was a pronounced move toward the Democrats. In 1964, for the first time, Democrats outnumbered Republicans (in terms of self-identification) throughout many high SES cohorts, and majorities of these groups backed Democratic congressional candidates. While there was some temporary falling off in Democratic support among these groups immediately after 1964, the overall secular progression has not been interrupted. Substantial portions of the high socioeconomic strata in the United States are consistently displaying absolute Democratic majorities in both self-identification and congressional balloting.[16]

Particularly ominous for the long-run prospects of the GOP is the disaffection of young high status whites. During the New Deal era, this group was solidly, indeed in many instances massively, Republican. By the mid-1970s, it has become solidly, indeed massively Democratic. These voters will grow older, of course, and perhaps relatively more conservative, swinging somewhat toward the Republicans, apart from what happens as a result of changing issues and changing party positions. But Figures 5.3 and 5.4 make clear that we are dealing with a long-term secular shift, not simply an artifact of Watergate. The Republicans have lost their grip on the American establishment, most notably among young men and women of relative privilege. They have lost it, we know, in large part because the issue orientations which they manifest are somewhat more conservative than the stratum favors. More generally, they have lost it because they appear an essentially reactive party, even more than the Democrats lack-

---

[16] Not all high SES groups show Democratic majorities, of course. People in the very highest income groups—over $25,000 a year—and business executives, still display Republican majorities, although the extent of the GOP advantage has been reduced even here.

ing a public philosophy suited to the demands of the times.

The Republicans are unable even to exploit fully this reactive stance. As Kevin Phillips and other proponents of a neopopulist, "new conservative" Republican party have noted, the GOP's leaders and activists represent far too narrow a slice of the socioeconomic and the ethnic-religious spectrums. At the activist level, the Republicans remain remarkably the party of upper-middle–class white Protestants. The party is especially poorly equipped in style and tone to articulate the frustrations of the newer, emergent American petit bourgeoisie—southern white Protestant, Catholic, black, and the like.

At times, notably between 1966 and 1972, when social issue resentment has been greatest, Republican candidates have been beneficiaries of it. But the party's leadership, national and local, appears very uncomfortable with the constituents of George Wallace and the "cop candidates." Some conservatives now speculate that the symbol *Republican* puts off many natural supporters of a conservative party and hence that the symbol should be scrapped. In fact, it isn't the symbol but the social composition of the party, especially the composition of the party's leadership cohorts, which puts off these putative supporters.

The Republicans won four of the six presidential elections between 1952 and 1972, and narrowly missed winning a fifth, in 1960. But as Figures 5.5 and 5.6 demonstrate, the GOP has occupied a weak position everywhere outside presidential voting. The Democrats have had a big edge in congressional seats. With the exception of 1966–1968, they have controlled the large majority of the governorships over the last decade and a half. Voting for candidates for the House of Representatives has without exception gone in the Democrats' favor. Comparing Figures 5.5 and 5.6 to Figures 3.7 and 3.9 (pp. 152, 158) we see that outside presidential voting the Republican position in the 1960s and 1970s has been weaker than at any point during the New Deal era, except the years immedi-

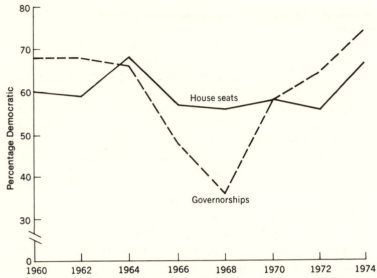

Figure 5.5. Democratic Percentage of U.S. House of Representatives Seats and Governorships, 1960–1974

SOURCE: U.S. Bureau of the Census, *Statistical Abstract of the United States: 1966*, 377; *1970*, 366; *1974*, 431, 434; *Congressional Directory*, *1975*, pp. 216, 415.

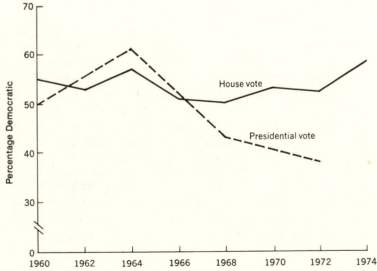

Figure 5.6. Democratic Percentage of the Popular Vote for President and U.S. House of Representatives, 1960–1974

SOURCE: U.S. Bureau of the Census, *Statistical Abstract of the United States: 1974*, p. 422; the 1974 data were compiled from the official voting returns as reported in the *Congressional Directory*, *1975*, pp. 406–412.

Figure 5.7. Distribution of Party Identifiers, 1960–1974

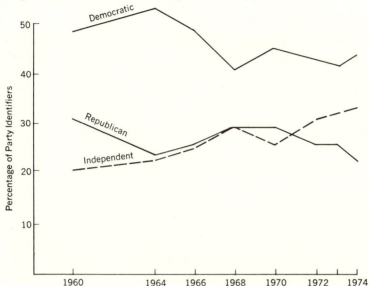

SOURCE: Data from the following AIPO surveys: *1960*, 635, 636, 637, 638; *1964*, 697, 698, 699, 701; *1966*, 724, 729, 737; *1968*, 768, 769, 770, 771; *1970*, 814, 815, 816, 817; *1972*, 852, 853, 854, 855, 856, 857; *1973*, 862, 863, 875, 876; *1974*, 889, 897, 899, 903, 906.

ately following the economic collapse of the Great Depression.

Data on party self-identification reveals a similar Republican weakness and decline. Figure 5.7 shows that both the Democrats and the Republicans had their ups and downs over the past decade and a half, with the Democratic margin over the GOP larger around the Johnson-Goldwater years, smaller at the time of Nixon's two presidential victories, and larger again after Watergate. The only line going steadily up over this span is that for independents, whose numbers increased rather dramatically, from 20 percent of the total electorate in 1960 to 33 percent in 1974. Still, the margin between Democrats and Republicans in terms of their respective proportions of all identifiers, was greater over the 1960–1974 period than at any time during the New Deal era.

IV. The Two-Tiered Party System

The Democrats have become far more vulnerable in presidential politics than they were during the New Deal era; there has been a dramatic inversion of the New Deal relationship of class and vote; and the Republican party, despite presidential victories, has seen its overall electoral position deteriorate, especially within the burgeoning ranks of the professionals and the college educated. All of these are important components of the contemporary realignment. There is yet another factor implicit in the materials which we have presented, that electoral behavior centered around the presidency differs sharply from that in other sectors, such as congressional voting, or the party self-identification of the citizenry. Over the last decade, the United States has had in effect a two-tiered party system, with one pattern applying at the presidential level and another everywhere else. The Republicans have had notable success in the presidential arena, winning four of the last eight contests, winning the 1972 election by the largest margin a minority party has ever obtained in American history, and the second largest margin anyone has ever achieved, and recovering sufficiently from the Watergate debacle so as to come within an eyelash of victory in the 1976 presidential sweepstakes. But outside presidential contests, the Democrats look like a majority party. What has happened? Is the present situation likely to persist?

For one thing, presidential contests have become the principal electoral arena in which broad policy or ideological differences are fought out. After examining a body of survey data on the bases of electoral choice, Gerald Pomper oberved that "in the last decade, after a series of political shocks, ideological conflict has been resurrected, and consensus has been severely disrupted, if not destroyed. Basic issues have been raised again, and the electorate has shown itself able to comprehend and respond to such conflicts." [17] With the political system in turmoil, and with contending candidates taking stands on the various issues which are reasonably clear and which matter to large numbers of voters, one finds a very substantial correlation between the issue orientation of voters and their candidate choice. Nie and Andersen found a much higher level of ideological constraint among political attitudes in the mass public in the late 1960s and early 1970s than there had been in the 1950s, and concluded that this change resulted from a much higher saliency of politics.[18] Nie and Andersen offer essentially the same interpretation as Pomper did: The electorate has been presented recently with the picture of a society in flux, with all sorts of important issues; and when candidates have taken clear positions on these issues a high correlation between political attitudes and the vote naturally emerged.

We agree. But it is important to note that what Pomper, Nie and Andersen, and others are describing applies largely to the presidential arena. Individual gubernatorial, senatorial, and congressional contests may manifest highly salient ideological divisions between contenders, but below the presidential level one cannot locate anything approaching coherent Democratic and Republican positions on the great issues of the day. In particular, the great social and cultural issues comprising the political agenda of postindustrialism, then, have dominated presidential voting, but appear only marginally and imperfectly to have left an imprint in other sectors of electoral choice. The presidency serves as the one coherent policy office. Presidential elections, not those for Congress, have functioned as referenda on the most divisive new issues spun off from the structure of contemporary conflict.

In the 1964 presidential contest, Lyndon Johnson and

---

[17] Gerald M. Pomper, "From Confusion to Clarity: Issues and American Voters, 1956–1968 *American Political Science Review*, 66 (June 1972), p. 427

[18] Nie with Andersen, "Mass Belief Systems Revisited: Political Change and Attitude Structure," pp. 571–578.

Barry Goldwater presented the American electorate with a clear ideological choice, and voters responded. The Goldwater position was rejected by a large majority of the electorate, and Johnson received a higher percentage of the total vote cast than any other candidate for president in American history. Eight years later, Richard Nixon was reelected with 60.8 percent of the popular vote, the second highest proportion of the total ever to go to one candidate. This massive alternation in eight years, from a record landslide Democratic victory to a record landslide Republican triumph occurred in part because the electorate has been cut loose from traditional ties to party and is behaving more independently, in part because a new dynamic to American electoral politics encourages—which is not to say dictates—presidential candidacies which are ideologically distinct and thereby have a high potential for coming up decidedly minoritarian. In any case, the 1964 and 1972 presidential results occurred largely in the context of candidates and issues, not parties. Nixon's 1972 triumph was not a Republican victory, nor was Johnson's 1964 landslide a Democratic party mandate. With the prominence of issues, and with a presidential system, in contrast to a cabinet-type executive, which focuses on the major party contenders as individuals, results like those of 1964 and 1972—massive alternating landslides—can readily occur.

It is not by chance, however, that recent presidential contests have seen an edge for candidates put forth on the Republican label. The country has been in the midst of extraordinary changes, and large segments of the white bourgeoisie, including many who in the 1930s were associated with the Democratic working class, have adopted a position of resistance if not reaction. There has been too much cultural change, too fast. There have been demands for an extension of equalitarianism, as in the area of race relations, perceived to go beyond the bounds of what is proper. In short, a white bourgeoisie, possessed of a desire to preserve a position deemed broadly satisfactory against demands for change considered excessive, has in a manner

not uncommon to such middling classes in the twentieth
century, adopted a kind of positional conservatism. They
have not, as such observers as Louis Harris and Ben Wattenberg have pointed out, sought a return to policy positions rejected in the course of the development of the New
Deal.[19] But they have said, "go slower," confronted with a
social and political passage of unusual scope and rapidity.
There has been, then, a neopopulistic—for the white
bourgeoisie contains the many, not the few—resistance to
components of change, a resistance centered in presidential contests rather directly and only in scattered instances
and hence in a confused melange in electoral contests
below the presidency. Of the two major parties, only the
national Democratic alignment is capable of producing
nominees who invite neopopulist resistance on the
grounds that they are too supportive of social and cultural
change. The Republicans have been well situated to generate candidates able to harness at least in part this neopopulist resistance. The result has been a presidential party
system in which contests have not really been determined
by party at all, but which has nonetheless tended to favor
nominees under the Republican banner.

Things are very different below the presidential level.
Both the Democratic and Republican congressional
parties, for example, manifest an extraordinarily diverse
ideological array. A Democrat running in New York can
take one set of positions, while his counterpart in South
Carolina can fashion a very different appeal. Ideological
choices are indeed presented in many of the subpresidential contests, but the Democratic party has found it easy to
avoid location on the newer social and cultural issues such
as to invite any uniform neopopulist retaliation. The Republicans have not experienced, at the congressional or
gubernatorial levels, for example, anything comparable to

---

[19] Harris, *The Anguish of Change;* and Wattenberg, *The Real America*
(Garden City, N.Y.: Doubleday, 1974).

the opportunity which the McGovern candidacy offered
them in the 1972 presidential voting.

With personalities less distinctinctly emphasized than in
the presidential arena, and with the ideological divisions
thrown up by the new agenda far more blurred and ambiguous, subpresidential contests have turned on older issues,
and older underlying images of the parties. During the
New Deal, the Democrats achieved the reputation as the
party better able to manage the American economy and to
sustain prosperity. The Republicans have never succeeded
in dislodging this popular conception. Gallup has regularly asked his survey respondents which party they believed to be best able and most likely to keep the country
prosperous, and with very few exceptions over the last
three decades has found the Democrats enjoying a wide
margin in favorable responses. Thus, in November 1951,
37 percent of the respondents named the Democrats as the
party most likely to keep the country prosperous, compared to 29 percent naming the Republicans; in February
1958, the margin was 47 percent to 22 percent; in January
1963, 46 percent to 21 percent; in February 1966, 48 percent to 19 percent; in September 1970, 40 percent to 25
percent; and in April 1974, 49 percent to 19 percent—in
each instance with the majority favoring the Democrats.[20]

None of the new divisions which have followed entry
into postindustrialism have been or are likely to be disruptive of these perceptions. The Republican party may lend
itself to neopopulistic appeals in the social and cultural
arenas, but it has remained economically elitist—relatively
more supportive of interests associated with economic
privilege.

The presidency by its exceptional prominence in American political life has become the focal point around which
struggles over new items entering the political agenda
have been joined. The neopopulist resentments and resis-

---

[20] *The Gallup Opinion Index,* No. 88 (October 1972), p. 16; and *The
Gallup Opinion Index,* No. 106 (April 1974), p. 17.

tance of the white middle classes have invited representation through Republican presidential candidacies. But
Congress and state administrations have not been drawn
as prominently into these social and cultural cleavages;
where they have been brought in, it has not been easy to
locate a general pattern of party responsibility. Big city
mayors have been engulfed by the new cleavages, but the
impact on the national party system has been minimal.
Older images of the parties, rooted in the New Deal era,
have continued to loom large in congressional voting,
then, and the general perception that the Democrats are
"better for prosperity" has unquestionably worked to
maintain that party's congressional majority.

So, too, has the fact that party means much more in congressional than in presidential voting, because personalities are less prominent, because candidates can accommo-
date themselves to the wishes of local districts and thus
avoid the disruptive impact on traditional party loyalties
which national issues sometimes entail. In 1975, a large
majority of the southern congressional delegation is still
Democratic, even though the white South has repudiated
the national Democratic party since 1964.

Finally, it appears likely that the Democrats have retained ascendancy at subpresidential levels because they
have a broader leadership base on which to draw. Recruit-
ment for presidential candidates is hardly a matter of numbers. Only one per party is required every four years. But
as one moves throughout the various state and local contests, the relative thickness or thinness of a party's leadership cadre can be crucial. The fact that the upper socioeconomic classes have moved toward the Democrats,
especially that the intellectual stratum has become decisively Democratic, would suggest a broader leadership
base for Democrats than for Republicans at subpresidential levels.

However this may be, a prominent feature of the re-
aligned party system is its two-tiered structure. There is no
majority party at the presidential level, but disaffection

from the Democrats stemming from that party's leadership in areas of social and cultural change, coupled with Republican success in articulating neopopulist resistance and resentment, has produced a situation in which contenders running under the GOP label are at least competitive. Outside presidential politics, the Democrats operate as the majority party. Their base has changed somewhat from the New Deal era, as they have lost ground among some of their old constituencies, such as trade unionists, big city whites, and southern whites; while they have made up for such losses with gains among the burgeoning upper–middle-class cohorts.

There is some indication that Americans are not unhappy with the operations of a two-tiered party system. In 1972, for example, they returned a Republican incumbent to the presidency with a record landslide, while increasing the already substantial Democratic majorities in Congress and among the governorships. The 1976 elections produced a similar, massive disparity between presidential and subpresidential voting. The Democrats' big congressional victories can be attributed in part to the advantages of incumbency in the age of weak party loyalties, but there is more to it than that. Surveys conducted by Gallup, Yankelovich, Harris, among others, show that in the month or two before the November 2, 1976, elections, large numbers of people were prepared to vote for Gerald Ford and then, in an almost abstract fashion, would choose "the Democratic candidate" for Congress.

How much does the populace perceive a certain functionality in the two-tiered system, whereby resistance to social and cultural change deemed excessive is expressed in balloting for its great national fulcrum, the presidency; while general support for extending the managerial/welfare state is sustained by maintaining the Democratic majority at the subpresidential level? The question cannot be satisfactorily answered from available information. What seems most likely is that component groups of the New Deal majority, notably the white working-classes-now-middle-class, are genuinely torn and ambivalent before contradictory demands of the new agenda. They appear to reject a perceived overenthusiasm within segments of the national Democratic party for social and cultural transformations; while at the same time rejecting the old and persisting economic elitism of the Republicans. The two-tiered party system becomes the vehicle, however consciously or unconsciously, for expressing this ambivalence.

V. A Note on Continuities

One of the recurring problems of studies which treat realignment is that they are led by their emphasis upon things which are new to understate the prominence of continuities from the old. This is understandable. To examine a realignment is to consider those things which set the partisan present apart from the past. Still, every realignment in American political history has comprised continuities as well as change, and it is good that we remind ourselves of the former lest we create unrealistic expectations about the magnitude of change. Important components of the New Deal alignment continue into the contemporary realignment, just as the New Deal party coalitions borrowed heavily from alignment patterns which took shape during the era of Republican ascendancy. *Beaucoup de choses changent, beaucoup restent pareil* is an apt depiction of the realigning process.

Business is still markedly more Republican than labor, although not as much so as during the New Deal. Young voters (under thirty years of age) have given Democratic presidential candidates a higher proportion of their ballots than the more senior electors (those over fifty years of age) in every presidential election since 1932—indicating a persistently higher backing for the more liberal and change-favoring party among the young, and a relative conservatizing with age.

Black voters, we have noted, moved into the Democratic

coalition during the New Deal, and they have remained there. Blacks now provide the Democrats, in both presidential and congressional contests, with a higher measure of support than any other identifiable ethnic collectivity. In the 1972 presidential balloting, blacks backed McGovern by a margin of roughly four to one (82 percent to 18 percent, according to the 1972 CBS Election Day Survey), and they supported Democratic congressional candidates by a margin of better than nine to one. Class differences in voting are small within the black electorate in presidential politics, but higher status black voters show up consistently more Republican than those of lower socioeconomic status. In 1972, 80 percent of black Americans in white-collar positions backed McGovern, compared to 86 percent of those employed as blue-collar workers.

Jews are another group who came heavily into the Democratic camp during the New Deal and who have remained there. There was considerable discussion in 1972 about a Jewish defection from McGovern, supposedly in part because of the association of his candidacy with support for quotas—going back to McGovern Commission recommendations, implemented for the 1972 Convention, which provided de facto quotas for blacks, women, and young people, groups markedly underrepresented in all previous Democratic quadrennial conclaves. As a group which had so often seen quotas turned against them, Jews were seen reacting negatively against McGovern because of his link to a kind of quota system. Then, too, the Israeli government was unusually direct in making known its preference for a Nixon victory, and it lobbied on Nixon's behalf with leaders of the American Jewish community. However important these considerations may have been in leading some Jews to reject McGovern's candidacy, the American Jewish electorate on the whole remained notably faithful to the Democratic side. According to the 1972 CBS News Election Day Survey, which contained a larger sampling of Jews (641) than any other single study, 65 percent of Jews backed McGovern, a proportion 27 points higher than the Democratic candidate's support in the electorate at large.

For well over a century, Catholics have shown a higher measure of allegiance to the Democracy than white Protestants outside the South. For much of this period, the Democrats gave something concrete to the ethnocultural groups we describe by one of their characteristics, *Catholic*. When they made Alfred E. Smith, an Irish Catholic, their presidential nominee in 1928, they extended recognition, acceptance, and legitimacy. With the New Deal, Catholic ethnocultural attachments to the Democracy were reinforced by economic attachments, since most Catholics were in the economic classes which benefited most from the new social policies. By the 1960s, however, the position of Catholics in American life had changed. Many had moved up the economic ladder, had become haves rather than have-nots. Perhaps even more important, most Catholics were no longer have-nots in status terms, having gained a large measure of acceptance into national life.

It is not surprising, then, that some Republican strategists such as Kevin Phillips (*The Emerging Republican Majority*) saw the Catholic vote "ripe for picking," and suggested that Catholic voters could be brought in large numbers to the Republican standard. Some such movement clearly has occurred, as with Irish Catholics in New York. But overall, as Figures 5.8–5.10 show, the historic gulf between the electoral attachments of Catholics and white non-South Protestants has not diminished notably. Catholics were as much more Democratic than the electorate at large in the 1972 congressional voting as they had been in 1948; and white Protestants outside Dixie backed Republican congressional candidates as heavily, compared to the general public, in the 1972 voting as they had a quarter of a century earlier. Indeed, with the exception of the 1960 elections, when Kennedy's candidacy produced a short-term Protestant-Catholic polarization, the graph lines comparing Protestant and Catholic congressional voting to that of the total electorate have not been essentially flat. In terms of partisan self-identification, Catholics were more Democratic than the public at large in the late 1960s and early 1970s, by a margin roughly comparable to that of the New Deal years.

In presidential balloting, we find a slight relative lessening of Catholic preference for Democratic nominees. Catholics lost some of their electoral distinctiveness in the Eisenhower years, became massively more Democratic than the total electorate in the 1960 Kennedy election, then returned to the Eisenhower level again. The margin by which Catholic and white non-South Protestant voters were differentiated in 1972 was smaller than in any preceding presidential election for which we have survey data, and quite probably smaller than in any preceding contest over the past century.

Still, the main conclusion which Figures 5.8–5.10 sustain is that Protestant-Catholic electoral distinctiveness has persisted. Catholic voters continue to back the Democracy more heavily than does the entire electorate; and Protestants, blacks excepted, everywhere outside the South (and now in presidential politics within Dixie as well) are consistently more faithful to the Grand Old Party than the remainder of the electorate.

VI. Toward a Conclusion

As we have moved from the New Deal party system to that of the postindustrial era, we find continuities aplenty, the persistence of many traditional patterns in social group distributions. Changes defining the new party system are nonetheless impressive. The New Deal class relationship, in which higher status groups were more Republican and lower status more Democratic, has been substantially although still incompletely inverted. The supremacy which the Democrats enjoyed in presidential politics throughout the New Deal era has gone, partly through a dramatic increase in independent electoral behavior, partly as constit-

Figure 5.8. Percentage Point Deviation from the National Democratic Congressional Vote, 1940–1974

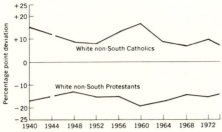

SOURCE: Data from the following AIPO surveys: *1940*, 215; *1948*, 430, 431; *1952*, 506, 507, 508, 509; *1956*, 572, 573, 574, 576; *1960*, 635, 636, 637, 638; *1964*, 697, 699, 701, 702; *1968*, 769, 770, 771, 773; *1972*, 857, 858, 859, 860; *1974*, 915, 916.

Figure 5.9. Percentage Point Deviation from the Proportion of All Votes Identifying as Democrats, 1940–1974

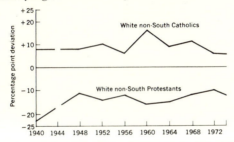

SOURCE: Data from following AIPO surveys: *1940*, 208, 209; *1948*, 430, 431, 432, 433; *1952*, 506, 507, 508, 509; *1956*, 572, 573, 574, 576; *1960*, 635, 636, 637, 638; *1964*, 697, 699, 701, 702; *1968*, 769, 770, 771, 773; *1972*, 857, 858, 859, 860; *1974*, 889, 897, 899, 903, 906.

Figure 5.10. Percentage Point Deviation from the National Democratic Presidential Vote, 1940–1972

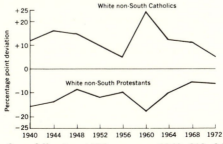

SOURCE: Data from following AIPO surveys: *1940*, 219, 248; *1944*, 328, 329, 336, 337; *1948*, 430, 431, 432, 433; *1952*, 506, 507, 508, 509; *1956*, 572, 573, 574, 576; *1960*, 635, 636, 637, 638; *1964*, 697, 699, 701, 702; *1968*, 769, 770, 771, 773; *1972*, 857, 858, 859, 860.

uent groups of the old New Deal coalition have defected before new cleavages brought about by social and cultural issues now crowding the agenda. But the Republic base remains weak, and the GOP's claim on the loyalty of high status groups is weaker than it ever was in the New Deal years. A two-tiered party system has emerged, with the presidential and subpresidential levels reflecting different electoral alignments.

There are yet other features of the parties-elections system, apart from the alignment of social groups, which have changed and thus help define the contemporary partisan transformation. Before turning to these in Chapter 7, however, we should examine in some detail the voting patterns of 1976. Are the alignments which we located against the backdrop of 1968 and 1972 still evident?

6

On the 1976 Elections

"The Old New Deal Coalitions": Requiescant in Pace

Much of the commentary which followed immediately upon the 1976 elections stressed "restoration." That legendary creature, "The Old New Deal Democratic Coalition"—and hence, presumably, its equally fabled though less illustrious Republican antagonist—had been put back together "one more time." Thus, *Newsweek* insisted that "Jimmy Carter's victory was not a personal triumph: he won because of the revival of the old coalition that first sent Franklin D. Roosevelt to the White House in 1932. . . ." [1] *Congressional Quarterly* asserted that "Carter won by welding together varying proportions of Roosevelt's New Deal coalition—the South, the industrial Northeast, organized labor, minorities, and the liberal community." [2] Writing in the *New York Times*, Robert Reinhold concluded that "Jimmy Carter, in the final analysis, won the presidency by holding together the basic elements of the old Democratic coalition, drawing back many of those who had strayed in recent years. . . ." [3]

---

[1] "The Old Coalition," *Newsweek* (November 15, 1976), p. 29.
[2] "A New Candidate Wins with an Old Coalition," *Congressional Quarterly* (November 6, 1976), p. 3116.
[3] Robert Reinhold, "Carter Victory Laid to Democrats Back in Fold, Plus Independents," *New York Times* (November 4, 1976).

Such conclusions, together with the more specific observation that prompted them, raise obvious questions about
the argument we have been presenting. At a minimum, if
they are valid, the 1976 voting contained some unexpected
revivals of old patterns—which must be explained. Given
their most expansive application, they argue that we have
been guilty of "overextrapolation," of making too much of
temporary, short-term movement in the political landscape. The view that the politics of the late 1960s and
early 1970s were essentially an aberration, the interruption of a persisting pattern rather than early etchings of a
new pattern, has been effectively presented by James Sundquist. Race, Vietnam, and "the social issue," he recognized, cut across the New Deal alignment and scrambled
voting alignments. But even as they were culminating in
Nixon's 1972 landslide victory, Sundquist saw them fading, and he confidently predicted that electoral configurations of the Roosevelt era would reassert themselves.[4]

I. The 1976 Elections: Continuities from the 1930s . . . or the 1960s?

It is appropriate that we look carefully at the voting patterns of 1976, to determine their fit or lack of fit with the
electoral developments we have thus far described. As we
do so, it would be well to bear in mind a few general distinctions and conceptualizations. First, we have argued
that the United States has experienced over the last
quarter-century or so various social and political changes
which together have transformed the party system and
which, specifically, have so eroded the voting configurations of the 1930s, 1940s, and 1950s as to preclude political
explanations based on "the New Deal Coalitions." This interpretation does *not*, of course, require a total disappear-

---

[4] James L. Sundquist, *Dynamics of the Party System: Alignment and
Realignment of Political Parties in the United States* (Washington, D.C.:
The Brookings Institution, 1973).

ance of the voting relationships of the Roosevelt era. The 1960s and 1970s appear to us to manifest at once enough common electoral features and sufficient differences from time past to require their recognition as a new political setting. But elements, substantial elements, from the old surely persist into the new. This does not get us around the inevitable argument as to when, and through what developments, there has been sufficient change to constitute "something distinctly new." It does caution us against insisting that a new electoral setting must involve starting with a clean electoral slate.

Second, our argument that a broad transformation of the American party system has been effected over the last decade and a half demands appreciation of the character of social trends. Rarely if ever in the real social and political world are there simple straight-line progressions from one status to another. Assume, for example, that some group in the U.S. electorate is shifting from securely Republican to Democratic in party support. Its movement over a series of elections is almost certain to resemble the pattern illustrated by Model B rather than that of Model A, below. Over a set of elections, a secular progression can be detected, but the movement is hardly uniform from each election to the following one. The line shows peaks and valleys *as various short-term factors influence group voting even as the underlying changes producing the secular*

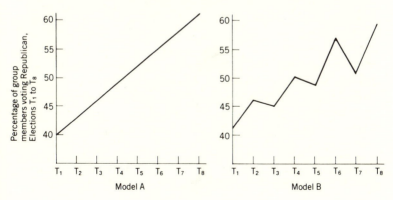

modifications of group loyalties remain evident. This observation is so very basic that we are a bit reluctant to make it here. But there seems to be a tendency to interpret any falling off from a trend line in a given election as indicating an apparent trend may not in fact be real. A group's voting in one election must be compared not just to that in the preceding contest but to its preferences over a long series of elections. Only the latter comparison is sufficient, obviously, to tell us whether there has been real underlying movement in the group's attachments.

It is important to bear in mind that presidential voting is especially susceptible to short-term influences. There are, typically, only two individuals in any contest for the presidency with any chance of victory, and there is intense national attention to the personal attributes and policy commitments of these two candidates. Whatever long-term movement there may be in the policy orientations of the two national parties and hence in the type of nominee each is *apt* to bring forth, and however social groups may be realigning themselves vis-à-vis the national parties, the contenders in a given election and the "nature of the times" are quite capable of greatly scrambling the electoral alignments. This is especially so in an era of relatively weak citizenry attachments to parties. And there is not the slightest indication it will be otherwise in the foreseeable future.

Again, it should be possible to detect broad patterns in presidential voting. We should expect election-specific variations or fluctuations, however, to be very large.

The 1976 Democratic presidential nominee over his long campaign attempted quite successfully to muffle the various' social and cultural issues which have been transforming the meaning of liberalism. He did not seek to mobilize—indeed, he sought to avoid mobilizing—a distinctively New Liberal coalition. After eight years in the presidential wilderness and especially because of their overwhelming 1972 defeat, the Democrats generally were willing to follow Carter's lead and sheathed ideological

knives in the interest of appeals at once more diffuse and
more traditional in their economic emphases. Vietnam was
fading from national attention and Watergate haunted the
Republicans. The Democratic contender was a white
southerner of moderately liberal inclinations, while the
Republican standard bearer embodied moderate, pragmatic conservatism. In view of all this, it would have been
wondrous indeed if the 1976 presidential vote configurations were a carbon copy of those in the McGovern-Nixon
contest of four years earlier. We must ask whether the
1976 electoral alignments fit into the general pattern
emergent over the 1960s and early 1970s, or if instead they
fit into the earlier New Deal mold. We begin this exploration, though, as it would seem anyone must, with the firm
expectation *that 1976 presidential voting would not simply reproduce the 1972 configuration.*

II. The South

In Chapter 3, we observed that "a rural, agrarian radical
Dixie could rest comfortably in the Democracy in the
economics-dominated agenda of the 1930s. A newly industrializing, petit bourgeois South could not remain Democratic as the agenda came to include civil rights and a host
of extensions of the liberal and equalitarian vision [p.
176]." In Chapter 5, we again noted "the long secular decline of support for the national Democratic party among
southern whites . . . [p. 233]." Was the 1976 voting an exception to the pattern thus described?

That 1976 saw some departure from the immediately
preceding presidential contests in the South is obvious.
The Old Confederacy had given Hubert Humphrey only
25 (Texas) of its 127 electoral votes in 1968; four years
later, George McGovern was completely shut out in the
South. But Jimmy Carter won 118 southern electoral votes,
compared to just 12 (Virginia) for Gerald Ford. The Democratic popular vote in Dixie had been 9.3 percentage

points *below* the party's proportion nationally in 1964, 11.3 percent lower in 1968, and 8 percent lower in 1972. Carter won 54.1 percent of the ballots cast in the South in 1976, however, 4 percent *above* his 50.1 percent share of the national popular vote. This was no return to the massive regional edge enjoyed by the Democrats until 1948—the South had been 18.9 points more Democratic than the country at large in 1932, 15.7 points more Democratic in 1944—but it was a sharp reversal of the 1964–1972 vote distribution and a return to roughly the regional advantage of 1948–1956.

Having noted these important characteristics of southern voting in the Carter-Ford contest and the element of "restoration" they contain, we still must conclude that the 1976 results are—from the standpoint of the party coalitions though obviously not in terms of who won the electoral votes—basically consonant with the 1964–1972 pattern. The pull of southern regional pride or loyalty in 1976 has not been measured with any precision. It can be noted, though, that Jimmy Carter was the first politician from a Deep South state to win a major-party presidential nomination since Zachary Taylor of Louisiana in 1848; and there are many informal indications the implications of the Carter triumph in terms of a full "acceptance" back into the Union were not lost on his co-regionists. Moreover, in his religious attachments, ethnic background, and style— he was the first major-party presidential nominee in more than a century who did not "talk with an accent"—Carter was part of the southern mainstream.

Even with these advantages, however, Carter failed to win a majority of the vote among southern whites. Every "Yankee" Democratic nominee from Samuel Tilden through Adlai Stevenson won majority backing among white southerners—and most by overwhelming margins. Southern white Protestants were a loyal and numerically substantial component of the Roosevelt coalition. They gave a higher proportion of their ballots to FDR than any other large, politically relevant social collectivity. The erosion of Democratic support within this group began in 1948 and accelerated greatly in the 1960s. In 1976, even with a southern white Protestant heading the ticket, southern white Protestants were 5 percentage points *less Democratic* than was the national electorate.[5]

On only five occasions since the Civil War has a Democratic presidential nominee lost majority support in the white Protestant South. And these are the last five presidential elections, 1960 through 1976. In many ways, the 1976 results provide even more dramatic proof of the scope and permanence of the realignment than does the McGovern-Nixon contest. If a centrist white southerner starting with an extraordinarily high margin of support in his native Deep South state, contesting against a Republican party that had been mauled by the most dramatic political scandal in the country's history and burdened with a poorly performing economy and pitted against a Republican nominee who was the second choice of his own party in the region and scarcely the most forceful or charismatic of contenders, cannot win majority backing in the white Protestant South—what Democratic nominee can?

Jimmy Carter ran well and won substantial support from most social groups, including white southerners. He ran especially well, as have all recent Democratic presidential nominees, among blacks. His strong, though minoritarian, base in the white South, together with heavy backing among relatively recently enfranchised southern blacks, combined to give him a near sweep of the region's electoral vote. But southern whites, a mainstay of the New Deal Democratic party, simply are not a principal Democratic contributor in the new party system.

---

[5] Carter gained 45 percent of the vote among southern white Protestants, compared to 50 percent among all voters. This estimate is based upon analysis of data from American Institute of Public Opinion studies 959, 960, 961, and 962 (1976); from the *New York Times*/CBS News election day poll (1976); from Yankelovich surveys 8540, 8550, and 8560 (1976); and it draws as well upon an examination of aggregate vote data. The authors wish to acknowledge the assistance of the Joint Center for Policy Studies, Washington, D.C., in the aggregate vote analysis.

III. The Persisting Absence of a Presidential Majority Party

We have argued that Democrats lost their New Deal status as the majority party in part because the national electorate is now too much up for grabs, probably too weakly attached to parties to ever again provide the base for a secure and persisting ascendancy. But we also maintained that the Democrats' position nationally as the principal partisan instruments for the new liberalism and its extensions has brought them a long-term disaffection among various groups which have seen their status shift from claimants or "have-nots" to (at least, marginal) "haves" with movement into the postindustrial era. This latter element has been blurred in subpresidential voting, but it has been dramatically evident in the great presidential "plebiscites."

Viewed first in the most general fashion, the results of the 1976 presidential balloting would seem consistent with the above interpretation. Blessed with an unusually favorable set of electoral circumstances, the Democratic nominee barely edged out his Republican opponent. A number of factors were centrally involved in the 1976 outcome, of course, but it is worth noting that this election fits into the post–World War II mold. Only once in the past eight presidential contests has the "majority party" been able to decisively defeat its "minority party" opposition.

From a closer perspective, too, we see many 1976 vote distributions which resemble those of other recent presidential elections. The Democrats did not regain in 1976 the large margins within the white working classes which contributed so importantly to their New Deal–era ascendancy—just as they did not recover majority status in the white South. Figure 6.1 reiterates data from Figure 5.1 and adds voting information from 1976 for several key "New Deal coalition" groups. Urban white Catholics, blue-collar workers other than those who are blacks and hispanics, like southern white Protestants, were somewhat more

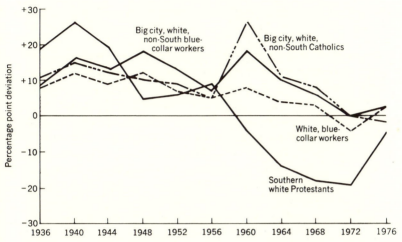

Figure 6.1. Percentage Point Deviation from the Democratic Presidential Vote; Selected Social Groups, 1936–1976

SOURCE: The 1976 data are from AIPO surveys: 959, 960, 961, and 962. Analysis of 1976 Yankelovich data, surveys 8540, 8550, and 8560 shows virtually identical distributions.

Democratic in 1976 than they had been in the McGovern-Nixon election, but their electoral standing remained consonant with that of the last decade and a half. There was no return to the Roosevelt-era high Democratic performance.

So the "old New Deal Democratic coalition" was not "put back together one more time" in 1976. Jimmy Carter surely received substantial backing from groups that were the building blocks of the Rooseveltian alignment, and he improved markedly on McGovern's electoral performance, but the Carter coalition had a quite different base than FDR's. The times have changed and so, permanently, has the Democratic presidential party. The big pluralities once provided by the white South and the blue-collar (white) ethnic North will not easily be regained by the Democratic presidential party.

IV. The Class Inversion

We demonstrated in Chapter 4 that a pronounced inversion of the New Deal class-ideology relationship has occurred in the contemporary period—with the result that high socioeconomic groups in the U.S. are now more *liberal*, given the current construction of that category, than are the middle-to-lower status groups across a wide array of issues. This inversion, we reemphasize, involves *class* and *ideology*, and extends to *class* and *party* only in those cases and to the extent one party is clearly associated with the present variant of liberalism. The national Democratic party, far more than its Republican opposition, is home to "the New Liberalism," but it is a large, highly disparate alliance and it hardly offers identical appeals and emphases in each presidential election. One may reasonably conclude, without need of extensive elaboration, that the McGovern candidacy of 1972 distinguished itself far more than the 1976 Carter candidacy by a commitment to the style, programs, and constituencies of the New Liberalism. The tendencies to an electoral inversion paralleling those of class and ideology, then, should have been more pronounced in 1972 than in 1976. And so they were.

But the elements of electoral inversion we described in Chapter 5 were not wiped away in 1976. The effects of the inversion were sharply evident in the 1976 Democrat presidential nomination contest. Throughout the primaries, it was a case of the more liberal the contender, the greater the proportion of his overall support drawn from among people of high socioeconomic status. For example, the NBC News survey of Massachusetts Democratic primary voters found that "two candidates—Harris and Udall—seem to be competing at the liberal end of the party spectrum. Both men appeal to upper socioeconomic status voters in the suburbs." [6] Bayh and Shriver occupied intermediate positions, in terms of the perceived extent of their

---

[6] NBC News, "The Election Newsletter," February 11, 1976.

liberalism and the education-occupation-income status of their supporters. Jackson, Carter, and Wallace did best among lower-status Democrats. Other NBC News polls and those of the *New York Times*/CBS News located similar distributions over the Winter–Spring 1976 primary season.[7]

Various national surveys confirm these state-by-state findings, adding, of course, a measure of overall precision. For example, the April 1976 study of Yankelovich, Skelly and White shows the most prominent Democratic contenders thus arrayed by the self-defined liberalism or conservatism of their supporters (among Democrats and independents): Udall, who had the highest proportion of liberal and the smallest percent of conservative backers; Humphrey; Jackson; Carter; and Wallace, whose backers were decidedly the most likely to think of themselves as conservatives.[8] (The differences in the Humphrey, Jackson, and Carter voter profiles, it should be noted, are modest.) And the candidate array by the socioeconomic status of their adherents is largely the same. Thus 35 percent of the Udall people were from families where the head of household held a professional or executive position, compared to 26 percent of Carter's backers and 14 percent of Wallace's. An extraordinary 50 percent of those favoring Udall claimed to have completed at least three years of college, the status of 26 percent in the Jackson camp, 25 percent of those supporting Humphrey and Carter, and only 11 percent of the Wallace loyalists.

---

[7] For reports on these surveys documenting the above conclusion, see Robert Reinhold, "Poll Finds Voters Judging '76 Rivals on Personality," *New York Times* (February 13, 1976); R. W. Apple, Jr., "New Political Universe," *New York Times* (March 3, 1976); Maurice Carroll, "Jackson Won in New York by Narrowly Based Voting," *New York Times* (April 8, 1976); and Reinhold, "Poll Links Udall Strength to Low Vote in Michigan," *New York Times* (May 20, 1976).

[8] These data were made available by Yankelovich, Skelly and White, and the author wishes to express his appreciation to Ruth Clark, vice-president of that organization. Democrats and independents in the April 1976 survey were asked: "If you had to make a choice among Jackson, Carter, Udall, Wallace and Humphrey as the Democratic candidate for the Presidency, whom would you choose?"

In the general election itself, 1976 was hardly a typical New Deal contest. According to the NBC News election day survey, college students—still a relatively privileged group in social background—continued their recent Democratic ways in both presidential and congressional balloting. The national election day survey conducted by the Associated Press indicates that a large majority of college-educated Americans voted for Democratic House of Representatives nominees.[9] Fifty-six percent of those with advanced degrees backed Democratic congressional candidates. While persons with a high school education or less were more heavily Democratic than the college-educated groups, the differences found by the AP survey were modest, on the order of 6 percentage points. Gallup surveys found higher-income Americans (with family earnings of $20,000 a year and more) dividing 56–44, Democratic and Republican, in the 1976 congressional balloting—surely not the New Deal distribution.

That there was a continuation of the pronounced weakening of class voting in congressional races is evident from an extensive analysis of 1976 Gallup data. Table 6.1 reviews the pattern for earlier contests and adds the 1976 results. High-status groups were less Democratic than their low-status counterparts again in 1976, but not by very much. The massive differences evident in the Roosevelt years continued through the 1950s and early 1960s. In 1948, for example, low-SES whites were 30 percentage points more Democratic than those of high socioeconomic standing, while in 1964 the difference was 26 percentage points. The gap had narrowed to just 13 points in 1968, however, and 10 points in 1974, and it remained at this reduced level in 1976.

It is also important to note that the Democrats in 1976 enjoyed a secure congressional margin among all of the distinct social strata identified in Table 6.1 This is one fur-

[9] These data were made available to the authors by Evans Witt of the Associated Press, and his assistance is gratefully acknowledged.

Table 6.1. Democratic Percentage of the Congressional Ballots, White Voters by Socioeconomic Position, Selected Years, 1948–1976

	1948	1960	1968	1972	1976
ALL					
High SES	33	46	42	48	55
Middle SES	49	60	51	49	58
Low SES	63	66	55	54	68
WOMEN					
High SES	35	41	42	48	58
Middle SES	49	57	49	45	58
Low SES	64	64	55	56	69
UNDER 30 YEARS OF AGE					
High SES	36	49	46	60	65
Middle SES	54	54	51	53	61
Low SES	66	59	54	51	71
COLLEGE EDUCATED	42	51	46	55	54
NONCOLLEGE	60	55	52	53	63

SOURCE: The 1976 data are from AIPO surveys 958 and 962. Data sources for earlier years are shown in Table 5.3, p. 243.

ther datum on the secular weakening of the GOP in sub-presidential balloting, of course, but it adds as well to an understanding of the distinctive character of the contemporary, post–New Deal alignment. When the "top," however defined, is solidly Democratic in voting for Congress—even if somewhat less so than the "bottom," one sees how far the country has moved from the sharp class divisions that characterized the previous party system.

In view of the number of congressional candidates, the contrasting policy stands those within one party take, the extent to which nonprogrammatic considerations determine how people vote for Congress, and the like, a *class-ideology* inversion will never be translated perfectly into a *class-party* inversion. That there has been movement toward a transposal in congressional voting patterns is evident from the 1974 and 1976 data. The exceptional Republican weakness everywhere outside presidential balloting, however, has meant that the inversion is taking shape more through marked Democratic gains at the top than Democratic losses at the bottom.

At the presidential vote level, there was a somewhat different pattern in 1976 than we saw in 1968 and 1972—and one more in keeping with the early 1960s. There was a fairly steady increase in the Ford proportion with movement up the socioeconomic ladder, however SES is measured. But any suggestion that class voting was as distinct in the 1976 presidential contest as in those of the New Deal years is, quite simply, *wrong*. There were clearer differences between high- and low-status voters in 1976 than in 1972 or 1968, but these groups were much less differentiated in 1976 than in the 1936–1948 period, less than in 1960.

Louis Harris found that grade school–educated whites were about 14 percentage points more Democratic in 1976 than were their college-trained counterparts. Whites from families earning less than $5,000 a year were approximately 16 points more for Carter than were whites with family incomes of $15,000 and higher per year. Data made available from the election day "intercept" polls of the *Times*/CBS News and NBC News show similar distributions. In the 1930s and 1940s, by way of contrast, high- and low-status whites were separated by between 30 and 40 percentage points in presidential preference. In the same article in which he argued that the distinctive feature of the 1976 presidential election was the holding together of the Roosevelt alliance, Robert Reinhold noted a secular erosion of the class voting which distinguished Roosevelt's alliance. He observed that "Mr. Carter succeeded in eating into groups that normally tend to vote Republican. For example, he did better among professional and managerial people than any Democrat in the last quarter century except Lyndon Johnson." [10] Actually, it could be extended to the last century.

---

[10] Reinhold, "Carter Victory Laid to Democrats Back in Fold, Plus Independents."

Gallup also called specific attention to Carter's strong showing within the business and professional strata:

Among professional and business people, while he did not win a majority of their vote, Carter proved exceptionally strong. Among Democrats, only Johnson . . . has outdrawn the Georgian during the last quarter century.[11]

Gallup data data do confirm, nonetheless, that there was a drawing back from the sharp tendency toward inversion of 1968 and 1972. Table 6.2 compares the presidential vote of

Table 6.2. Democratic Percentage of the Presidential Ballots, White Voters by Socioeconomic Position, Selected Years, 1948–1976

	1948	*1960*	*1968*	*1972*	*1976*
ALL					
High SES	30	38	36	32	41
Middle SES	43	53	39	26	49
Low SES	57	61	38	32	53
WOMEN					
High SES	29	35	42	34	41
Middle SES	42	52	40	25	46
Low SES	61	60	39	33	53
UNDER 30 YEARS					
OF AGE					
High SES	31	42	50	46	46
Middle SES	47	49	39	32	48
Low SES	64	52	32	36	52
COLLEGE EDUCATED	36	45	47	45	44
NONCOLLEGE	56	49	33	30	51

SOURCE: The 1976 data are from AIPO surveys 959, 960, 961, and 962. Data sources for earlier years are shown in Table 5.2, p. 240.

various socioeconomic groups in the Carter-Ford race to their vote in earlier contests. It shows clearly that the 1976 distributions were essentially what one would have expected them to be—assuming the general validity of the argument and analyses presented in the previous chapters,

---

[11] *The Gallup Opinion Index,* December 1976, p. 4.

and knowing the campaign approaches of the two main contenders in 1976. Lower-status cohorts were relatively more Democratic, compared to their upper-status counterparts, in the Carter-Ford race than in either of the two preceding elections. But there was no return to the relatively sharp class divisions of the New Deal years, not even to that of 1960. Carter ran a campaign which minimized rather than heightened the "social issue" concerns of lower-status whites. And it should be noted that actual social conditions in 1976 made it far easier for a Democratic nominee to accomplish this than it had been in 1968 and 1972. Still, the altered meaning of liberalism and hence of the national Democrats as the liberal party, together with the changed social position of the white working classes and the professional-managerial cohorts, had precluded a return to the class-voting patterns of the New Deal epoch.

College-trained professional and managerial people, especially the younger age cohorts, are consistently more liberal than the noncollege, blue-collar groups on a wide range of social and cultural issues. On matters of economic policy, however, they are often more conservative, although much less decidedly so than during the New Deal period. The Democratic party is associated with both "social liberalism" and "economic liberalism," and as a consequence it is evoking contradictory responses within both the upper and the lower SES groups. The decline in class distinctiveness in voting, and the tendencies toward inversion, come as a result—among white Americans. Black Americans must be treated separately because their electoral choices are not accounted for by the *class-ideology* dynamic we have been describing.

Middle-class and lower-class blacks may differ fully as much as middle- and lower-class whites in expectations, life styles, social and cultural values, etc.; but in their general orientations to the two major parties, blacks—whatever their socioeconomic position—are responding to a common stimulus. The sociology and politics of race, specifically the pattern of discrimination that has affected virtually all black Americans, have resulted in a set of electoral commitments that is singularly untouched by income, occupational, educational, and other such status components.

We created three large merged data sets—one containing fifteen Gallup surveys conducted in 1976, another of seven 1976 Yankelovich national surveys, and the third comprising the five NORC General Social Surveys of 1972–1976.[12] The number of cases provided by these combined studies has permitted attention to subgroups that are too small for reliable analysis in conventional-size cross-sectional surveys. In particular, here, we have been able to look at the electoral preferences of black Americans by socioeconomic position. Blacks have not only been consistently and heavily Democratic, they have sustained this Democratic preference with remarkable uniformity across class lines. Thus, in congressional voting, in both the 1972 and the 1976 presidential contests, and in party identification, middle-class blacks have been no more or less Republican than their lower-class counterparts. Differences may well appear in specific elections, especially when two black candidates are contending against each other. But in the broader arena of national party politics, the black vote is both massively and *uniformly* Democratic.

V. Republican Weakness; Democrats as the "Everyone" Party

The point is often made that the GOP experienced a big decline in support during the Depression decade. Its backing did drop off substantially in that period, of course, as the party fell from majority to minority status. But the Re-

---

[12] The number of cases (*n*) in the combined NORC data set is 7590. The fifteen Gallup studies—done from April 20 through December 7, 1976—have a total *n* of 23,086. The seven Yankelovich surveys, covering the January–October 1976 span, have a combined *n* of 7977.

publicans were a very healthy minority party—in their ability to provide sustained competition—throughout the period from 1932 to the 1960s. Even in 1936, with the Democrats riding high and the Republicans perceived as the party of economic failure, the Democrats had a lead of only 15 percent in party identifiers. And this lead shrank to just 4 or 5 percent in the early 1940s. It took the Republicans but a decade after their 1932 rout to return to a really competitive position in Congress. Of the 436 representatives elected in 1942, for example, 208 bore the GOP label. The Republicans captured both houses of Congress in 1946, again in 1952, and they stayed close to the Democrats throughout the 1950s until the 1958 recession-year election.

Looking at state legislative races, we find a Republican party which was similarly competitive up to the early 1960s. By 1938 the GOP had recovered from its Depression debacle to the extent that it claimed 43 percent of state legislators in the country. In 1948, the Republicans actually gained a state legislative majority by a 53 to 47 percent margin over the Democrats. In 1956, 44 percent of state legislators carried the Republican label.

Over the last decade and a half, however, the GOP has slipped into its "half-party" status. Little more than one-fifth of all Americans now identify as Republicans. In 1977, only 32 percent of state legislators in the country are Republicans and this low has been reached through a steady secular erosion. The GOP state legislative contingent has actually declined slightly from its 1974 lowpoint. The Republicans have become—and this is only the second time in American political history that we have had such a development—a permanent minority party in Congress, one unable to secure a majority in either house, no matter what the prevailing conditions are in the country.

For a full quarter-century, then, the Democrats have had at least a nominal majority in both houses of the national legislature, and for the last decade and a half that majority has been essentially unchallenged. The only other period in which one party controlled Congress over a comparably prolonged period was that between 1801 and 1825 when the Jeffersonians reigned. Need we remind ourselves that that period saw the death of the Federalist party and the inauguration of a temporary "era-of-good-feelings" one-partyism? The present-day Democrat control of Congress has already exceeded in number of years the domination of the Democratic-Republicans.

In 1972 when Nixon was winning by 17.5 million votes, the Democrats were winning a majority of the popular vote in U.S. House of Representatives' contests, a forty-seven–seat edge in the House, and 60 percent of all state legislative seats. In 1976, when Ford contested evenly for the presidency, the Republican congressional position dropped below that of 1972 and showed only the slightest revival from the 1974 Watergate low. Just 42 percent of all congressional ballots cast in 1976 went to Republican nominees.[13]

The Republican party cannot find, outside of the performance of its presidential nominee, a single encouraging indicator of a general sort from its 1976 electoral performance. (Obviously, individual Republican contenders did very well in certain 1976 contests.) We have criticized the common tendency of political commentators to overreact to the last election, but what we see manifested here is a *secular deterioration* of the GOP position.

The Democrats have emerged almost everywhere outside the presidential arena as the "everyone party." The depiction is not intended literally, of course. Rather, it is meant to describe an absolutely unprecedented situation in which one party shows more strength than its opposition across virtually the entire range of politically relevant groups. The Republicans do better among some groups than others, but there are few social collectivities indeed that give them regular pluralities either in party identification or in the sweep of subpresidential voting.

---

[13] The 1976 Republican congressional percentage of 42.1 is from computations of *Congressional Quarterly* (March 19, 1977), p. 4.

An examination of the party identification of various age strata, social groups, and ideological clusters in 1976 offers confirmation of the above argument. The Democrats are, for example, well ahead of the GOP in every age cohort, from the youngest segments of the electorate to the oldest, and their margin is remarkably uniform. The proportion of self-described independents does rise steadily with movement from the oldest to the youngest voters. The latter have had less time to establish regular preferences. College-trained people, more inclined to see themselves as "independent," are more heavily represented in the younger cohorts. Finally, the young have "come of age politically" as partisan attachments are weakening, and they reflect the current swing more than older voters who had established party loyalties in times when such identifications were stronger. Still, our exhaustive analysis of 1976 survey data reaffirms the presence of a big, rather even Democratic lead over the Republicans, one that extends to people whose earliest political memories are from the 1910s and 1920s, to those who first saw U.S. politics in the years of Kennedy, Johnson, and Nixon.

Tables 6.3 and 6.4 testify to the breadth of the Democratic appeal as against that of the Republicans, and hence the legitimacy of our depiction of the Democracy as the "everyone" party. Wage workers are less Republican than businessmen and executives, but a *plurality of even the latter now identify with the Democrats*. Less than one third of the business-professional stratum claims attachment to the GOP. *All* educational groups show a Democratic margin.[14] So do *all* income cohorts—up to the very

---

[14] The Yankelovich surveys show more Democratic adherents than do Gallup's, and report fewer independents. The combined Yankelovich data ($n = 7,977$), for example, indicate these partisan distributions by education:

	Republican	Democratic	Independent
Less than high school	20	63	17
High school graduate	25	54	20
Some college	27	48	24
College graduate	31	42	27

Figure 6.2. Party Identification by Year of Birth, the American Electorate in 1976

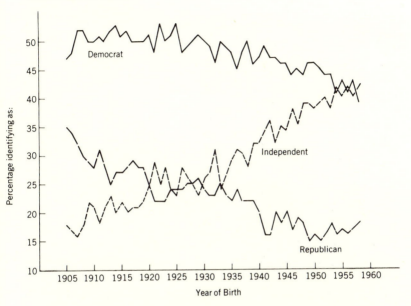

SOURCE: These data, comprising a total number of cases of 23,086 are from AIPO surveys 950 through 964, April–December 1976.

prosperous. The Democrats lead the Republicans in *every* region, among *all* religious groupings, among virtually *all* ethnic groups. People who come from wealthy family backgrounds prefer the Democrats by a two-to-one margin. Yankelovich, in fact, finds that not only are the Democrats far outdistancing Republicans among voters who think of themselves as liberals and among moderates, but they have a comfortable edge among self-described conservatives as well! [15]

[15] Ideological self-description distributions are:

	Republican	*Democratic*	*Independent*
Conservative	35	45	20
Moderate	25	51	25
Liberal	13	66	22
Radical	7	64	28

Table 6.3. Party Identification of Selected Social Groups, Gallup Data, 1976

	Republican	Democratic	Independent
OCCUPATION			
Professionals	27	39	34
Business, Executives	29	37	34
Sales	29	36	35
Clerical	23	45	32
Skilled blue-collar	17	49	34
Semiskilled; unskilled	15	55	30
Service	18	53	29
Farm owners	36	41	23
Farm laborers	14	59	27
RACE AND SEX			
White males	23	42	35
White females	26	45	28
Black males	5	79	16
Black females	6	79	16
EDUCATION			
Less than high school	19	57	24
High school graduate	22	47	31
Some college	26	41	34
College graduate	29	37	34
RELIGION			
Protestant	27	45	27
Catholic	17	53	30
Jewish	10	59	31
FAMILY INCOME			
Under $2,000 a year	19	60	21
$2,000–2,999	17	58	24
$3,000–3,999	19	56	25
$4,000–4,999	19	57	24
$5,000–5,999	18	54	28
$6,000–6,999	20	54	26
$7,000–9,999	21	50	29
$10,000–11,999	21	48	31
$12,000–14,999	21	45	34
$15,000–19,999	23	45	32
$20,000 and higher	29	39	31
REGION			
Northeast	26	46	29
Midwest	24	41	34
West	27	46	28
South	16	57	28

SOURCE: The combined 1976 AIPO data set ($n = 23,086$).

Table 6.4. Party Identification of Selected Social Groups, NORC Data, Combined 1972–1976 (Percentages of *n*)

	Republican	Democratic	Independent
SELF-DESCRIBED			
SOCIAL CLASS			
Lower class	15	61	25
Working class	18	49	34
Middle class	28	38	34
Upper class	38	31	31
ETHNICITY			
Irish	21	44	36
German, Austrian	30	34	36
Italian	17	44	39
Scandinavian	30	36	34
Eastern European	13	54	33
English, Scottish, Welsh	36	31	34
Other European	24	38	38
Latin American, Spanish surname	3	75	22
Black	7	72	21
FAMILY INCOME, WHEN AGE 16			
Far below average	16	61	24
Below average	22	47	31
Average	23	43	34
Above average	27	33	41
Far above average	21	38	41
OTHER SELECTED GROUPS			
White New England Protestants	40	22	39
White Northeastern Protestants	45	25	30
Northeast; English, Scottish, Welsh	52	16	32
Midwest; English, Scottish, Welsh	38	27	35
West; English, Scottish, Welsh	36	35	30
South; English, Scottish, Welsh	27	38	35

SOURCE: The combined NORC surveys (*n* = 7590).

There are only a few Republican bailiwicks left. After extensive analysis of the huge collections of data available to us, we are struck by the prominent role of region and ethnicity in defining the remaining GOP bastions. White Protestants in the Northeast have remained strongly Republican, continuing a regional-ethnic tradition that reaches far back into U.S. history. And no group is more decisively Republican than the "Yankees," if the term is taken to mean white Protestants, especially those of British stock, residing in the northeastern states.

Kevin Phillips has argued that the GOP was torn from its deep Yankee roots in the 1960s. So long securely Republican, the Yankees are now, Phillips maintained, deeply divided electorally.[16] He could not have been more wrong. To be sure, the Yankees deserted Goldwater in 1964—but so did many other groups. In their party identification and as well in most recent elections, the Yankees have manifested strongly Republican loyalties.

The "Yankee Northeast" has moved away from the GOP, of course, and the region now is rather decisively Democratic. But this is not because the Yankees have wandered from their ancestral partisan home. New England is simply no longer Yankee territory. According to NORC data, less than 20 percent of the New England population is of British stock today, and less than 30 percent is white Protestant. Yankelovich and Gallup data sustain this same description. White Protestants are now a smaller proportion of the population of New England than of any other section of the country. Probably in part because of this minority status, they have maintained the historic party ties more than their co-religionists elsewhere in the U.S.

Tables 6.3 and 6.4 show only party identification. Data on congressional voting, however, reveal the same pattern. The Democrats have surpassed their GOP opponents across most of the social spectrum. Party conflict, as a result, looks very different today than it did in the New Deal

---

[16] Kevin P. Phillips, *The Emerging Republican Majority* (New Rochelle, N.Y.: Arlington House, 1969), pp. 93–105.

era. In the latter period, each party had its reasonably secure bases among certain social groups. The Republicans
were the party of New England, of business, of the middle
classes, and of white Protestants. The Democrats enjoyed
a clear majority among the working classes, organized
labor, Catholics, and the South. This distinctiveness has
disappeared in the contemporary party system as the Democrats have assumed their "everyone" status. The middle
classes may be more Republican than the working classes
today, but both groups produce large Democratic pluralities.

At the presidential level, thanks to the pronounced
"nonparty" flavor of the competition, the intense media
emphasis on two individuals, and widespread popular ambivalence if not hostility to policy extensions involving the
"New Liberalism," Republican contenders have occupied
a highly competitive position. But elsewhere in the
contemporary U.S. electoral competition, the Republicans
have seen their social base eroded and their ability to sustain even competition with the Democrats diminished.
One should not discount the importance of election rules
and "monopoly-of-opposition" status—together, of course,
with historic loyalties—in keeping the GOP ship afloat.
The Democratic-Republican two-party system is written
into the formal electoral machinery in most states across
the country, and the second party in a two-party system,
however weak, can always find backing as people turn
against the performance of majority party officeholders.
Still, the Republicans have experienced a marked deterioration of their electoral position, and questions about their
electoral viability must be entertained.

VI. Conclusions

On December 10, 1976, Patrick H. Caddell, pollster to
the Democratic nominees of 1972 and 1976, delivered to
the man who was about to be installed as the "Prince" and

to his principal courtiers a lengthy discourse titled "Initial Working Paper on Political Strategy." The prescriptions contained in this much-leaked document cover a wider range of topics than we are exploring in this chapter. But Caddell does address at length the status of "the old New Deal coalitions."

Caddell argued that it is a mistake to attribute Carter's 1976 victory to the "traditional" alignments. "There has been a desire in recent elections to reconstruct the 'New Deal' coalition. It has been a problem since the New Deal coalition is essentially premised on carrying a majority of the White electorate, something the Democratic candidate has been unable to do since the 1940s with one exception—Johnson's victory in 1964." [17] After reviewing the electoral performances of various social groups, Caddell concluded that "it seems clear that while Carter benefited from their support [that of traditionally Democratic groups], he may owe his election more to the nontraditional groups that helped him to do better in unexpected places. Carter's performance among traditional groups is impressive when compared to McGovern's showing in 1972, but when placed in long-term historical perspective, it simply cannot explain the victory.[18]

Caddell then described the "nontraditional" groups to which the president-elect owed his victory: "white Protestants"; "better-educated, white-collar people"; and "rural, small-town voters." The pollster was especially sensitive to the long-term implications of the voting preferences of the college-trained professional cohorts. "If there is a 'future' in politics, it is in this massive demographic change. We now have almost half the voting population with some college education, a growing percentage of white-collar workers and an essentially 'middle-class electorate.'" Carter "did well" among these voters, although not as well as "we had hoped." [19]

---

[17] Patrick H. Caddell, "Initial Working Paper on Political Strategy," December 10, 1976, p. 9.

[18] *Ibid.*, p. 13.

[19] *Ibid.*, p. 14.

Summing up, Caddell wrote his own epitaph for the New Deal alignment:

> If we first look at the definition of policy, we see that the Democratic party can no longer depend on a coalition of economic division. Whatever our short-term economic troubles of the "haves" versus the "have-nots," a tremendous growth in economic prosperity has produced more "haves" in our society than "have-nots." Many older voters are becoming more conservative, if not in an economic sense at least in a social-cultural sense. Younger voters . . . are more likely to be social liberals and economic conservatives. More importantly, they perceive a new cluster of issues—the "counter-culture" and issues such as growth versus the environment—where old definitions do not apply. In short, the old language of American politics really doesn't affect these voters.[20]

We would take issue with aspects of Caddell's analysis, but basically, it seems, his "Prince" was well advised on the state of the contemporary coalitions. There are important continuities from the New Deal era, but the discontinuity is more impressive. Viewed at the level of the coalitions, the American party system has indeed been transformed.

---

[20] *Ibid.*, p. 19.

7

The Changed Fabric
of American
Electoral Politics

Twice now in the last four elections, presidential candidates who might have normally expected to win at best modest majorities have become the recipients of massive victories, winning by margins at the upper limits in American presidential history. Perhaps more impressive than the issues of 1964 and 1972, and personal attributes of the victorious and vanquished candidates, is this fact of landslides which by conventional rules of American presidential politics should not have been—"unnatural" landslides.

To refer to the unnatural landslide supposes that there is such a thing as a natural landslide, and further that there are reasons for describing the massive victories of 1964 and 1972 as "outside the norm." American two-party politics has in the past assumed, with fair correspondence to reality, the following sequence: Both the Democratic and the Republican parties, confident in the support of their respective faithfuls, have looked among their presidential nominees for candidates able to build from the secure base to a majority. The search for supporters has typically produced appeals to sectional, ethnic, and class groupings supposedly susceptible to courtship. To the extent there has been an issue base, it has involved an effort to capture the ground where most of the people are.

In other words, our working model has assumed two national parties engaged in *accommodationist* politics. Clinton Rossiter put it this way, that

> they [the two major parties] are creatures of compromise, coalitions of interest in which principle is muted and often even silenced. They are vast, gaudy, friendly umbrellas under which all Americans, whoever and wherever and however-minded they may be, are invited to stand for the sake of being counted in the next election. The parties, moderate and tolerant and self-contradictory to a fault, are interested in the votes of men, not in their principles. . . . The task that they have uppermost in mind is the construction of a victorious majority, and in a country as large and diverse as ours this calls for programs and candidates having as nearly universal an appeal as the imperatives of politics will permit. It calls, that is to say, for a gallant attempt by each party to mirror the entire American electorate. . . .[1]

The model which emerged from observation of the American parties nationally, then, has seen them as coalition-minded, seeking a majority from the extraordinary heterogeneity of the country, searching for a majority on the bases of loose appeals (in contrast to sharply defined, ideologically structured programs). The parties have been seen operating from an assumption of multi-structured mobilization. A majority could not be secured by drawing lines neatly around any single axis; so it was pursued by attempting to mobilize varying segments of the electorate through diverse appeals across a series of axes of conflict.

This point is sometimes made by stating that the national parties have competed for the center. But the concept of a center in issue or ideological terms is somewhat confusing because it suggests a single continuum upon

---

[1] Rossiter, *Parties and Politics in America* (Ithaca, N.Y.: Cornell University Press, 1960), p. 11.

which voters are arrayed. In post–New Deal nomenclature, this would mean that Republicans as the more conservative party, and Democrats as the more liberal, have
sought in their presidential appeals to attract voters whose
issue concerns are neither decisively liberal or conservative, but rather are near the center of the continuum. The
notion of a search for the center would be fine if the mix of
issues in fact generally would fit a single such continuum.
We know, however, that reality does not submit to such
analytic neatness. For example, in the principal Republican issue appeals in 1952 involving "communism, corruption, and Korea," where was the center? What is the liberal or conservative position on corruption? What was it on
the Korean War?

The issue mix, typically, does not lend itself to "more
than" or "less than" along a single ideological or quasi-
ideological dimension. Donald Stokes caught a facet of
this when he emphasized the difference between "position" and "valence" issues. The former "involve advocacy
of government actions from a set of alternatives over which
a distribution of voter preferences is defined"; while valence issues are those which "involve the linking of the
parties with some condition that is positively or negatively
valued by the electorate." [2] Concern over governmental
corruption in 1952 serves as an example of a valence issue:
Republicans and Democrats did not take opposite sides on
it, and neither were some voters in favor of corruption
while others stood against it. Corruption was a perceived
condition which, at the time, was linked in the minds of
many voters to the performance of the Democratic administration. Stokes argues, correctly we think, that valence issues have often been decisive in electoral choice.
It may be possible in a general way to locate the center on
a cluster of related position issues; but there may be other
clusters each with quite different centers. Furthermore,

[2] Stokes, "Spatial Models of Party Competition," as reprinted in Angus
Campbell, *et al.*, *Elections and the Political Order*, pp. 170–171.

the notion of a center makes no sense at all with reference to valence issues. For these reasons, it is more precise to describe the traditional mechanics of American two-party politics as comprising a series of issue appeals designed to be majoritarian.

So much of the literature on the American parties historically has noted their efforts to put together a majority by being "all things to all people." Thus, the parties are described as "Tweedledum and Tweedledee," imagery which connotes superficial dissimilarity masking essential similarity. There is not, we have been told by various critics such as George C. Wallace, "a dime's worth of difference" between the Republicans and Democrats.

The contrast between accommodationist and ideological parties has often been made. The former, including the Republicans and Democrats in the United States, are engaged in what Maurice Duverger described as "a conflict without principles."

The two parties are rival teams, one occupying office, the other seeking to dislodge it. It is a struggle between the *ins* and the *outs*, which never becomes fanatical, and creates no deep cleavages in the country.[3]

"Typically," Dwaine Marvick has observed, "the primary characteristics of American parties are said to be cooperation with certain enduring special interests rather than political convictions about complex issues, emotional attachments to symbols of regional or ethnic origin, rather than concern with philosophies."[4] Ideological parties, by way of contrast, are primarily distinguished by conflict over principles, either subsidiary or those basic to the very fabric of the regime.[5]

---

[3] Duverger, *Political Parties* (New York: John Wiley, 1959), p. 418.
[4] Marvick, "Party Organizational Personnel and Electoral Democracy: the Perspectives and Behavior of Rival Party Cadres in Los Angeles from 1963 to 1972" (paper delivered at the Ninth World Congress of the International Political Science Association, August 1973), p. 14.
[5] Duverger, *op. cit.*, p. 418–419.

I. Natural Landslides

If both parties competing for the presidency conform to the accommodationist model described above, under what circumstances can, indeed have, landslides occurred? [6] Two principal circumstances, alone or in concert, have been decisive. In one instance, salient valence issues may be decisively stacked against one party. Neither the Republicans nor the Democrats in 1932 were in favor of economic collapse and depression, but the Republicans were in office when the collapse occurred and were necessarily associated with it. A second, different source of landslides, even when both parties are actively and effectively pursuing majoritarian appeals, occurs when one of them is blessed with a candidate of unusual personal standing and popularity—or more generally, when there is a decisive gap between the personal appeal of the contenders. Thus, Eisenhower's victory of 1956 appears more than anything else as a personal tribute, product of his exceptional individual popularity. And Alton B. Parker was no match for dynamic "Teddy" Roosevelt. It should be added that a more modest advantage in candidate appeal or in the weight of valence issues is required on behalf of the majority party, than for the minority party, to secure a big victory. The party with the larger share of identifiers begins with a built-in advantage. The elections of 1904, 1932, and 1956, in any event, may be taken as examples of natural landslides. They are perfectly compatible with the accommodationist politics model.

The elections of 1964 and 1972 do not, however, present these conditions. Neither Johnson nor Nixon benefited from high personal affection across the electorate, or projected charismatic appeal. In 1972, sensing the voters did not particularly like either Nixon or McGovern, the Daniel Yankelovich survey organization gave respondents a

---

[6] For convenience, we may think of a landslide election as one in which the winning candidate enjoys at least a 10 percentage point margin over his principal rival.

chance to express their dissatisfaction. And an exceptionally high proportion—about a third—"voted" for "neither one" in polls taken less than a month before election day.[7] In 1972, with the country at war, the economy unsettled, with a climate of considerable pessimism concerning the adequacy of American institutions and processes, with the emerging Watergate scandal, one could hardly argue that the Republicans were linked to an overall national circumstance so positively valued by the electorate as to make them, as the incumbent party, virtually impregnable.

Table 7.1. "Now, Forgetting about Politics, Whom Do You Find More Attractive as a Personality, Nixon, McGovern, or Neither One?"

	Nixon	McGovern	Neither One	Not Sure	n
Survey of October 1–12, 1972	34	26	32	8	2323
Survey of October 15–24, 1972	33	23	37	7	3010

SOURCE: Surveys conducted by Daniel Yankelovich, sponsored by the *New York Times* and *Time*, cited by Natchez, "The Unlikely Landslide."

Here, then, is the basis for the feeling, variously expressed, that the 1972 Nixon landslide, like that of his predecessor eight years earlier, was unlikely or unnatural. They should not have occurred if the behavior of both parties had conformed to the accommodationist model. But occur they did. These two elections are among the most one-sided in American electoral history, as Table 6.2 demonstrates. Ordered by the percentage point spread between the winner and the runner-up, the 1972 and 1964 elections ranked fourth and fifth respectively in all-time standings. Measured simply in terms of the victor's per-

[7] Peter B. Natchez, "The Unlikely Landslide: Issues and Voters in the 1972 Election" (paper presented before the New England Political Science Association at Northeastern University, Boston, Mass., April 27, 1973), p. 3.

Table 7.2. The Ten Presidential Elections in Which the Winning
Candidate's Margin over His Closest Challenger Was Highest
(Rank Ordered)

Year	Principal candidates	Winner's percentage of the total vote cast	Winner's margin (in percentage) over his principal challenger
1920	Harding, Cox	60.3	26.2
1924	Coolidge, Davis	54.0	25.2
1936	Roosevelt, Landon	60.8	24.3
1972	*Nixon, McGovern*	60.8	23.2
1964	*Johnson, Goldwater*	61.1	22.6
1904	Roosevelt, Parker	56.4	18.8
1932	Roosevelt, Hoover	57.4	17.8
1928	Hoover, Smith	58.2	17.4
1832	Jackson, Clay	54.5	17.0
1956	Eisenhower, Stevenson	57.4	15.4

centage of the total vote cast, the Johnson and Nixon victories were the two largest in American history.[8] Two of
the most imposing presidential victories were achieved,
then, by nominees not known for their personal popularity
with the electorate, and not the beneficiaries of decisive
mixes of valence issues. Nixon's 1972 landslide is all the
more striking because it was achieved by a nominee of the
minority party. The only other one-sided triumph listed in
Table 6.2 going to a minority party nominee was Eisenhower's 1956 victory; and Eisenhower had built his political career upon being "above [partisan] politics,"
whereas Nixon had been the quintessential Republican
partisan leader.

    That the landslides of 1964 and 1972 did in fact take
place requires one of two explanations: either they were

---

    [8] While the subject cannot be examined here, it should be noted that
nine of the ten record landslides in American political history have occurred in the twentieth century. On the whole, presidential contests were
much closer in the nineteenth century, especially between 1876 and
1900.

deviant cases, products of a peculiar mix of personalities and events not likely to reoccur and hence of interest solely as aberrations, as political museum pieces; or they followed from some fundamental structural changes bearing upon party role in national electoral politics which point to a significant weakening if not a collapse of assumptions and practices associated with accommodationist politics. Either the old rules hold and the landslides were merely flukes, or the old rules are being rewritten. If it is the latter, then perhaps most observers a decade hence, in their retrospective analysis, will consider them far from unnatural. Unlikely under the old rules, they may conform easily to the dictates of a new structure of national interparty competition.

II. The "Accident" Thesis

The argument that Nixon's landslide of 1972, and that achieved by Johnson in 1964, were accidents, products of nothing more than a bundle of short-term forces, deserves serious consideration. It underlies, implicitly if not explicitly, a lot of commentary on the two elections. The Republicans, we are told, made a mistake in 1964 and subsequently showed that they had learned from that mistake. Similarly, the Democrats made an error in 1972, and it is possible that they will also profit from their error and avoid it in the future. The notion of error or mistake suggests temporary aberrations. As far as we know, no one has advanced an interpretation of these two elections which treats them strictly in terms of short-term electoral accidents, but the general lines of such an argument are readily apparent.

First, it can be noted that neither party which was to be the ultimate loser had any prospective nominee who clearly established himself as the popular choice. This was due in part, certainly, to a string of coincidental developments. Richard Nixon, the GOP standard-bearer four years earlier, had temporarily eliminated himself in 1964 as a result of his gubernatorial defeat in California. Nelson Rockefeller suffered liabilities attendant on his divorce and subsequent remarriage. George Romney made disastrous campaign gaffes. William Scranton of Pennsylvania waxed indecisive at strategic moments. And Goldwater had tied himself to the Republican right. As a result, two weeks before the 1964 Republican Convention no potential contender for the party's nomination was endorsed by more than one-fifth of Republican identifiers.[9] In a divided field, with no clear popular choice, Goldwater who had a strong, highly committed, well-mobilized grass-roots organization, linked to a movement with ideological adherence, possessed a distinct advantage.[10] Besides this, the conservative wing of the Republican party had been claiming for two decades that there was a conservative majority in the United States waiting to be mobilized, and that the Republicans had failed to exploit this because, beginning with the rejections of Ohio Senator Robert Taft, they had failed to give their nomination to an avowedly conservative leader. Now, it was the conservatives' turn.

By an unusual chain of circumstances, then, the Republicans came to nominate a man who started with the disadvantage of being distinctly the minority choice of the minority party. Gallup reported in December 1963 survey findings which showed Goldwater the preferred candidate of only 27 percent of Republican identifiers.[11] Two months later, in February 1964, the Arizona senator was backed by just one-fifth (20 percent) of Republicans.[12] And as we have noted, in late June, shortly before the Republican

[9] *The Gallup Poll: Public Opinion, 1935–1971* (New York: Random House, 1972), vol. 3, p. 1894. This late June Gallup survey showed Goldwater the choice of 22 percent of Republicans, Nixon backed by 22 percent, Lodge by 21 percent, Scranton by 20 percent, Rockefeller by 6 percent, with 9 percent undecided.

[10] F. Clifton White, National Director of the Draft Goldwater Committee in 1964, has emphasized this. See his *Suite 3505: The Story of the Draft Goldwater Movement* (New Rochelle, N.Y.: Arlington House, 1967).

[11] *The Gallup Poll, op. cit.*, vol. 3, pp. 1854–1855.

[12] *Ibid.*, p. 1864.

Nominating Convention, Goldwater's minority position had not been improved: He was the favorite of just 22 percent of Republicans in the national electorate.

Even with the alternatives narrowed to two, Goldwater was unable to move above, indeed even to approach, the 50 percent mark in Republican support. In a survey conducted between June 11 and June 16 of 1964, Gallup posed the question: "Suppose the choice for President in the Republican Convention narrows down to Senator Barry Goldwater and Governor William Scranton, which one would you prefer to have the Republican Convention select?" Fifty-five percent of Republicans chose Scranton, 34 percent Goldwater, with 11 percent undecided.[13] And only two weeks before the Republican National Convention, 60 percent of Republicans told Gallup interviewers they preferred Scranton, while 34 percent endorsed Goldwater, and 6 percent were uncertain.[14]

Backed by a minority of the minority party, Goldwater also labored throughout the campaign under the label "extremist." He was widely perceived as a radical, an image which he helped cultivate, and which the Democrats scarcely failed to exploit. Michigan's Survey Research Center asked respondents to a preelection survey, "Is there anything in particular about [the candidate] that might make you want to vote against him?" No leads were provided; respondents were asked to free-associate as to negative attributes of the contenders. (A comparable question asking for positive attributes was also included.) Large numbers of respondents offered criticisms of Goldwater which were variations on the extremism theme: fanatic, too radical, too militaristic, reactionary, impulsive, etc. This type of negative image was held by many Republicans—who were far more likely to label their own party's candidate as a radical than they were the nominee of the opposition.

Surveys conducted by the Louis Harris organization

---

[13] *Ibid.*, p. 1890.
[14] *Ibid.*, p. 1893.

show a similar picture. In October 1964, 45 percent of respondents in a national sample agreed with the proposition that Goldwater "is a radical." (Another 45 percent disagreed, with 10 percent undecided.) That same month, Harris found 51 percent of the electorate agreeing that Goldwater "would get America into a war," (33 percent in disagreement); while 57 percent were of the opinion that if president he could be expected to use nuclear weapons in Asia, an action they massively disapproved.[15] The Republican nominee, then, was widely perceived as out of the mainstream in his approach to both domestic economic and foreign policy matters, as too conservative and as too bellicose.

When the minority party nominates as its candidate a man who is not even the first choice of a majority of his own party and who is widely perceived as unstable, too conservative, too militaristic, and the like, it is obviously in serious electoral trouble.

The intensity of the 1964 Republican nomination struggle fractured the party, and leaders disenchanted with Goldwater attacked him with a virulence which was to increase his popular image as an extremist, and which provided a critique at least as devastating as any the Democrats could mount. For example, William Scranton's supporters released in his name a letter charging:

You [Goldwater] have too often casually prescribed nuclear war as a solution to a troubled world. You have too often allowed the radical extremists to use you. You have too often stood for irresponsibility in the serious question of racial holocaust. . . . In short, Goldwaterism has come to stand for a whole crazy-quilt collection with absurd and dangerous positions that would be soundly repudiated by the American people in November.[16]

Once nominated, Goldwater hurled a now-famous thunderbolt at party moderates in his acceptance speech: "Ex-

---

[15] *The Harris Survey*, release of October 26, 1964; and *The Harris Survey*, release of October 30, 1964.

[16] Quoted by Theodore H. White, *The Making of the President, 1964* (New York: Atheneum, 1965), p. 239.

tremism in the defense of liberty is no vice. . . . Moderation in the pursuit of justice is no virtue." Control of his campaign was vested in the hands of men and women relatively inexperienced in national politics, an "Arizona Mafia" seemingly more interested in preserving their own position of power in the Goldwater campaign and in the Republican party than in building an effective national base required for victory or a creditable showing.[17] Further, Goldwater selected as his vice-presidential candidate Congressman William Miller of New York, a man who singularly lacked the national stature and breadth of appeal needed to strengthen the ticket.

Example can be piled upon example, but doing so adds little to the basic point: A minority candidate of a minority party, strongly identified as a conservative ideologue throughout his career, was locked in a contest for his party's nomination where charges and countercharges solidified his popular image as dangerous and extreme, and launched the campaign with the party more bitterly and deeply divided than at any time in this century.

Despite obvious differences, one can find many parallels in McGovern's 1972 candidacy. As in 1964, there was a crowded field. No contender for the Democratic nomination was able to command a clear mandate among the supporters of his own party. Hubert Humphrey, a longtime party leader, might well have commanded such support, had he not been so badly bruised by Vietnam and events surrounding the Democratic Convention of 1968. Edward Moore Kennedy almost certainly would have enjoyed massive popular support, had it not been for the events of Chappaquiddick. As it was, no Democratic contender could claim a clear popular mandate within his party. A late June 1972 Gallup survey showed McGovern the choice of 30 percent of Democrats (his high-water mark), Humphrey of 27 percent, Wallace at 25 percent support,

---

[17] F. Clifton White, obviously an interested party to these events, provides what is nonetheless an interesting discussion of this problem with inexperience. See White, *op. cit.*, especially pp. 263–279.

Muskie at 6 percent, with the remainder scattered among other candidates or uncertain.[18] Kennedy was excluded from this list, as an avowed noncandidate. A Harris survey of about the same time, however, included Kennedy and showed the following distribution of support among Democrats: McGovern, 23 percent; Kennedy, 22 percent; Wallace, 21 percent; Humphrey, 18 percent; Muskie, 7 percent; with the remaining 9 percent for other contenders or not sure.[19] In a field so divided and with no obvious popular choice, the advantage went to the candidate with a strong grass-roots organization, with active, ardent supporters highly participant in party caucuses and in primaries to select convention delegates, who led a movement with some ideological distinctiveness. With George Wallace widely considered far "beyond the pale" (apart from the severe injury he was to sustain in an assassination attempt), McGovern in 1972 was that candidate.

Proponents of the accident thesis also point out, as a related matter, the impact of the actions of the Democratic party's Commission on Delegate Selection and Party Structure, set up subsequent to the 1968 Convention, and first chaired by Senator McGovern himself. His opponents, it has often been remarked, did not realize until too late how substantial an impact the new rules and procedures bearing on delegate selection would have; "the McGovern forces . . . benefited . . . from the sheer confusion into which party leaders were thrown."[20]

Besides the crowded field, the new rules, and a large cadre of spirited grass-roots workers, McGovern appeared to benefit from a variant of the "potential conservative majority" argument which had worked for Senator Goldwater eight years before. There was, it was claimed, a new majority in the country waiting to be tapped, one composed of youth, blacks, and the poor in general, with a good leav-

---

[18] *The Gallup Poll*, release of July 10, 1972.

[19] *The Harris Survey*, release of July 6, 1972.

[20] Penn Kemble and Josh Muravchik, "The New Politics and the Democrats," *Commentary*, 54 (December 1972), p. 82.

ening from the burgeoning intellectual stratum. The Democrats had failed to provide a candidate in 1968 able to mobilize this majority; now, in 1972, the opportunity should not be missed.

All these things considered, the fact remains that the Democrats nominated in 1972 a man who was the first choice of only a distinct minority of his party, and who had managed to secure only a quarter of the votes in Democratic presidential primaries. In December 1971, when Gallup interviewers presented respondents with a list of potential Democratic presidential nominees and asked who among them they would like to see nominated, McGovern was the choice of only 5 percent of Democrats.[21] Three months later, in March 1972, McGovern's position remained unchanged; he was the first choice of just 5 percent of his party's rank and file.[22] Then, following primary election successes (a strong second place finish in the New Hampshire primary, with 36 percent of the vote, victory in the crowded Wisconsin primary, with 29.5 percent of the vote, etc.), unexpected demonstrations of strength in nonprimary states, and the collapse of the candidacy favored by a majority of the regular Democratic leadership, that of Edmund Muskie—and the concomitant rise in media attention and in general public recognition—McGovern's standing among the Democrats improved notably. Still, his backers remained a distinct minority in the party, never numbering more than three in ten. Even with the choice compressed to two or three alternatives, McGovern was unable to achieve the endorsement of a majority in the Democratic citizenry party. Humphrey was backed by 43 percent, McGovern by 28 percent, and Wallace by 24 percent of Democrats, when respondents were asked to choose among the three in a May Harris survey.[23] The same survey recorded 50 percent for Humphrey, 38 percent for McGovern (with 12 per-

[21] *The Gallup Opinion Index*, Report No. 79 (January 1972), p. 6.
[22] *The Gallup Opinion Index*, Report No. 82 (April 1972), p. 3.
[23] *The Harris Survey*, release of May 29, 1972.

cent uncertain), with the choice narrowed to two. In mid-June, Gallup did report McGovern with a slight plurality over Humphrey among Democrats when they were asked to make a choice between these two men only—46 percent to 43 percent—the South Dakota senator's closest approach to a majority.[24]

More damning for the success of his candidacy than his minoritarian status in his own party, was McGovern's reputation as someone too radical, too extreme—an assessment held not only by a majority of the entire electorate but even by a majority of Democrats. A June 1972 Harris survey found just 38 percent of all voters, and 44 percent of Democrats, agreeing with the proposition that "McGovern stands for the right kind of change in this country." [25] In August, 56 percent agreed (while 27 percent disagreed) that McGovern was "too radical and too quick to agree to 'way out' ideas." [26] The same survey found voters by a plurality of five to three accepting the charge that the South Dakota senator had "too many ties to radical and protest groups." A September Harris survey reported that voters, by a margin of two to one (54 percent agreeing, 26 percent disagreeing, with 20 percent not sure), felt the Democratic nominee offered "too extreme liberal views." [27]

An August 1972 Gallup survey adds to this picture of voters' perception of ideological incongruence between their views and those of the Democratic nominee. Forty-three percent of all voters identified themselves as conservatives, while only 13 percent considered McGovern a conservative; on the other hand, 25 percent of the electorate described its views as liberal, while 61 percent saw McGovern as left-of-center. Republicans, of course, displayed a much larger gap between their collective political self-portrait and that which they painted of McGovern, than did Democrats; but even for the latter the disparity was strikingly large. Thus, the proportion of Democrats

---

[24] *The Gallup Poll*, release of June 22, 1972.
[25] *The Harris Survey*, release of July 10, 1972.
[26] *The Harris Survey*, release of August 28, 1972.
[27] *The Harris Survey*, release of October 3, 1972.

identifying themselves as conservatives was nearly twice as large as the percentage seeing the South Dakota senator as conservative. Not surprisingly, the very large bloc of Democratic adherents who indicated in this August survey that they planned to defect and support the Republican nominee showed an especially wide gap between their collective ideological stance and that which they attributed to their party's nominee. Forty-five percent of these defecting Democrats labeled themselves political conservatives, while only 12 percent located McGovern on the conservative end of the political spectrum. In general, the American electorate in August 1972 saw itself more conservative than McGovern and more liberal than Nixon; but the disparity between its collective self-portrait and its McGovern portrait far exceeded that between the electorate and the Republican incumbent.

In 1972, then, the majority party was led by a partially fortuitous set of circumstances to select as its nominee a candidate who never achieved majority support among the rank and file and who was widely perceived at the time of his nomination—that is, even before the inter-party campaign had begun in earnest—as too liberal or too extreme.

Again as in 1964, a series of circumstances, some of his own making, some inflicted upon him, weakened McGovern still further. As the attacks of Rockefeller and Scranton upon Goldwater had provided at least as devastating a critique as the Democrats themselves could muster, so the assault of Jackson and Humphrey—the latter notably in the California primary—provided powerful confirmation of the Republican charge of McGovern's unsteadiness and extremism. The 1972 Convention, far from helping to heal wounds, intensified them. The exclusion of the elected Chicago delegation headed by longtime Democratic leader Richard Daley on highly specious technical grounds [28] could hardly increase the sense of confidence and well-being of Democratic party regulars.

Then there was a matter of the "one thousand" cam-

---

[28] The challenge rested upon a technicality in the McGovern Commission stipulations. While it had been chosen in an open election in which

paign gaffes: The ill-thought-out and subsequently withdrawn incomes proposal calling for governmental distribution of a thousand dollars per person; and the ill-
thought-out and subsequently withdrawn "one thousand
percent" endorsement of then vice-presidential nominee
Thomas Eagleton following disclosures that the Missouri
senator had undergone psychiatric treatment. The entire
"Eagleton affair," with all the attention it commanded, the
prolonged period of immobilization which it inflicted
upon the McGovern campaign, the obvious difficulty
which the Democratic standard-bearer experienced in finding a replacement, detracted enormously from the momentum of the campaign. And such wafflings and errors could
hardly add to the electorate's confidence in the capabili-
ties of the Democratic nominee to manage the executive
branch. Thus, Gallup found in late September, 1972, that
the electorate believed Nixon could "do a better job" in
handling Vietnam than McGovern, by a margin of 32 percentage points; that the incumbent could do a better job
than his opponent in "dealing with inflation and the high
cost of living," by 14 points; and that Nixon could do better than McGovern with "the problem of crime and law-
lessness," by a two-to-one proportion (50–26 percent, with
the remaining 24 percent either having no opinion or
showing little confidence in either candidate's ability).

The accident thesis has a certain measure of plausibility,
for it is rooted in a number of actual conditions: crowded
fields; candidates supported by distinct minorities within
their own parties, perceived as too radical and unstable
and lacking in ability to manage the affairs of state, burdened with, indeed contributing themselves to divided
parties; and campaigns encumbered by a series of errors

over 900,000 votes were cast, the Daley organization had not invited its
opponents to participate in drawing up its slate. (The McGovern Commission had stipulated that state parties must assure that bodies making
up candidate slates permit widespread participation and establish appeals safeguards.) Ironically, the challenge slate which replaced that
headed by Daley had been drawn up at closed meetings from which
Daley supporters had been excluded.

that were in no way intrinsic to the Goldwater and McGovern candidacies respectively.

III. The Thesis of a Changing Dynamic

When the candidate of one of the major parties loses by 16 million votes (as Goldwater did in 1964), or by 17.5 million votes (McGovern in 1972), it is hard to avoid the conclusion that something went wrong. And it is not at all hard to locate a variety of specific circumstances, events, and errors which are associated with the devastatingly lopsided results. While some of the problems experienced by the losers are obviously chance occurrences—few would argue, for example, that any structural attributes of American politics accounted for McGovern's selection of a vice-presidential running mate who would subsequently be embarrassed by revelations of previous mental illness—the possibility must be seriously entertained that many of the specific events associated with the record defeats were but surface reflections of some underlying alteration of the fabric of American national politics. When twice in eight years, first a Republican and then a Democratic presidential nominee lose by near record proportions to opponents not known for their high personal popularity and not blessed by especially favorable political circumstances, and when the losing candidacies manifest strikingly similar patterns, serious exploration of whether there is some fundamental, long-term causation becomes important. This is so especially since the consequences of such unnatural landslides for American political life are so profound. In effect, large numbers of voters in 1964 and 1972 concluded that they did not really have a choice—that there was only one acceptable, though not especially appealing, alternative.

As we have examined the possibility that the recent unlikely landslides reflect a changed dynamic, two broad sets of developments have been identified as potentially the

most significant. One starts from recognition that the citizenry parties as bundles of electoral loyalties are coming
apart. The other focuses upon the political role of the intelligentsia, of the college-educated new middle class generally; on the growth of one stratum of party activists, and
upon an ideological polarization of ascendant Republican
and Democratic activist cohorts.

AN EMERGING "NO MAJORITY": THE EXTENT OF THE
WEAKENING OF PARTY LOYALTIES

Intermittently over the last two decades, some politicians, journalists, and scholars alike have been attracted to
the idea that the United States again stands on the brink of
a critical realignment, a massive restructuring of electoral
loyalties in which the relative strength of the contending
parties is significantly altered for the long term. A major
transformation is in fact proceeding, but it is not manifesting itself in some coherent new majority—comparable to
the Democrats' meteoric rise during the 1930s.

No facet of the current transformation assumes greater
importance than the pronounced weakening of citizenry
ties to political parties. Groups are relocating across party
lines, to be sure, in response to new conflict structures.
But equally impressive is the movement of voters away
from firm partisan ties generally. We are becoming a nation of electoral transients.

Evidence of a weakening of party loyalties is abundant.
For one thing, a growing proportion of the electorate,
when asked the now-familiar "Generally speaking in politics as of today, do you consider yourself . . . ?" has come
to answer *independent* rather than *Democrat* or *Republican*. Both Gallup and the Survey Research Center of Michigan found that self-described independents began outnumbering Republican identifiers by the end of the
sixties, for the first time since the inauguration of systematic voter surveys. By 1974, about one third of the popula-

tion was consistently selecting the independent label, with about one quarter describing themselves as Republicans and something over four in ten as Democrats. Throughout the 1940s and 1950s, independents had hovered around 20 percent of the electorate (Figure 6.1). Within Wisconsin, a state long noted for its high level of political independence, the proportion of the electorate identifying with one or another of the political parties declined from 70 percent in 1960 to 58 percent in 1974.[29]

Figure 7.1. Partisan Identification in the United States, 1937–1974

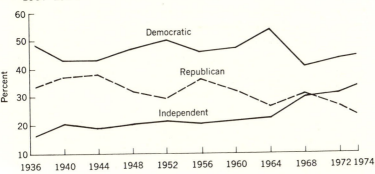

SOURCE: Data from following AIPO surveys: *1937*, 72, 104; *1940*, 208, 209; *1944*, 328, 329; *1948*, 429, 431, 432, 433; *1952*, 504, 505, 507, 508; *1956*, 571, 572, 573, 574; *1960*, 635, 636, 637, 638; *1964*, 697, 698, 699, 701; *1968*, 768, 769, 770, 771; *1972*, 852, 853, 854, 855, 856, 857; *1974*, 889, 897, 899, 903, 906.

College-educated voters have consistently comprised a higher proportion of self-described independents than the public at large, but the growth of independent status in the former cohort has increased dramatically in recent years. In 1944, according to Gallup surveys, 47 percent of college-trained voters identified as Republicans, 31 percent as Democrats, and 22 percent as independents. As recently

---

[29] Jack Dennis, "Trends in Public Support for the American Political System" (paper delivered at the Annual Meeting of the American Political Science Association, Chicago, Ill., August 29–September 2, 1974), p. 4.

as 1960, there had been relatively little change in the college cohort: the proportion of Republicans was down
slightly, that of Democrats up modestly, while independents had remained constant at 23 percent of the total.
Over the last half-decade, however, independents have
become the largest "party" among college-educated Americans. According to 1973 Gallup data, 38 percent of voters
who had attended college thought of themselves as independents, 30 percent as Republicans, and 32 percent as
Democrats.

Not only are larger numbers of voters describing themselves as independents, but we are seeing as well an actual increase in independent electoral behavior: specifically, in split-ticket voting, where an elector casts his
ballot for the Republican candidate(s) in one set of offices
and at the same time supports the Democratic nominee(s)
for others. This is the crucial variable, for "the real test of
the voter's independence is whether or not he splits his
ticket. A voter may say he is an independent, but this can
be confirmed only by his actual voting behavior." [30]

Walter Dean Burnham has plotted the number of congressional districts producing split-party outcomes (the
vote for president going one way and the vote for congressman the other) throughout the twentieth century. His
data show a marked secular increase in this manifestation
of split-ticket voting in the contemporary period. Thus,
voters gave a majority to one party in the presidential balloting and to another in House contests in fewer than 20
percent of the congressional districts in 1952. By 1968, 32
percent of the congressional districts displayed this split-
party outcome pattern; and in 1972 it reached an all-time
high of 42 percent.[31] Burnham maintains that while data

[30] Walter DeVries and V. Lance Tarrance, *The Ticket-Splitter: A New
Force in American Politics* (Grand Rapids, Mich.: William B. Eerdmans,
1972), p. 23. This volume provides a useful collection of data on the actual increase in the incidence of split-ticket voting.
[31] Burnham, *Critical Elections and the Mainsprings of American Politics*, p. 109. The 1972 data were made available to the authors by Professor Burnham.

have not been compiled prior to 1900, it can be assumed
that between the Civil War and the turn of the century,
split results existed normally in less than 5 percent of the
congressional districts, and rarely, if ever, exceeded 10
percent of such districts. There has been a long-term expansion in the number of split presidential-congressional
outcomes, then, but the big increase has come over the last
decade.

Howard Reiter provides data on the incidence of split
outcomes involving two other offices, governorships and
U.S. Senate seats. In the 1920s, he found, there was a
divergent outcome (Republicans victors in the Senate
vote, Democrats in the gubernatorial balloting, or vice
versa) on average in about 20 percent of the states holding
these two elections simultaneously. The proportion of split
outcomes in the 1940s remained essentially the same, and
while there was an increase in the 1950s, it was modest.
But since 1960 the level has been notably higher: Thus, 44
percent of states with simultaneous gubernatorial and senatorial elections in 1960 produced split results, 56 percent
in 1964, 59 percent in 1966, 60 percent in 1968, 46 percent
in 1970, and 50 percent in 1972.[32]

These general aggregate data are suggestive, but the
measure of the level of split-ticket voting which they provide lacks precision. An election in which 49 percent of
voters in a district give their support to a Republican presidential nominee and a Democratic congressional candidate, for example, and one where 70 percent of the electorate endorse a Republican for president while 70 percent
vote Democratic in the House contest, are classified as the
same. Both are described as involving split-party outcomes, even though the apparent incidence of ticket splitting was minimal in the first case, and very large in the

[32] The data through 1968 are from Howard Reiter, (an unpublished
paper presented at the John Fitzgerald Kennedy School of Government,
Harvard University, 1969) and have been reprinted in DeVries and Tarrance, *op. cit.*, p. 31.

second. Survey data serve as a useful complement, especially as they permit us to assess the incidence with which *individuals* engage in independent voting—defined variously in terms of a split ticket in a single election, and of moving back and forth between the parties over time.

In each of their presidential election year surveys since 1952, researchers at the University of Michigan's Survey Research Center have asked respondents whether they "have . . . always voted for the same party or have . . . voted for different parties for President." In 1952, 71 percent of respondents in the national sample indicated that they had always or "mostly" voted for the same party. Sixteen years later, the SRC reported that the proportion of consistent Democratic and Republican presidential voters had dropped to just 56 percent of the electorate.

The best indicator, perhaps, of the level of independent voting is the frequency with which individual electors support Democrats for some offices while backing Republicans for others in a given election. We have no fully reliable data prior to the 1940s, but DeVries and Tarrance have estimated that proportions of only 20 percent or so of the electorate in the split-ticket category were common.[33] In 1948, Gallup for the first time asked a national sample a question permitting systematic assessment of the incidence of straight-ticket voting: "Did you vote a straight ticket—that is, did you vote for all candidates of the one party—or did you vote a split ticket, that is, did you vote for some candidates of one party and some of the other?" Sixty-two percent of respondents described themselves as straight-ticket voters, 38 percent as ticket-splitters. Gallup repeated essentially the same question in subsequent surveys in the 1950s and early 1960s, and found little change in the proportions.[34] Thus, in 1964, a post-election survey

[33] DeVries and Tarrance, p. 22.
[34] After 1948, the Gallup question was worded: "For the various political offices, did you vote for all the candidates of one party—that is, straight ticket—or did you vote for the candidates of different parties?"

showed 59 percent having voted a straight ticket, 42 percent having split their ballots (Table 6.3). Since 1964, however, the percentage of ticket-splitters has increased dramatically: According to Gallup, it reached 56 percent of the electorate in 1968 and 62 percent in 1972. Over the last decade, then, the proportion of the electorate splitting their ballots in presidential election years has jumped from roughly two-fifths to nearly two-thirds.

Table 7.3. Proportions of the Electorate Voting Straight and Split Tickets, 1948–1972; in the Country at large, and by Region (Column Percentages)

	1948	1960	1964	1968	1972
NATIONALLY					
Split	38	34	42	56	62
Straight	62	66	59	44	38
NORTHEAST					
Split	27	23	45	54	60
Straight	73	77	55	46	40
MIDWEST					
Split	42	40	39	58	56
Straight	58	60	61	42	44
SOUTH					
Split	30	24	34	55	64
Straight	70	76	66	45	36
WEST					
Split	56	57	50	57	72
Straight	44	43	50	43	28

SOURCE: Data from following AIPO post-election surveys: *1948*, 432; *1960*, 638; *1964*, 701; *1968*, 771; *1972*, 860.

This striking increase in split-ticket voting did not occur evenly across the country, but was substantially greater in the Northeast and in the South, while less pronounced in the Midwest and West. In view of the region's dissatisfaction with Democratic presidential nominees, it is not surprising that the South manifested the biggest drop in straight-party voting, from 76 percent in 1960 to 36 percent in 1972. But the drop was almost equally precipitous in the northeastern states, from 77 percent to 40 percent over these four elections. While there was less change in the West, this section consistently produced the highest proportion of ticket-splitters. Legacies of the Progressive era, involving both cultural orientations toward party regularity and specific legislation designed to weaken the hold of parties on the electoral process and to encourage independent voting, were more prominent in the western states than elsewhere in the country. Back in 1948, when ticket-splitters numbered only 27 percent of the eastern electorate, 30 percent in the South, and 42 percent in the Midwest, they encompassed a clear majority (56 percent) of western states voters. The most important conclusion supported by the data does not relate to regional *differences,* however, but to the *similarities:* there has been a secular increase in ticket splitting in all sections; and the South has not contributed disproportionately to the overall rise.

Michigan's Survey Research Center has asked a question similar to Gallup's, but limited to state and local races below the gubernatorial level.[35] Since presidential elections, with their focus on candidate personality and programs, are known to manifest the highest incidence of nonparty-oriented voting, we would expect the SRC question to yield higher proportions of straight-ticket voters than the Gallup item which included the total spectrum of contests. This was indeed the case. But the underlying pattern, comprising a substantial drop in straight-party voting in recent years, remains the same. Thus, the 1952 SRC Survey reported 74 percent of the electorate as "party regulars" at the state and local level. In 1956, the proportion was 71 percent, and in 1960, 73 percent (Table 6.4). By 1968, however, it had fallen off 20 points, to 52 percent; and reached its all-time low—so far as we can tell—in

---

[35] In 1952, 1966, and 1968, the question read: "How about the elections for other [than governor] state and local offices—did you vote a straight ticket or did you vote for candidates from different parties?" The question was framed essentially the same in the other years.

Table 7.4. Proportions of the Electorate Voting Straight and Split Tickets for State and Local Offices, 1952–1972; in the Country at Large, and by Region (Column Percentages)

	1952	1956	1958	1960	1962	1964	1966	1968	1970	1972
NATIONALLY										
Split	26	29	31	27	42	40	50	48	52	58
Straight	74	71	69	73	58	60	50	52	48	42
NORTHEAST										
Split	15	20	24	22	36	37	50	40	50	48
Straight	85	80	76	78	64	63	50	61	50	52
MIDWEST										
Split	33	41	37	33	45	46	53	54	55	63
Straight	67	59	63	67	55	54	47	46	45	37
SOUTH										
Split	17	16	22	16	35	32	39	44	40	56
Straight	83	85	78	84	65	68	61	56	60	44
WEST										
Split	42	41	39	47	55	47	58	58	66	67
Straight	58	59	61	53	45	53	42	42	34	33

SOURCE: Data from the Survey Research Center/Center for Political Studies surveys for the ten election years.

1972, when just 42 percent of the electorate voted a straight ticket for the lesser offices. Again, there are regional variations, but the national sweep of increased party irregularity in the 1960s and 1970s is the most impressive datum.

In view of the rupture which occurred within the national Democratic party during the late sixties and early seventies, we are not surprised by the finding that self-described Democrats show a greater rise of independent voting than Republican identifiers. But it is substantial for both party groups. Gallup reports that the ranks of ticket-splitters expanded by 25 percentage points among self-identified Democrats between 1960 and 1972, and by 15 points among Republican adherents.[36]

The weakening of party loyalties and hence of party regularity is clearly evident at all levels of the electoral process—local, state, and national. But the most dramatic effects have centered around presidential balloting. The magnitude of McGovern's 1972 defeat, occurring together with notable Democratic successes in congressional and gubernatorial contests, serves as the prime case in point. *Only one-fourth* of those who identified themselves as Democrats in November 1972 had performed such an elementary act of party regularity as voting for Democratic presidential nominees in both 1968 and 1972.[37] And in 1972 just 55 percent of the national electorate were "consistent partisans"—either self-described Democrats voting Democratic in the presidential contest, or Republican identifiers voting for the GOP nominee; this compares to the 81 percent classified as consistent partisans in 1936, 72 percent in 1948, and 78 percent in 1960.

Jack Dennis has developed a complementary set of data on public orientations toward political parties as institutions, based upon surveys of the Wisconsin electorate between 1964 and 1974.[38] Illustrative of these materials is the question of whether party labels should be stricken

---

[36] These data are from the same AIPO surveys cited in Table 6.3.

[37] AIPO Survey No. 857.

[38] Dennis, *op. cit.*, pp. 8–19.

from the ballot.[39] Supporting use of partisan labels to identify candidates is surely a modest expression of general
confidence in parties and attachment to them. In 1964, 67
percent of Wisconsin voters favored keeping party identification on the ballot—a figure which in itself seems low,
but over the past ten years the proportion has dropped off
massively, reaching just 38 percent in 1974. Just over one
Wisconsinite in three professed to care enough about parties to want to know with which ones the candidates were
affiliated.

All measures lead to the same conclusion. There has
been a long-term decline of party allegiance, and a dramatic drop-off over the last decade. A large segment of the
electorate now describes itself as independent, and an
even larger proportion is behaving independently, showing little regard for party in electoral choice. Why, then, is
this change occurring? What are its precipitants?

One set of answers involves the changing character of
the electorate, and related to this, changes in the structure
of political communications. One effect of the higher education explosion has been to extend dramatically the proportion of the population which feels no need for parties
as active intermediaries in the voting decision. Higher
levels of information bearing on political issues and hence
a higher measure of issue orientation, and a general feeling of confidence in one's ability to judge candidates and
their programs apart from party links, are promoted by the
experience of higher education. College-educated voters
tend to have more varied and extensive sources of political
information than the population at large, and are thereby
more likely to respond to stimuli other than those which
the party provides. We have already noted that a much
higher proportion of college-educated Americans, than of
the public generally, describe themselves as independents. The greater incidence of split-ticket voting among
those with exposure to higher education is even more

---

[39] The proposition presented respondents, inviting their agreement or
disagreement, was: "It would be better if, in all elections, we put no
party labels on the ballot."

striking. In 1968, according to Gallup, just one-third (34 percent) of the college educated voted a straight ticket, in comparison to nearly half (48 percent) of the high school and grade school educated. The extraordinary gains in formal higher education have contributed to a growing reservoir of people inclined to independent voting.

The emergence of the electronic communications media as the principal source of political information is yet another precipitant of independent electoral behavior.[40] The prominence of the electronic media serves to promote partisan irregularity in two ways. Party activists are displaced as the primary source of political information relevant to candidate assessment for the rank and file of the population. And with attention focused so much on the style and personal attributes of the contenders, the role of party ties is necessarily weakened. In an age of television, candidates are brought into voters' living rooms. As personal images become more salient, the importance of the party label to the voting decision must lessen.

Parties surely continue to be prominent political entities, because they are broadly appreciated vehicles for organizing elections, reducing the alternatives to a manageable number; but they are less critically needed—or at least are perceived to be less needed—by the contemporary electorate, as some of their old functions get taken over by new structures. Historically, parties have performed important linkage functions, connecting a populace with the centers of governance. Communications passed up and down this linkage structure as, for example, people in elected office used party organization and personnel to

[40] The Survey Research Center has asked respondents in its election year surveys, "Of all these ways of following the campaign, which would you say you got the most information from—newspaper, radio, T.V., or magazines?" In 1952, just 32 percent indicated that television was the prime source. By 1968, however, the proportion was nearly two-thirds (64 percent). John S. Saloma and Frederick H. Sontag note that in the 1960s television replaced newspapers as the most widely followed media; and that television is rated as the most believable news source by a large margin over newspapers, its closest competitor. *Parties* (New York: Vintage Books, 1973), p. 251.

communicate information on government programs and to generate electoral backing. Increasingly today, the communications linkage is performed by the national communications media. The press and president, not the parties, vie for influence in agenda setting. Ad hoc campaign organizations—of which the Nixon Committee to Reelect the President simply is thus far the supreme manifestation—are set up to harness the national communications structure and deal directly with voters, without the intermediate intervention of regular party apparatus.

An electorate which is highly educated, which secures a personalized view of contenders through the intervention of television, and which deals with parties that have experienced a severe erosion of one of their great historic functions, will be bound less by partisan identification in its electoral behavior. This precipitant of party irregularity is unlikely to recede. Rather, it should become ever more prominent.

Another quite different source of the weakening of party ties stems from the breakup of a series of group alignments with the parties, some extending back to the New Deal, others to the early years of American political experience—a subject discussed in the preceding chapter.

Any period distinguished by the erosion of long-standing group alignments to the parties, by definition a period of partisan disaggregation, must be characterized by a high level of independent electoral behavior. Old loyalties are breaking up, but have not disappeared. Voters find themselves cross-pressured between old ties and new interests. The sources of the collapse of old alignments manifest themselves in certain electoral contests, but not in others. Thus, in the contemporary period, white southerners have abandoned the national Democratic party en masse but continue to express their historic loyalties by heavy Democratic voting in many state and local contests.

The breakup of old group ties with the parties does not, however, necessarily contribute to *long-term* weakening of partisan attachments. In the past, the collapse of old alignments has been followed by the rise of new ones—that is, the establishment of new partisan identifications for significant segments of the electorate.

In the present period, groups surely are crossing party lines, but it is unlikely that this will lead to a new party alignment structure comparable in scope, strength, and stability to that of the New Deal. Instead, the unraveling of the New Deal alliances seems to be resulting in what Samuel Lubell described as "a new alignment of two incomplete, narrow-based coalitions. . . ." [41] The key here is that party loyalties are now so lightly held. A Roosevelt era–type realignment necessarily requires a condition of rather strong and persisting group *alignments*. That both the Democrats and the Republicans probably will be unable to establish decisive majority party status in national politics in the foreseeable future reflects not ineptness, or a failure to deal adequately with pressing national problems (although inadequacies there are and will surely continue to be), but the unwillingness of decisive portions of the citizenry to give the unvarnished loyalty such a coalition requires. The massive increase in formal education and the role of the electronic media—along with a more diffuse set of changes attendant on entry into a society characterized by affluence, advanced technology, high physical mobility, and impersonalization—have produced an electorate which is so fluid as to obviate the old "star and satellite" majority and minority party relationship.

It is a simple fact that Americans need parties much less now than in the past as intermediaries in shaping their electoral decisions. The electorate has become, for the long run, more issue oriented and more candidate oriented, and necessarily, then, less party oriented. As such, it is up for grabs. Or as Daniel Patrick Moynihan has put the matter, "we are getting an atomized electorate, by definition an unstable one." [42]

---

[41] Lubell, *The Hidden Crisis in American Politics*, p. 278.

[42] Moynihan, "My Turn: The Lessons of '72," *Newsweek*, 80 (November 27, 1972), p. 17.

In this situation, alternating landslides—achieved first by one party, then by the other—become more ordinary occurrences. Less anchored by party loyalties, more inclined to independent electoral behavior—the American electorate can be moved massively by the events of the day: the particular mix of candidates, programs, and problems prevailing in a given election. Extreme alternations in party fortune will occur most frequently, of course, in voting for highly visible offices where candidate personality and issues become readily manifest. This weakening of party loyalties does not by itself explain why we have entered an era of unnatural landslides; but it does account for a context in which landslides can occur with greater ease than in the past.

ACTIVISTS, IDEOLOGY, AND PARTY STRUCTURE:
A CHANGING DYNAMIC FOR "THE MAKING"
OF THE PRESIDENTIAL NOMINEE

The 1972 presidential election occurred in a setting distinguished by a confrontation of new problems and the juggling of new collections of interests—and all this with an electorate cast adrift from its partisan moorings. The electoral instability is understandable enough. Important as this is, however, it is only part of the puzzle. For what may be the key piece, we must look to developments converging around those segments of the electorate most influential in nominating politics, especially the stratum of party activists.

One of the first attempts to locate a new dynamic in American national politics within changes affecting the activist stratum was Aaron Wildavsky's study of the Goldwater candidacy.[43] Wildavsky concluded that the Goldwater phenomenon "is not a temporary aberration, but

---

[43] Wildavsky, "The Goldwater Phenomenon: Purists, Politicians, and the Two-Party System," *Review of Politics*, 27 (July 1965), pp. 386–413.

represents a profound current within the Republican party," and insisted that "it becomes impossible for me to join the wishful thinkers who believe that the moderates and liberals in the party will automatically gain control after Goldwater's severe defeat in the election." [44]

In Wildavsky's view, the Goldwater movement developed near the outset of a new cycle, distinguished by "the beginnings of ideology in the United States." [45] For the first time on the stage of American national two-party politics, a cadre of highly involved people whom Wildavsky labeled "purists" were emerging in significant numbers to influence if not dictate the outcomes of contests for presidential nominations.

Central to this interpretation was the view that the Goldwater activists shared with an emergent activist stratum on the left a distaste for the compromising, accommodationist tendencies which had generally prevailed in U.S. politics. Distinguished by an ascendant orientation to issues, purists left and right were more sensitive to integrity of program than to maintenance of the party organization, more concerned with getting an ideologically "right" candidate than with nominating a winner.

On the basis of extensive interviews with Goldwater delegates, Wildavsky constructed a portrait of a type of activist whom he expected to become influential in both national parties:

Here we begin to see the distinguishing characteristics of the purists: their emphasis on internal criteria for decision, on what they believe "deep down inside"; their rejection of compromise; their lack of orientation toward winning; their stress on the style and purity of decision—integrity, consistency, adherence to internal norms.[46]

The old activist strata, the "politicians," had a very different characteristic approach to political life. "The belief

---

[44] *Ibid.*, p. 411.

[45] *Ibid.*, p. 413.

[46] *Ibid.*, p. 393. The empirical base for Wildavsky's observations comprised interviews with 150 delegates to the 1964 Republican Convention.

in compromise and bargaining; the sense that public policy is made in small steps rather than big leaps; the concern with conciliating the opposition and broadening public appeal; and the willingness to bend a little to capture public support are all characteristics of the traditional politician in the United States." [47]

In a study published in 1962, James Q. Wilson had developed essentially the same distinction between two sets of activists, although in a very different context. He was examining the Democratic club movement in New York City, California, and Illinois.[48] A sharp division had emerged among Democratic activists in these areas, although one which Wilson did not then believe would move out to dominate national politics. On the one hand, were the party regulars, rejected by their opponents as "hacks," "organization men," "bosses," and "machine leaders." The regulars in turn labeled their opposition "dilettantes," "crackpots," "outsiders," and "hypocritical do-gooders." [49] Such tension was by no means novel, but as Wilson saw it, the division between the "amateur Democrat" and the "professional" had taken on a new, greatly extended dimension.

Wilson's amateur Democrat was the intellectual kin of Wildavsky's purist. The amateur was an issue-oriented activist. He wanted political parties to be programmatic, internally democratic, and largely free of patronage incentives. His programmatic party would offer a real alternative. To vote for it would be to choose a clear set of policy proposals linked to a coherent philosophy of government.

Like Wildavsky, Wilson saw the strengthening of issue activists having powerful implications for American electoral politics. Indeed, separating them from the regulars is an alternate conception of the nature of democracy gener-

---

[47] *Ibid.*, p. 396.
[48] Wilson, *The Amateur Democrat* (Chicago: The University of Chicago Press, 1962).
[49] *Ibid.*, p. 2.

ally. When the amateur Democrats were able to succeed, Wilson argued, they weakened the capacity of their party to engage in broad-based, diffuse, accommodationist, coalition-building activities.

> If American parties have traditionally been sources of social coherence, this has in part been due to the fact that occasionally, and for very fundamental reasons, they have become identified with the opposite sides of crucial issues. . . . The amateur is . . . interested in reducing the center-seeking, consensus-building tendency of parties.[50]

Recently, Arnold Kaufman has nicely described characteristics of the issue-oriented activist stratum—although he was referring only to its left-of-center, "new politics" branch:

> The new politics is principally a politics of issues, not candidates. Loyalty to party, loyalty to candidates and winning elections are important only as they contribute to the fulfillment of the radical liberal's program and values. Those who practice the new politics are therefore ready to exercise an electoral veto on Democratic candidates when doing so serves their concern for issues. . . . The new politics implies predominant concern with the overall dynamic of the political process, not with the grubby ambitions of the lesser-evil politicians.[51]

The labels may vary but the distinction is essentially the same, whether one speaks of *purists vs. politicians* or *amateurs vs. professionals*.[52] One ideal type, the *issue-*

---

[50] *Ibid.*, pp. 357, 359, 360.

[51] Arnold S. Kaufman, *The Radical Liberal* (New York: Simon and Schuster, 1970), pp. xii–xiii.

[52] The literature in which this distinction is variously interpreted and assessed now has grown to considerable size. Besides the pieces already cited, see Wildavsky, "The Meaning of 'Youth' in the Struggle for Control of the Democratic Party," in his collected essays, *The Revolt Against the Masses* (New York: Basic Books, 1971), pp. 270–287; John W. Soule and James Clarke, "Amateurs and Professionals: A Study of Delegates to the 1968 Democratic National Convention," *American Political Science Review* (September 1970), pp. 888–898; Soule and Clarke, "Ideology and Amateurism: The 1968 National Conventions" (paper prepared for the Brookings Institution, 1971); C. Richard Hofstetter, "Organizational Ac-

oriented activist, is primarily concerned with the advancement of a program. He evaluates candidates not so much as potential winners or losers, but on the basis of whether their issue commitments are correct. The model which he holds up for the proper functioning of a party is not one of accommodation, consensus-building, being "all things to all people"; but rather a conflict model which posits the role of parties as sharpening the divisions around crucial issues in the interest of resolving rather than papering over them. His opposite is the *party-oriented activist,* a role which has been dominant in American politics throughout much of our history and is intimately associated with "our expectations concerning the behavior of parties and politicians." The latter type is occupied with the maintenance of the organization, and its success. It is more important that a candidate be a potential winner than that he meet tightly defined issue or ideological standards. The task of party is accommodation of the broadest range of groups and interests on behalf of a majority.

This distinction between issue-oriented and party-oriented activists relates directly to another which Theodore Lowi has developed, as to two alternate functions of political parties. The American parties historically, Lowi argues, have been of the *constituent* variety, concerned with organizing and structuring the context in which conflict occurs. Put somewhat differently, the American parties have not been programmatically coherent or much concerned with policy processes and outputs. They have been vehicles for *organizing the government, not for governing.* In opposition to the constituent party is one which Lowi refers to as *responsible.* The latter variety is oc-

tivists: The Bases of Participation in Amateur and Professional Groups," *American Politics Quarterly,* 1 (April 1973), pp. 244–276; Vicki G. Semel, "Ideology and Incentives among Democratic Amateurs and Professionals" (paper delivered at the 1973 Annual Meeting of the American Political Science Association, September 1973); and E. Gene De Felice, "Purism vs. Professionalism among Party Leaders in a Semi-Competitive Party System" (paper delivered at the 1973 Annual Meeting of the American Political Science Association, September 1973).

cupied with constituent functions, but as well with policy shaping and policy making, "it stands for something." The party-oriented activist is comfortable with a constituent notion of the political party; the issue activist, in contrast, is attracted to the "responsible party" model.[53]

Both Wildavsky and Wilson identified issue-oriented activists with a rather distinctive socioeconomic position: highly educated (in terms of formal attainment), upper–middle-class, drawn heavily from professional occupations, with important leavening from the intellectual stratum. The commitment of the issue activist to his role and to his definition of the responsibilities of party are linked directly, then, to objective characteristics of his socioeconomic position. He (or she) has the formal training necessary to participate effectively in a "politics of ideas," and his social status and economic position are such as to make unappealing or unnecessary a politics of organization maintenance and patronage.

Is it valid to describe the issue activists as "ideologues," in contrast to more pragmatic, "nonideological" party-oriented activists? Well no, at least not exactly. To do so seems to confuse more than clarify. If one is comfortable with the prevailing lines of party and/or national programs, one is not likely to stress policy considerations. Those emphasizing issues almost necessarily are ideological dissenters—which is what "ideologue" often connotes.

Just how the discomfort with existing policy comes about involves some interesting considerations, and admits contrasting interpretations. One view is that a group of activists simply finds current approaches insufficient in terms of its values, interests, and perspectives. So they advance programs designed to change things. Other activists who are generally content with existing programmatic stances can afford to emphasize organization maintenance, can afford to be moderate—in the sense of

---

[53] Lowi, "Party, Policy, and Constitution in America" in Chambers and Burnham (eds.), *The American Party Systems: Stages of Political Development*, pp. 238–239.

not calling for broad new policies which by definition are divisive, which shatter the prevailing policy structure.

A variant of this interpretation seems closer to the mark, however, especially as it links up with the argument which we have advanced on the orientations of the intelligentsia, and which Wilson, Wildavsky, et al, have brought up in their analyses of purists or amateurs. People with a high measure of training in abstract ideas are more inclined thereby to probe established programs. The probing sensitizes them to insufficiencies, to gaps between the calling and the coming. The college-trained, affluent professional is more likely to scrutinize policies-as-they-are, and *the very act of careful scrutiny is apt to promote dissatisfactions,* beyond whatever might result from the basic substantive values which are held.

Within the Democratic party nationally, issue activists are likely to manifest a new left or new liberalism posture, since the Democracy has been securely committed to old liberalism for several decades. Dissatisfaction with policies-as-they-are for national Democrats means dissatisfaction with the established ideological structure and response of the New Deal. The long-standing equalitarianism of Democratic leadership assures that a rejection of the old will carry, predominantly, to commitments further left. By way of contrast, Republican issue activists are inclined to push against the established policies of moderate, eclectic conservatism, toward a conservatism at once more pure and coherent. So Democratic issue activists are heavily "left ideologues," and their Republican counterparts "right ideologues" only to the extent that they articulate discontent with existing approaches *in directions consistent with, determined by the established commitments* which have defined the stances of the respective parties.

The success of the Goldwater candidacy for the Republican nomination in 1964 appears in significant measure the product of an enormous strengthening of the position of issue activists. It was, in the final analysis, a candidacy of grass-roots, issue-oriented, conservative activists in the Republican party. The Arizona senator conformed superbly to the standards of this group. He carved out a distinctive, avowedly conservative program. He confronted issues directly. He made no effort to paper over differences, but rather sharpened them. His was a politics of morality, of ideological coherence, of presenting a conflict-inviting choice rather than an accommodation-inviting echo.

The parallels in McGovern's 1972 candidacy, again, are compelling. The South Dakota senator was not the choice of a majority of his party's rank and file. His support among the regular leadership of the party never approached majority status. But he was backed by a decisive majority of issue-oriented, left-of-center activists within the Democracy. Both friend and foe acknowledged that here was the fulcrum of McGovern's support. Thus, Michael Harrington (a friend) wrote in the *Nation* of "McGovern's basic constituency" as "issue-oriented, white, college-educated." [54] And Jeane Kirkpatrick (a foe) pointed to the same issue-conscious, upper–middle-class activists as the core of the movement which secured for McGovern the Democratic presidential nomination—although in terms hardly designed to be flattering:

Intellectuals enamored with righteousness and possibility; college students, for whom perfectionism is an occupational hazard; portions of the upper classes freed from concern with economic self-interest; clergymen contemptuous of materialism; bureaucrats with expanding plans to eliminate evil; romantics derisive of *Babbitt* and *Main Street*. [55]

Like Goldwater's, McGovern's politics was one of discontent with things as they are, and of principle and moralism. The electorate, he argued, wanted a candidate who would confront issues directly, who would take clear and

---

[54] Harrington, "The Myth That Was Real," *Nation*, 215 (November 27, 1972), p. 521.

[55] Kirkpatrick, "The Revolt of the Masses," *Commentary*, 55 (February 1973), p. 61.

principled stands. "I think the American people want me to say what I believe," McGovern told an interviewer from a San Diego television station shortly before the California primary, "I'm not trying to get in line with Dr. Gallup. You can't straddle the issues any more." [56] The issue-oriented activists of the left, Tom Wicker observed, "had more nearly nominated an Idea—a man of courage and integrity and candor who had stumped the country for three years attacking the 'old leadership' as straddling and ducking the issues [i.e., promoting a continuance of the old liberalism], compromising with principle, clinging to outmoded formulas and deceiving the people." [57]

The neatness of the issue-oriented–party-oriented distinction is naturally clouded in the real world of political life. What is evident is the emergence of an activist stratum, heavily college-educated and middle-class, inclined to substitute a conflict for an accommodation model, and preoccupied with the politics of issues and principles. No word ranks higher in the lexicon of party-directed participants than *compromise*. For the issue activist, by way of contrast, the country had paid a severe programmatic price for an excessive fealty to a politics of compromise.

The McGovern coalition, and that around Goldwater in 1964, were to a notable degree bottom- rather than top-directed. They comprised movements seeking candidates; instead of being coalitions engineered by candidates. There was, of course, an important element of leadership, in that the South Dakota and Arizona senators were hardly pawns. But to a striking extent, both were cases of movements searching out spokesmen. For the Democrats, Eugene McCarthy had filled that role in 1968; in 1972, with considerably greater energy and commitment, George McGovern rode the movement to his party's nomination. It is important to see the extent to which right-of-center, issue-concerned activists on the one hand, and left-

[56] As quoted by Wicker, "McGovern With Tears," *New York Times Magazine* (November 5, 1972), p. 99.
[57] *Ibid.*

of-center activists on the other, moved by fairly clearly defined issue concerns, sought out suitable nominees; Theodore White described this nicely when he referred to Goldwater as not so much the captain as "the emblem of a major coup d'état in American politics." [58]

The McGovern movement in 1972 did not spring miraculously from the dissent and turmoil surrounding Vietnam. Its precursors are clearly evident, in Democratic club movement of the 1950s, and as well, although in a different party, in the 1964 Goldwater triumph within the Republican party. For two decades, an activist stratum— split into right and left—which focuses upon a politics of issues has been gaining strength in American national politics.

THE WEAKENING OF PARTY ORGANIZATION

This activist stratum has been aided, of course, by the weakness of regular party organization. American party structures have never been strong compared to their counterparts in Europe, and have weakened steadily in the twentieth century under repeated assaults. Most notable was the Progressive movement of the early years of this century. In their wars with the party bosses, Progressives, in a very real sense the intellectual precursors of the Goldwater and McGovern activists of the last decade, managed to deal party organization a number of severe blows, especially in the introduction on a wide scale of the direct primary as the vehicle for nominating candidates for state and local office. Rather than by the party organization, nominations would be controlled by voters who turned out in the primaries. An issue-conscious, activist stratum, blocked by the regular party machinery, substituted a theory of *intra-party* democracy for one which saw democracy *between* the parties. The fact that much of the United States was in an era of massive one-partyism, Democrats dominant in the South and the Republicans in wide areas

---

[58] White, *The Making of the President, 1964*, p. 250.

of the North, obviously strengthened the Progressives'
case. If inter-party democracy was made a sham by one-
partyism, perhaps intra-party democracy was the only alternative.

In any case, the capacity of regulars to control party life
was decisively weakened and a theory of intra-party democracy, compatible with the American value system
which has stressed participation and equalitarianism, took
root to an extent not found in any other democratic system.
The widespread, casual description of party leaders able to
dominate the affairs of their organizations as at least
slightly sinister bosses, is indicative of the underlying legitimacy of the claim to intra-party democracy.

Over the last half-decade, a new era of party reform activity has opened, one which may achieve results quite as
substantial as those of the Progressive years, and one
which surely has much in common intellectually with that
led by the Progressives. This new surge of party reform
originates largely within the Democratic party, but in a
less rapid and dramatic fashion it is engulfing the Republicans as well.

The rallying cry of contemporary reform, like that of the
early years of the century, is *democratization*—opening
the party structure to broader participation, reducing the
opportunities for dominance by party regulars. The tumul-
tuous 1968 Democratic Convention created two commissions, one headed by George McGovern to study and
make recommendations bearing on delegate selection (a
commission subsequently chaired by Representative Donald Fraser of Minnesota), the other led by Representative
James O'Hara of Michigan to study convention rules and
operations. Recommendations of the McGovern-Fraser
Commission, implemented for the 1972 Convention,
proved particularly important and generated rancorous
intra-party debate.[59]

The commission insisted that internal party democracy

---

[59] For the full text of the recommendations, see *Mandate for Reform: A
Report of the Commission on Party Structure and Delegate Selection to
the Democratic National Committee*, 1970.

was the primary value to be promoted. And in this context, it attacked such prevailing practices as (1) the absence of clear rules governing delegate selection (in twenty states), a condition which left "the entire process to the discretion of a handful of party leaders"; (2) the ability of majorities to use "their numerical superiority to deny delegate representation to the supporters of minority presidential candidates"; (3) frequent recourse to "secret caucuses" and other vehicles of "closed slate-making"; (4) underrepresentation of blacks, women, and youth at the national conventions; and (5) frequent use of the "unit rule," a practice whereby a majority at a party meeting could bind a dissenting minority to vote in accordance with majority wishes. The achieved changes required that state Democratic parties "overcome the effects of past discrimination by affirmative steps" to assure the representation of blacks, women, and young people at the national conventions and other party functions "in reasonable relationship to [the group's] presence in the population of the State." They stipulated that state parties must adopt rules which facilitate "maximum participation among interested Democrats in the processes by which National Convention delegates are selected"—through such devices as broad publicization of the time and place of all selection meetings. Use of the unit rule was banned. Minority views were to be represented in slate-making sessions, including those in states where final selection of delegates was left to statewide primary elections. The practice whereby "certain public or Party officeholders are delegates to county, State and National Conventions by virtue of their official position" was proscribed. If a state Democratic party insisted on permitting its central committee to choose delegates to the national convention, it was required to limit the number of delegates thus selected to not more than 10 percent of the total.

Many party regulars called foul in 1972, insisted that they were victimized by a McGovern coup, and in particular attacked the use of a de facto quota system for blacks,

women, and youth. Some groups variously troubled by the
1972 reforms and opposed to the ideological slant of the
McGovern wing of the party organized themselves as the
Coalition for a Democratic Majority (CDM). The AFL-CIO
leadership was a prime mover in the CDM. After the 1972
electoral debacle, Robert S. Strauss replaced Jean West-
wood as Democratic National Chairman, with the blessing
and sponsorship of organized labor. In this context of a
massive election setback following after the work of the
"reformed" 1972 Democratic Convention and a vigorous
counterattack by labor and other groups of party regulars,
many observers believed that many of the changes in
intra-party operation would be compromised away. In fact,
they have not been. The basic thrust of the changes has
been firmly embedded in party structure.

Two commissions set up by the 1972 Convention continued the changes in party organization and procedures:
the Democratic Charter Commission, chaired by Terry
Sanford; and the Commission on Delegate Selection and
Party Structure, headed by Barbara Mikulski. After nearly
two years of argument befitting in its complexity the internal heterogeneity of the Democratic party, the work of
these commissions culminated in decisions of the Democratic National Committee and of the 1974 Conference on
Democratic Policy and Organization, the so-called Kansas
City miniconvention.[60]

The 1972 requirements that delegates be selected
through open processes (primaries or caucuses) in which
any party adherent wishing to participate could do so—at
the expense of the influence of party regulars—was continued. Winner-take-all schemes of delegate selection
were banned, with proportional representation required:

At all stages of the delegate selection process, delegations shall
be allocated in a fashion that fairly reflects the expressed presi-

---

[60] The conference was held in Kansas City, Missouri, December 6–8,
1974, and was attended by some 2,000 delegates. This off-year meeting
had been mandated by the 1972 Democratic Convention.

dential preference, uncommitted, or no preference status of the primary voters, or if there be no binding primary, the convention and caucus participants, except that preferences securing less than 15 percent (15%) of the votes cast for the delegation need not be awarded any delegates.[61]

Even in the area of minority group representation—where emotions ran particularly high—the only achievement of the regulars was a rejection of "mandatory quotas." The 1972 affirmative action requirements were continued, and in the case of a challenge the burden of proof rested with the delegation: it must prove that it had been open to minority involvement under affirmative action stipulations.[62]

The historic 1974 Democratic meeting, which formally adopted a charter for the national party, sustained virtually all the 1972 reforms, and in fact served to extend them. While depicted as a "compromise conference"—which in a sense it was since no party group achieved *all* that it wanted—the charter meeting served largely to publicly acknowledge a changing of the guard in Democratic national politics, and to implement changes favored by the ascendant reform faction.

The Democratic party changes of the 1970s are largely in the spirit of the earlier Progressive reforms. By this we mean, (1) that they reflect a distrust of party organization and established leadership structures, and (2) that they involve efforts of ascendant middle-class groups—notably college-educated professionals—to achieve a measure of influence in party affairs comparable to what they were attaining in the larger society. The reformers of the Progressive era were profoundly anti-party—in the sense of opposing the ascendancy of party organizations and their

---

[61] "Delegate Selection Rules for the 1976 Democratic National Convention," adopted by the Democratic National Committee, March 1, 1974.

[62] As the Democrats were making these rather dramatic changes, the Republicans were plodding in much the same direction of openness and democratization. The low-profile Delegates and Organizations (DO) Committee served as the McGovern-Fraser Commission counterpart, and the Rule 29 Committee paralleled the Mikulski Commission.

leadership, and favoring instead a higher measure of internal democracy and rule by the people. This commitment to internal party democracy and the antipathy to organization control was highly functional in terms of the interests of the Progressives, and so it is for the 1970s' reformers. Ascendant middle-class strata in both eras confronted party organizations substantially unresponsive to their claims for influence and their policy perspectives. They proceeded, then, upon a highly rational course: They attacked the legitimacy of the ascendancy of the bosses, in the name of an irresistible American value, democratization. That these highly educated, well-informed, relatively prosperous cohorts possessed the requisite skills for a high level of participation in more open party processes should not be overlooked. In the late 1960s and the 1970s, segments of the new middle class, their numbers swelled by the economic-occupational transformations of postindustrialism moved for greater party influence. This brought them into conflict with older activist cohorts, firmly entrenched in party organizational structures (such as they were). They proclaimed the need for more openness and democracy, and spoke on behalf of deprived minorities, but the new middle-class bias of the reforms was clear. As John Saloma and Frederick Sontag have pointed out, "the Miami Beach Democratic National Convention [1972] . . . was . . . a predominantly middle-class, affluent, college-educated convention which underrepresented other elements of the traditional Democratic coalition." [63] In the Great Democratic power struggle of the 1970s, older party leadership groups—such as organized labor—were losers.[64]

---

[63] Saloma and Sontag, *op. cit.,* p. 393.

[64] It should be acknowledged that the thrusts of Democratic reform in the 1970s were not all in one direction. At the same time as party organization control of the presidential nominating process was being so substantially weakened, party reformers were as well calling for a stronger party in some regards—one with more programmatic coherence, national conventions committing the party to policy positions, etc. The Progressive suspicion of party organization, and the "More Responsible Party"

Formal structural changes are not the only developments weakening party organization, and particularly the
role of party apparatus in the presidential nomination process. A more highly educated electorate feels less in need
of organization as an active intermediary. As Moynihan
has noted, "with the educated middle class ever more involved with politics, the inclination to disdain coalition as
unedifying is vastly enhanced, and as a result coalitions
are collapsing everywhere. . . . For a good half-century
now, the concept of party reform has basically involved
the weakening of party. The vocabulary of political
science no less than that of political journalism reinforces
this notion. Party officials are 'bosses.' Outsiders who want
their power without their responsibility are 'reformers,'
selfless, progressive, and, above all, democratic." [65] In a
climate of ever-extending egalitarianism, the claim of established party leadership, working through such formal
mechanisms as state committees and conventions, to a privileged place in the determination of party affairs—and
most notably the question of who secures the party nominations—becomes increasingly hard to defend.

The crumbling of party has made it easier for waves of
issue activists to overwhelm the regulars and temporarily
take over the party, imposing their preferred nominees.
The ease with which the McGovern movement over-
whelmed much of the regular apparatus of the Democratic
party in 1972 testifies to the numbers and influence of the
new activist stratum, to the immediate effects of the
McGovern Commission reforms, but as well to the general
weakness of party organization in the United States.

argument for strengthening partisan structures, were sometimes blended
together in a confusing way. Mark Alan Siegal, who served as chief assistant to DNC Chairman Robert Strauss for charter business, argues that
there always was a basic inconsistency in the goals of the reformers—
between more open, democratic participation on the one hand, and a
more programmatically coherent national party on the other. See Chris-
topher Lydon, "Democrats Face Disputes on Three Issues at Parley this
Week," *New York Times* (December 3, 1974), for a discussion of Siegal's
views.

[65] Moynihan, *op. cit.*, p. 17.

THE POLARIZATION OF COLLEGE COHORTS

To understand the strength of what we have called the issue-activist stratum in the contemporary United States, and why its expansion may contribute so substantially to the potential for unnatural landslides, one needs to look at developments within that principal reservoir from which issue activists are drawn—the college educated.[66] Not that all issue activists are persons who have attended college, but reports seem to concur that the expansion of formal higher education, the changed orientation to issues it promotes, the changing mix of needs and interests which it reflects, more than anything else precipitated the new role.

For one thing, as Philip Converse has so effectively demonstrated, higher education correlates significantly with an ability and inclination to evaluate politics in terms of systematic issue concerns—or, to put it differently, to view politics ideologically.[67] Ideological thinking—in the sense of actively applying "a relatively abstract and far-reaching conceptual dimension as a yardstick against which political objects and their shifting policy significance over time [are] evaluated"—is to a striking degree coterminous with possession of standard college training.[68]

---

[66] We would prefer to use *intelligentsia* in place of *college educated*, but the former is not readily located in survey data, while the latter is precisely measured. It seems evident that formal higher education is the principal vehicle through which people move into that group directly involved in the application of trained intelligence. So *college educated* serves as a convenient analytic surrogate for the intelligentsia.

[67] Converse, "The Nature of Belief Systems in Mass Publics," in David Apter (ed.), *Ideology and Discontent* (New York: The Free Press, 1964), especially pp. 213–216, 255.

[68] *Ibid.*, p. 213. Some recent research argues against this interpretation. Nie and Andersen assert, for example, that "the growth of attitude consistency within the mass public is clearly not the result of increases in the population's 'ideological capacity' brought about by gains in educational attainment." Nie with Andersen, "Mass Belief Systems Revisited," p. 570. In large part, the disagreement is more apparent than real, the result of investigators speaking to *two different questions*. Converse is concerned, as we are, with the capacity to manipulate abstract concepts,

Besides this, separating out college-trained Democrats and Republicans is a reasonably good shorthand way of identifying groups in the citizenry disproportionately endowed with resources necessary to be active participants. As people of relatively high socioeconomic status, the college educated have more money, more time, more information, more political skills, hold more influential occupational positions, overall possess substantial resources for influencing the course of public decision making.

In this context—of the college trained as the natural reservoir and constituency for issue activists—a recent development involving the ideological perspectives of the former seems especially important. To appreciate it, some background is necessary. In the 1940s, 1950s, and early 1960s, college-educated Democrats and Republicans differed from the parties' rank and file in a consistent pattern: Both college cohorts were more conservative than their respective parties on economic matters, more liberal on civil liberties and civil rights, and more internationalist and interventionist in foreign affairs. For example, college Democrats in 1940 were much less supportive of the Wagner Act than their citizenry party as a whole; and similarly, college Republicans disfavored the act more than the Republican rank and file. In 1952, college Democrats and Republicans gave less backing to government health insurance, and in 1964 to medicare, than their citizenry parties at large.

These distributions seem natural enough in view of the

---

while Nie and Andersen are looking simply at the level of attitudinal consistency involving specific policy items—a phenomenon which can be heavily influenced by the saliency of such items in contemporary public argument. A high level of attitudinal consistency necessarily follows from ideological thinking—the application of abstract conceptual dimensions to order a disparate array of policy choices—but the presence of a high level of attitudinal consistency is not proof of the presence of meaningfully applied abstract conceptual dimensions. People with little interest in abstract ideas can demonstrate high correlations in their responses to items A, B and C, if these items are central in public argument, and if it is made evident that their interests are linked to each in some consistent fashion.

class interests of the college educated. On the whole more affluent, they were less inclined to applaud economic measures designed to help the lower income strata, more in sympathy with business interests. There was an exact reversal in civil rights and foreign policy matters, with the college cohorts more liberal (or internationalist-interventionist) than their respective coalitions. The foreign affairs distributions are especially interesting. In 1952, the college contingents were somewhat more in favor of sending troops to Indochina if Communist China invaded the area. They were more willing to furnish American money and manpower for the defense of western Europe against the Soviet Union than were the entire citizenry parties. Rank-and-file Republicans and Democrats were much more of the opinion that entry into Korea had been a mistake than were the college-educated segments of the parties. In the early 1960s, those exposed to formal higher education in both party coalitions expressed greater optimism about the possibility of arranging a peaceful settlement with the Soviet Union. In economic matters, common class interest led college-educated Democrats and Republicans to the right of their parties. On the other hand, the educational background and social position of the college cohorts made them, in a manner commonly encountered and described, more sensitive to and supportive of civil liberties and civil rights; and generally more internationalist as they looked at the world outside.[69]

By the late 1960s, however, a significant change had occurred. Among the issues which have come to dominate the American political agenda over the last decade or so, we typically find that the opinion distance between the college strata, relative to that between the parties' rank and file, has become much larger than in the past.[70] Col-

---

[69] This subject has been explored at length in a previous publication. See Ladd and Hadley, *Political Parties and Political Issues: Patterns in Differentiation Since the New Deal.*

[70] *Opinion distance* refers to the percentage point difference between the citizenry parties, or comparable subgroups of these parties, in support

lege-educated Republicans and Democrats appear rather consistently more dissimilar in issue orientations than do their respective citizenry parties. Furthermore, there has been a decided trend toward polarization—with college Republicans often more conservative than the general membership of their party, and college Democrats regularly much more liberal than their party's rank and file.

In 1968, only 1 percentage point separated the Republican and Democratic parties (defined by self-identification) in the proportion of Vietnam hawks, whereas there was a margin of 24 points between the college cohorts.[71] A year later, in October 1969, the percentage of self-described hawks had declined in all party groups, but the distance between the college contingents was much larger than between the rank and file.[72] College Republicans were more hawkish than their citizenry party, but college Democrats were decidedly more dovish than their party. Fifty-one percent of college Democrats, compared to 41 percent of all Democrats, accepted the Kerner Commission conclusion that the United States was moving toward two societies, one white and one black, separate and unequal; on the other hand, the proportion of college Republicans concurring with this judgment (31 percent) was smaller than among all Republican followers (36 percent).[73] Seventy-four percent of the college Democrats in June 1969 said they wanted liberal nominees to the Supreme Court, as against just 21 percent of college Republicans—a 53 point margin of difference. But the margin was just 18 points between the rank and file of the two parties (defined by self-identification).[74] In 1972, party distance was a massive 47

---

for a specified policy position. Opinion distance scores are arrayed from zero to 100. If 60 percent of both Democratic and Republican adherents endorsed a given position on an issue, the party distance score would be zero; conversely, if all Democrats but no Republicans took the position, party opinion distance would be 100.

[71] AIPO Survey No. 769, September 24, 1968.
[72] AIPO Survey No. 792, October 28, 1969.
[73] AIPO Survey No. 761, April 30, 1968.
[74] AIPO Survey No. 781, May 20, 1969.

points for the two college cohorts on the question of am-
nesty for draft resisters, in comparison to just 18 points for
the identification parties at large.[75] Ninety-four percent of
college-educated Democrats indicated that they would be
more likely to vote for a candidate if he backed a government health insurance program for all ages, the position
taken by 53 percent of college Republicans.[76] The Republican citizenry party was generally *more favorable* to national health insurance than its college component, while
the Democratic rank and file were *less supportive* than
college Democrats.

There is a consistent pattern across a broad range of issues: foreign policy, race relations, support for liberal or
conservative domestic policies, questions about the propri-
ety of the use of violence by aggrieved groups, the legalization of marijuana, the eighteen-year-old vote, and continued military aid for South Vietnam. In every instance,
the college cohorts are more dissimilar in issue orientations than are their respective citizenry parties. In most
cases, college Democrats are to the left of their party. And
college Republicans are either more conservative or about
as conservative as their partisan coalition.[77]

Closer examination of data on college cohorts of the two
parties shows that not only are they typically further apart
on issues than are the ranks and file, but in many cases

---

[75] Center for Political Studies (Michigan) 1972 Election Study.

[76] AIPO Survey No. 856, August 1, 1972.

[77] It was possible that the growing polarization of the college-educated
cohorts in the late sixties and early seventies might have resulted largely
from a disproportionate entry of young graduates into the Democratic
party. If the young among college graduates are decisively more liberal-
left than the old, and if the young have recently turned heavily to the
Democratic party, then the wide gulf between the two college cohorts
might represent largely a generational cleavage. In the earlier publication
cited above (Note 68), this possibility was systematically explored. We
found that whatever the future pattern of partisan behavior of the college
trained, the recent polarization is not a function of age differences between the two college cohorts. The most dramatic evidence here is the
fact that the opinion distance between younger college-trained Republicans and Democrats is greater than that separating the older cohorts.

they occupy opposite sides of a question where majorities of both Republican and Democratic supporters at large are on the same side. Rank-and-file Republicans and Democrats alike agree that a professor who is an admitted Communist should be fired, favor use of the death penalty for convicted murderers, oppose open housing legislation, agree that blacks shouldn't "push themselves where they're not wanted." [78] On these and many related issues, however, college Democrats take the liberal position, with majorities of college Republicans on the conservative side.

Our analysis makes clear that the polarization of the college (or generally, high SES) cohorts in the two parties has been accelerated substantially these past few years. The better-educated, more highly informed segments of the electorate are expected to have more constrained belief systems. But there is no reason why upper status groups persistently must be polarized on questions of policy. Data from the 1940s and 1950s, in fact, show that they were not; the degree of differentiation between the college cohorts then was no greater on the whole than that between the rank and file. In the late 1960s and now in the 1970s, however, the upper strata are found regularly at the extremes of their respective parties. College-trained, high income Democrats and Republicans, class equals, differ very sharply on a wide range of policy choices.

We have used college-educated Democrats and Republicans as surrogates for the activist cohorts of the two coalitions in part because there is a much richer collection of survey data on the former than on the latter precisely defined and located. A number of recent investigations, however, do permit us to get at the activists directly. In conjunction with the Center for Political Studies of the University of Michigan, Jeane Kirkpatrick conducted a study in which the policy perspectives of all Democratic identifiers were compared to those of delegates to the 1972

---

[78] National Opinion Research Center (Chicago), General Social Surveys, 1972 and 1973.

Democratic Convention.[79] She noted that previous research, such as that of Herbert McClosky, had shown party leaders to be more sharply differentiated ideologically than the respective ranks and file, and specifically Democratic leaders more liberal than the mass of Democratic identifiers.[80] But the convention delegates of 1972 stood much further to the left of all party supporters than is the norm. *"In 1972, the difference between Democratic mass and elite so far exceeded the norms that on a range of issues central to the politics of that year, the Democratic elite and rank and file were found on opposite sides. . . ."* [81]

A 1976 survey inquiry by the *Washington Post* points up very nicely the pronounced polarization of the activist cohorts of the two parties, in the absence of any such sharp differentiation of all Democratic and Republican adherents:

Republican party workers by majorities of more than 4 to 1 believe that poor people are almost always to blame for their poverty. Their Democratic counterparts, by margins of more than 5 to 1, believe just the opposite: that the American system is to blame, in that it does not give all people an even chance. Republican party workers, by margins of more than 3 to 1 say that justice is administered equally to all in the United States; their Democratic counterparts by margins of more than 4 to 1, say that justice favors the rich. By margins of almost 4 to 1, Republican party workers oppose public financing of elections, while by more than 5 to 1 their Democratic counterparts favor it. . . . If the two parties are poles apart [the activist cohorts, that is] the electorate stands almost midway between the poles. . . . The result, almost invariably, was a positioning of this kind: at the far left were the Democratic party workers. In the middle were the citizens who identified themselves as Democrats; to the right of

---

[79] Jeane Kirkpatrick, *The New Presidential Elite* (New York: Russell Sage Foundation and the Twentieth Century Fund, 1976).

[80] Herbert McClosky, *et al.*, "Issue Conflict and Consensus Among Party Leaders and Followers," *American Political Science Review*, 54 (June 1960), pp. 406–427.

[81] Kirkpatrick, *op. cit.*, p. 297. The emphasis is in the original.

them were those who identified themselves as Republicans. At the far right were the Republican party workers.[82]

Why has this pattern become so sharply etched? For one thing, it appears that a fracturing of the higher social strata has occurred—with the influx of new groups in the wake of developments linked to postindustrialism, and with the salience of social and cultural issues described in the preceding chapters.

One can now distinguish two broad strains among high SES Americans: one, the older and more traditional, revolving around business corporations and the associated line executive occupations; and the other, newer and expanding, extending to the upper governmental bureaucracy, the research and development community within business and outside, intellectuals and other components of the knowledge industry. The business upper strata continue to be ascendant in the Republican party, while the postindustrial upper social cohorts have grown vastly more influential in national Democratic circles. These upper status groups, although possessed of generally similar economic standing, confront each other with widely differing ideological perspectives.

As the class dimension of politics has been muted, and social and cultural issues have become more prominent, we encounter a conflict situation in which the most ideologically inclined party segments are apt to display the greatest opinion distance. So long as the American political agenda was dominated by issues with a direct pocketbook component, less informed, less ideologically inclined voters could be as sharply divided as those who tend to see politics in ideological terms. But with a relative decline of class conflict, and the substitution of more diffuse divisions over a broad array of social questions having heavily symbolic overtones, it is the most ideologically oriented components of the two parties who are most sharply at odds.

[82] Barry Sussman, "Electorate More Moderate than Poles-Apart Party Workers," *Washington Post* (September 27, 1976).

High status Republicans and Democrats have the greatest resources for participation and influence in party decision making. And the steps to democratize candidate selection procedures, along with the general erosion of party organization, are likely to further strengthen the position of these cohorts. As control over nominations is more removed from the regular party organization and delivered to those citizens who choose to be highly participant either through caucuses or primaries, the role of college-educated, upper SES groups is enhanced because they are best equipped to intervene in the more open processes.

Both the 1964 and the 1972 presidential elections appear to show the influence of the developments we have been discussing—the polarization in issue terms of major segments of the high SES cohorts of the two citizenry parties, and the enhanced role of these groups in party decision making. Goldwater's appeal was commonly described as to the right not only of the Democratic but of the center of the Republican party as well; and McGovern's positions have been depicted as more liberal than many in his citizenry party would accept. Our data provide support for the conclusion that both candidates, however, struck responsive notes in ideology or issues among the respective upper status components of the two parties.

This is not to suggest that we should expect Republican leaders who are relatively more conservative than their party's rank and file, or Democrats more liberal than their citizenry party, to capture nominations in all cases in the immediate future. Even if our findings as to the polarization of highly educated, highly participant cohorts of the two parties are fully valid, and if this condition persists,[83]

---

[83] Some observers argue that the condition will not persist. James L. Sundquist, for example, agrees that the type of ideological polarization we have described has indeed developed, but maintains that is is unlikely to last. Extreme times invite extreme positions. "If the mood of the country is extreme, the parties cannot 'fly' off toward moderation either." Sundquist, *Dynamics of the Party System*, p. 305. Such a situation developed in the 1960s but comparable situations were present at earlier points in American history. During the Civil War period, and in the

there are still a variety of other considerations bearing upon presidential candidate selection—from personal appeal outside the realm of issues to such events as assassinations—which can deliver the nomination to leaders who do not correspond to the above specifications. Our point is only that the apparent polarization of the college-trained and highly participant segments of the citizenry parties may well prove to be a factor of fundamental importance for the future of party conflict: *it may increase pressures within each party to select candidates, as in presidential contests, who hold sharply differing issue positions, rather than candidates competing for the center, playing accommodationist politics.*

SUMMARY OBSERVATIONS

From the above analysis and commentary we move inescapably to the conclusion that the unnatural landslides of 1964 and 1972 were not unnatural after all. Rather, they appear products of the emergence of a new dynamic in American national politics. In 1965, Wildavsky observed of the Goldwater-Johnson contest that "we are surprised that our expectations concerning the behavior of parties and

Bryan years, deep cleavages appeared, and "political policies were invested with moral absolutism (p. 278)." Inevitably, leaders arose to champion a programmatic politics, and to eschew accommodation on behalf of party organization maintenance. But these times passed, and the factions which had organized around absolutist stances faded. By the early 1970s, there were clear signs, according to Sundquist, of the weakening of the polarizing issues of the 1960s (pp. 308–331). This general line of argument, which has much to commend it, leads Sundquist to assume that the elite polarization we have detected will now weaken. We think not. Sharp conflict surely is not new, and comes in ebbs and flows. But what is peculiar to the present setting is the presence of a large and growing cadre of people with enough time and education to indulge permanently in a politics of issues. College-educated Democrats and Republicans have come to occupy polar positions not just because of the depth of feeling generated by current issues, but because they comprise large strata sensitized to ideological distinctions which abound in the diffuse, heavily symbolic conflict structure of postindustrial society.

politics have been violated." [84] Our expectations were violated in 1964, and again in 1972, because they were based on a model in which both parties rather consistently adhere to accommodationist politics.

The old dynamic seems to have been upset. The strength of party organization has continued its long-term secular decline, with the weakening intensified in the contemporary period. Issue-oriented participants in both parties, committed to a more programmatic politics, are stronger—vis-à-vis the older party-oriented activists—than at any earlier point in American history. The prospects, then, for their capturing either the Republican or the Democratic nomination for president (an presumably for other major offices as well) and committing the party to a more doctrinally distinctive politics, with the prospect thereby of presenting a minoritarian appeal, is greater than ever before. The polarization of issue activists of the two parties has occurred in a larger context: a more ideologically divisive national politics, and a polarization of college-educated (and generally high SES) Republicans and Democrats—the principal constituency from which issue activists are drawn.

There is no indication that rank-and-file voters are less receptive to the old accommodationist politics today than they were two decades ago. But important segments of the more active and highly participant membership of the citizenry parties are less supportive of this approach and of candidates committed to it. The situation, then, in which a major party nominates a candidate who is the minority choice of the rank and file, considered too extreme by many, and hence who submits to a massive defeat even in the absence of that mix of candidate personal attributes and valence issues which have in the past been associated with landslides, appears to have been elevated to the position of a natural occurrence. It follows readily enough under the new dynamic.

---

[84] Wildavsky, op. cit., p. 386.

What, then, for the future of American presidential politics? Lubell's prediction, made in 1970, of "a new [partisan] alignment of two incomplete, narrow-based coalitions, polarized against each other," seems likely to be borne out. With party identification greatly weakened for a growing segment of the electorate, with independent voting a more frequent occurrence, and with major party candidates perceived as ideologically extreme likely a common occurrence, massive alternating landslides are in prospect.

There is a distinct possibility, of course, that in a given election *both parties* might nominate candidates seen by large segments of the electorate to be away from the center. In such instances, low levels of electoral turnout, a diminished sense of the legitimacy of the outcome, and frequent sorties by third party candidates can follow as readily as a massive victory by one of the major party contenders.

As long as the United States operates, with a one-man executive (in contrast to the cabinet type) and with a winner-take-all electoral system (the electoral college), prospects for a regularized multi-party system appear dim. Much more likely is the continuance of a greatly weakened but still, ostensibly, two-party system, characterized by frequent reversals of massive proportions and nothing approaching a stable presidential majority. With dominant activists more programmatically concerned and less in sympathy with a politics of accommodation, the prospects are also high that the majority of the electorate will find itself confronting presidential contests in which the stakes appear greater than they have typically in the past. Wildavsky's point with regard to Goldwater's candidacy stands as a likely guide to many future presidential elections: "The Goldwater candidacy . . . visibly increased the cost of losing the election to those who disagreed profoundly with him. As a result, there was a much more bitter campaign fraught with much greater anxiety than in the past. Will the comforts of a political system which is ordi-

narily kind to losers (because campaigns are fought between parties and candidates which differ somewhat but
are not separated by too large a gulf) be more highly valued [in its absence] in the future?" [85]

We hold no "apocalyptic" visions for the future of American politics. It appears, simply, that elections like 1972
will be not uncommon occurrences in the future. The most
striking feature, and the lasting importance, of the unnatural contest between Richard Nixon and George McGovern
is not that McGovern lost and lost badly; not just that a
large segment of the electorate found itself unimpressed
by both candidates and wound up either not voting or
choosing with reservations; not only that a new politics
wing of the Democratic party came of age and succeeded
in imposing its choice; but that a dynamic is now at work
which makes such occurrences natural.

IV. Accounting for the 1976 Nomination Experience:
A Concluding Note

". . . th' Supreme Court," said Mr. Dooley, "follows th'
iliction returns." Picture a moistened finger thrust boldly
into the prevailing breeze. Finley Peter Dunne might better have had his illustrious creation speak thus of political
commentators. We are often too quick to set a new direction. Thus, every "iliction" summons a bold theory to explain what *has just happened.*

Has our own private limb been sawed off by the 1976
nomination experience? At first inspection, it might seem
so. When the preceding sections of this chapter were written in 1973 and 1974, the backdrop was formed by the
"ideological" McGovern candidacy. New actors had
seized power in the Democracy, had commanded the nomination of the party but not its heart—not the approval of
the rank and file—and in the process had handed the Re-

---

[85] *Ibid.*, p. 413.

publican nominee a landslide endorsement the electorate had really not intended to give. At the present time, though, it is the Carter-Ford "battle of the centrists" that is fresh in mind. Both parties delivered their nominations in 1976 to moderates who fudged on the issues which divided us, argued mostly about who would better pursue objectives everyone wanted, thereby waged a "pedestrian" campaign, and produced one of the closest elections in U.S. history.

Looking upon the 1976 presidential contest, Richard Scammon saw a return to normalcy.

This year we have the first really normal election in a generation. We had Eisenhower—a big charismatic figure—in 1952 and 1956. We had Roman Catholicism as a disturbing issue in 1960, when John Kennedy ran. In the last three elections, we've had a perceived extremist on the ballot—Goldwater, Wallace, and McGovern. What we've got this time is a moderate conservative running against a moderate liberal, neither of them greatly charismatic figures. It amounts, frankly, to a feeling of pedestrianism. Now, pedestrianism may not be a good thing to stimulate voters, but it's not necessarily a bad thing for the future of the Republic.[86]

In fact, we would argue that the 1976 nomination politics fit easily into the story which has been written since the early 1960s. They are a new chapter, but not a different book. The interpretation which has been advanced thus far in this chapter needs to be enlarged, not rejected.

A PROBLEM OF REPRESENTATION

First, we would note that it has now been *four* consecutive presidential elections which have seen successful (in the sense of being able to secure the party's nomination) and near-successful candidacies of a very distinctive ideo-

[86] "What Will Sway Voters When Election Day Comes; Interview with Richard M. Scammon, Director, Elections Research Center," *U.S. News and World Report* (October 25, 1976), p. 30.

logical character: Goldwater in 1964, McCarthy in 1968, McGovern in 1972, and Reagan in 1976. In each case the contender enjoyed the support of only a tiny fraction of the regular party leadership and was the first choice of only a distinct minority of all party identifiers. But two of these candidates managed to capture their party's nominations, and the other two came very close indeed. In each instance, the candidate enjoyed disproportionate support among the middle-class and upper-class cohorts which are the prime beneficiaries of the weakening of party. These strata tend to be issue-emphasizing and party-organization eschewing.

The ideological distinctiveness of activist cohorts becomes most consequential, of course, in the context of low turnouts in primaries and caucuses. Participation in the 1976 presidential primaries was 28 percent, about half that in the same set of states (not all states held primaries) in the subsequent general election. And the most highly participant Americans manifest an extraordinary over-representation of the college educated and the above average in income.[87]

The slice actually voting in the new open processes is

---

[87] "Sidney Verba and Norman H. Nie, *Participation in America: Political Democracy and Social Equality* (New York: Harper and Row, 1972). Verba and Nie note that "if participants came proportionately from all parts of society . . . then political leaders who respond to participation will be responding to an accurate representation of the needs, desires, and preferences of the public at large" (p. 12). But in fact, they quickly observe, "the participants are by no means representative of the public as a whole but come disproportionately from particular—especially upper-status—groups . . ." The most highly participant Americans, whom Verba and Nie label "complete activists," manifest an extraordinary over-representation of the college educated and the above average in income (p. 100). In general, the correlation between participation rate and socio-economic status is exceptionally high, dwarfing the relationship between participation and any other aspect of social status. When we examine the social standing of 1976 presidential primary voters, we find the expected skewing toward the higher socioeconomic classes. In every state, NBC and CBS–*New York Times* survey data show, the primary voters came disproportionately from the ranks and these overlapping groups: the college trained, the professional middle class, and those of upper-middle to high income.

small *and* unrepresentative of the population generally. Not surprisingly, in view of this, extraordinary warpings of public wishes can occur. In 1976, the Republican president was found consistently from March through June to outdistance his California rival in popular support among all Republicans and independents, by margins up to two to one. Yankelovich, for example, showed Ford leading Reagan by 71 to 29 percent among Republicans and independents who declared a preference in April 1976; in June, the Ford margin was 62–38.[88] According to Harris, Ford was ahead of Reagan—again, among Republicans and independents—60 to 40 percent in late February, 66–34 in late March, 67–33 in May, and 61–39 in July.[89] Ford and Reagan split the primary vote almost evenly, however. Democratic crossovers accounted for only a small part of the discrepancy between survey descriptions of rank-and-file preferences and the actual primary distributions. And it should be noted that Reagan actually did somewhat better in the polls with self-described independents than with Republicans. The main factor was simply that the primary voters were not a microcosm of the mass of Republican adherents.

Much of the recent commentary on choosing presidential candidates displays an unfortunate insensitivity to the distinction between *participation* and *representativeness*. The scope of the former has been extended by the new nominee-selection mechanisms—more primaries, open caucuses, and the like—but the latter may have been diminished. In 1976, we see ample evidence of a persisting representativeness problem.

Gerald Ford was the choice of a large majority of GOP-elected officials around the country. If they, together with party organization leaders, were still in charge of the candidate-designation process, Ford would have easily won

---

[88] Yankelovich, Skelly and White, Survey No. 8510, April 1976; and Survey No. 8520, June 1976.

[89] *The Harris Report*, March 18, 1976; April 29, 1976; June 3, 1976; and August 2, 1976.

the nomination in 1976. The Republican leaders wanted Ford, not because they were strongly attached to him personally, but because they concluded partisan *raison d'état* required his nomination. He was the incumbent, had not done badly, was well positioned between the main ideological camps, was accepted by a broad spectrum of the electorate, had at least an outside chance of winning, and almost certainly would not lose badly. And the rank and file wanted Ford. It seems that the established leadership was more representative of the general public than was the primary participant stratum whose elevation had been achieved over the past decade and a half. To understand fully the problem thus posed and the special democratic dilemma presented, two things must be appreciated. One applies to party regulars; the other to the activist stratum.

Party regulars—the leaders of the "organization," such as it is—have been inclined in the American two-party system to use what control they have over the nomination process to advance rank-and-file preferences for candidates. People who spend their lives within party organizations necessarily want to assure the survival and promote the growth of these enterprises. In some fashion, their individual aspirations have been attached to the fate of the party—the reason why they have been willing to labor on the party's behalf.[90]

In a multi-party system, of course, interest in party maintenance may lead to an espousal of particularistic appeals. With many contenders, the party survives by distinguishing itself and thereby maintaining the loyalties of its own special slice of the electorate. The distinctive base must be defended at all costs. But party organization leaders in the American two-party system have been conditioned to think very differently. Success requires regularly attaining the votes of at least 50 percent plus 1 of the general public. Particularistic appeals might bring the in-

---

[90] The analysis of Jeane Kirkpatrick, while confined to 1972 national convention delegates, supports this general line of interpretation. Kirkpatrick, *op. cit.*, especially chapters 4 and 5.

tense approval of, say, 30 percent of the public; but if the rest were thereby lost, there would be a massive debacle for the party one is committed to maintain. Success requires a promiscuous search for supporters. Thus the psychological attachment to party is translated into an intense majoritarianism which eschews ideological distinctiveness and enthrones accommodation.

There are times when hard choices must be made. The party organization leaders of the U.S. system have long been socialized to be suspicious of principled appeals which cannot be generalized. They have been "taught" that the pursuit of party success requires that they be mushy majoritarians. Presumably those not psychologically inclined to such a stance—those for whom a principle must be pursued whatever the national majority may desire—frequently have "selected themselves out" of party leadership positions thus defined, or have tried to stay in but have failed in struggles with more flexible (less principled?) rivals.

Thus a special type of party leader has been produced by the U.S. party system historically. He has had his attractive and not-so-attractive features. Here, one characteristic stands out: He has been willing—nay, eager—to subordinate personal ideological predilections in the interest of articulating majority preferences.

This is why "boss-dominated" national conventions so often have produced nominees with high support and low resistance standing among the rank and file. The "bosses" have not been candidates for democratic sainthood. But they have pursued party maintenance, which in a two-party system has required pursuit of the majority.

When one moves outside that small slice of the population tied to party maintenance into the rest of the activist or participant stratum, one finds a mix of participation motivations which do not on the whole mesh so easily or consistently with complete majoritarianism. Some of the activists may be strongly wedded to advancing a program. Others articulate the claims of an interest group. Still others may be moved by the personal attributes of a leader. And so on. None of these are incompatible with majoritarianism, and one can entertain any of these motivations and still devoutly seek electoral victory; but there is no necessary structural link between the motivation for participation and majoritarianism.

So it is not surprising that the Richard Daleys of the United States tried to articulate majority wishes in the choice of candidate. And it is not surprising that the present ascendancy of a participant stratum frequently produces a disjunction between popular wishes and party nomination decisions.

The new nominating processes, in which the elite "filter" has been largely removed, are not more democratic, in the sense of being more representative of popular wishes. But they reflect the current conception of democracy and the participation demands of an expanding professional middle class.

Any party must be expected to include groups more inclined to the selection of nominees whose public philosophies are compatible with the group's, than to the choice of nominees with views which best fit the expectations of the rank-and-file party supporters. But effective aggregation and conversion of popular wishes requires that each major party begin general election campaigns with candidates broadly representative of the wishes (style, policy perspectives, and the like) of those voters making up its "regular expected majority." To the extent selection processes and mechanisms advantage sectors of the party with particularistic (as opposed to catholic) preferences for candidates, the ability to be representative is diminished. Such a diminution has occurred in the U.S., especially at the presidential level.

THE INABILITY TO PLAN

There is another, related deficiency in the current nominee-selection mechanisms. It was apparent before 1976 but we did not call attention to it—because the matter of ideologically distinctive and unrepresentative candidacies was more dramatically evident. In particular, the disappearance of party organization as the decisive intermediary in the selection of presidential nominees has made *planning* virtually impossible.

Whatever the song may claim, it's a big world after all, specifically a big country. The potential electorate in the U.S. (persons of voting age) numbered about 150 million in 1976. This public comprises a considerable range of interests, hopes and fears, values, preferences as to candidate style, and the like. It will never be possible for two national parties (or three, or four) to offer presidential nominees who will seem "an ideal choice" to everyone, and in some electoral circumstances it may be hard to avoid frustrating many voters. The chances that any given pair of presidential contenders will produce various *unforeseeable* dissatisfactions among the electorate are also high—whatever the selection system. But for there to be a reasonable prospect that the candidates will be seen regularly by most people as a good distillation of their interests and expectations, the parties must have a mechanism which is at once able *to assess popular wishes and to convert those wishes into candidates.* This is what, in our usage here, *planning* requires. The capacity of the Democratic and Republican parties to plan for presidential nominee selection, in particular, has diminished notably over the last fifteen years.[91]

Earlier in this chapter, we noted the pronounced weakening of the organizational parties effected by the contemporary "reform" movement, and observed that this made it easier for successive waves of issue activists to impose their nominee selections. The observation still seems

---

[91] We should specify precisely what is meant by *party* in the context of this discussion. The term very often refers to symbol and identification. But party is also *organization*—by which we mean leadership and the structure and processes through which leaders operate. When we refer to the diminished capacity of party to plan, it is the latter usage that we intend.

valid, but it now appears to locate only one principal facet of a more general condition—the preclusion of planning.

It is simply no longer possible for the parties to plan for presidential nominee selection. Party leaders can still contemplate the question of who is best suited to be the nominee, but *they are not able now to assure the implementation of their judgment.* Factions—meaning groups wedded to a given candidate—can engage in intricate strategies, of course, but the sum total of factional calculations does not equal planning for the party. At the same time, we have not achieved—probably because it is not possible to achieve—a mechanism through which "the people," meaning popular majorities, pick the candidate who is their considered choice. All sorts of bizarre outcomes are thus possible in party candidate selection and subsequently in the elections themselves. The 1976 contest is a case in point.

Were political parties still intact, were the Democratic party an organizational entity still controlling nominations for the presidency, Jimmy Carter would not have been chosen. This would have been partly for the wrong reasons—he lacked an established network of "old-boy" ties—but it would have been in part for the right reason. In the context of national presidential politics, Carter was unproved. We Americans have now created a party system which is extraordinarily contemptuous of the notion that leaders are to be "brought along," tried and seasoned gradually, rather than suddenly tossed upon the national leadership stage.

In reviewing the weakness Carter displayed and his inability to enthuse the Democrat-inclined electorate of the nation in 1976, there has been much commentary on personal weaknesses or errors. He made mistakes, of course, but it seems more productive to emphasize problems of the mechanism rather than those of the man. Is there any reason to expect a candidate chosen through the presently employed procedures to be a notably strong contender in the general election? There is no place at present to intro-

duce coherently the standard of the candidate's ability to
bring together the various groups and interests in the national party and to convince the electorate he is well fit to
govern. One may get a strong candidate, but since there
are presumably many indifferent candidates for every
strong one, a mechanism which eschews planning is risky
indeed.

Jimmy Carter was not perceived by the American public
during the 1976 campaign as either a fool or a knave. The
public mood—with regard to both contenders in fact—was
one of doubt and skepticism, not hostility. Carter was seen
as an inexperienced person in the context of presidential
politics. The voters were not sure how he would handle
the presidency. They were somewhat dissatisfied with
things as they were, but they remained quite unsure that
things would be better if Carter were elected. Since only 3
or 4 percent of the electorate knew who Carter was nine
months before the November voting, since the vast majority of voters lacked any behavioral base on which to assess
him, since most electors had seen him only on the campaign trail, is it surprising that they considered him something of an unknown, something of a question mark?

Jimmy Carter's 1976 march on Washington can properly
be described as an electoral tour de force—or as an indifferent showing. To come from so far back and capture the
nomination of a major party (and then the presidency) is an
extraordinary achievement, one that surely should not be
dismissed lightly. But Carter also manifested striking
weaknesses.

He led the field by only 4300 votes in New Hampshire,
or by 5.5 percent. If Jackson, Wallace, Brown, or
Humphrey had entered the New Hampshire primary, it is
almost certain that Carter would not have attained the plurality which gave him a badly needed bit of early momentum. Carter had "right field" all to himself in New Hampshire, while the liberal vote was divided. After getting
only 14 percent of the Massachusetts vote and running
fourth, Carter won Florida with one-third of the popular

vote and a lead of only 4 percent over George Wallace. Humphrey was not entered. Neither was Brown. Jackson got going late. Carter then won the Illinois popular vote handily (with 48 percent of the total vote, and a 20 percentage point lead), but only Wallace, Shriver, and Harris were on the ballot with him. The *Times*-CBS News Poll indicated that Hubert Humphrey would have swept the Illinois primary had he been entered.

With all the momentum thus generated, Carter won Wisconsin by only one percentage point, Michigan by two-tenths of a point. He lost in Nebraska, was trounced in Idaho, Nevada, and Maryland, was solidly beaten in Oregon, was defeated in the New Jersey delegate voting, was swamped in California. He had much earlier done poorly in the New York delegate race. Out of these raw materials one could easily build a hypothetical progression of early defeat, loss of momentum, drift back into the pack, and disintegration.

There is also the largely forgotten fact that after Carter had acquired a lead during the primary season, he was typically unable to hold it. Thus in state after state, from Florida through Michigan and Wisconsin, he saw his lead over contending Democrats weaken in the last days before the primary voting—a datum indicated by the surveys of the candidates' own pollster, Patrick Caddell—just as once his nomination appeared well nigh irresistible, he began to get beaten badly by a young California governor.

One may argue, still, that winning primaries is the best test of electability, and that Carter won more of those in 1976 than any other Democrat. The weakness of the claim that presidential primary victories indicated a popular mandate is revealed most clearly by the following: only 20 percent of the voting-age public in the states which held presidential preference contests actually cast ballots in the Democratic primaries of 1976; Carter received the votes of about 8 percent—and this in the context of crowded fields and a changing mix of possible alternatives from one state to another. This 8 percent was more than any other Democrat received, and as translated through the party's current delegate selection procedures it gave Carter the victory. But it hardly indicates he was the choice of "the people."

We have been reduced presidentially to an overweaning individualism. Each individual entrepreneur (candidate) sets up shop and markets his wares—himself. The buyers—the voters—don't find the same choice of merchandise in all the states, and one seller, who may attract only a small segment of all the buyers, is finally granted a monopoly. Candidates are able to win, then, because of crowded fields, low turnouts, strategic miscalculations by their opponents—but above all because there is no one to mind the store.

The 1976 presidential election did not, of course, produce a landslide victory for either of the major-party contenders. The Democratic nominee enjoyed a slight edge, but the election remained in doubt until the early hours of November 3. Still, the 1976 election appears to be part of the series begun in 1964. With this twist. Rather than an "unnatural landslide," 1976 produced "unnatural deadlock."

The Democrats by all rights should have *won easily* in the 1976 presidential balloting. They came out of their presidential nominating convention in New York a relatively united party. At the same time, the Republicans were laboring under exceptional burdens. Both the president and the vice-president elected under the Republican banner in 1972 had been forced to resign in disgrace amid major scandal. The economy suffered through high unemployment and high inflation under the Republican administration. The body of core supporters of the Republican party had reached its lowest point since 1856.

Were this not enough, the Republicans were led in the 1976 election by a relatively weak candidate. While widely admired on personal grounds, Gerald Ford never showed any signs of capturing his party, much less the presidency, until a beleaguered Richard Nixon nominated him for the vice-presidency in the wake of Agnew's resignation. Ford's initial weakness in presidential leadership followed because he had never, in a quarter-century of public life, become really a *national* leader—the head of a faction seriously contesting for control of the presidential party. After assuming the presidency, Ford continued to suffer from a widespread perception, held by both elites and by the mass public, that he was insufficiently "presidential," lacking in those leadership qualities demanded by the office.

This public perception was dramatically reinforced by the events of spring and early summer, 1976. While Carter was locking up the Democratic nomination, Ford was in deep trouble within his own party. He lost the North Carolina primary of late March, was clobbered in Texas and Georgia, lost Indiana and Nebraska, was trounced in Nevada, dropped South Dakota, and was solidly defeated in Montana and California. In between these setbacks, there were triumphs, of course, but an overall image was reinforced: Ford was seen to be "weak," not a leader. He could not master his own party—how could he expect to lead the free world?

This list of Republican debits and initial Democratic advantages in 1976 can be extended, but the point is evident enough. When a united majority party confronts a divided, incumbent minority party, beset by one of the most celebrated political scandals in U.S. history, by a deteriorating economy, and by a citizenry clearly inclined to changes in leadership—it should have been no contest. Nineteen seventy-six presented a situation where the "ins" should have been trounced. But the "ins" were not trounced in 1976, they were barely beaten. This virtual deadlock was as "unnatural" as were the landslides of 1964 and 1972.

CONCLUSION

The United States, like any polity with a high level of popular participation, has asked much of its party system.

Such changes as the development of a pervasive electronic communications system, a significant further elaboration of interest groups, and an increasingly leisured, educated, and hence independent-minded citizenry, distinguish the contemporary context for party activity from that of earlier periods in the country's first two centuries. But the party system retains exclusive custody of one core democratic function—*aggregating* the preferences of a mass electorate for political leadership and thereby *converting* what was general and diffuse into specific electoral decisions.

Performance of this aggregation-conversion function is the *raison d'être* of a democratic party system. Because this function is so critical to a democracy like the U.S., it matters much how well or how poorly the parties perform it. And though other institutions have come forward to claim certain of the functions associated historically with the American parties—such as the transmission of political information and assessment, which has been assumed increasingly by the national communications media—there is no rival claimant in sight for the aggregating-converting role. The parties must play it, or it does not get performed.

To do an effective job of aggregating and converting popular wishes, the American party system must be able to plan for nominee selection, and the mechanisms for choosing candidates must assure representativeness. It is unfortunate, then, that both of these capacities have been diminished over the past fifteen years.

Postscript

Transformations of the Party System

When the Great Depression broke, there were a variety of lags in the sociopolitical system which, apart from what contributions they may have made to the severity of the collapse, fueled a much more rapid and sweeping set of political transformations than would otherwise have occurred. In a space of a few short years, the American political agenda was rewritten. An unusually distinct policy cleavage appeared. And the parties dug into wholly new positions in a political battlefield so greatly altered. Neither before or since the 1929–1936 period can one find partisan transformations of comparable magnitude occurring with such speed.

The New Deal party developments were also uniquely conclusive. In 1929 the Republicans were the national majority party. By 1936, they had been shoved firmly, decisively, into minority status. In 1929 they spoke for an ascendant public philosophy. By 1936 a new public philosophy was ascendant, with a new partisan home. Nothing so neat and definitive has prevailed in the contemporary transformations, nor did it occur earlier in the formation of the party system of the industrializing era.

Despite such ample evidence to the contrary, the notion

that a single pattern underlies each of the American party transformations has crept into the literature on the subject, with unfortunate analytic consequences. In particular, we have been mesmerized by the New Deal experience, to the point of taking it to be a model. And since realignment was the most dramatic and visible components of the New Deal party transformation, realignment has become the prime focus in studies of partisan change. The New Deal model is so tantalizing, so compelling in its neatness and simplicity. The electorate was subjected to an overriding new issue. Under the impact of this new issue, the old structure of partisan alliances crumbled. A new majority party marched forth boldly, rallying a majority of the populace to the urgent business of the nation. Here was a realignment! When shall we see such another?

The search was on. Insightful observers detected a striking rhythm to the pattern of party realignment. Some came to believe that there was a natural interval of roughly a third of a century between realignments—the period of time required for a new generation of voters to come of age politically with perceptions sufficiently free from the searing experiences of the preceding realignment to be receptive to the call of a new. Count off thirty to thirty-six years from 1932 and what do you find? The United States is now overdue!

Alas, there is no realignment cycle, no striking rhythm, no necessity that the old majority party will be replaced by a new majority, no reason even to be particularly attentive to the prospects of the latter development. Over the course of American history, we hear only the ceaseless hum of societal change, detect only the intermittent accumulation of change sufficient to usher in a new sociopolitical period. And such a momentous shift in social setting requires basic transformations of the party system which may, or may not, feature prominently the type of transition which the classic New Deal realignment entailed.

We are now living through a transformation of the American party system. In its own way, it is quite as exciting and dramatic as that of the New Deal years. It is not as rapid, not as conclusive, not possessing of such elegant simplicity.

It surely has not, and will not produce a new Republican majority. There has been a pronounced weakening of Democratic presidential support in a number of that party's old strongholds. If a solid Republican South is not in the offing, a solid Democratic South, so long a fixture in American politics, has now become an impossibility. But at no point in the last fifteen years has any set of indicators justified the conclusion that a coalition calling itself Republican would become majoritarian. The Republicans have shown no signs of becoming anything other than a reactive party. They have not approached articulation of a public philosophy comparable to the business nationalism of the old Republican majority or the governmental nationalism of the New Deal Democrats. And as a reactive party in a rapidly changing social setting, the Republicans have seen their support weaken steadily among ascendant political classes. Intellectuals, the college educated, the professional and managerial upper-middle classes, and privileged youth, have all moved decisively toward the Democrats.

The United States lacks a competitive two-party system at present primarily because of the exceptional weakness of the Republican party.[1] The now-common observation that the two-party system in the U.S. has been replaced by a "one-and-a-half-party system" does not contain much exaggeration.

In those contests where one gets media-utilizing and media-assessed candidacies of such visibility that voters attend to candidates' personal attributes rather than to party—and this includes in many instances elections to state governorships and to the national Senate—Republicans can win without particular difficulty when

---

[1] The Republican weakness to which we refer here is, of course, primarily that of the "party in the electorate," rather than of party organization.

they nominate attractive candidates (and sometimes when they don't). But everywhere outside such contests, everywhere party is a prominent element in voting, the Grand Old Party is weaker today than it has been at any time since 1856.

For all of the Republicans' problems and weakness, there is no indication of a new Democratic majority, comparable in policy coherence, scope, and regularity to that of the New Deal era. The Democrats have become an establishment party, in the sense of being home to major segments of the high socioeconomic and political classes of the contemporary United States. And in particular, their ascendant position within the intelligentsia permits them, much more than the Republicans, to be a generator of new responses rather than simply a reactor to past events and frustrations. Like the post–Civil War Republicans and the New Deal Democrats, they are a party of "new ideas." But the leadership of social and cultural change which the Democrats have assumed brings them into continuing tension with the white, middle-class majority of what remains—even in a time of inflation and recession, and the ongoing energy crisis—an affluent society. In the tentative, qualified manner which seems inevitable in so enormously diverse and multi-layered a party system as that of the United States, the Democrats will function as a top-bottom alliance, strongest among intellectuals and high status professionals, and among the deprived underclasses. Their vulnerability to neopopulist resistance and resentment, evident in 1972, will be recurring.

Another, very different reason why both new majority forecasts are in such grievous error involves an inherent blind spot in the realignment focus. Important facets of the contemporary partisan transformation simply do not comprise the movement of groups of voters from one party to another. The claims of any party, present or future, to majority status are blocked by the long-term weakening of popular partisan attachments. To a greater extent than ever before, the American electorate is candidate and issue oriented, rather than party oriented.

Political parties in the United States are now buffeted by an unusually powerful, and disparate, set of forces. However much advocates of disciplined, programmatic, responsible parties may lament this situation, increasing numbers of voters simply feel less dependent upon party-provided cues. An affluent, by all historical standards enormously leisured, highly educated populace, able to draw political information from an extraordinary national communications structure, will never bestow the kind of coherent and persisting attachments to parties which electorates of times past freely gave.

As the current thrusts of reform testify, what the ascendant professional classes want is not some strong party organizational structure able to barter, bargain, and dictate nominations, but open parties, porous electoral instruments which they can capture easily and use to advance favored candidates and the concerns which at a given moment seem to be of the most compelling importance. The reforms of the McGovern-Fraser, Mikulski, and Sanford Commissions, and of the 1974 Kansas City mini-convention, carry a clear message from the professional classes to the party regulars, organized labor, and other old claimants: "We want a permeable party, responsive to the kind of free-lance intervention in which we excel. Give us that and we will probably stay. Deny it, and we will leave." The party gave.

Current talk of a "Europeanization" of the parties is absurd. A European-type party isn't merely ideological. It is central-office directed, responsive to a party bureaucracy. Nothing done in the reforms of the 1970s is leading to such a development. Issue-oriented candidates and middle-class constituencies, not a muscular party apparatus, are the beneficiaries.

Even if the citizenry were not so inclined to independent electoral behavior, the weakening of political parties in the United States would be ordained by the extension of a national communications complex. Television news, not party handouts or doorbell ringing by precinct committees, is the primary source of information on candidates for much of the populace. The national media are candidate-and issue-emphasizing vehicles, not party emphasizing. Political parties have become ancillary structures in the whole process of communications between candidates and elected officials on the one side, and the electorate on the other.

In a perceptive essay, David Broder, the distinguished journalist of the *Washington Post*, has emphasized the extent to which the media have increasingly assumed, more through the unfolding of technology than by conscious design, various facets of the communications function which rested historically with political parties. Media personnel, Broder observes, serve as the principal source of information on what the candidate is saying and doing; act the part of talent scouts, screening candidates for national (and on another tier, state) office, conveying the judgment that some are promising, while dismissing others as of no talent; operate as the race-caller or handicapper, telling the public how the election contests is going, and why X is ahead of Y; function at times as self-perceived public defenders, bent on exposing what they consider the frailties, duplicities, and sundry inadequacies of a candidate; and in some instances serve as assistant campaign managers, informally advising a candidate, and publicly, if indirectly, promoting his cause.[2] The press has long been linked in some way to such communications activities. But Broder is right in insisting that the preeminence of the media, vis-à-vis the parties, is something very recent and very important.

If substantial segments of the public feel much more confident than they did before in reaching electoral choices without the intervention of parties, and if the role of parties in the communications function has steadily diminished, is it surprising that citizenry loyalties or

[2] David S. Broder, "Political Reporters in Presidential Politics," in Charles Peters and Timothy J. Adams (eds.), *Inside the System: A Washington Monthly Reader* (New York: Praeger, 1970), pp. 3–22, *passim*.

attachments to political parties have diminished? The lessened capacity of parties to organize and mobilize the electorate is a major feature of the contemporary partisan transformation. And, in the context of the American political system, it appears irreversible.

Some observers see coherent party government as the only realistic answer to policy drift and governmental inertia. And they insist that political parties are the only available instrument through which the many who are individually weak can be organized and mobilized against the few who are powerful individually or organizationally. We do not share this view. An electorate which engages with abandon in ticket splitting is much more volatile than one marked by party regularity, but it does not seem to us inherently less capable of effective democratic participation. The contemporary party system displays this dimension: nominee-oriented, issue-directed, media-utilizing, and media-assessed candidacies operating within the formal structure of political parties. Not only does this general development appear well-nigh inevitable—in the sense that it is a response to fundamental features of the contemporary sociopolitical setting in the United States—but we see no necessary reason why it must pose a crisis of democracy. What *is* unfortunate is the absence of an appropriate "countercyclical response." A number of factors are eroding citizenry loyalties to parties and weakening party organization. Still, we require a party system that can effectively aggregate and convert popular preferences for political leadership. There is need, then, to preserve mechanisms which promote representativeness and the capacity to plan in the face of somewhat hostile tendencies. But the party "reform" of the past decade has, in many instances unthinkingly, pushed in precisely the opposite direction. It has unnecessarily and inappropriately sacrificed planning and representativeness on the altar of participation.

If the new Republican and new Democratic prophesies are inaccurate and inadequate, they appear fortunate when compared to the prediction of long life and good health for the New Deal coalitions. In fact, the New Deal party system has vanished as certainly as that which featured the old Republican, post–Civil War majority. Could the indicators of this be clearer? Republicans and Democrats during the New Deal era grouped themselves rather nicely on opposite sides of the liberal-conservative polarity and were sharply distinguished thereby. The substantial inapplicability of this ideological division—focusing as it did on governmental nationalism vs. business nationalism, and the question of how expansive a role government should play—now has been widely noted. The class dimension of conflict was unusually salient (in terms of American experience) throughout the 1930s and 1940s, and as a consequence the class character of voting and party differentiation was unusually pronounced. There has been a long secular decline in class voting, however, since 1950, a decline which accelerated notably after 1964. The point was reached by the 1970s at which, within the white population, actual inversions of the New Deal class order began appearing frequently. In the New Deal context, the white working class provided regular, powerful sustenance for liberal programs. By the late 1960s and early 1970s, this social collectivity, its social and economic position so substantially altered, had come to occupy a position of persisting resistance to many of the claims for extensions of liberalism—involving new beneficiary groups in some instances, and altered policy objectives in others. (Support for busing on behalf of integration, and support for a minimum wage, both receive in the casual nomenclature of American politics the description "liberal"; but these policies obviously impact most directly on different population groups and evoke contrasting ideological dimensions.)

In the New Deal context, the Republicans qualified as the establishment party, representing the business elites. But in postindustrial America, the elite structure of the society has been substantially changed, and the composition of the upper classes has been massively altered by an expansion of college-educated, professional, and managerial cohorts. In 1977, the Democrats, more than the Republicans, can lay claim to being an establishment party—in the sense of representing collections of prominent, established interests and a large, apparently growing proportion of persons of high socioeconomic status. Big business, "big science," "big education," the big governmental bureaucracies—all of these, as much as big labor, are dependencies of the New Deal Democratic state. How could an establishment so closely tied to governmental interventions championed more effectively by the Democrats than the Republicans fail to applaud the ascendancy of the Democratic party?

Both Republicans and Democrats in the New Deal era enjoyed a high measure of regular support from their respective "believers." But all indicators now reveal major increases in the levels of independent electoral behavior, a pronounced weakening of party loyalties, and a general decline in the capacity of parties to organize and mobilize the electorate. The growth in numbers and influence of issue activists, a stratum polarized ideologically, conservative activists gravitating to the Republican party while liberal activists are ascendant in Democratic affairs—with the profound implications this has for the shape of intra-party and inter-party competition—comprises a development with no counterpart in the New Deal party system.

Change in the fabric of conflict has been the principal precipitant of all transformations of the American party system. And with movement from industrial to postindustrial, exceptional alterations of conflict have occurred. This is nowhere more evident than in the fracturing of American liberalism. New Deal liberals were occupied primarily with the need for economic reform: Imposing controls on corporate business; organizing the industrial labor force; using government to bolster the economic position of the working class, to provide it with a larger measure of economic security, and to extend the range of social services. Such objectives are still pursued today, of course, and to some extent receive the endorsement of a large majority of the population. But as primary concerns, these remain the property of what must now be called *old liberalism*.

A *new liberalism* has now grown up. Nurtured by a climate of affluence in which such values have been significantly realized, it places less emphasis upon economic well-being and security, is less materialistic. It rather more emphasizes civil liberties and civil rights. It looks to a more participant, less hierarchical society. It stresses the importance of self-development of the individual, even at the cost of some further economic expansion if that is necessary. It is less attentive to the demand for economic growth, stressing environmental costs of such growth. Not rejecting governmental nationalism, it is nonetheless much less sympathetic to it than is the old liberalism, and reveals a suspicion of the state and of the workings of bureaucracy not found in the latter. The new liberalism shares the equalitarian commitments and flavor of the old (surely the only excuse for attaching "liberal" to both positions); but its equalitarianism is more sensitized to the needs of deprived (often ethnic) minorities. The new liberalism is attracted to the socially and culturally avant-garde, to experimentation and change in life styles, personal values, and ethical or normative codes.

Ronald Inglehart has explored this old liberalism-new liberalism distinction, applying the categories "Materialist," which he associates with the traditional "Left" of industrial society, and "Post-Materialist," a perspective of the "post-industrial Left." [3] Using survey data from a number of countries, Inglehart comes to the conclusion that "Materialists tend to be recruited from lower income groups, which traditionally have supported the Left—while the Post-Materialists come mainly from middle-class

---

[3] Ronald Inglehart, "Industrial, Pre-industrial and Post-industrial Political Cleavages in Western Europe and the United States" (paper delivered at the 1973 Meeting of the American Political Science Association, New Orleans, La., September 4–8, 1973).

families. . . ." [4] In the United States, the old liberalism draws its support disproportionately from the working-class-now-middle-class and the trade union movement, while the new liberalism gains its principal backing from segments of the college-educated upper-middle classes.

Since the objectives of the old liberalism have in many regards been substantially met, it is not surprising that it often reflects a kind of positional conservatism, a resistance to demands for change emanating from the new liberalism. And the latter is a much more substantial force for change in the contemporary United States. This point has been made by Richard Flacks who argues that opposition in postindustrial America comes to a substantial extent from *"those whose social position is already post-industrial*—who have been able or aspire to be able to make a life outside of the goods producing sector—i.e., in the production and distribution of knowledge, culture and human services, or as free persons—and those whose needs in a material sense have been satiated by the existing system." [5]

Liberalism was a united camp in the New Deal era, but it is now divided; and with its fracturing has come a rending of the Democrats as the great American liberal party. Important segments of organized labor, reflecting a core constituency for the old liberalism, find their position notably weakened as groups attached to the new liberalism achieve more prominent representation in the national Democratic party. The 1972 presidential election was the first to present a real quandary for the old liberal, trade union leadership and its mass clientele. These groups could not respond enthusiastically to a Republican party and presidential candidate never supportive of the economic egaliatarianism of the old liberalism; but they re-

---

[4] *Ibid.*, p. 8.
[5] Richard Flacks, "On the New Working Class and Strategies for Social Change," in Philip G. Altbach and Robert S. Laufer (eds.), *The New Pilgrims* (New York: David McKay, 1972), p. 88.

sented the growing influence of the new liberals who had nominated McGovern, and rejected the style, social and cultural concerns, and many of the social groups sympathies embodied in the new liberalism. The presidential election of 1972 was the first to manifest this split. It will not be the last.

In view of such sweeping changes in the structure of conflict within which the parties live and function, insistence that the New Deal party system is somehow still substantially intact can be accounted for only by a highly formalistic analytic focus. That is, a political party calling itself Democratic enjoyed a substantial lead over another party calling itself Republican in many sectors of electoral behavior in 1977, as it did in 1937. In both years, Democratic identifiers outnumbered Republican adherents by a large margin. Control of Congress and of state capitols was securely Democratic in both periods. Looking to party registration data, we find that the Democratic position was actually much stronger in 1977 than forty years earlier. Such data are, of course, important. But what they demonstrate is the persisting weakness of the Republican party, not the persistence of the New Deal party system.

The key feature of a party transformation involves the search for electoral organization and expression of a new conflict configuration generated by a new social setting. That is what we have tried to attend to—more than to the subsidiary although not unimportant matter of which party is coming out on top. From the perspective applied here, we see reasonably steady and coherent progression of partisan change, even while immediate electoral results bounce wildly, this way and that, from one election to the next.

In the absence of analysis which locates parties amid the larger context of change in the social system, one is left with short-term forecasting which inevitably overemphasizes currents in the last election. We have had altogether too much of this. In the Eisenhower years, there was much

talk of a new Republican majority. But just a few years
later, following the 1964 Goldwater debacle, some observers questioned whether the GOP could survive as a
serious electoral contender. Then, in the early Nixon
years, forecasts shifted once more, and visions of a Republican revival were again seen throughout the land. And
now, after Watergate, economic woes, and the massive setback administered to Republicans in the 1974 elections,
and the 1976 GOP loss of the presidency, we see a revival
of assessments with a 1964 flavor. To bend in this fashion
before the prevailing breezes is sheer nonsense.

There have been a number of basic, long-term changes
which collectively define a new party system. These have
grown out of the gradual transformations of the society,
however, and the responses of the parties to such change.
They have not occurred as functions of the last election.

The party coalitions in 1977 look very much like they
have over the past decade. Of the two, the Republican is
clearly the weaker. The political agenda continues to reflect the influx of issues and concerns peculiar to the postindustrial era. Although they presided over the creation of
the New Deal programs and display something of the pre-
servatism most parents feel toward their offspring, the
Democrats are still the party of change and experimentation—in large part, we think, because of their success in attracting the intelligentsia, the idea generating
and consuming community. Both party structures are weak
and porous; in an age of ideologically polarized activist
cohorts, they are notably susceptible to take-overs by
movements and candidates which eschew a politics of accommodation, as well as to walkouts when they appear insufficiently responsive. And conditions are such that the
volatility displayed in national electoral politics over the
last decade or so will surely persist through the next.

"The more things change, the more they are different,"
violates the French aphorism, but better approximates political experience. By the 1970s, enough had changed to

usher in a basic transformation of the American party system. Let us, then, bid fond farewell to the old New Deal coalitions. The system of which they were parts, along with the social era which nurtured it, having served us well, have slipped into history. And let us read well the new chapter that is opening, in the hope that by understanding it we can proceed intelligently in the quest for a full and secure democracy.

A Note on Data Sources

The Social Science Data Center of the University of Connecticut houses data from hundreds of opinion surveys of the American public, conducted from the mid-1930s up to the present. We have drawn heavily upon these materials, particularly on some one hundred and fifty American Institute for Public Opinion (AIPO) surveys, commonly known as the Gallup Polls.[1]

There are several reasons for our reliance upon the AIPO studies. They constitute the longest continuous stream of survey information on the American public—covering the entire span since the New Deal. In overall quality and consistency, the Gallup Polls deserve very high marks. So numerous are these surveys, moreover, with more than twenty conducted each year, that it is possible to "check in" on the electorate with a high measure of regularity. It is also possible to combine several AIPO surveys in a limited time span—a strategy used by George Gallup in many of his own analyses, and by a number of other investigators—to create a national sample with very large numbers of respondents among strategic subgroups, and to minimize sample bias. Routinely we pooled four AIPO surveys conducted just before and after a presidential or congressional election.

For the years since 1952, we also relied upon the University of Michigan biennial election studies.[2] Our debt is greater than the reader might suspect, since relatively little of the Michigan data actually appears in the text. We

---

[1] AIPO surveys were made available to the Social Science Data Center by the Gallup Organization directly and through the Roper Center for Public Opinion Research.

[2] These survey data are made available through institutional membership in the Inter-University Consortium for Political Research (ICPR) (Ann Arbor, Michigan).

regularly compared Gallup and Michigan findings, as an additional way of determining the secrurity of the base on which our conclusions were built.

Our analysis was supplemented and enriched by the availability, beginning in 1972, of the annual General Social Surveys of the National Opinion Research Center (NORC) of the University of Chicago. Other valuable surveys made available to us include those conducted by CBS News in 1972 and 1974, and by Daniel Yankelovich, Inc., in 1972.

We made use of a number of political leadership surveys: the 1968 Democratic and Republican National Convention delegate surveys by James W. Clarke and John Soule; the 1972 Democratic and Republican National Convention delegate surveys conducted for the *Washington Post* and released through the State Data Program of the University of California, Berkeley; the 1972 Republican National Convention delegate survey sponsored by the Knight Newspapers, and the 1972 Democratic National Convention delegate survey conducted for CBS News. Surveys of the general public, and of state and local political leaders, carried out by Louis Harris and Associates for the Senate Subcommittee on Intergovernmental Relations added yet another dimension to the analysis.[3]

After examining thousands of variables from hundreds of separate surveys, and a modest mountain of computer printout, we came away with two strong feelings—apart from the various substantive conclusions which we have reported. The first is added appreciation of both the values and the limitations of systematic opinion surveys, and particularly the sense that a good approximation of the state of the U.S. electorate comes not from single studies but in the patterns etched by many separate inquiries. The second relates to the first, and involves the enormous debt we

---

[3] For a published report on these surveys, see *Confidence and Concern: Citizens View American Government.* The raw data were furnished by the Louis Harris Political Data Center of the University of North Carolina (Chapel Hill).

owe the many investigators who preserved their survey findings and made them available to us, thereby creating an overall collection sufficiently large and varied to sustain the kind of study we felt was necessary.

Index

Index

conflict, 203, 354–6
forecasts, 2, 3, 5, 7–8, 10–11, 14, 19, 21, 201–2, 238, 249, 252–8, 332, 359–74, 379–82, 386–8
grass-roots activists, 310, 314, 340
information, 301–2, 330–1
input, 17, 85, 184, 187, 190–1, 192, 193, 199, 205, 229–30, 258, 346–8, 350, 356, 379–80
insurgency, 137. *See also* Party insurgencies; Third parties
majorities, 11–12, 14–15, 48, 84–87, 176, 344–5, 349*n*–50*n*
model, outmoded, 358–74
organization, 144, 314
participation, 58, 60–61, 114–15, 344–7, 383–4
party challenges, 2, 6, 8, 114, 135–7, 154–6, 378–80
power structure, 84, 128–36, 138–9, 142–3, 159–60, 177, 181, 202, 330, 343–4
primaries
  presidential, 315
  white, 157
process, 174–5, 336, 357
scandals, xvii, xxi, 2, 3, 5–6, 176, 190, 207, 210, 211*n*, 236, 258, 261, 262, 307, 386–7
science, 3, 24, 49*n*, 201, 348
style, 386
system, 22, 201
  racially, 230
theories, 24, 200–2, 262–4, 309–19, 360
views of 205 359–74, 380–1
Political-economic context, 105, 106–7, 137–42, 249–50
Politicians, 3, 16, 20, 102, 103, 107, 116, 124–6, 127, 135, 199, 233, 249, 262–6, 306, 320, 333–4, 335, 336
Politics, U.S., xxii, 1, 4, 11–12, 13, 15, 18, 31, 37–41, 91, 106, 129, 263, 269, 276, 305, 307, 309, 320, 328, 331, 342, 356, 359, 378–9
  accommodationist, 303, 305, 306, 307, 309, 334, 336, 337, 340, 357*n*–8*n*, 358–9, 360, 387–8
  class, 356
  flux of, xx, xxi, 1, 15–16, 35–41
  of issues, 339–42, 349–59
  and labor unions, 384–6
  local, 44, 92, 146, 267, 342
  national, 358–74
Pomper, Gerald M., 262–3
Popular
  opinion, 209–10, 266
  vote, 11–12, 126–7, 136, 146, 152, 154, 233, 260, 263–4, 273, 279
Population, xix, 33, 44, 60–61, 94, 139, 142
  black, 57, 58–59, 114, 157, 230–1
  economic standing, 194–8, 202
  groups, income, 93, 103, 104, 122
  metropolitan-rural defined, 164*n*
  movements, 94, 139, 142, 163, 332
  nonsouthern, redefined, 58*n*
  "old stock" (white), 47
  rank and file, 353–4
  sampling methods, 99*n*, 103*n*
  student, 253–4, 349–54

Populism, 34, 39, 48, 130–1, 137
  neo, 259, 265–6, 378–9
  "spoiled," 140
Pornography, 215
Postindustrial U.S., xviii, 7, 27, 140, 142, 177, 182, 206, 266, 282, 356
  blacks in, 229–30, 239
  described, 183–4, 384–5
  distinguishing features of, 185–6, 191, 251, 255
  labor needs, 198, 199
  Left in, 384–5
  new issues, 387
  party system changes, 181–274, 347, 356, 358*n*, 380–2
  unionism, 195, 230
"Post-materialists," 384–5
Poverty, 4, 9, 12, 13, 61, 64, 66, 68, 71, 94, 95, 97, 104, 113, 114, 115, 168–9, 193, 194–7, 199, 200, 314
Power, 17, 18, 32, 184, 380–1
  business, 191
  one-man, 318, 331, 360
  political, 177, 191, 203, 204
Presidential
  arena, 26, 264–6
  campaigning, 16, 20
  conventions, *see* by name of party
  elections of:
    1896, 65, 70
    1900, 43, 61
    1904, 306
    1912, 35
    1916, 61
    1920, 163
    1924, 49, 84
    1928, 43–44, 49, 50, 61, 151, 152, 154, 271
    1932, 8, 9, 38, 42–44, 58–60, 66, 153, 269, 275, 280, 306
    1936, 52–53, 56, 59, 61, 64, 66, 67, 70–71, 72, 74, 83, 84, 85, 116, 119, 159
    1940, 52–53, 59, 61, 62, 64, 67, 70–71, 82, 83, 85, 86, 100, 153, 159, 234
    1944, 73, 100, 107, 135, 280
    1948, 74, 85, 100, 102, 107, 124, 136, 153, 154, 157, 162, 163, 242, 243, 280, 286
    1952, 116, 154, 362
    1956, 306, 308, 362
    1960, 116, 119–20, 124, 128, 153, 154, 158, 234, 362
    1964, xx, 12, 18, 83, 136, 153, 154–5, 157, 162, 164, 166, 235, 263–4, 286, 302, 306, 307, 308, 359, 386–7
    1968, 74, 107, 155, 159, 233–4, 235, 242, 279, 286, 287, 290
    1972, xviii, 3, 6–9, 11, 12, 17, 18, 74, 107, 136, 146, 158, 159, 163, 164, 229, 233–4, 235, 242, 262, 264, 266, 268, 270, 271–2, 276, 278, 279, 280, 281, 283, 284, 287, 290–1, 300, 302, 306, 307, 308, 333, 345, 358, 360, 374, 385–6
    1976, 247, 275–301, 362, 372–3
  majorities, 360
  nominations, 333–4, 341, 344, 347*n*, 348, 356–60